BONFIRES
TO
BEACONS

FEDERAL CIVIL AVIATION POLICY

UNDER THE AIR COMMERCE ACT,

1926–1938

Nick A. Komons

Smithsonian Institution Press
Washington, D.C.   London

in association with Airlife Publishing
England

Printed in the United States of America
96   95   94   93   92   91   90   89
                    5   4   3   2   1
⊗ The paper used in this publication meets the
requirements of the American National Standa   /or
Permanence of Paper for Printed Library
Materials Z39.48-1984.

This book is part of the Smithsoniar   story of Aviation Series. Published in the Uni   states by the
Smithsonian Institution Press   s series of books is
distributed in the United K gdom, Europe, the Middle East, and Africa by Airlife Publishing Ltd.

Library of Congress Catalog-in-Publication Data

Komons, Nick A.
      Bonfires to beacons.

      (Smithsonian history of aviation series.
Classics of aviation history)
      Reprint. Originally published: Washington :
U.S. Dept. of Transportation, Federal Aviation
Administration.
      Includes bibliographical references and index.
      1. Aeronautics and state—United States.
2. Aeronautics, Commercial—Law and legislation—
United States. I. United States. Air
Commerce Act.   II. Title   III. Series.
[HE9803.A4K64 1989]   387.7'068   89-6416
ISBN 0-87474-727-9   Smithsonian
British Library Cataloguing-in-Publication Data is
available.
ISBN 1-85310-134-6   Airlife

BONFIRES
TO
BEACONS

Smithsonian History of Aviation Series

On December 17, 1903, on a windy beach in North Carolina, aviation became a reality. The development of aviation over the course of little more than three-quarters of a century stands as an awe-inspiring accomplishment in both a civilian and a military context. The airplane has brought whole continents closer together; at the same time it has been a lethal instrument of war.

This series of books is intended to contribute to the overall understanding of the history of aviation—its science and technology as well as the social, cultural, and political environment in which it developed and matured. Some publications help fill the many gaps that still exist in the literature of flight; others add new information and interpretation to current knowledge. While the series appeals to a broad audience of general readers and specialists in the field, its hallmark is strong scholarly content.

The series is international in scope and includes works in three major categories:

SMITHSONIAN STUDIES IN AVIATION HISTORY: *works that provide new and original knowledge.*

CLASSICS OF AVIATION HISTORY: *carefully selected out-of-print works that are considered essential scholarship.*

CONTRIBUTIONS TO AVIATION HISTORY: *previously unpublished documents, reports, symposia, and other materials.*

Contents

Editor's Introduction

Clement Keys, chief executive of the Curtiss Aeroplane and Motor Company, once remarked that "ten percent of aviation is in the air, and 90 percent is on the ground." Keys's statement is as true today as when it was first uttered. Public perception of flying during the twenties and thirties as merely a glamorous and dangerous enterprise filled with colorful characters who risked their lives to perform aerial feats ignores the complexity of the struggle to make aviation a viable business.

Before aviation could become profitable, the public had to be convinced that it was safe to fly; the way to accomplish this was to move aviation away from the reckless barnstorming tradition into the realm of the professional. Part of aviation's untold story during this period has to do with the federal government's role in helping to make flying safe and put it on a sound footing financially. To a great extent, this work took place behind the scenes in corporate boardrooms and government offices.

The first offering in the Smithsonian Institution Press's Classics of Aviation History reprint subseries, *Bonfires to Beacons: Federal Civil Aviation Policy under the Air Commerce Act, 1926–1938,* by Nick A. Komons, is one of the few scholarly books to elucidate the federal government's critical role in the development of commercial aviation during the twenties and thirties, aviation's so-called Golden Age.

In this most unique and exhaustive treatment of federal civil aviation policy, Dr. Komons analyzes the background of the pivotal Air Commerce Act of 1926, which ushered in the era of modern commercial flying by setting stringent standards for aircraft and pilot licensing and air safety. He then examines in some detail the aviation policies of Republican presidents Calvin Coolidge and Herbert Hoover. Finally, he assesses the impact of Franklin D. Roosevelt's New Deal on federal aviation policy to 1938, when the Civil Aeronautics Act was passed.

Komons's opening chapter, "The Chaos of Laissez Faire in the Air," sets the context for the rest of the book by pointing out how badly in need of regulation American aviation was during the period immediately after

World War I. Chapters two and three lay out the background for the Air Commerce Act of 1926, which Komons justifiably calls "the legislative cornerstone," including the deliberations of the Morrow Board, the most important and most neglected presidential advisory board on aviation in the 1920s. In subsequent chapters, Komons turns to the rather differing approach toward civil aviation policy taken by the Republican administrations of Coolidge and Hoover versus that taken by the Democratic New Deal of Roosevelt. Komons also devotes considerable attention to the government's part in the advent of radio navigation and in one of the important technological landmarks of the era, illumination of the airways— hence the title *Bonfires to Beacons*.

Those who believe that institutional history is of necessity boring or doctrinaire will be pleasantly surprised by *Bonfires to Beacons*. The work is a model for professional historians working in the area of aviation policy. Komons has interpreted the regulatory environment in a lively, engaging, and far-reaching way. By continually bringing the reader in touch with the broader events of American history during the interwar years, Komons reminds us that the development of civil aviation in the United States did not take place in a vacuum.

The cumulative effect of Komons's book, as Peter Clapper so aptly commented in the first edition of *Bonfires to Beacons,* is that, among other things, "it is . . . the story of government and private interests forming a symbiotic relationship that promotes a new industry and advances the public good." Eleven years after it was first published, Komons's work can still lay claim to being the standard work on the government-industry relationship during this formative period.

What is more, it stands as the best institutional history of the government's role in aviation during the interwar years.

Dominick A. Pisano
Series Editor

Foreword

The airplane is a liberating force—a force that released man from his earthly tether and helped ease the demands of time and distance. Thanks to this machine, mountains, oceans, and vast stretches of desert, which man had previously traversed with time-consuming effort and often at his peril, today are daily conquered with speed, ease, and safety. Yet, though a liberating influence, the airplane is itself a highly dependent machine. In order to serve man's purposes safely and efficiently, it must operate in a controlled and regulated environment, and requires the support of a far-flung and complex ground organization to monitor and direct virtually its every move.

In the following narrative, Dr. Komons tells how the U.S. Government came to recognize the dependent nature of the airplane and how, between 1926 and 1938, it organized itself to foster and regulate civil aviation's development. The tale is not without inner contradictions. At times it is the story of a Federal bureaucracy—seemingly menacing yet eager to please—serving a constituency of businesses, professional fliers, and aviation enthusiasts, who recogize their dependence on Federal regulation and benefaction but often prefer to be left alone. But it is also the story of government and private interests forming a symbiotic relationship that promotes a new industry and advances the public good.

Though this is an official history and the author is a Federal employee, the opinions expressed herein do not necessarily represent an official point of view; Dr. Komons was given complete freedom to interpret events as he saw them.

Peter R. Clapper
Assistant Administrator for Public Affairs
Federal Aviation Administration
May 20, 1977

Author's Preface

Tell them, tell them that the old man says that writing any history is just pulling a tomcat by its tail across a Brussels carpet.

Charles A. Beard to Eric F. Goldman

In my bout with my particular tomcat, I was fortunate to have the assistance of many generous people. My colleagues on this project, Richard J. Kent, Stuart I. Rochester, and John R. M. Wilson, besides being my most spirited critics, were a constant source of encouragement. To Ellmore A. Champie I owe more than I can possibly acknowledge here; suffice it to say that he painstakingly read every word of my manuscript in draft and saved me many an embarrassing blunder. Glyndon P. Bennett responded to my every demand in a fashion that went beyond the normal call of duty. Charles W. Hazelwood spent the summer of 1975 doing research for me in the periodical literature. Samuel Milner took a week off from his regular duties to identify pertinent documents for me at the Herbert Hoover Presidential Library. Colonel M. A. Roth, Assistant Executive Director of the National Aeronautic Association, assembled for my use two large crates of NAA files. Richard K. Smith, Alex Roland, and William M. Leary, Jr., read and criticized portions of my manuscript; in addition, Professor Leary made available to me some of the findings of his research. Tom D. Crouch allowed me to read a preliminary draft of his article on Eugene Vidal's low-priced airplane. Fred D. Fagg, Jr., graciously consented to read portions of my manuscript; he also corresponded with me about a number of events of which he has first-hand knowledge. The chapter on air traffic control would have been the poorer had not Chester A. Church, Glen A. Gilbert, Hugh H. McFarlane, Emerson R. Mehrling,

Walter B. Swanson, Lee E. Warren, James B. Watson, and the late William H. Cramer read it or made materials available to me. Lane Moore, of the National Archives and Records Service, extended me many courtesies. *Time* Magazine granted me permission to reproduce a number of its covers. Finally, I would be remiss not to mention Robert E. Whittington and Louis J. Churchville, whose interest and support helped bring this project to fruition.

Nick A. Komons
Agency Historian
Federal Aviation Administration
May 11, 1977

Bonfires to Beacons

1926–1938

Federal Civil Aviation Policy under the Air Commerce Act

Prologue

Time had brought all manner of change — change enough for the world power observing its Sesquicentennial to be scarcely recognizable as the onetime nation of rebelling colonials. Indeed, in some respects, the transformation had been so dramatic and thorough that 1776 appeared eons away.

Much of the change, spiritual as well as material, had been wrought by technology. The machine tilled farms and harvested crops, ran factories, generated power, built roads, and moved people and goods. It helped make the United States the greatest producer of agricultural products in the world. At the same time, it transformed America from a country that was agricultural and rural to one that was predominantly industrial and urban. But the machine had not done it alone. The presence of a large land mass bountifully endowed by nature had been crucial, as had a helpful government and an enterprising spirit.

The dominant spirit in 1926 was unmistakable. Economic enterprise absorbed the attention of the nation. Fired by a booming economy, Americans went on an acquisitive binge. The country, as Robert L. Heilbroner put it, "was drunk with the elixir of prosperity." Some men believed the good times would never end and poverty would become only a dim reminder of a cruel and unenlightened past. "We shall soon with the help of God be within sight of the day when poverty will be banished from the nation," Herbert Hoover asserted. That elusive pot of gold at the end of the rainbow was not only within reach, but within the reach of all. "Everybody Ought to be Rich," argued John J. Raskob in an article bearing that title. He laid down a simple formula: "If a man saves $15 a week and invests in good common stocks, at the end of twenty years he will have at least $80,000 and an income from investments of around $400 a month. He will be rich." The eternal verities — piety, hard work, and frugality — resurrected and given new, if spare, expression by Calvin

1

Coolidge — would triumph in the end and lead the American people to the promised land of milk and honey.[1]

It didn't work out quite that way. A cavernous gap separated rhetoric from reality. No one, with the possible exception of Calvin Coolidge, seemed to believe in the eternal verities. Coolidge had abandoned the global commitments and political experiments of the previous decade and offered, in place of the heady idealism of Theodore Roosevelt and Woodrow Wilson, time-worn copy-book maxims. Americans echoed Coolidge's litany; but temperance, thrift, probity, and simplicity, though they rolled glibly off the tongue, were empty words in an age of hip flasks and speakeasies, raccoon coats and speedy roadsters, dance marathons and all-night galas, frothy land schemes and runaway stock prices. A strain of hypocrisy tainted the times.

What eventually took hold, what eventually replaced Roosevelt's New Nationalism and Wilson's New Freedom, was a gospel of materialism. "The man who builds a factory builds a temple. . . . The man who works there worships there," Calvin Coolidge said. But in spreading this creed, Coolidge was also displaying an insensitivity to the realities of the workingman's lot. In economic matters, as in others, promise and performance went their separate ways. The mass of the American people never made it to the promised land. Admittedly, there were riches aplenty; but under the prevailing philosophy of every man for himself (and the devil take the hindmost), there was never enough to go around. One percent of the total population collected 73 percent of all corporate dividends. Among American families, the top fifth earned 54.5 percent of the national income; the bottom two-fifths, 12.5 percent. Translated into dollars and cents, 40 percent of U.S. families lived on a mean income of $725 a year (or $55 less than the annual savings required by Raskob's get-rich formula). In the end, even the rich fell on hard times. As the decade came to a close, the American economy, bloated with unwanted or unaffordable goods, burst like an overinflated balloon. Speaking of the 1920's, Henry Steele Commager and Richard B. Morris noted: "The mark of failure is heavy on these years: failure in the sense of responsibilities evaded, and of opportunities missed."[2]

But it was not a wholly barren decade. F. Scott Fitzgerald, Ernest Hemingway, Sherwood Anderson, and Sinclair Lewis wrote some of the best literature of the century in the 1920's. Robert F. Wagner, Fiorello H. La Guardia, and Bronson Cutting, though only voices in the wilderness, enunciated social themes and political possibilities that would influence coming generations. Nor were all responsibilities evaded, nor all opportunities missed. The nation, brimming with people on the make and fascinated by the machine, possessed a sharp eye for the main chance, the genuinely progressive economic opportunity. One such opportunity not overlooked was presented by the airplane, that marvel of American inventiveness that had not been exploited as a tool of commerce in the land of its birth. Beginning in 1926 — nearly 23 years since Kitty Hawk and nearly eight since the end of World War I, when aviation demonstrated it was an industry laden with potential — Americans turned their attention in earnest to the airplane's commercial prospects. In doing so, they touched off yet another technological revolution — a revolution that would change the United States still more.

But the airplane's potential would not — in fact, could not — be realized by a community of businessmen acting alone. The Federal Government would stand at their side, becoming, in effect, civil aviation's indispensable partner. The partnership flourishes to this day.

I

Background to the Air Commerce Act

1918–1926

1. "The Chaos of Laissez Faire in the Air"

Prior to 1926, an American engaged in flying either for a livelihood or for pleasure could go about his business and scarcely notice the existence of Federal, state, or local authority. A few minor exceptions aside, his access to the air was totally unencumbered. He needed no pilot's license, nor a license to carry passengers or goods in commerce. The school or individual that taught him to fly was also unlicensed. The aircraft he flew possessed no airworthiness certificate. If he chose, he could build his own machine in his own backyard and fly it — if it would fly — without conforming to any mandatory set of engineering standards. "Any would-be birdman can throw together a flying machine and soar skyward with passengers who are oblivious to the first aerial law laid down by Sir Isaac Newton," complained a newspaper editor.[1] Once in the air, this birdman was not required to abide by any rules of flight. There were none. Thus, he could take off and land whenever and wherever he chose and without following any prescribed procedures. He could dive, spin, buzz, or do a figure 8 — perform any outrageous stunt — and answer to no one for his actions.

If government did not regulate activity in the air, it also did nothing to encourage it. Indeed, the very absence of regulation was a deterrent to civil aviation growth. Other transportation modes benefited not only from Federal safety regulation, but also from generous Federal subsidies. Civil aviation received nothing, whether direct or indirect in character. Though municipalities were slow to establish airports, Federal officials did nothing to encourage the development of these facilities. With one notable exception, the Federal Government established no civil airways, maintained no civil air navigation aids, and made no provision for emergency landing fields.

Some men, no doubt reflecting the prevailing climate against governmental interference in business affairs, were satisfied to keep things as they were. "What we want is progress — not red tape!" asserted a flier from Cincinnati. "I think regulation will put the average commercial aviator out of business," declared a small fixed-base operator from Freeport, Ill. An aviator from Philadelphia expressed a similar concern: "As sure as the sun rises and sets, strict government regulations will retard commercial aviation ten to fifteen years, if not kill it entirely." At such times as the Federal Government appeared ready to embark on air regulation, it was met by the usual barrage of criticism. "It seems somewhat absurd," went a typical reaction from a commercial operator, "to have all this hullabaloo and endeavor to set the massive and ponderous machinery of the law on a measly 120 [commercial] airplanes."[2]

But it was a contrary view that was taking a firm hold both in and out of Government towards the middle of the 1920's. It seemed less than evenhanded for the Federal Government to support and encourage the development of other modes of transportation — modes that appeared mature enough to stand on their own feet — while doing nothing to encourage civil aviation, which was still in its infancy and badly in need of governmental benefaction. An increasing number of people were, moreover, beginning to sense the preposterousness of the Federal Government's allowing no steamboat to take passengers across, say, Long Island Sound unless captain, mates, engineers, boilers, hull, lifeboats, and life preservers had passed the scrutiny of Federal inspectors, while permitting anyone — and all too often with tragic results — to fly passengers over land or water without any scrutiny whatever.[3] "Time is at hand," declared the Buffalo *Courier* in 1924, "to bring some order out of the chaos of laissez faire in the air, where constantly increasing numbers of . . . flyers . . . disport without let or hindrance."[4]

"The chaos of laissez faire in the air." Such words must have had an incongruous ring in the 1920's. Yet they took hold. They took hold among hardheaded businessmen, who called for Federal aviation regulation at a time when unbridled business activity was a high economic virtue. They took hold among highly placed Federal officials, who seriously proposed that the Federal Government foster and encourage the development of commercial aviation while Calvin Coolidge — the undisputed champion of individual initiative — still occupied the White House. They even took hold within the White House itself. It was a curious, uncharacteristic twist, perhaps, for a period in American history

noted for its sermons on self-help. But in another context the drive for
Federal regulation of aviation was of a piece with the character of
transportation development in the United States.

II

America ran on wheels. In 1925, every man, woman, and child in the
United States — 115 million strong — could be moved simultaneously by
a combination of rail and motor vehicle. Later in the decade, automobiles
would be capable of performing this feat alone.[5]

Rail was the dominant transportation mode. Nearly 250,000 miles of
track, enough to span the world 10 times, was owned and operated by
American railroads. In 1925, railroads carried 902 million passengers
over this intricate network, while chalking up 36 billion passenger-miles.
At the same time, they hauled 417.4 billion ton-miles of freight. Passenger revenues came to $1.1 billion; freight revenues, to $4.6 billion. The
book value of all U.S. railroads added up to $23.2 billion. Railroads
employed 1.8 million people, or 4 percent of the total labor force.[6]

But if the railroad was the dominant transportation mode, it was also
a fully mature mode. It was in fact beginning to go into a slow but steady
decline — a decline not significantly interrupted except during the
Second World War, and then only temporarily. The peak for miles of
track in operation had been reached in 1916; the peak for number of
passengers carried, in 1920. Why railroads should experience a drop in
activity during a business boom had a relatively simple answer, the
emergence of the motor vehicle. Competition from trucks, buses, and
automobiles began to cut heavily into rail traffic in the 1920's. Trucks
and buses, however, were not yet accounting for a significant portion of
this loss; actually, in long distance transportation, they were barely
making themselves felt. But the damage that the private passenger car
was inflicting on the railroads was both extensive and permanent.[7]

In 1925, the manufacture of land vehicles powered by internal
combustion engines was the largest industry in the United States.
Though other industries — radio, for example — grew at a faster rate,
none could approach the automobile in its overall importance to the
economy, particularly in its impact on other industries. By the midtwen-
ties, motor vehicles were accounting for 90 percent of the petroleum

products consumed in the United States, 80 percent of the rubber, 75 percent of the plate glass, 25 percent of the machine tools, and 20 percent of the steel. The impact of the automobile on the road construction industry was nothing short of dramatic.[8]

A number of factors made the expansion of the automobile industry possible, not the least being an increase in the purchasing power of the average American that ignited a broad, rapid, and unprecedented expansion in the consumption of durable goods. It is true that the nation's farmers, owing in great measure to a precipitous drop in the price of nearly all agricultural goods, faced hard times throughout the 1920's. But what was bad for the farmer appeared to be good for the rest of the population. Indeed, at a time when the average annual wage remained stable, consumer prices were undergoing a significant decline — all of which meant that Americans could buy more for less. In 1920, the consumer price index, reflecting a soaring postwar inflation, stood at 85.7 (100 = 1947–49); by 1925, it had dropped to 75. Between 1920 and 1925, only one important cost-of-living barometer had shot up: the index for housing rose from 100.2 to 126.4. But the index for food dropped from 83.6 to 65.8. At the same time, the average annual income for all workers — farm and industrial — remained relatively constant, standing, in 1925, at $1,473 per year, down only slightly from $1,489 in 1920. Unemployment was low. Among a total labor force of 45,000,000, only 1,800,000 (or 4 percent) were unemployed. In 1926, perhaps the peak year of the Coolidge prosperity, unemployment dropped to 880,000 — an incredibly low 1.9 percent of the total labor force.[9]

The automobile industry did its part to promote its product by keeping its price within the reach of the average worker. In 1926, for example, the retail price of a new Ford Model T touring car was a mere $290. Credit, available to both consumers and dealers on liberal terms, contributed mightily to the sales boom, as did massive Federal and state financing of highway construction.[10] Thus, while in 1920 the auto industry produced 2,250,000 vehicles, five years later it rolled 4,266,000 off its assembly lines. Motor vehicle registrations more than doubled during the period, jumping from 9.2 million to 20.1 million. In 1925, Americans drove these vehicles 122.3 billion miles.[11]

III

Beside the activity of rail and motor car, aviation activity — or what there was of it — paled. Even inland water transportation, which had matured many decades before, was a more significant force in the nation's economy. Earlier generations did not see the airplane as we see it today. Far from being viewed as a mode of transportation crucial to the nation's economic well-being, it was regarded as late as 1924 as having limited commercial application. "For the most part," William P. Mac-Cracken, Jr., said, "people thought of flying as somewhere between a sport and a sideshow."[12]

This view was not far off the mark, though, admittedly, the airplane had come a long way from the days when flying was akin to a death-defying feat and men just flew for the hell of it. Gone were the birdmen and the likes of the irascible Lincoln Beachey ("The most wonderful flyer I ever saw," Orville Wright said of him), who had gained instant but fleeting notoriety testing the indulgence of fate with his spellbinding antics. Gone was the dauntless, accident-plagued Calbraith Perry Rodgers, who, in a 49-day period in 1911, suffered 12 major crashes and a number of lesser mishaps in flying between New York and Pasadena, Calif., in a fragile Burgess-Wright flivver. Gone, too, were Arch Hoxsey and Ralph Johnstone, the famed "Star Dust Twins." They had excited thousands for a few brief glory-filled months in 1910 with their reckless aerial acrobatics and daring attempts to establish new altitude records. It had been Hoxsey who, in October 1910 — a month before Johnstone's fatal crash and two months before his own — had taken Theodore Roosevelt up for his first and only flight. T.R., his famous teeth flashing, waved his arms so excitedly at the crowd below that he came dangerously close to tripping an overhead cord that would have short-circuited the engine. No President, former President, or Presidential candidate was to take to the air again until Franklin D. Roosevelt did so 22 years later.[13]

The First World War was a watershed in aviation's history. It was then that a substantial aircraft manufacturing industry, force fed by military procurement orders, first sprang up. At the same time, the state of the art was substantially advanced, both in airframe and engine design. The war, moreover, had provided the airplane with a utilitarian function, albeit a destructive one. It had also taught thousands of young Americans to fly and given many thousands more their initial firsthand experience with the airplane.

The war over, the military services discharged many an airman who liked and still wanted to fly. As matters stood, it was relatively simple for these men to satisfy their urge. Peace had left both the Army and Navy with a vast stock of surplus aircraft and engines. The Government put this stock on the market at bargain-basement prices. A Jenny (i.e., a

Curtiss JN-4H trainer) complete with engine could be purchased for as little as $300. A slightly used Curtiss OX-5 engine could be bought for $75. Some flying schools offered an attractive package: pilot training and a Jenny for $500.[14]

Flooding the market with surplus machines had a devastating effect on the aircraft manufacturing industry, and, indeed, retarded the development of new aircraft and engines. But it put airplanes in the air — airplanes that were poorly fitted for commercial operations. The owner of a surplus Jenny or a de Havilland DH-4 wishing to earn a living with his craft could do little more than peddle the thrill of an airplane ride to the curious, just as an amusement park operator peddled rides on a roller coaster. A rented cow pasture or a town lot was his usual base of operations. To attract a crowd he might perform a few stunts in the air — twisting, tumbling, and skimming tree tops in a daring, hell-for-leather exhibition — and then solicit customers from among those gathered. His charge rarely exceeded 50¢ per minute. When patronage fell off in one location, he would pack his ship and fly off in search of greener pastures, thus earning the epithet of "gypsy flier."[15]

It was a rough existence, reserved exclusively for hardy, carefree souls. A gypsy flier had to be pilot, mechanic, barker, and business manager all wrapped in one. Because of the need to be constantly on the move, his life was fraught with physical hardship. It was also fraught with danger. Carelessness, foolhardiness, inadequate landing fields, and machines that were often less than airworthy took their toll in human life. And the returns were meager. Competition kept profits to a minimum, as did the constant demand of rickety, outworn aircraft for parts and repairs. One barnstormer, on being asked what was the most dangerous thing about flying, retorted: "The risk of starving to death."[16]

A flier, or course, had options other than barnstorming for applying his skills. And though these options were limited, they were definitely increasing in number.

Hollywood directors were quick to realize that the motion picture was an exceptionally good medium for capturing the excitement of flight, and they began grinding out films in which airplanes were prominently featured. "Sky Highwayman," "Speed Girl," "Broken Wing," "The Go-Getter," and other, mostly undistinguished, offerings entertained movie audiences of the twenties. A motion picture about flying, "Wings," won the first Oscar ever presented by the Motion Picture Academy for best picture of the year. For a former barnstormer, performing stunts before a live audience was only a short step from performing them before a movie camera. But it was equally dangerous: witness the fate of Ormer Locklear, the first of the fearless wing walkers, who met an untimely death during the filming of a movie in 1920.[17]

The utility of the airplane in advertising had been recognized even before the Great War. One of its earliest uses in this field was in the dropping of handbills. Later, airplane owners (including gypsy fliers) began advertising products on the sides of their fuselage and the bottom of their wings. In the 1920 political campaign, Democrats, Republicans, Farm-Laborites, and Prohibitionists, ranging from presidential aspirants to candidates for sheriff, utilized the airplane in this way, usually employing a simple legend saying no more than "Vote for . . . ." But it was not until the advent of skywriting that aerial advertising began taking on the characteristics of an organized business. The first public demonstration of this technique had been given in England in May 1922 by a Major Jack Savage. It quickly spread to the United States, where, in January 1923, the Skywriting Corporation of America was formed. With 12 aircraft at its disposal, this company performed over some 300 U.S. cities before an audience numbering in the millions during its first year of operation.[18]

Aerial photography also assumed the characteristics of an organized business in the 1920's. The technique had some overtones of a fad during its early development. Photographs taken from an airplane were in demand by newspapers and magazines because of their novelty. But with the entry of such concerns as Fairchild Aerial Camera, Hamilton Maxwell, and Underwood & Underwood, the field began to take on more substantial aspects, the most important of which were mapping and surveying. For sheer speed and fidelity to detail, aerial mapping was unrivaled (though it was not without drawbacks at this stage of its development). In 1920, the entire City of New York was photographed in 69 minutes. Four years later, a giant sectional wall map of Greater New York, comprising an area of 620 square miles, was produced on a scale of 600 feet to the inch. The map portrayed the city in the minutest detail, showing everything from skyscrapers to privies. Fairchild, which owned its own airplanes and built its own photographic equipment, was the largest operator in the field and undertook the most ambitious projects. One of the more notable was the aerial survey of vast Canadian timberlands. By 1924, aerial surveying was the largest single privately organized endeavor in commercial aviation, grossing some $500,000 a year.[19]

Crop dusting was not far behind. The U.S. Department of Agriculture had pioneered in the use of the airplane in entomological work in 1919. The earliest efforts in this field, however, were in neither spraying nor dusting, but in locating remote cotton fields in south Texas that had escaped inspection for pink bollworm. An Army pilot, an entomologist, and one aircraft comprised the entire project, which was abandoned in August 1919 when the airplane crashed, killing both men. Two years later, the State of Ohio successfully applied lead arsenate by air to a grove of trees infested with the catalpa worm. This inspired the U.S. Department of Agriculture to go airborne again, this time over cotton fields in Louisiana and Mississippi in an effort to combat the bollweevil. The Bureau of Entomology had been fighting this scourge of the cotton fields with ground-based dusting equipment. Progress was so slow that it would have taken many years before the fields were brought back to desired production levels. The U.S. Army again lent a hand, providing both aircraft and pilots. The experiment was a decided success. A single Army airplane, which had not even been designed as a crop duster, could do the work of 40 ground-based machines. This success brought commercial firms into the field, most notably the Huff-Daland Airplane Company of Bristol, Pa. By 1925, Huff-Daland had 20 airplanes dusting cotton, peach and pecan orchards, and sugar cane fields.[20]

More indicative of future commercial activity was the limited and selective use the airplane was being put to in transporting light cargo. A flying boat might be chartered, for example, to transport from Florida to New York a cargo of grapefruit "at a time of year when that delicacy was rare to even the choice menus of the north." Or an aircraft might be chartered, as had been done in 1920, to carry between Cleveland and Washington, D.C., a container of ice cream that would occupy a place of special prominence at a banquet of the Retail Ice Cream Dealers' Association. But, as might be expected, such uses of the airplane were rare, depended on people with pronounced proclivities for conspicuous consumption, and were in no way organized on a regular basis.[21]

Far more organized was the use of the airplane as a carrier of contraband — notably, bootleg whiskey. How much liquor was run by air over the Canadian and Mexican borders during the Prohibition era is

anyone's guess; but if the testimony of some contemporaries is to be
believed, trade was brisk and relatively safe from detection. One small-
time aircraft designer, who sold his first airplane to a bootlegger,
maintained that the illicit liquor trade was "the thing that held up
aviation's pants" during the early 1920's. Another maintained that rum-
running by air had an important educational impact; it opened the eyes
of many potential investors to the "great possibilities for legitimate
commercial flying."[22]

Prior to 1925, the opportunities for private carriers to transport mail
were strictly limited since the U.S. Post Office Department carried
domestic airmail in its own ships manned by its own crews. The Post
Office did have, however, foreign airmail contracts with private carriers
over two relatively short routes. In 1919, Hubbard Air Transport was
awarded a contract to fly mail between Seattle, Wash., and Victoria,
British Columbia. Four years later, the Gulf Coast Air Line contracted
to carry mail between New Orleans and Pilottown, La., on the Mississippi River, where it was transferred to ocean-going vessels bound for
Latin America. Both these lines were virtually one-man operations. They
used small aircraft and carried no passengers. But they operated in the
black, demonstrating, if nothing else, that carrying mail by air could be a
profitable business.[23]

Barnstorming, performing before Hollywood cameras, skywriting,
crop dusting, aerial photography, running liquor to a thirsty nation —
though all this activity in combination amounted to very little in an
economic sense, making scarcely a ripple in the 1925 gross national
product, it did give a hint of the diverse commercial uses that the airplane
could — and would — be put to. What this activity did not give a hint of
was the prominent role the airplane would come to play as a mover of
people. If the airplane ever filled a niche, it was this one.

In 1925, the United States decidedly lagged behind other industrial
nations in the development of commercial air-passenger transportation.
The most conspicuous carrier of air passengers — conspicuous because
of his presence in sheer numbers and not because of the traffic he carried
— was the small fixed-base operator. As often as not, he was a former
gypsy flier who had accumulated capital, bought or rented a promising
location for his operations, incorporated, and settled into business in
what he hoped to be a permanent location. His operation bore more of a
resemblance to the modern day air-taxi operator than to the certificated

route carrier. He had no schedule and he flew anywhere, though rarely long distances. He provided, in other words, an intercity taxi service.[24]

While the small fixed-base operator was present in numbers, the operator of scheduled passenger service scarcely existed. The first known scheduled air-passenger carrier in the United States was the St. Petersburg-Tampa Airboat Line, which was established in January 1914 and ran between the two Florida cities borne in its name. For three winter months this line shuttled passengers back and forth across 23 miles of water on a more or less regular basis. Then, with the coming of spring, tourists moved north, and the airline went out of existence.[25]

It was not until after the war, in August 1919, that another airline made its appearance. This was Aero Limited, which, like St. Petersburg-Tampa, passed but briefly over the scene. Aero Limited began operating between New York and Atlantic City, transporting vacationers to and from the New Jersey seaside resort. In the winter of 1919–1920, attracted by the prospect of helping Americans escape the trammels of Prohibition, Aero Limited moved its operations to Florida. Using Curtiss flying boats, the airline made some 40 flights between Miami and Nassau during that winter, then ceased operations.

The attempt of Aero Limited to exploit the effects of Prohibition prompted another airline, Aeromarine Airways, to enter the Florida-West Indies market. One of the financial backers of this carrier, which had been flying between New York and nearby summer resorts, decided to form another airline, West Indies Airways, to fly between Key West and Havana. West Indies began operations in November 1919. Eventually, Aeromarine absorbed West Indies and, shortly thereafter, took over the Miami-Nassau route that had been served by Aero Limited. In November 1920, Aeromarine was awarded a U.S. Post Office contract to carry mail between Key West and Havana. Cuba awarded a similar contract for the return run.

The Key West-Havana and Miami-Nassau routes were operated only during the tourist season, between November and May. Beginning in 1921, Aeromarine moved its equipment — converted U.S. Navy F-5L flying boats capable of carrying 11 passengers — north each summer to serve a route between Detroit and Cleveland. The line also continued to shuttle passengers between New York City and Long Island and New Jersey summer resorts.

The service was strictly for the affluent, and for those willing to pay a premium for speed. The one-way fare between Key West and Havana was $50 (compared to $19 by steamer); between Miami and Nassau, $75 ($25 by steamer); between Detroit and Cleveland, $25 ($9 by rail). But Aeromarine did provide real passenger transportation on a regular schedule for those who could afford the price of the ticket. In the four years that the line remained in operation, it carried 30,000 passengers over one million passenger-miles. It was, by far, the most substantial commercial air-passenger enterprise in the pre-1926 period. The line shut down in 1924, but it is likely that it would have survived into the period of Federal regulation had the United States and Cuba not withdrawn their airmail payments. The lesson seemed clear. At this stage of aviation's development, passenger service could be maintained only in combination with airmail carriage.[26]

The fate that befell Aeromarine was the fate that befell most commercial air transport enterprises. Indeed, by 1924, commercial air transportation was clearly an economic disaster area. The mortality rate among fixed-base operators was unbelievably high. In 1920, for example, there were 88 fixed-base operators in the United States; in 1921, their number rose to 125, and the following year to 129. But of the 129 operators in 1922, only 17 had existed in 1920, and only 56 in 1921. Remaining in business longer than two years was extremely difficult. Twenty-four months later, in 1924, the number of fixed-base operators dropped to 60, a decline of more than 50 percent from the 124 of the previous year. The aircraft manufacturing industry fared no better. "Today the aircraft industry . . . in America has almost disappeared," lamented one observer in 1923. "Of the $100,000,000 invested in aircraft plants at the time of the Armistice certainly not one-tenth remains." Aviation had problems.[27]

IV

But if private enterprise was not making a go of the airplane, the Federal Government was. If there was any single civil aviation activity in 1925 that could clearly be called a success, it was the U.S. Air Mail Service. In the eyes of many, this service constituted the only substantial civil aviation undertaking. "There has been little or no coordinated, systematic, supervised development in commercial aviation in this country . . ., providing the operation of the air mail is excluded," said Chance M. Vought, an aircraft manufacturer, in 1925. The airmail, according to Vought, was "the single most interesting use of nonmilitary [aviation] and the most successful recorded anywhere." Paul Henderson, the Second Assistant Postmaster General, was of the same opinion: "I do not believe it improper to state my conviction that all that has been done for commercial aviation in this country thus far has been performed by the Post Office Department." A panel of aviation experts agreed. "The outstanding application of aircraft to transportation in the United States," the panel declared, "is the Air Mail Service."[28]

Before the airplane was even 10 years old, any number of rudimentary airmail demonstrations had been conducted in the United States, usually as part of the fare at aviation meets. The first such demonstration conducted with the official blessing of the U.S. Post Office Department was held during the week of September 23–30, 1911, at an aviation meet on Long Island, N.Y. Earle L. Ovington, duly appointed an airmail carrier for the duration of the demonstration, picked up the mail at a temporary post office near an airfield just off Nassau Boulevard and dropped it from his small monoplane at the Mineola, N.Y., post office, at which point the mail continued on its way by train. This process was repeated on a regularly scheduled basis during the entire week of the demonstration. In the seven days, Ovington carried 32,415 post cards, 3,993 letters, and 1,062 circulars.[29]

The Post Office, pleased with the results of the demonstration, asked Congress for $50,000 to launch a regular airmail service. Congress denied such funds until 1916, when it authorized the Post Office to initiate an airmail service by contracting with private carriers. The Post Office invited bids for one route in Massachusetts and seven in Alaska. It found no responsible takers. Private interests were unwilling to risk their capital in an unproven venture.[30]

In the ensuing months, the Post Office's belief in the airplane as a potentially important transportation vehicle continued to be reinforced, particularly by the role aviation began to play on the European war front. This belief was shared in other circles, including the National Advisory Committee for Aeronautics (NACA), which suggested that the Post Office itself undertake to develop an airmail service. Accepting the suggestion, Congress appropriated $100,000 for fiscal year 1918 for the establishment of an experimental airmail route.[31]

The Post Office inaugurated this service on May 15, 1918, flying mail between New York and Washington, with a stopover in Philadelphia. The Army cooperated in the venture by providing both the flying equipment and the pilots. Three months later, on August 12, the Post

Office took over the entire operation of the route, furnishing its own aircraft and pilots.[32]

The Washington-New York route proved a commercial failure. The distance covered — only 218 miles — was too short to permit any substantial time-saving advantage over existing surface transportation. In consequence, once the novelty wore off, mail planes were carrying, on the average, about seven pounds of special airmail per trip; the rest of the load was regular mail put on to make the trip worth while. Subsequently, the airmail postage rate was reduced from 24 to 16 cents per ounce, but again the response was disappointing. Accordingly, the special postage rate was abandoned and quantities of first-class mail were more or less arbitrarily chosen for the airmail run.[33]

But if the service was a commercial failure, it was proving a decided operational success. During the first 120 days of operation under the Post Office Department, 80 percent of the scheduled trips were completed in less than four hours. During one 90-day period, every trip scheduled was started, if not completed. This demonstrated to the satisfaction of the Post Office that an airmail route could be run. "But if the service was ever going to amount to anything," postal officials concluded, "it had to be undertaken on a much greater scale . . . and between points far more distantly separated." Hence, the Department now turned to establishing a permanent route spanning the continental United States and connecting New York with San Francisco.[34]

The first segment of the transcontinental route opened on May 15, 1919. It ran between Chicago and Cleveland, with a service stop at Bryan, Ohio. Six weeks later, on July 1, the New York-Cleveland segment, with a stopover at Bellefonte, Pa., opened, thus effectively connecting New York and Chicago. The route was extended west from Chicago to Omaha (with a service stop at Iowa city, Iowa) on May 15, 1920, and from Omaha to San Francisco (with stops at North Platte, Nebr., Cheyenne, Rawlins, and Rock Springs, Wyo., Salt Lake City, Utah, and Elko and Reno, Nev.) on Spetember 8, 1920. These 15 fields, spaced approximately 200 miles apart over a 2,680-mile route, made up the original transcontinental airway. To them were later added Des Moines, Iowa, and Sacramento, Calif.[35]

Beginning in July 1924 with the lighting of the Chicago-Cheyenne segment of the transcontinental, service was conducted on a regular 24-hour, day-night schedule. In the next 12 months, airmail pilots flew 2.5 million miles, carrying 9.3 million pieces of mail.[36]

The Post Office Department not only pioneered in the development
of civil aviation operations; it also pioneered in the development of civil
aircraft — or more precisely, the conversion of military aircraft to civil.
The Army had used Curtiss JN-4's to inaugurate the Washington-New
York route. The Jenny, equipped with a 150-h.p. Hispano-Suiza engine,
was capable of carrying about 6,000 letters, or 150 pounds. When the
Post Office took over the operation of the route, it discarded the Jennies
in favor of Standard E-4's, also equipped with Hispano-Suiza engines,
capable of carrying 8,000 letters, or 200 pounds. Then, on the transcontinental, the Post Office switched to de Havilland DH-4's, which had an
even greater carrying capacity.[37]

The British had developed and introduced the DH-4 in 1916 as a day
bomber. The craft performed creditably enough, but with a 60-gallon
fuel tank between its two cockpits making an easy target for enemy
gunners, it was soon dubbed "The Flaming Coffin." The sobriquet
notwithstanding, the U.S. Army built its own version of the aircraft, wed
it to the Liberty-12 engine, and used it as an observation plane. Vast
numbers were produced in America, most of which came off the
assembly line too late for war service. At war's end, they went on the
market as surplus and were grabbed up at bargain-basement prices by
aviation enthusiasts, and by the U.S. Post Office Department.[38]

A number of modifications were required to convert the aircraft into
a mail carrier. Its body was rebuilt for strength. It was outfitted with a
new undercarriage. The front cockpit, which had been meant for the
pilot, was converted into a water-tight compartment capable of holding
400 pounds of mail. The craft was now flown from the rear cockpit as a
single-seater.[39]

The U.S. Air Mail Service was one civil aviation enterprise that was
not a part of the chaos of laissez-faire in the air. Airmail pilot applicants
were required to have 500 flying hours and had to pass qualifying
examinations. Once hired, pilots were given periodic medical examinations. Aircraft were inspected at the end of each four- or five-hour trip —
and not in any haphazard manner. Postal mechanics checked the
airplane's condition against a list of 180 items before declaring it
airworthy. Engines were overhauled after every 100 hours of service;
airframes were given similar treatment after 750 hours. The emphasis
that the service put on preventive maintenance is illustrated by the fact
that it employed 353 mechanics and mechanics' helpers to care for a fleet

of 96 aircraft. Indeed, it was the Post Office's recognition of the importance of ground organization to organized flying activity that made the operation a success. Of the 745 people employed by the Air Mail Service in 1925, 699 (or 94 percent) were ground personnel. This bore fruit not only in the efficiency of the service rendered, but also in safety. In flying some 7.9 million miles between 1922 and 1925, the service suffered 10 fatalities (or one fatality for every 789,000 miles flown) — the best safety record of that day for any category of aviation activity.[40]

So the Post Office ventured into the air. There was no thought, however, that this enterprise, once established on a sound footing, would remain permanently under Federal auspices. "The general theory upon which the Air Mail Service is operated is that of demonstrating the practicability of aviation and thereby stimulating its commercial development," Paul Henderson explained. To Postmaster General Harry S. New, the idea was to perform an important public service in a manner that would "demonstrate to men of means that commercial aviation is a possibility." Charles D. Walcott, Chairman of the National Advisory Committee on Aeronautics, seconded the notion in a letter to Herbert Hoover, then serving as Secretary of Commerce. "We must develop efficiently the Air Mail Service," Walcott wrote, "making it serve not only to carry the mails, but in the more important capacity of an experimental laboratory for the development of civil aviation."[41]

By 1925, this objective had been attained. U.S. Air Mail Service operations over the transcontinental airway had clearly demonstrated the utility of the airplane as a transport vehicle. But mere example was not enough to propel the airplane into the mainstream of commerce. The Government still had to create an atmosphere in which commercial aviation could flourish. And it had to provide businessmen with appropriate incentives to enter the field.

V

An increasing number of people were coming to the conclusion in the early 1920's that aviation could not develop into a viable transportation mode without Federal safety regulation. These were not concerned citizens seeking safety for safety's sake. These were people within the aviation community — aircraft manufacturers and operators, and others, who, in one way or another, depended, at least in part, on aviation for a livelihood.

"It is interesting to note," Herbert Hoover wrote in 1921 to Congressman Frederick C. Hicks (R-N.Y.), "that this is the only industry that favors having itself regulated by Government." When the Senate Committee on Commerce held hearings on an ill-fated air-regulation measure, it was surprised to find that no one appeared or asked to appear in opposition to the bill. Indeed, aviation industry representatives were the bill's most enthusiastic supporters. "Congress has been denounced unsparingly for passing legislation regulating and controlling business," the committee noted in its report. "It is rather startling, to say the least, to have an industry . . . asking and urging legislation putting the business completely under Federal control."[42]

The committee exaggerated somewhat. The aviation industry did not wish to be completely under Federal control. In 1921, an aide to Hoover attended a flying meet with a number of prominent businessmen, including Howard E. Coffin, vice president of the Hudson Motor Car Company, C. M. Keys, president of Curtiss Aeroplane & Motor Corp., and S. S. Bradley, manager of the Manufacturers' Aircraft Association. These men, Hoover's aide discerned, believed the development of civil aviation depended "on the establishment of some sort of a federal governmental agency which shall immediately codify and present rules for interstate flying . . . ." Economic regulation was not even hinted at. That would come a decade or so later.[43]

The clamor for safety regulation spread. In 1922, the Merchants' Association of New York adopted a resolution calling for "national control" of commercial aviation. The Chamber of Commerce of the United States regularly reiterated at its annual meetings a position favoring the establishment of a Federal civil aviation regulatory agency. The National Aircraft Underwriters' Association and the National Aeronautic Association openly lobbied for the creation of such an agency.[44]

It was not the first time — nor the last — that businessmen advocated and sought Federal regulation of commercial activities. But the usual pattern that this advocacy had taken in the past was for one set of commercial interests to seek the regulation of a competing set. Shippers had been in the vanguard of those who advocated granting the Interstate Commerce Commission the power to fix reasonable railroad rates. Businessmen from the South and Midwest supported the Federal Reserve Act as a way of decentralizing and equalizing the distribution of the nation's monetary resources. With aviation, however, the industry itself, as Hoover had noted, was asking to be regulated. And though other businessmen had, in rare cases, sought Federal regulation of their own activities as a way of protecting themselves from dominant forces either within or without their industry, the call here as in other instances arose from an interplay of competing economic interests.[45] No such interplay was present to any significant extent in the call for Federal air regulation.

One more point. The demand for aviation regulation was not a popular, grassroots movement as was, say, women's suffrage or Prohibition. It did not even command the level of support enjoyed by such relatively esoteric legislative measures as the Sherman, Hepburn, Elkins, or Clayton Acts, which aroused passions well beyond the confines of the business sectors they were designed to regulate. Congress, in other words, had no popular mandate to act. When it did act, it responded to the pleas of a special interest group, which believed, with some justification, that its industry was in chaos and dying and could only be rescued by Federal intervention.

The narrowness of the base of support for Federal intervention is explained by the fact that commercial aviation, unlike other industries that had been subjected to regulation, had not yet grown sufficiently to perpetrate abuses of substantial scope or consequence.[46] Even counting the airmail service, which was in any event a controlled Federal enterprise, civil aviation activity was scant. And though what activity that did exist was not without sin, its sins did not pose a sufficient threat to arouse broad public concern. There was little in flying that represented a direct or personal threat to the man on the street. To the great majority of Americans, aviation was a rich man's or a daredevil's game. And while sensational newspaper accounts of this or that crackup may not have been devoured by the public with total callousness, the necessity of saving flying enthusiasts from themselves must have appeared exaggerated. (To others it appeared pointless. "If a man wants to kill himself . . . ," asserted a delegate to the Second National Aero Congress, "let him do it.") In 1925, 83 people lost their lives in aircraft accidents; in the five-year period 1921–1925, 354 (or an average of 70.8 per year) perished. As one wit cracked, the hind legs of mules annually claimed a larger number of victims than did air crashes.[47]

VI

This is not to say that men did not argue that a threat to life and property existed. "Lives and property can be saved by a national law regulating movement of aircraft," *Aero Digest* contended in 1922. Without Federal safety regulation, declared an official of the Huff-Daland Airplane Co., the public "is likely to suffer from badly engineered, badly built or badly repaired aircraft . . . ." Charles J. Glidden, publisher of an aeronautical journal, wrote to President Coolidge in 1923 that "a great many fatal accidents are daily occurring to people carried in airplanes by inexperienced pilots using aircraft that has [*sic*] not been inspected." The solution, according to Glidden, was the immediate enactment of a Federal aviation law. Charles M. Schwab, the steel magnate, agreed.[48]

In 1925, a joint committee composed of representatives from the Department of Commerce and the American Engineering Council declared that "flying is unnecessarily dangerous" because of a lack of Government regulation. "In all the discussion of the need for air law," observed the editors of *Aircraft Year Book*, reflecting on the events of 1925, "there was advanced no argument more consistently convincing than the necessity for protecting public life and property." Orville Wright joined the chorus. "I believe the examination and licensing of every pilot who engages in the transportation of passengers or merchandise for pay should be required," he said. "I also believe that proper precautions must be taken to insure the safe condition of the planes so used."[49]

Fiorello H. La Guardia was of the opinion that the state of the art had overtaken the skills of many a pilot. He had learned to fly in 1914 at a small field in Mineola, N.Y., in a tiny, 35-horsepower Bleriot with a class that included, in his words, "a Chinaman, two Japs, a farmer boy from Vermont," and a New York City policeman named "Mile-a-Minute" Murphy. "We were perfectly happy to sit in that thing, and . . . circle that field and think we were flying," he recalled. And though he had served as a U.S. Army flyer in the First World War, he told a congressional committee in 1925, "I do not consider myself a pilot anymore. . . ."[50]

Others, with less training than La Guardia, had no hesitation in taking to the air. In consequence, advocates of Federal regulation had a field day pointing to a record of incompetence and irresponsibility among private pilots. During the brief period of a single week, in July

1922, the residents of New York City were treated to the following hair-raising incidents: (1) an aircraft buzzed an automobile traveling the Long Island Speedway, causing the frightened motorist to lose control of his car and crash, with fatal results; (2) another aircraft, in the course of performing stunts over Far Rockaway Beach, went out of control and crashed, sending bathers scampering to safety; (3) yet another aircraft, flying out of control over the Hudson River, nearly collided with a ship and then an express train before crashing to the ground.[51]

That same week, a former Army reserve officer, whose commission had been revoked for reckless flying, crashed in Washington, D.C., killing a passenger. On Memorial Day 1922, this same pilot had been involved in another incident during the dedication of the Lincoln Memorial. With the President in attendance, the ceremonies had drawn a large crowd. While Harding was delivering the dedication address, the former reserve pilot buzzed the gathering, drowning out the President's words. "Had the machine gone wrong while flying over the great assemblage and fallen it would probably have caused the deaths of many people," the Washington *Evening Star* observed editorially. With no flying regulations on the books, the pilot was not subject to discipline, and was allowed to continue his errant ways. To the *Star*, the incident pointed "to the need of a regulation governing all planes of private as well as official character."[52]

S. S. Bradley, writing to Herbert Hoover in August 1922, drew attention to the contrasting safety records of unregulated private flying and the U.S. Air Mail Service, which, in fiscal 1922, had a "continuous operation under proper Federal inspection and control . . . without a fatality." A U.S. Senate subcommittee, after examining the fatality figures for 1924, found that itinerant commercial flyers had one fatal accident for every 13,500 miles flown; during the same period, the U.S. Air Mail Service had one fatality for every 463,000 miles, and the U.S. Army an even better record. "Both the air mail and the Army airways use only pilots and planes approved by Federal authority," the subcommittee said in its report. "The inference is obvious."[53]

VII

The reluctance of the United States to embark on a course of regulation contrasted with the involvement of European nations. "We are the only nation having any considerable aeronautical interests that

does not have . . . national legislation" regulating aviation, declared
Godfrey L. Cabot, president of the National Aeronautic Association. As
early as 1911, the British Parliament had granted the Secretary of State
the power to prohibit flying over such areas as he might prescribe; his
powers were augmented by acts in 1913 and 1919, granting him the
authority to regulate air navigation, issue, revoke, and suspend pilots'
licenses, and certificate aircraft. In 1920, France created an Under
Secretary of State for Aeronautics and Air Transportation and made him
responsible for, among other things, constructing airways and regulating
air commerce. Germany, Austria, the Netherlands, Switzerland, and
some Balkan states had statutes in force regulating flying to one extent or
another. Moreover, the air navigation rules set down by these states
conformed with the International Air Convention, which had been
drafted by an international aeronautical commission during the peace
conference at Versailles. By 1925, there were 20 parties to this convention. The United States, though one of the original 16 signatories, had
failed to ratify it.[54]

Only for a brief period during the First World War did the United
States have anything resembling Federal control over civil aviation. In
February 1918, President Woodrow Wilson issued a proclamation forbidding civilian pilots to fly over an area proclaimed a war zone unless
they possessed a license from the Joint Army and Navy Board on
Aeronautical Cognizance. Since the United States, its territorial waters,
and all its possessions fell within such a zone, every civilian pilot who
intended to fly had to secure a Federal license. The proclamation was
lifted in July 1919.[55]

Outside of state and municipal governments, the only control over
civilian flying of any consequence was exercised by the Aero Club of
America and, beginning in 1922, by its successor, the National Aeronautic Association (NAA). The NAA was the sole representative in the
United States of the Federation Aeronautique Internationale (FAI),
which, among other things, acted as the world authority for the certification of all flying records. The NAA exercised control over pilots by
forbidding anyone who had not been licensed by it to participate in flying
meets held under its auspices. These licenses provided a modicum of
order, though scarcely more. Indeed, the FAI licensing test was woefully
inadequate as a measure of pilot proficiency, and the license itself was
little more than a nice card for a gentleman aviator to carry in his pocket.

To Godfrey Cabot, the NAA president, the test was "antiquated" and suitable for a time when "engines were punk" and airplanes far less capable. Hence, according to Cabot, an FAI license was "not of much value"; he confessed that he had never applied for one himself.[56]

Some state and municipal governments tried to fill the void left by Federal inaction. Connecticut bestirred itself first, enacting a statute regulating air navigation in 1911. This statute, which required licensing and registration of aircraft, owed its existence to the efforts of Simeon E. Baldwin, the Connecticut governor. At the annual meeting of the American Bar Association in 1911, Baldwin had offered a resolution urging, among other things, that Congress "regulate by statute flights in the air between states . . . ." The ABA, believing there was no reasonable necessity for such legislation, rejected the resolution, and Baldwin returned home to secure state legislation. Two years later, Massachusetts passed a law similar to Connecticut's. Other states were slow to follow. By 1926, only seven more — California, Kansas, Maine, Minnesota, New Jersey, Oregon, and Wisconsin — had put regulatory statutes on their books, some of which were of a very minor nature.[57]

The reluctance of states to act and their tendency to be less than comprehensive when they did act prompted some municipal and county governments to pass local ordinances governing flying activities. Los Angeles County enacted an ordinance providing for the licensing of pilots. New York City prohibited flying at an altitude below 2,000 feet. Towns as small as Nutley, N.J., and Kissimmee, Fla., had local ordinances regulating aviation to one extent or another.[58]

But aviation was not an activity that was readily amenable to state or local regulation. In the opinion of one contemporary observer, local flying ordinances were an "undesirable expedient" that was "productive of much confusion." The problem of flight in the United States, observed a special committee of the American Bar Association in 1921, was peculiarly a problem of uniform law. "Any people who are so organized as to permit or to compel regulation of air flight by local ordinance," the ABA committee continued, "are headed for a confusion which will retard the development of the art." The net effect of state law was scarcely better. Like local ordinances, state laws spread confusion because of their lack of uniformity and were, perhaps, more of a hindrance than a help.[59]

The National Conference of Commissioners on Uniform State Laws drafted a uniform aeronautical statute and urged its passage by state governments. Ten states had adopted the measure by 1926. The trouble with this statute, however, was that it dealt exclusively with such questions as ownership of the airspace, lawfulness of flight, liability for injury, and related legal matters. It contained no regulatory provisions. A set of such provisions, applied uniformly throughout the 48 States, was the need of the day. As William P. MacCracken, Jr., pointed out before a meeting of the National Air Institute in October 1922, "Uniform regulation of aeronautics . . . is not only desirable but absolutely indispensable to the effective development of aerial transportation as an instrumentality of interstate commerce."[60]

VIII

Clearly, MacCracken, the ABA, and others who looked askance at the confusion of state and local laws were not talking about safety as an end in itself. They were concerned, to use MacCracken's phrase, about aviation's development into "an instrumentality of interstate commerce."

"One of the severest handicaps to the normal development of transportation by air is the belief that it is extremely dangerous," observed the Manufacturers' Aircraft Association. "This belief is strengthened by the knowledge that no laws or regulations governing such traffic exist . . . ." To Godfrey Cabot, the chief deterrent to aviation's development was the fear of flying — a fear "chiefly caused by ever-recurring accidents due to defective airplanes and incompetent pilots." Aviation would never reach its "fullest possibilities," argued Aero Digest, until the public was convinced of its safety. And the public would never become convinced "while incompetent pilots" were allowed to fly unsafe aircraft. "No business can prosper under dangerous conditions," observed Aircraft Year Book, an organ of the Aeronautical Chamber of Commerce. Some form of Federal regulation and inspection was needed, said Herbert Hoover, to give the public "a feeling of safety."[61]

Aviation had only itself to blame for the public's distrust of flying. "The gaping crowds gaze wide-eyed at the acrobat, wing walker, parachute jumper and such abnormalities, in quaking wonder . . . ," wrote one observer. And when people did venture forth for their first ride, they did so with the feeling of having offered themselves up "to the god of excitement . . . , very much as a man feels when he rides on a roller coaster to get a thrill . . . ." Much of the onus for implanting fear in the public mind was placed on the shoulders of the gypsy flier — "the care-free and often too careless itinerant" whose "irresponsible flittings" had embarrassed the responsible fixed-base operator and "left a trail of fear" from "coast to coast and from Mexico to Alaska." Aviation needed a new image, and a good place to begin the rebuilding process was the gypsy flier, making him accountable to authority. Then and only then would the "sane thinking and sane living persons" — those who were not interested in "looping the loop or falling down in a spiral" — begin patronizing aviation. Tomorrow's airlines would be built on the patron-age of such people.[62]

The absence of Federal regulation, besides creating a reluctance among the public to fly, had also created a reluctance among the financial community to invest in aviation. Aviation desperately needed new capital. But before anyone "would think of investing any substantial amount of money in the air business," Paul Henderson told a congres-sional committee, "he must first have some basic law" — a law defining the rights of the aviator and the man on the ground, a law regulating who may fly, where he may fly, and in what sort of aircraft. The British Air Attache in Washington, in reviewing the U.S. aviation scene, reported in his annual report for 1922, "No financial backing and consequently no real development can be hoped for in [the United States] until Civil Aviation receives legalised status and protective regulation through Federal Legislation."[63]

Another factor standing in the way of aviation's development was the inability to secure insurance at reasonable rates. "Insurance is almost prohibitive because of the lack of Federal law," noted *Aircraft Year Book* in describing conditions in 1923. "The underwriters, suffering heavy losses from crashes by irresponsible fliers, pass the burden on by increasing the premium from the responsible operators." Insurance costs for Aeromarine Airways, which had only one fatal accident in its four years of operation, came to 17.25 percent of total operating expenses — more than went for fuel and labor. Flight insurance for air passengers was also difficult to acquire and extremely high when acquired. In 1923, Aeromarine was the lone commercial carrier able to secure special flight insurance for passengers. The insurance, which could be bought at the time tickets were purchased, cost $1.00 for each $1,000 of insurance.[64]

Insurance companies could scarcely be blamed. To begin with, liability in air. accidents was a legal no-man's-land. Without either Federal or state laws on the books, the insurance industry, according to one underwriter, was "at a loss to know what legal principles and jurisdiction will apply in fixing the degree of liability." What really kept rates up, however, was the total lack of control over flying activities. But Federal regulation, when it came, would "make it possible for airplane owners and operators to procure insurance at lower rates," wrote H. P. Stellwagen of the National Aircraft Underwriters' Association to Herbert Hoover. In the meantime, the member companies of the National Aircraft Underwriters' Association took matters into their own hands. They arranged for the Underwriters' Laboratory to establish airworthiness and pilot standards and examine prospective policyholders. This was scarcely the answer since uninsured aircraft and pilots — and they were in the majority — affected everyone's safety. Insurance rates remained high.[65]

The advocates of Federal safety regulation, then, advanced an argument for social control as a way of furthering the economic prospects of an infant and sickly industry. Their position was somewhat similar to that of the city fathers of a frontier town overrun by lawlessness. Stamping out disorder would not only secure their persons and their property; it would also improve the town's economic prospects. Federal regulation of aviation safety would not only protect life and limb; it would also produce paying customers. Disorder was bad for business.

IX

But order was not all that the aviation community and its friends wanted of the Federal Government. They wanted it to play a more direct role in fostering the development of their industry. Government had done no less for other modes of transportation. "I do not think that many people appreciate that aids to [water] navigation have been provided by the Government," noted Senator Hiram Bingham in arguing for similar Federal assistance to aviation. He could have added that between 1917 and 1925, the Federal government had expended $484 million on rivers and harbors. Railroads had also come in for their share of Federal benefaction. By 1871, they had received from the Federal Government

land grants totaling more than 170 million acres — an empire, according
to one expert's calculation, amounting to more than four-fifths of the
area comprising the five states of the Old Northwest. Nor had the
development of the automobile as a popular transportation mode been
left to happenstance. In 1916, Congress passed the first of many Federal-
aid highway acts. Over the ensuing nine years, the Federal Government
expended $425 million for highway development. By 1925, some 180
million miles of the nation's highways had been built with Federal
assistance.[66]

Government subsidy of commercial aviation was the rule rather
than the exception in Western Europe. British and French air passenger
lines, which were far more stable than their American counterparts, had
been propped up from the beginning by generous government handouts.
"Should we subsidize commercial aeronautics?" asked *Aero Digest.*
"Why not? Did we not subsidize with all sorts of grants and privileges
our railroads and our merchant marine?" Why not, indeed, thought
Clarence W. Barron, a *Wall Street Journal* editor. Congressman Clarence J. McLeod (R-Mich.) proposed a different approach. He introduced
a bill that would have set aside $100 million in loans at 3 percent interest
to corporations or individuals engaged in commercial air
transportation.[67]

But proposals for this kind of direct assistance — subsidy in the form
of cash outlays — were rare and taken seriously mainly by the people
who made them. Most of the industry and its supporters in and out of
Government agreed with Chance M. Vought that "a direct subsidy
would be inconsistent with American ideals." But, Vought was quick to
add, "an indirect subsidy . . . would not be distasteful . . . ."[68] What
Vought and others had in mind was the establishment and maintenance
of ground-based navigational aids by the Federal Government. "There is
no question that the development of commercial aviation requires that
these things be done just as surely as there could have been no extensive
motor-car development . . . except that the States and Federal Government provided good roads," Vought said. It was the Federal Government's duty, argued Vincent Burnelli, the noted aircraft designer, to
provide these "basic elements" for aviation's use. Paul Henderson, newly
embarked on a commercial aviation venture, suggested that the Government take over all existing interstate airways and "maintain them for the
benefit of all who wish to properly navigate over them." Charles M.

Schwab, himself on the brink of entering the aviation field, offered the same suggestion.[69]

Herbert Hoover picked up the argument's loose ends and constructed what was perhaps the most compelling rationalization for Federal involvement. The Federal Government, he stated in 1925,

> provides for lighting and marking the channels of water navigation; it provides for accurate study of these channels and publication of charts of them; it maintains constant advice to navigators as to the shifting of channels and the changing of weather . . . .
> It gives aid in the development and improvement of ports and waterways.[70]

If the Federal Government suddenly ceased to provide these services, "our entire water-borne traffic would stop instantly." Hence, commercial aviation could not be expected to develop in any substantial way before airways were charted; before an aviation weather service was established; before provision was made for landing fields; and if real economy of time was to be attained, before airways were lighted for night flying. "Without such services my belief is that aviation can only develop in a primitive way," he said.[71]

Only the Federal Government could reasonably be expected to provide these services. "We can no more expect the individual aviator or the individual shipping company to provide them on sea." Should a private developer establish these facilities, he would not be able to regulate their use. He would thus be forced to allow any and all comers to fly over them free of charge. This would be unfair. On the other hand, the Government could concede a monopoly to him. But such a course "would be the negation of equal opportunity and of stimulative competitive development," Hoover argued. Why take such a course when every precedent for Federal action was at hand?[72]

There was a higher purpose for Federal involvement than merely helping establish an assortment of aspiring entrepreneurs in a new enterprise. The airplane appeared capable of adding an important new dimension to America's transportation system. If every city in the United States of 25,000 people or over were linked by a network of three or four transcontinental airways and a half dozen north-south airways, said Edward B. ("Eddie") Rickenbacker, the World War I ace, the nation would be tied together and brought, in terms of hours of travel, "down to the size of Texas." According to Charles D. Walcott, the Chairman of NACA, the development of commercial aviation would advance civilization itself.[73]

That was not all. Commercial aviation, in addition to providing an important transportation service, would become a valuable adjunct to America's air defense. By fostering the development of civil aviation, the argument went, the government would be producing a large body of skilled pilots, mechanics, and aeronautical engineers, as well as a vigorous airframe and engine manufacturing industry — all of which could be turned quickly to military use in the event of war.[74]

This, then, was the rationale for abandoning "the chaos of laissez faire in the air." By 1925, the Federal executive and legislative branches were convinced of the validity of this rationale. But, while there was substantial agreement concerning the need for Federal action, there was dispute over the precise form this action should take. This — not the broader imperative — would be the principal obstacle before the passage of Federal civil aviation legislation.

2. Prelude to Federal Regulation

How the nation should set aviation's house in order was a long-smoldering issue. In the seven years between 1918 and 1925, it was one of the most intensely discussed and debated questions on the national scene. Three Congresses — the 66th, 67th, and 68th — and diverse instrumentalities of the Federal executive investigated and reinvestigated the subject. By the end of the 68th Congress, in March 1925, no fewer than 26 probes of both civil and military aviation had been conducted. At the same time, countless measures were introduced in the Congress looking to the solution of the issue. Yet, despite the fact that the aviation community had launched a well-organized campaign to secure Federal legislation, and despite the support of three successive Presidents — Wilson, Harding, and Coolidge — all of whom saw the necessity of the Federal Government's regulating and fostering civil aviation, no regulatory statute had been enacted by the time Calvin Coolidge took his second oath of office. Nevertheless, these seven years were not without accomplishment. They saw the issue aired and defined. They saw contending solutions put forth. And they saw the principal protagonists in the aviation drama emerge. All this had to precede the final solution.

II

The Federal role in regulating and fostering civil aviation was first considered and debated on the national level while the First World War was raging in Europe. In consequence, civil aviation was entangled at the outset with the companion question of how to organize military aviation. The pattern had been established by Congressman Charles Lieb (D-Ind.), who, in March 1916, introduced a bill providing for the creation of a department of aviation with cognizance over both military

35

and civil aviation. Lieb saw his legislation as a national defense measure, reasoning that a separate aeronautical department was required to effectively mobilize the nation's air arm in time of war. But with the nation still at peace, albeit a precarious peace, and the Wilson administration lending no support, the bill died in committee.[1]

The interest of the Aero Club of America, however, had been aroused. The following spring, only days before Woodrow Wilson asked for a declaration of war, this organization of aviation enthusiasts, spearheaded by Rear Admiral Richard E. Peary, drafted a bill similar to Lieb's and persuaded Senator Morris Sheppard (D-Tex.) and Congressman Murray Hulbert (D-N.Y.) to introduce it in their respective houses. Secretary of War Newton D. Baker took a firm stand against the measure. The War Department's position, as expressed by Assistant Secretary Benedict Crowell, was that a separate aeronautics department, with military responsibilities not under the control of the Secretary of War, was "wrong in principle." The Aero Club, the only force of consequence behind the measure, was clearly no match for the War Department. Two similar measures, introduced by Congressman Norman J. Gould (R-N.Y.) and Senator Harry S. New (R-Ind.) prior to the Armistice, fared no better than the Sheppard-Hulbert bill.[2]

The problem with this small flurry of legislative activity was that it was being conducted in a political vacuum. Individual legislators were taking off on their own without support from congressional leaders, committee chairmen, or administration officials. Without such support, there was no prying legislation out of committee.

The war over, the quest for legislation took a more serious, if no more effective, turn. Woodrow Wilson, like his Secretary of War, was adamant in his opposition to a new cabinet department. He also opposed the idea of lumping civil and military aviation activities into one organizational unit. He sought, therefore, a legislative solution for civil aviation that was separate and distinct from any military legislation.

The 12 men who sat on the National Advisory Committee for Aeronautics (NACA) were like-minded. This agency, the sole Federal instrumentality outside of the armed services with a clear mission in aviation, had come to the conclusion as early as 1918 that "Federal legislation should be enacted governing the navigation of aircraft in the United States . . . ." At its behest, an interdepartmental committee composed of representatives from NACA and the Departments of War,

Navy, and Commerce was formed to study the question. Though this committee's recommendations were ultimately rejected, NACA's executive committee, headed by Dr. Joseph S. Ames, put together a bill creating a civil aviation regulatory body within the Department of Commerce. In February 1919, Wilson endorsed the measure.[3]

The principal features of the NACA legislative proposal ultimately appeared in the form of an administration-backed bill introduced by Congressman Julius Kahn (R-Calif.) in May 1920. A bill differing from Kahn's in a few minor details was introduced days later by Frederick C. Hicks (R-N.Y.) in the House and by James W. Wadsworth (R-N.Y.) in the Senate.[4] But by this time the 66th Congress had been flooded by bills dealing with aviation. The majority of these measures called for the creation of a department of aviation with responsibilities in both military and civil aviation.

In the forefront of the drive for a separate aviation department were the officers of the Army Air Service. These men, led by Brig. Gen. William ("Billy") Mitchell, an outspoken, charismatic figure who had made a brilliant record as an air combat commander in Europe, wished to free themselves from the control of the Army's General Staff. "From General Mitchell down to the hundreds of service lieutenants who wear wings," declared Laurence Driggs, president of the American Flying Club, "comes the unanimous counsel to take American aviation out of the hands of its enemies and place it entirely within the protection of its friends — the aviators." The "enemies" were the infantry and artillery officers that made up the General Staff and their civilian overlords, who, presumably, knew next to nothing, and cared even less, about aviation.[5]

The idea of an aviation department had been revived in the midst of a controversy over the wartime aircraft production program. This program, launched with high hopes and an enormous budget, never came up to expectations and began to draw fire from a number of quarters, particularly from Wilson's detractors, who suggested that the program, besides being mismanaged, was riddled with corruption. Mismanagement there was aplenty. The program's initial difficulties were due in large measure to an effort to introduce mass-production techniques to aircraft manufacturing. Wilson and Baker had handed the job of running the aircraft production program to automobile manufacturers. The Aircraft Production Board was headed by Howard E. Coffin, a vice president of the Hudson Motor Car Company. Coffin brought into the program such people as Harold E. Emmons, a Detroit lawyer associated with the automobile industry, Jesse G. Vincent, a Packard Motor Car Company executive, and Edward A. Deeds, who had pioneered in the use of mass-production techniques both at the National Cash Register Company and Delco, a producer of electrical ignition systems for automobiles. These men quickly applied the manufacturing techniques of their industry to the aircraft program, with the result that a great many unexpected production snags, some of monumental proportions, developed. Worse, their methods had a particularly stultifying effect on creativity. Their greatest achievement was the development of the Liberty-12 engine, which, by most accounts, was the outstanding aircraft engine produced anywhere during the war. But this achievement was diminished by their decision to make the Liberty the standard engine for all aircraft, whether bombers, fighters, or low-flying observation craft. Since airframes are planned around engines, aircraft designers were forced to conform to the characteristics of a single engine, the intended function of the airplane notwithstanding.[6]

By April 1918, after a full year of war and expenditures in excess of $600 million, the United States had produced a grand total of 15 aircraft. The following month, Wilson overhauled the program and installed new people in command. For the first time, men with experience in aircraft development were called in. The production machine swung into high gear. By the end of the war, 32,000 aircraft engines and 12,000 aircraft had been produced, not to mention vast facilities that had been built virtually from scratch. The trouble was that most of this came too late. The war ended, and the United States was left with an enormous arsenal of unused aerial equipment. Fewer than 200 aircraft were actually produced in time to reach the front. And all of them were trainer or reconnaissance craft. With $1.25 billion in appropriations, the program had failed to produce an airplane that could be used in aerial combat, forcing the United States to rely on its European allies for pursuit planes. In terms of its overall contribution to the war effort, the cost of the program had been enormous. Since fewer than 1,000 American aviators crossed enemy lines during the war, committing a single man to combat cost more than one million dollars.[7]

There was plenty in this mixed bag of failure and achievement for the critically disposed to seize upon. There was even more, it appeared, under the surface. Some of the men in charge of the production program, particularly Deeds, were accused of deliberately funneling Government contracts to favored firms — firms in which they had an active financial interest.[8] Wilson was embarrassed by the affair. In May 1918, he persuaded Charles Evans Hughes, his Republican opponent in the 1916 Presidential race, to conduct an investigation of the aircraft program. A subcommittee of the Senate Military Affairs Committee, headed by Charles S. Thomas (D-Colo.), initiated its own probe. Both Hughes and Thomas found ample evidence of waste, mismanagement, and inefficiency. And the Hughes report, released 10 days before the Armistice, caused something of a sensation by recommending that E. A. Deeds be prosecuted under the criminal statutes.[9] But by the time these charges had been digested, the war was over and public attention turned to other matters, temporarily.

The Thomas subcommittee, though overshadowed by the Hughes investigation, did manage to join the issue of a department of aviation. In his May 1918 overhaul of the aircraft program, Wilson had reorganized the Army's air arm into the Army Air Service, which he divided into two coequal components, the Division of Military Aeronautics and the Bureau of Aircraft Production. The scheme did not work well, for the two components could operate independently of each other. Troubled by this disjointed organization, the subcommittee cast about for an alternative. A visiting official of the British Air Ministry, General William S. Brancker, suggested publicly that the United States might well follow Britain's lead and create a single Cabinet level department in charge of all aviation activities, including civil. This suggestion had provided the inspiration for Senator New's 1918 aviation bill. Thomas and his colleagues bought the suggestion and recommended the creation of a new department in their report.[10]

Air Service officers headquartered in Washington believed they had found in this recommendation a way out of their predicament. This was the way to rid themselves of the heavy hand of ground officers. In November 1918, a memorandum urging the air staff to support a Cabinet-level aviation department made the rounds at Air Service Headquarters. In March 1919, Mitchell returned home from the war, and the call for a separate department received new impetus. Mitchell, through his wartime association with Maj. Gen. Hugh Trenchard, the Chief of the British Air Staff, had become convinced that the United States should adopt Britain's organizational scheme. He began expounding his ideas first within the War Department and then, to Newton Baker's chagrin, before congressional committees.[11]

By no stretch of the imagination was either Baker or Wilson wedded to the status quo. Both knew that aviation's house was in disarray. But, conservative in their approach, they believed that the legislation advocated by Mitchell and the Air Service was too far-reaching, that it went well beyond the needs of the present.

In May 1919, as a way of putting the wartime experience into concrete legislation, Baker dispatched Assistant Secretary of War Benedict Crowell to Europe at the head of a factfinding mission to report on aviation development in the United Kingdom, Italy, and France. This delegation, named the American Aviation Mission (or more popularly the Crowell Commission), included in its membership Howard E. Coffin, the former head of the defunct Aircraft Production Board, C. M. Keys, president of Curtiss Aeroplane & Motor Corp., Samuel S. Bradley, general manager, Manufacturers' Aircraft Association, and four members of the armed services. Crowell, it will be recalled, had opposed the creation of an independent aviation department, which may explain his selection by Baker to head the mission. Baker, however, unwittingly surrounded Crowell with people of different persuasions. Coffin, for example, had gone on record in 1917 in favor of the Sheppard-Hulbert bill. And Keys and Bradley, who were eager to see the Federal Government regulate and foster the development of civil aviation, were sympathetic to the legislative prescription advocated by the Aero Club of America. Hence, when the commission arrived in England and met and talked with General Trenchard and Winston Churchill, who, among other things, was serving at the time as Secretary of State for Air, Coffin, Keys, and Bradley found an organizational concept to match their tastes.

Whether it was these men, or Churchill and Trenchard, or a combination of both that persuaded Crowell to change his mind is anyone's guess; but change his mind he did. Crowell, in his report to Baker, asserted that Britain had "the most comprehensive governmental mechanism yet set up by any nation in the world for the encouragement, upbuilding, direction and control of its air resources." This mechanism had been built from "five bitter years of trial, mistake, experience and progress" and was the product of Britain's best minds. "America may well study it carefully." From here it was only one short step from the mission's recommending (with only the two naval representatives dissenting) that the air activities of the United States — military, naval, and civil — be concentrated in "a single Government agency created for the purpose, co-equal in importance with the Departments of War, Navy, and Commerce . . . ."[12]

Baker had not gotten what he had bargained for. He reacted by shelving Crowell's handiwork. Finally forced to release the report when Crowell made its contents known to a congressional committee, Baker had no choice but to openly disavow it.[13]

Meanwhile, the gulf separating the Air Service and the General Staff was being pointed up in a study ordered by General John J. Pershing, the Army Chief of Staff. A board from each branch of the Army conducted the basic study. The findings and recommendations of these individual boards were then reviewed by a board of senior officers, headed by Brig. Gen. Joseph T. Dickman, which wrote the final report. "No greater lesson can be drawn from the World War than that the unity of command is absolutely vital to the success of military operations," concluded the Dickman Board. The Army, in other words, required control of its own air arm. Baker clearly had the General Staff on his side.[14]

The divergent views within the Military Establishment were soon being aired in public. In July 1919, a House subcommittee chaired by Congressman James A. Frear (R-Wis.) began a 2-month-long investigation into wartime aviation expenditures. The Frear hearings, unlike the Thomas and Hughes investigations of the previous year, brought the full scope of the production scandals into the open.[15] The hearings also created interest within the Congress in the proper relationship between the Army and its air arm. The release of the Crowell Report, coupled with the known dissatisfaction of Air Service officers with their lot, convinced a number of legislators that an aviation department was the best device for correcting the deficiencies of the existing system. The result was a crop of bills establishing a new department.

The most important of these measures was a bill introduced by Senator New in August 1919, and reintroduced two months later. It alone out of 17 similar measures introduced during the first and second session of the 66th Congress managed to clear committee. Mitchell and Brig. Gen. Benjamin D. Foulois vigorously supported the bill. The General Staff, in an effort to prove that Mitchell represented a minority point of view, conducted a poll among a selected number of Army officers and displayed the results, which came out overwhelmingly in opposition to the bill. The trouble with this poll, as Foulois pointed out publicly, was that from among the fifty officers polled, only four were fliers; the rest were infantry and artillery officers. "The lines are clearly drawn," wrote one contemporary. "Upon one side are the aviators — upon the other, West Point or the military machine."[16]

Baker moved to defuse a potentially dangerous situation. He convened a five-man board of general officers to look into the merits of the New bill and similar legislative proposals. This board, on which sat four artillery officers and the Director of the Air Service, Maj. Gen. Charles T. Menoher, who, curiously enough, was not an aviator, predictably rejected the idea of an aviation department. "It would be a serious mistake," the board said, in an obvious rebuttal to the Crowell Report, "to blindly follow any system that was adopted by a European nation under the circumstances such as led to the adoption of the Air Ministry in Great Britain." The board concluded that "there should not be created any military air force independent of Army or Navy control." Baker sent this report to Congress along with a legislative proposal looking to the reorganization of the Air Service along lines that would guarantee the air wing's closely integrated status with the rest of the Army.[17]

The New bill got rough treatment on the Senate floor. Carrying an authorization of nearly $100 million, it was raked over by such fiscal conservatives as Reed Smoot (R-Utah) and William E. Borah (R-Idaho). "This bill creates a new department," Borah told his Senate colleagues. "We all know what this means . . . . It means opening up the Treasury . . . ." New, seeing the cause was lost, requested that his bill be sent back to committee. But Baker did get the legislation he wanted. The Army Reorganization Act of 1920 reorganized the Air Service along the lines recommended by the Menoher Board. The rest of the legislation, including the Kahn and Hicks bills, died in committee.[18]

It had not been a favorable time to secure civil aviation legislation. The 66th Congress was, after all, a Republican Congress, the first since William Howard Taft left the White House, and it was in no mood to follow the leadership of a Democratic Chief Executive. Other issues, moreover, loomed larger. This was particularly true in the Senate, where the debate over the League of Nations took an eternity. Then, too, the 66th Congress, like its immediate successors, was economy minded. To many legislators, aviation had led a profligate existence during the war.

Establishing either an aviation department or an aviation bureau in the Department of Commerce was no way to put a stop to spending. The reputed failure of the wartime aircraft production program did not help. Indeed, the conduct of this program, which had filled the air with the smell of scandal, was the primary aviation issue. By the time the Frear committee swung into action, in July 1919, legislators appeared more interested in dredging up the shortcomings of wartime aircraft production than in establishing the relationship between the Federal Government and civil aviation.

There was also a widespread feeling that aviation had not yet reached a stage of development that would justify Federal action. Assistant Secretary of the Navy Franklin D. Roosevelt, in challenging Billy Mitchell's call for a department of aviation, conceded that the day would come, sometime in the distant future, when aviation would grow to deserve the status Mitchell wished to confer on it. "But," Roosevelt said, "[General Mitchell's] inference is that [that day] will come about immediately." Senator Gilbert M. Hitchcock (D-Neb.) struck a variation on this theme. "Aviation is too little known and too little understood to justify the paternal attention of the government," he asserted. This kind of logic left aviation in a Catch-22 predicament. Commercial aviation could not grow and prosper without Federal benefaction; but such benefaction would not be forthcoming until civil aviation grew and prospered and developed a sufficient degree of importance. To these impediments were added the philosophical divisions between those wishing a separate, but unified, aviation establishment and those insisting that civil aviation belonged in the Department of Commerce. Even if no other impediment existed, the fact that those who did want legislation could not agree on its form was alone a formidable barrier against Federal action.[19]

III

Warren G. Harding, while campaigning for the Presidency in 1920, had not been unmindful of the aviation issue confronting the Congress. But he chose not to address himself to it; indeed, he said little about anything during the entire campaign. As President-elect, however, he ventured to say that he favored the creation of a department of defense made up of three separate and equal components — Army, Navy, and Air Force. To nearly everyone's surprise, the conservative Harding appeared to be favoring an approach as radical as Billy Mitchell's. But on assuming office the new President quickly dropped the idea of a new Cabinet department.[20]

On April 1, 1921, Harding directed Dr. Charles D. Walcott, the Chairman of the National Advisory Committee on Aeronautics, to organize a NACA subcommittee composed of representatives from the Departments of War, Navy, Post Office, and Commerce and from "civil life." The kind of recommendation that would come out of a committee handpicked by Walcott could be fully anticipated. Indeed, shortly after Harding's inauguration, Walcott had taken steps to acquaint key officials of the new administration with NACA's views on aviation policy. On March 23, in a letter to Herbert C. Hoover, Harding's Secretary of Commerce, Walcott reiterated NACA's position that "aviation is insepa-rable from the Army and the Navy . . . ." As to regulating civil aviation, there was "no question of the authority or the duty of the Federal Government in this respect." To exercise this authority, Walcott recommended that "a Bureau of Aeronautics should be established in the Department of Commerce . . . ." The administration knew what it could expect from NACA.[21]

Walcott moved at double time in organizing the subcommittee. Holding its first meeting on April 5, the subcommittee hammered out a report in four days — a report that reflected the policy in Walcott's letter to Hoover. NACA's executive committee approved the report in a special session on April 8, a pro forma affair at best since three members of the subcommittee also sat on the executive committee. Walcott transmitted the report to the President the following day.[22]

On April 12, in an address before a joint session of the Congress, Harding declared that it had become "a pressing duty of the Federal Government to provide for the regulation of air navigation." He briefly outlined NACA's recommendations, which, he delcared, "ought to have legislative approval." A week later he transmitted NACA's report to Congress. Thus, in short order, the Harding administration had adopted a civil aviation policy that was virtually indistinguishable from the Wilson administration's.[23]

Harding's performance may have appeared curious to some observ-ers. After all, his administration was an unabashed exponent of unfettered business enterprise. To the Mellons and the Hoovers of his cabinet, nearly everything of importance about political economy ended with the classical economists. Yet, in one of its first policy declarations, the Harding administration advocated plunging the Federal Government into a new regulatory field. Herbert Hoover, a believer in businessmen settling their own affairs through voluntary associations, told the National Association of Manufacturers shortly after assuming office: "It is my feeling that in order that this Department shall be of the greatest service to commerce and industry, it should be maintained on a non-regulatory basis . . . ." But to this he made an exception. "Matters in connection with the safety of human life" should be regulated. When an aviation industry lobbyist told him that the absence of Federal air regulations was contributing to "the needless loss of lives throughout the country," Hoover did not hesitate to tell an influential Congressman that Federal regulation of civil aviation was a "matter . . . . of a pressing order." And Harding, who was more conservative, though less doctrinaire, than his Secretary of Commerce, could readily agree, as could his successor to the Presidency, Calvin Coolidge.[24]

Harding had acted swiftly, but neither he nor his Secretary of Commerce, whose job it would be to assume the proposed new Federal responsibilities, displayed much of an inclination to follow up. It was not in their character, or in the character of this administration, to push hard on issues and tackle the grubby details associated with seeing a piece of legislation through. They appeared cooperative enough when their cooperation was sought; but for the most part, they restricted themselves to benign utterances. In consequence, the principal burden of pushing an aviation bill through Congress over the next four years was carried by private interests.

Following Harding's legislative initiative, the aviation community turned to Hoover for leadership in securing an acceptable law. "I feel that I voice the opinions of many leaders in expressing the sincere hope that aviation will soon have the benefit of your personal interest and direction," wrote Samuel S. Bradley to Hoover in July 1921. Bradley, his stint with the American Aviation Mission over, was back in the fold of the Manufacturers' Aircraft Association. Also back from wartime service was Benedict Crowell, who now sat on the Board of Governors of the Aero Club of America. Since leaving his War Department post, he and Bradley had, according to Crowell, "been in frequent — I might say almost constant — contact." Howard E. Coffin, now helping run the Hudson Motor Car Company, also sat on the Aero Club's Board of Governors. These men and others, representing the Aero Club, the Society of Automotive Engineers, the National Aircraft Underwriters Association, and the Manufacturers' Aircraft Association, soon sought a conference with Hoover. The initial impression at the Department of Commerce was that these men would wish to impress on the Secretary the advantages of creating a department of aviation — an understandable misimpression considering the presence of Crowell and Coffin. A Hoover aide, who had gone to witness Army-Navy bombing tests held off the Virginia Capes, soon determined otherwise. Finding the Washington-bound delegation in attendance, he discerned that these men "have changed their mind and do not believe that [a separate aviation department] should be established . . . ." They wanted, rather, a civil aviation bureau in the Department of Commerce. Crowell, the Aero Club, and the aviation community in general had flip-flopped, some for the second time. They would, however, hold to this course to the end.[25]

The meeting with Hoover, held on July 18, went smoothly. Hoover listened patiently to what these businessmen had to say and asked merely to be reassured that Federal action was required to save lives. Assured that it was, Hoover agreed to cooperate in securing legislation. The meeting broke up with the understanding that the delegation would take responsibility for drafting an appropriate bill.[26]

The bill that ultimately emerged from these people's hands conformed in its general outline to the recommendations made by NACA in April. In delineating Federal authority, however, it went beyond anything NACA had ever recommended by giving the Secretary of Commerce control over both interstate and intrastate aviation. At the beginning of the second session of the 67th Congress, in December 1921, James W. Wadsworth introduced this measure in the Senate, Frederick C. Hicks in the House. That same month, Harding again called upon Congress to establish a bureau in the Department of Commerce "for the regulation and development of air navigation."[27] Wadsworth's bill (S. 2815) went to the Senate Commerce Committee, where it was ripped apart by state rights advocates. Charles D. Walcott, anticipating trouble, had asked a New York law firm to review the bill's constitutionality. The firm's lawyers found the bill "within the constitutional powers of the Congress under the commerce clause." This opinion made no impression on the Southerners sitting on the committee. Thus, the committee's report characterized the bill as "most sweeping in its terms and scope." Wadsworth retreated. On January 26, 1922, he introduced a new bill (S. 3076), which was quickly reported out of committee. The new bill had successfully allayed the fears of the state righters, but it was not what the aviation community wanted.[28]

Five days before Wadsworth introduced his second bill of the session, the Aero Club had adopted a resolution asking for "immediate and decisive consideration" of S. 2815. But when S. 3076 emerged from committee, some members of the aviation community began having second thoughts. Bradley, seeing the bill's teeth had been extracted, characterized it as "nothing but a scrap of paper . . . ." To Maj. Gen. Mason M. Patrick, the Chief of the Army Air Service, who sat on NACA's executive committee, the Senate bill did not even constitute half a loaf. "We have asked for bread and they offer us a stone," Patrick declared.[29]

Despite their dissappointment, these men did not openly attack the measure. Senator Wesley L. Jones (R-Wash.), the Chairman of the Senate Commerce Committee, pleaded that he could do no better with his committee. He counseled that the bill should be seen through the Senate. Effort could then be concentrated on securing a better bill in the House, after which everyone would just have to trust to the good sense of the Senate-House conference. Though Patrick had his misgivings, this was the strategy followed. S. 3076 passed the Senate on February 14 and eventually found its way to the House Committee on Interstate and Foreign Commerce.[30]

V

During the last week of February 1922, two small groups of lawyers gathered for a joint two-day conference at the Willard Hotel, in Washington, D.C. Though they had had no hand in the recent legislative proceedings, they were vitally interested in them and would soon be involved in the effort to get a better bill in the House of Representatives. One group, the Aviation Law Committee of the National Conference of Commissioners on Uniform State Law, was chaired by George G. Bogert, the Dean of the Cornell Law School; the other, the Committee on the Law of Aeronautics of the American Bar Association, by an up-and-coming 33-year-old attorney from Chicago, William P. MacCracken, Jr.

This was MacCracken's first trip to Washington on aviation matters, and virtually no one in the Nation's Capital knew or had heard of this engaging young man who was destined to become a fixture in aviation circles. MacCracken would, indeed, become such a dominant figure that it is difficult to single out any personality, whether in private or public life, that left a greater imprint on Federal civil aviation policy during the 1920's.

MacCracken was born, reared, and educated in Chicago. His parents, a pair of homeopathic physicians, had more or less expected him to follow in their footsteps. But his talents, so evident on his high school debating team, lay elsewhere. He took his bachelor's degree from the University of Chicago (where, as a tall, lanky cheerleader, he helped whip up enthusiasm for Amos Alonzo Stagg's charges) and followed it in 1911 with a degree in law.

The qualities that had served him well as a high school debater were now brought into play in his chosen profession. He joined the Chicago law firm of Montgomery, Hart & Smith and ended up doing most of the firm's trial work. But it was not merely his quick mind and his considerable ability in courtroom presentation that made him a successful trial lawyer. There was something about this man — a certain charm mixed with earnestness, sincerity, and zestful good humor — that disarmed nearly everyone he came in contact with and set him apart from the common run of hail-fellow-well-met. Hugo Black was so taken with MacCracken that he struck up a friendship with him virtually on first meeting. "You could not see him and talk to him without laughing," Black said. These engaging qualities, so valuable in direct, interpersonal relationships, eventually worked to draw him away from the courtroom. He became a representative of special interests, perhaps the outstanding aviation attorney and lobbyist of his day, only to have his career abruptly and tragically cut short at its apex during the airmail scandals of 1934.

People could, and sometimes did, mistake him. It was difficult on first meeting to probe beneath the pleasant smile, the easy manner, and the good looks and sort him out as a man. Those who knew him best knew what they saw was genuine. They knew of his freedom from dissimulation (though he did have a pocket of reserve, albeit a small one, that he called upon from time to time); they also knew of his industry, his astounding capacity for work, and his willingness to get to the heart of a matter ("I wear one and we will get down to them — 'brass tacks'"). Though he hailed from a city dominated by Democrats, his politics were Republican, as were those of his parents and the majority of his clients. "It will always be a marvel to me," he said on the occasion of John W. Davis's nomination for the Presidency, "how the Democrats managed to nominate such a good man for president, but it goes to prove that the 'Divine Providence looks out for fools and children.'").[31]

MacCracken's interest in aviation began like that of many other Americans of his time, with his service as an Army flier in World War I. In the spring of 1919, having shed his military wings, MacCracken was asked by a local Chicago club to present a paper. For lack of anything better, he decided to talk on aviation law. To his surprise, when he began researching the subject, he could find nothing. Thus, on hearing that the annual convention of the ABA, meeting in St. Louis in August 1920, was holding a special session on aviation law, he determined to attend.[32]

The session was such a dissapointment to MacCracken that he wondered why he had ever bothered coming to St. Louis. The report, prepared by an aviation law committee appointed by the ABA the previous year, had rambled on about the law of the sea and other areas of "metaphysics." What disturbed MacCracken even more than the intellectual sterility of the report was the fact that the convention appeared satisfied to let the entire subject remain in limbo, which is where the committee had left it. With the help of a New York attorney, Charles A. Boston, MacCracken took matters in hand and succeeded in having a new committee appointed to study the question. He and George Bogert, among others, were picked to serve on the committee. Boston was selected chairman.[33]

Boston's committee did a more workmanlike job than its predecessor. Its report, submitted to the 1921 ABA convention in Cincinnati, was one of the most thorough reviews of aviation law attempted up to that time. The thrust of the report was that aviation law was in an unsettled state and, consequently, aviation existed in a legal vacuum — a vacuum that only the Federal Government could fill with the enactment of a comprehensive law extending Federal authority over all flying. But to secure such a law, in the opinion of the committee, would require a constitutional amendment — an opinion not shared by MacCracken.[34]

The report was attacked on the floor of the convention for a variety of reasons, particularly by members of the 1920 committee, who could not hide their displeasure at being upstaged in this manner. Hurt by the attack, Boston declared that he would not serve on the committee again. This led to MacCracken's being named chairman of a reconstituted committee, called the Committee on the Law of Aeronautics.[35]

George Bogert, selected to serve on MacCracken's committee, was occupied in yet another endeavor. He was chairman of a committee formed by the National Conference of Commissioners on Uniform State Laws to draft a uniform state aviation law. The report of the ABA aviation committee had taken a decidedly dim view of state regulation of aviation. And a draft uniform state law written by Bogert's committee had come under sustained attack from many quarters. It was obvious to MacCracken, whose committee was primarily concerned with Federal legislation, that his and Bogert's committees must come together and decide which powers properly belonged to the Federal Government and which to the states. Otherwise, the two committees might find themselves working at cross-purposes. The two men agreed to meet the following February in Washington.[36]

MacCracken and Bogert addressed themselves to two primary questions during their Washington conference. One question dealt with a practical matter: the extent to which states should regulate aviation in the absence of Federal regulation. The other was essentially constitutional in character: how far could the Federal Government go in regulating aviation under the commerce clause?

Aviation law in 1922 was in such an unsettled state that private rights, as well as Federal and state powers, were at issue. One of the more heatedly debated questions at the time was whether flight over private property without permission of the property owner constituted trespass. To put it another way, did the landowner own the space above his land in the same sense that he owned the soil? More than one reputable legal mind invoked an old common law maxim, *Cujus est solum, ejus est usque ad coelum* (Whose the soil is, his it is all the way to the heavens) and claimed that such flights, no matter at what altitude, constituted actionable trespass. This rule, like other legal aphorisms, had no basis in legislation; it had been adopted by the English courts as a comprehensive statement of landowners' rights at a time when any practical use of the upper air was thought impossible. Nevertheless, the legal profession spilled much ink agonizing over the implications of this maxim. Surprisingly, in 1921, the Chief of the Air Service published a circular holding that *Cujus est solum* stated the law. The ABA, though it took exception to this point of view, nevertheless recommended that the Congress resolve the matter by giving careful consideration to a constitutional amendment conferring control over the airspace to the Federal Government.[37]

MacCracken felt the ABA was too timid. He saw no necessity for a constitutional amendment. He believed Congress' powers under the commerce clause extended over the airspace; Congress, therefore, could regulate air commerce in the same way that it regulated other forms of interstate commerce. But the extent of Federal control over these modes was itself an unsettled question. Thus, there was no precise answer as to whether Congress could, for example, require the certification of aircraft or the licensing of pilots that never crossed state lines. The view of the Senate Commerce Committee was that Congress could not. Mac-Cracken, less concerned with constitutional niceties, believed that the Federal Government must regulate all phases of aviation, or else confusion would reign. Benedict Crowell, who had watched MacCracken's work at the ABA with favor, was in substantial agreement. Writing to MacCracken before the Wadsworth bill had been emasculated in committee, he admitted that the legislation posed some tough constitutional questions. He believed, however, that the bill should be passed as originally drafted and its constitutionality left up to the Federal courts, which he felt would interpret it "on the basis of public need."[38]

Feeling as he did about the Federal role in regulating aviation, MacCracken had little sympathy with efforts to enact state legislation. Bogert's bill, which provided for a state aircraft board with powers to license pilots and aircraft, make regulations, and enforce them, was particularly obnoxious to him. These were functions that could properly be exercised only by a single central authority, not by 48 separate units. Samuel S. Bradley, whom MacCracken had met through Crowell, also found Bogert's bill objectionable. "I can think of nothing that would more effectively paralyze the development of civil aviation in this country than the passage of this sort of legislation by the various states," Bradley wrote MacCracken two weeks before the Washington conference.[39]

MacCracken's views prevailed. The two committees decided that the uniform law should contain no provision for a state regulatory board; rather, it should deal with matters relating to aviation's legal status. Bogert did have his way in one matter. He insisted on and got a provision

making aircraft owners liable for damage caused by aircraft to property
on the ground. Federal legislation issues could not be dealt with so
conclusively. The conference did agree, however, that Federal legislation
was desirable and that the necessity for a constitutional amendment was
doubtful. This was clearly a stronger position than that advocated by
Charles Boston's committee in 1921.[40]

Far more important than what transpired at this conference were the
results of a meeting between MacCracken and Congressman Samuel
Winslow, a genial, easy-going New Englander who chaired the House
Committee on Interstate and Foreign Commerce. MacCracken had been
delegated by the conferees to visit the Congressman to discuss the
Wadsworth bill, which was before his committee. At first encounter
things went badly. Winslow manifested no interest whatever, in either
the bill or what MacCracken had to say. The conversation drifted to
other matters as MacCracken searched for a responsive chord. Recalling
that the Congressman was a harness racing enthusiast, he made a casual
reference to the sport. Winslow lit up and proceeded to deliver a
monologue on the subject. Presently, he ordered lunch for two and, more
importantly, sent for Frederic P. Lee, a lawyer on the staff of House
Legislative Drafting Service. He told the two men to get together and
draw up an aviation bill. "Whatever you agree upon, I'll introduce and
get through Congress," Winslow said.[41]

The members of the joint conference had no sooner checked out of
the Willard Hotel than MacCracken was greeted with more good news.
On February 27, the Supreme Court of the United States in a case
involving the Interstate Commerce Commission's power to set intrastate
railroad rates handed down a decision that said in part:

> Commerce is a unit and does not regard State lines, and while
> under the Constitution, interstate and intrastate commerce are
> ordinarily subject to regulation by different sovereignties, yet
> when they are so mingled together that the supreme authority,
> the Nation, can not exercise complete effective control over
> interstate commerce without incidental regulation of intrastate
> commerce, such incidental regulation is not an invasion of State
> authority or a violation of the proviso.[42]

Those who had worked for a strong aviation bill were delighted. And
others, such as George Bogert, who had been leaning toward a constitutional amendment, now saw no necessity for one. "I have been thinking
that the recent decision of the Supreme Court . . . makes it almost
certain that the same Court would sustain the constitutionality of a Bill

giving the Federal government exclusive jurisdiction over Aeronautics," Bogert wrote to MacCracken. Bradley, after canvassing a number of lawyers in New York City, was greatly encouraged. "Some men go as far as to say that there is no need for further consideration of the subject [of a constitutional amendment]," he reported.[43]

Thus, within a period of a month, between January 26, when Wadsworth introduced his "scrap of paper," and February 27, the day the Supreme Court ruled on the railroad rate case, matters had taken a surprising turn for the better. MacCracken had been handed an opportunity by an influential Congressman to repair the damage done by the Senate Commerce Committee. And he could now undertake this task relatively free of constitutional constraints. He could, in short, write the kind of bill he wanted. He had ample reason to believe that Federal regulation of aviation would not be long in coming. But MacCracken would have done well to temper his optimism with the knowledge that he was dealing with a man more interested in horses than airplanes.

VI

While MacCracken was in Washington he ran into Harold E. Hartney, a lawyer and World War I fighter pilot of some note. Hartney told him a of a project that was absorbing all his energies, the founding of a broad-based aviation association. MacCracken saw merit in the project and was soon engaged in its advancement.[44]

The task of promoting aviation's interests, including securing appropriate legislation, required organized activity — raising money, enlisting people in the cause, prodding and cajoling legislators and other public men. To those who gave the matter thought, it was clear that existing aviation clubs and trade associations were unequal to this task. The Manufacturers' Aircraft Association, besides being too parochial, was associated in the public's mind with the wartime production program. In an effort to put together a more representative body and one that would not revive unpleasant memories, the MAA helped found, in December 1921, the Aeronautical Chamber of Commerce (ACC). Samuel Bradley took on the task of managing this new association of aircraft manufacturers and operators. There was no hiding the fact, however, that the ACC was a child of the MAA, particularly since its membership embraced every aircraft manufacturer of consequence.[45]

The Aero Club of America, besides being the oldest private aviation organization, had the broadest membership base. But the Aero Club was also an organization in turmoil. As a functioning body, the Club was a mere shadow of its old self. The organization's decline began in 1920 with the election of Henry A. Woodhouse as its president. Woodhouse immediately unleashed an intemperate, unremitting assault upon the manufacturers and financiers involved in the wartime aircraft production program. Since many of the individual targets of this assault were also Club members, the organization was rent apart. But Woodhouse was not only disrupting the association internally; he was bringing the Club's members, and aviation itself, into public disrepute. Crowell, Howard Coffin, and Godfrey L. Cabot, a Boston Brahmin who had taken up flying at the age of 50, staged a revolt; they unseated Woodhouse and expelled him from the organization.[46]

But the damage had been done. "The scandalous attacks of Woodhouse on the Club and its Governors," wrote Philip A. Carroll, a Club member, "[have] destroyed its usefulness in promoting the cause of aviation." Nor was the Club's usefulness enhanced when Woodhouse initiated a series of suits that tied the Club up in seemingly endless litigation. These suits proved so knotty and cost the Club and its members so dearly in legal fees that Godfrey Cabot, not normally paranoid, strongly suspected that the Club's lawyers deliberately offered "rotten advice" in order to feather "their own nests at the expense of the Club to which they belonged."[47]

The Aero Club of America had clearly become a liability. Howard Coffin, encouraged by Herbert Hoover to do something, decided that the Club should be displaced by another organization — an organization "untainted with the animosities . . . of unsatisfactory ancient history." The new organization would be national in scope and catholic in outlook; it would embrace all segments of aviation, but would be subservient to none. Coffin was willing to contribute a substantial amount of his own money and time to this enterprise.[48]

The scheme ultimately decided upon was to disband the Aero Club, which was now securely under the control of Coffin, Cabot, and Crowell, transfer its assets, local affiliates, and its connection with the F.A.I. to the new organization — the National Aeronautic Association (NAA).[49]

It was in this project that Hartney had enlisted MacCracken's aid. Before long, MacCracken was performing the legal work connected with incorporating the organization and presiding at the October 1922 convention in Detroit that gave birth to the NAA. Things would be easier now, though not necessarily all the way. Dissension in the ranks did not die altogether; it was, however, kept to a minimum. The initial membership drive ("I understand that it was a complete fizzle," MacCracken informed an acquaintance) did not bring in enough dues-paying members to finance the organization's activities. But Coffin, elected the NAA's first president, made good the deficits. There was now money enough to finance lobbying expeditions to Washington and the activities of NAA's legislative committee, which MacCracken was persuaded to head, thus cementing ABA and NAA legislative policy. No longer would MacCracken, who was not independently wealthy ("I have to stick a little closer to my law practice than some people in order to connect up with three squares a day"), have to worry about who would defray his hotel and traveling expenses, as he and Bogert and their confederates had done during their two-day stay in Washington in February 1922. But more importantly, with the creation of the NAA, aviation now appeared to have an organization that could present a united front and effectively pursue aviation's best interests. Topping the list of these interests, in the view of the NAA, was securing a Federal civil aviation law.[50]

VII

Not everyone was happy with Winslow's decision to shelve Wadsworth's bill and substitute one of his own. Samuel Bradley believed it was a tactical error and a time-wasting procedure. Winslow, he felt, could do better by amending Wadsworth's bill. Otherwise, he thought, the hope of securing legislation during the 67th Congress could be abandoned. MacCracken, closer to the realities on Capitol Hill, saw things differently. "My private opinion is that [Winslow] wants the first aviation law to go down in history with his name attached to it . . .," he observed. When Howard Coffin made preparations for a trip to Washington, which included a visit with Winslow, MacCracken cautioned him: "Don't lay too much emphasis on the name Wadsworth, and above all else, refrain from mentioning Hicks," who had introduced a replica of Wadsworth's bill in the House. Given what he believed to be Winslow's ambition, MacCracken felt it was useless to hope that Wadsworth's bill would somehow emerge from Winslow's committee. Events would prove both Bradley and MacCracken right.[51]

The task of drafting Winslow's bill was long and arduous. Since the Commerce Department was an interested party, it was brought into the picture from the beginning. Hoover assigned William E. Lamb, the Department's solicitor, to work with MacCracken. The collaborators were like-minded and had few differences to resolve among themselves. Winslow, however, proved a source of difficulty. No sooner had the two men begun drafting than the Congressman changed signals in midstream. He would not, as he had promised, accept any bill MacCracken produced; he now wanted a bill establishing a department of aviation. Winslow had decided to join forces with Congressman Charles F. Curry (R-Calif.), an advocate of a united air service. Having little choice, MacCracken and Lamb followed instructions.[52]

By April 1922, they had a first draft, which, at Winslow's behest, was passed around informally among ABA officials. Despite the ICC rate case, these men had their doubts about the legality of Federal control over purely intrastate flying. It fell to MacCracken to remove these doubts. When the bill finally got to Hoover, in June, he bounced it back to Lamb. Hoover wanted no part of a British air-ministry setup. At the same time, he told Winslow that "a Department of Aeronautics looks to me to be a political dream." Though Winslow said nothing and left people wondering whether he would continue to insist on a department, Hoover's opposition had actually ended the chairman's flirtation with Curry.[53]

On June 19, a week or so before the House began a long summer recess, Hoover transmitted the revised bill to Winslow, who, in turn, handed it to Fred Lee for final revision, prompting Howard Coffin to voice the thought that "if we continue making changes in the Winslow Bill there will be no possible chance of getting it enacted at the coming session of Congress." The House was back at work on August 16, but when Winslow failed to bestir himself, Bradley reported detecting "increasing unrest" among those favoring Federal regulation. Congress, he believed, "has reached a stage where it is impossible for them to do business of any kind." The following month, when Hoover inquired about the bill's progress, Winslow replied that the bill in its present form would only attract unfavorable comment. He saw no possibility of introducing the measure until the end of the year. In November, MacCracken spent three days in Washington going over the bill with Lee. In the last week of December, Winslow distributed confidential prints to interested parties around the country.[54]

Comment was not unfavorable, though it should be remembered that it came from a limited, handpicked audience. The key section, which gave the Secretary of Commerce control over both interstate and intrastate commerce, appeared to please most respondents. W. Jefferson Davis, a member of the ABA aeronautical committee, thought it "a splendid statement of the powers Congress should have . . . ." George Bogert, still plagued by doubt, nevertheless believed it desirable that the Federal Government control intrastate air commerce. Six Federal deparments — Justice, Post Office, Agriculture, Treasury, War, and Commerce — endorsed the measure. NACA approved, though it did object to a provision giving the Secretary of Commerce power to establish and maintain airports. But again, this was merely a preview. The bill would not do so well before a wider audience.[55]

Finally, on January 8, 1923, Winslow dropped his bill into the House hopper. More than 10 months had elapsed since his initial talk with MacCracken. And less than two months remained in the life of the 67th Congress. The House Committee on Interstate and Foreign Commerce was engrossed in other legislation. Only a firm resolve on the part of the chairman to secure quick action could have guaranteed consideration of the measure. Winslow had no such resolve. The bill died, as Bradley had predicted. There was now an enforced wait until December 3, 1923, when the 68th Congress would convene.[56]

VIII

The 68th Congress was virtually a mirror image of the 67th. Wadsworth introduced his bill at the opening bell, and once again it was quickly passed by the Senate. Winslow, in turn, introduced his measure. When the Senate bill arrived before the House Interstate and Foreign Commerce Committee, Winslow struck out all but the enacting clause and substituted his own bill as an amendment. The next move was Wadsworth's. In a show of flexibility, he introduced a bill identical to Winslow's — a move explained by MacCracken to a confused observer as a piece of legislative strategy. Wadsworth was indicating his willingness to accept the Winslow bill. Things appeared to be looking up.[57]

But as the Winslow bill came under close public scrutiny it also came under critical attack. Form was a vital concern of the measure's critics. The bill, in truth, was a long, elaborate, complex document burdened with an overwhelming mass of detail. Previous legislative proposals stood in sharp contrast to it. The Wadsworth bill, for example, which, in Wadsworth's words, "was intended to be as simple as possible," sought to grant certain general powers that the Secretary of Commerce could exercise to devise, promulgate, and enforce a civil air navigation code — a code that would be refined with experience. The drafters of the Winslow bill approached their task differently, dealing with specific as well as general matters. In short, they drafted an aerial code into the legislation. This put Winslow in the position of trying to legislate air navigation rules that would stand for all time — or until Congress changed them. MacCracken, Lamb, and Lee, surrendering to the draftman's penchant for comprehensiveness, had overindulged themselves.[58]

Philip A. Carroll, a New York attorney who had served with MacCracken on the ABA's aviation committee, found the bill contained such a mass of useless and harmful provisions that he gave up trying to enumerate them. The Secretary of Commerce, he told MacCracken, should make the rules governing aerial navigation; otherwise, "the flexibility which is required in dealing with a subject as new as Aviation cannot be obtained." Howard Coffin agreed. The legislation should deal with "broad general principles of control," he said, and give the administering agency the broadest possible latitude in dealing with details. The art was too new and precedent too meager to permit any other approach. Clarence M. Young, another lawyer-aviator, told Hoover that the bill was "extremely complicated and arbitrary." W. Jefferson Davis, an ABA official, while he liked the bill on balance, conceded that "the minuteness of the details may provoke more than ordinary opposition." Perhaps, he wrote to a Department of Commerce official, the desired results could be achieved "by a somewhat more succinct statement of general legal principles," leaving the matter of the particular regulations to the Secretary of Commerce. This kind of criticism was coming from people who were leading the drive for Federal regulation — people MacCracken was in regular contact with.[59]

The bill precipitated a nasty fight within the NAA. Gypsy fliers and fixed-base operators had not exactly flocked to the NAA in droves. But those who did join began to wonder whose interests the association represented. They assumed, when they read the Winslow bill, that they had been singled out as special targets. After all, they reasoned, since no one else was engaged in flying, this elaborate bill of dos and don'ts could not be directed at anyone but themselves.

"It's surprising to note the amount of opposition [to the Winslow Bill] being encountered around the country, particularly among aviators . . . ," wrote John Ahlers, an NAA member from Dayton. "This Winslow Bill was calculated to eliminate the 'gypsy flyer' . . . ," charged an NAA delegate from Chicago. The president of a small fixed-base operation derisively referred to NAA's "after dinner aces," who were attempting to lay on the small operator the "vicious" hand of Federal regulation. To this man, the NAA was showing "an insolent disregard" for commercial aviation's real problems. When MacCracken tried to put a group of commercial fliers at ease his words fell on deaf ears.[60]

The dispute heated up to the point that NAA officers were accused of numerous and sundry sins. The NAA, it was reasoned, since it obviously did not represent the small operator, was the mouthpiece of the organized industry — in short, the monied interests. And MacCracken, the architect of the hated Winslow bill, was the tool of these interests.[61] More than one rank-and-file member wondered, moreoever, why Coffin and his two immediate successors to the NAA presidency, Frederick B. Patterson and Godfrey Cabot, were so generous in their financial contributions to the association. By one account, Coffin contributed $120,000 during his term of office, and Patterson, the president of the National Cash Register Company, $50,000 during his. Cabot, by his own admission, contributed substantial, though lesser, amounts during 1923 and 1924 and "footed the deficits" during his two-term presidency. This practice troubled not only rank-and-file members, but also such men as Lester D. Gardner, publisher of the respected and influential weekly *Aviation*, who told an offended Godfrey Cabot, "I don't believe in having rich men finance [the NAA]."[62]

The recruiting methods employed by the NAA also drew the fire of the rank and file and brought into question the association's integrity. Since NAA executives were also executives of large corporations, they found it convenient to bolster the association's rolls by recruiting members from among their own employees. Patterson, in particular, used such methods, signing up 500 members from the sales force of the National Cash Register Co. It appeared problematical that all these men were genuinely interested in aviation or that they would exercise independent judgment as NAA members. Rear Admiral W. F. Fullam, who was in charge of Patterson's recruiting drive, defended the practice by arguing that "membership is the sine qua non. Without membership . . .

this organization cannot live." But others suspected that these people were recruited to carry out policies dictated from the top, including the ramming of the Winslow bill down aviation's throat.[63]

All this was mere impression. The people who were instrumental in founding the NAA had little or no direct financial interest in aviation; indeed, a deliberate attempt was made to keep such people, particularly aircraft manufacturers, off the organization's governing board. Men like Coffin and Cabot, if they thought of their aviation activities at all in terms of financial returns, saw themselves creating the kind of environment that would eventually prompt a prudent man to invest in aviation as a system of transportation. (Coffin, for one, did eventually make such an investment.) And MacCracken and other NAA lawyers, who gave freely of their time and talent, were making important contacts and becoming experts in a field that had no experts, while looking forward to the day when they would earn fees representing new aviation ventures. But in this pre-1925 period, these men had not sunk their money in air transport. Men of means were not in air transport. Air transport was left to the small-time prospector with big dreams.

Far from being under the domination of aircraft manufacturers or any other interest group, the NAA was pursuing policies that were less than satisfactory to the manufacturers. F. H. Russell, president of the Aeronautical Chamber of Commerce, accused the NAA of being "timid," "cautious," and "prejudiced" toward the manufacturing industry. At the same time, the NAA contest committee was embroiled in a dispute with the Aeronautical Chamber of Commerce over the rules governing NAA-sponsored air meets. This dispute lead to Admiral Fullam's telling Russell categorically that the NAA was not surrendering to the organized industry at the expense of the independent builder. Moreover, though the NAA and ACC legislative policies were generally in agreement, not all aircraft manufacturers agreed with these policies. Grover Loening, for example, believed that the regulating provisions of the Winslow bill would "absolutely ruin" the aircraft manufacturing industry — precisely what fixed-base operators and gypsy fliers felt it would do to theirs. R. H. Fleet, president of Consolidated Aircraft Corp., saw the Winslow bill as an invitation to the Government to over-regulate. Thus, though the charge that the Winslow bill was designed to favor the organized industry tended to stick, it was a long way from squaring with the facts. Even as severe a critic of the NAA as Lester

Gardner had to admit that the NAA's interest in the bill was "purely unselfish."[64]

Deferring to its critics, the NAA leadership retreated from its categorical support of Winslow's measure. Coffin was not happy with the bill, and Cabot had second thoughts about the wisdom of granting the Federal Government control over intrastate air commerce. Patterson, concerned over "the enormous effort that is being brought to bear by people opposing the bill," believed a policy shift was in order. "Rather than . . . arouse widespread ill-feeling," he wrote MacCracken in May 1924, the NAA should "put the soft pedal" on the Winslow bill. Instead of supporting any specific measure, the NAA should merely approve the general policy of Federal control. "The most important thing just now is to create harmony in our ranks," he said. "There has been too much dissension and too much ill-feeling."[65]

MacCracken did not agree. "My personal opinion is that instead of pussy-footing on the bill we should still stand squarely behind it . . .," he said. Indeed, he disregarded Patterson's advice and secured the endorsement of the Winslow bill by the 1924 NAA annual convention, albeit with recommended amendments. He also secured the ABA's endorsement.[66]

Meanwhile, legislative activity on the state level was giving Mac-Cracken, Bradley, and other NAA and ACC members concern. The uniform state aviation law had been approved by the Commissioners on Uniform State Laws and then, in turn, by the ABA. If MacCracken and Bradley had had their way, all state legislation would have been deferred until Congress enacted a Federal statute. "Now, don't let us 'kid' ourselves," MacCracken told a group favoring state legislation; states would enact statutes that conflicted with each other and "you will have chaos." But as a practical matter, MacCracken knew that some states would not defer action; he therefore counseled at every opportunity that state legislators (1) oppose all measures except the uniform law, and (2) oppose any amendments to that law. Massachusetts ignored this advice by passing a measure drawn up by Edward P. Warner, an MIT aerodynamicist, causing Bradley to ask MacCracken why he had not done something about "our friend Warner" ("If a lot of these engineers and other regular fellows are wrong, it seems to me that you lawyer fellows should straighten us out").[67]

When the uniform law was introduced in the New York State

legislature, Hugh W. Robertson, at this time an employee of the Hudson
Motor Car Company, alerted MacCracken that "Professor Bogert is
busy again." What Robertson, a future operator, objected to was a
provision in the uniform law applying the doctrine of re ipsa loquitur to
aviation. "It will mean that when an airplane falls the owner or lessee
. . . is absolutely liable on the theory that merely because the plane fell
the owner or operator was guilty of negligence," Robertson pointed out.
Chester W. Cuthell, a New York attorney, who had handled the
Woodhouse case for the Aero Club, believed that this provision would
push insurance rates so high that it would seriously interfere with the
establishment of a practical air transport system. To Bogert's consternation, the ACC began lobbying against the New York measure and a
similar measure in Pennsylvania.[68]

Bradley, finding that 39 additional states were considering aviation
legislation, tried to persuade the NAA to oppose the measures. He wrote
B. H. Mulvihill, the NAA vice president, advocating an "aggressive
nation-wide" NAA campaign against state legislation. Mulvihill, caught
between Bogert's and Bradley's conflicting views, decided to call a
conference to settle matters. MacCracken was exasperated. "Why on
earth will you insist on taking off with your throttle half open?" he asked
Mulvihill. There was nothing to settle. All outstanding issues had been
ironed out in 1922. Mulvihill called the conference off, which satisfied
MacCracken but left matters in a state of confusion. Bogert continued to
support appropriate state legislation, while MacCracken, finding most
state legislation inappropriate, fought it. When the legislature in his
home state considered an aviation measure, MacCracken made three
trips to Springfield, the Illinois capital, to help block the measure, after
which he received a lecture from Cabot on the inadvisability of interfering in state affairs.[69]

IX

While MacCracken had his hands full controlling the enthusiasm of
state legislators, he had a difficult task instilling a sense of urgency on the
Federal level. To MacCracken's periodic inquiries about the status of the
Federal statute, Winslow would invariably make vague references to one
temporary impediment or another, all the while refusing to be pinned

down on a definite legislative timetable. MacCracken concluded that Winslow preferred to deliberate rather than act. When John Ahlers suggested that the NAA direct an extensive letter-writing campaign at Congress, MacCracken countered that the effort would be futile. The man to work on was Winslow. "If he wants to rush the bill through Committee onto the floor of the House, he can do so," MacCracken said. The trick was getting Winslow to act. Others, thoroughly frustrated by Winslow's unhurried pace, despaired of ever getting him off dead center. "Representative Winslow is nice enough, but that is about all you can say for him," said H. W. Karr, an assistant to Frederick Patterson. "He is pessimistic, too fat to have much energy, and I have been wondering how on earth the Bill ever got to him in the first place."[70]

In fairness to Winslow, he was not responsible for all the problems facing the measure. MacCracken himself, in his desire to be as comprehensive as possible, had contributed to the bill's difficulties. Thus, the subcommittee assigned the task of passing judgment on the bill was hard put to resolve all the differences between its members. Winslow, an easy taskmaster, allowed the subcommittee to do its work in its own good time. In consequence, it was December 1924 before the full committee held hearings on the bill. If anything became obvious at this late hour, it was that the measure was unpalatable to a significant segment of the House Commerce Committee membership. Olger B. Burtness of North Dakota, George Huddleston of Alabama, Homer Hoch of Kansas, and Sam Rayburn of Texas had serious reservations about extending Federal authority over intrastate commerce. Winslow brought MacCracken before the committee, and while the Illinois lawyer was brilliant in his recital of the bill's constitutional underpinnings, neither eloquence nor logic could convince a Huddleston that Federal authority could touch a citizen of Alabama plying his trade solely within the state's boundaries. The full committee reported the bill out on January 15, 1925, the section on intrastate commerce intact. Timing was atrocious, as it had been in the previous Congress. On this occasion, moreover, the measure, if it came to a vote, would have to compete for congressional favor with a bill introduced by Charles Curry establishing a department of aviation. Billy Mitchell's unification issue had flared up again. As it was, Winslow's bill did not come up for a vote in the seven remaining weeks of the 68th Congress. If there was any consolation for the bill's advocates it was in the knowledge that Winslow would no longer be around to contend with.

Coming close to losing his committee chairmanship in 1923, he had decided not to run for reelection.[71]

X

Those who had worked so hard for enactment could no doubt dredge up a long list of reasons for their failure. Winslow's ineffectualness had damaged the cause. So had the issue of state rights and MacCracken's propensity for comprehensiveness. The suspicions of the fixed-base operators that the Winslow bill was a piece of special-interest legislation did not help matters. Nor did the presence of a small, hard core of legislators in the Congress favoring the establishment of a department of aviation.

But none of this need have been fatal. Opponents of the Winslow bill were arrayed here and there in pockets of opposition that were, on balance, insignificant both in size and influence. Opposition did not defeat the Winslow bill. The subject of civil air regulation, though it was intensely debated by special interest groups, never caught fire; it never became a party issue. It was just another topic on the edge of legislative activity. Legislators could not become excited over an issue that lacked public sentiment (though they may have voted for it if given a chance). And such sentiment was lacking because commercial aviation did not exist on a scale that could attract public attention. As a matter of fact, commercial aviation was a declining rather than an expanding industry between 1921 and 1924. Senator Hitchcock's characterization of aviation as too little known to justify paternal attention was as valid in 1924 as in 1920.[72]

But the 68th Congress did not, as we shall see, ignore air commerce entirely. Indeed, it enacted legislation that would soon prove a boon to civil aviation activity. This legislation, when combined with a special set of circumstances, led the 69th Congress into the field of Federal air regulation.

3. The Legislative Cornerstone

On September 13, 1925, Dwight W. Morrow picked up his Sunday morning newspaper to discover that Calvin Coolidge had appointed him to a newly created Presidential board charged with investigating the state of U.S. aviation. The President's action, taken without the slightest attempt to sound out Morrow's feelings in the matter, had not come as a total surprise. In March, Morrow had received a curt message from Coolidge vaguely hinting at such an assignment. "I have in mind that I may like to have you look into the subject of airplanes for me," the President had written. Morrow heard nothing further about this particular Presidential inspiration until he picked up his newspaper six months later.[1]

Morrow's first inclination was to decline the assignment (after all, he reasoned, he knew nothing of aviation), though it is difficult to see how he could have ultimately refused the President. Dwight Morrow had known Calvin Coolidge since his undergraduate days at Amherst, where they had been classmates and friends. Both had gone on to law school, after which they pursued their separate careers, Coolidge entering politics in Massachusetts, Morrow eventually associating himself with J. P. Morgan & Company, where he earned, among other things, a high reputation in international finance. They remained friends, with Morrow giving his former classmate an occasional assist up the political ladder.[2]

The association left its mark. Morrow had a profound influence on Calvin Coolidge's life. And he knew Coolidge, his habits and his turn of mind, as well as anyone could know the deadpan Vermont Yankee. The President was not given to tilting at windmills; he abhorred the do-gooders in politics, who butted into everything and made every issue in the political arena their own. It was not the business of government to do good, Coolidge once explained to Morrow; its business was to prevent harm, and harm could normally be prevented by allowing matters to take their natural course. "If you see ten troubles coming down the road," he told Herbert Hoover, "you can be sure that nine will run into the ditch before they reach you . . . ." Public officials, then, should control their impulse to grapple with every issue in sight. "They should remain silent," Coolidge said, "until an issue is reduced to its lowest terms, until it boils down to something like a moral issue." Then and only then should they act. Apparently, in Coolidge's eyes, the aviation imbroglio had now assumed the aspects of a moral issue. And Coolidge was turning to his lifelong friend from the House of Morgan to help resolve it.[3]

II

"The general atmosphere of Aviation in America," wrote a visiting English journalist in January 1925, "impressed one as being in that state when something is just going to happen. Not so much the calm before the storm but rather the slump before the boom." The Englishman, C. G. Grey, had forecasted correctly; 1925 proved a fateful year for aviation in America.[4]

No event was more pivotal in the eventual assumption of civil air regulation by the Federal Government than the enactment of the Air Mail Act of 1925, signed into law by Calvin Coolidge on February 2, 1925. Federal air regulation now appeared a foregone conclusion, unless Congress intended the Air Mail Act to become a dead-letter law. This legislation, sponsored by Congressman Clyde Kelly (R-Pa.), authorized the Post Office Department to contract for the carriage of domestic mail with commercial air carriers. This undertaking would be doomed to failure without Federal airway development and regulation.[5]

The undertaking was also likely to fail without a willingness on the part of the business community to risk its capital. In the previous decade, a Post Office request for bids on a number of proposed domestic air routes had been met with silence by the business community. So the Post Office Department took it upon itself to demonstrate the feasibility of airmail carriage. This task fell largely upon Paul Henderson, the Second Assistant Postmaster General. Henderson constructed a superb transcontinental airmail service. He also worked closely with Kelly and with interested business leaders in preparing for the day when the service could be turned over to private interests. Kelly, chairman of the House Post Office Committee, largely represented railroad interests; his concern was to get the U.S. Government out of an enterprise that competed directly with private rail carriers — and the sooner the better. But Henderson persuaded Kelly to delay consideration of his bill for a year, until the Post Office had successfully demonstrated night flying. Meanwhile, Henderson urged business leaders to prepare for the eventual takeover. Samuel S. Bradley was soon involved in yet another private association, the Air Mail Extension Committee, founded in New York in 1924. The stated purpose of this organization was to promote the use of the airmail among large banks and business corporations. Obviously, Bradley was not trying to drum up business for the U.S. Air Mail Service; he and the interests he represented were looking ahead to the day when they would be flying airmail planes. Henderson did his job well. Within two months after the passage of the Kelly Act, the Postmaster General had received more than 2,000 inquiries from aspiring airmail carriers. Businessmen were now willing to invest their money in air transportation.[6]

No less a personage than Henry Ford himself was among them. "I feel it is now or never to get hold of commercial flying and make a success of it." With these words, Ford established, on April 13, 1925, an air-freight service between Detroit and Chicago. He had made his initial entry into aviation late in 1923, when he came to the financial rescue of William Bushnell Stout, who was experimenting with an all-metal monoplane. The Ford Motor Company began building this airplane itself in 1924 and eventually assumed complete control of Stout's company. But scarcely anyone had expected Ford to become an air transport operator. His entry into the air carrier business had a substantial psychological impact, for Ford was known as a hard-nosed businessman who eschewed the visionary and the impractical. Thus John Golstrom commented in his occasional column, "The example of Henry Ford's financial interest in air transport is certain to be felt increasingly in the coming year." To the editor of *Aero Digest*, Henry Ford — "this master genius of industry" — had lifted "the dark shadow that has hung over American commercial aviation . . . ." Lester D. Gardner advanced the opinion that "the magic of the name of Ford" was just the thing needed to bring the aviation industry out of its doldrums. "Now you know," wrote Will Rogers, "that Ford wouldent [*sic*] leave the ground and take to the air unless things looked pretty good to him up there."[7]

What looked good to Henry Ford apparently looked good to others. For the first time since Kitty Hawk, American capital began to flow in substantial amounts into the formation of air transport companies.

Perhaps even more important for the long run than the amount of capital was its source. Two airlines in particular were organized by some of the sharpest and wealthiest investors in the United States. Colonial Air Lines, which would eventually form the nucleus of American Airlines, was capitalized by, among others, William A. Rockefeller and Cornelius Vanderbilt Whitney. Rockefeller also invested in National Air Transport (NAT), the forerunner of United Air Lines, as did Philip K. Wrigley, Lester Armour, C. F. Kettering, Marshall Field, and Robert P. Lamont. C. M. Keys was installed as chairman of NAT's executive committee; Howard E. Coffin became the line's first president. William P. Mac-Cracken, who handled the incorporation, became the line's legal counsel. Paul Henderson was induced to leave the Federal service and become the line's general manager.[8]

The Post Office Department began to let airmail contracts in the fall of 1925. Ford, Colonial, and NAT were among the first half-dozen successful bidders. Ford was awarded two mail routes: Detroit-Cleveland and Detroit-Chicago. Colonial got the Boston-New York route; NAT, Chicago-Dallas. More awards would be made in the coming months when the Post Office opened up the transcontinental route to bids.[9]

A beginning had been made. Aviation was on the verge of moving into the mainstream of American transportation. What remained to make the transition complete was a Federal law providing for airway development and air regulation. With the likes of Ford, Rockefeller, Whitney, and Lamont now possessing a stake in the industry, there was little doubt that such a law would be soon in coming. But as events unfolded, a seeming complication intruded — "seeming" because what appeared at first blush to be a complication proved, in the final analysis, a powerful catalyst that eased the way to enactment of a Federal civil aviation statute.

III

Brig. Gen. Billy Mitchell was not easily diverted from his chosen course. The Assistant Chief of the Army Air Service had fixed his sights on aviation's attaining a strength and status appropriate to its military mission — a mission that he believed was coequal with that of land and naval forces. For six long, sometimes tumultuous years, Mitchell pursued this goal relentlessly, driven by a missionary zeal that seemed to mount in passion with each frustrating setback. The struggle had its peaks and valleys, but Mitchell occupied center stage throughout, keeping himself and his ideas before the public with a prodigious literary and oral outpouring. He hit the after-dinner circuit with all the energy, enthusiasm, and indefatigability of a Chautauqua lecturer. He wrote three books and an endless stream of articles and filled volumes in testifying before congressional committees. The winter of 1925 found Mitchell in his customary role of embattled knight-errant, engaging in another of his periodic forays against the military establishment.[10]

The Army Air Service, like the rest of the military establishment, had fallen on hard times during the postwar period. A penny-pinching Congress and an economy-minded Executive had allowed equipment to become obsolescent and personnel to drop far below the strength authorized by the Army Reorganization Act of 1920. The air arm found itself in this predicament, Mitchell believed, because it was under the control of people who did not appreciate the military value of aviation. He determined to impress aviation's value on military authorities, Congress, and the public at the expense of the Navy, for whom he reserved his boldest and most virulent attacks. The Navy, he argued, was no longer needed in coastal defense. Aircraft could sink any naval vessel. With aircraft of that day having an effective range of 200 miles, they were perfectly capable of protecting the nation's coastline. Accordingly, the Navy's defense mission should now begin beyond the perimeter of aircraft activity. Forcing the issue, Mitchell secured approval to validate his case in a series of bombing tests, which were conducted off the Virginia Capes in July 1921. Three captured German vessels, including the dreadnought *Ostfriesland*, were attacked and sunk. More tests were conducted in September 1921, and more in 1923.[11]

Mitchell had made his point (though the Navy had refused to concede it). The prospects of the neglected Air Service, however, failed to improve. Frustrated, Mitchell continued to upbraid the military establishment. Some of this criticism was unjustified. The establishment, from Maj. Gen. Mason M. Patrick, the Chief of the Air Service, to the General Staff and the Secretary of War, was not only mindful of the Air Service's predicament, but hopeful of doing something about it. In 1923, confronted by Patrick's plea for more funds, the General Staff convened a board of general officers headed by Maj. Gen. William Lassiter to consider the Air Service's plight. This board confirmed Patrick's and Mitchell's contention that the Air Service was in desperate straits. It recommended a 10-year spending program at $25 million per year to modernize equipment and bring personnel up to acceptable strength. The Secretary of War, John W. Weeks, approved the Lassiter Board's recommendations, but did not press the matter before the Bureau of the Budget or Congress when the Navy indicated its opposition. Thus, though the military establishment was timid in pursuing its goals, it was far from uniformly hostile, as Mitchell contended, to advancing aerial development.[12]

Mitchell's quest for funds went unfulfilled for reasons other than General Staff hostility. The plight of the Air Service was deeply rooted in America's disenchantment with the Treaty of Versailles and its resolve to refrain from further international entanglements. America's policy of isolation, men reasoned, would keep it out of all but defensive wars. With the nation flanked by two friendly powers on its northern and southern borders and by two oceans on its eastern and western flanks, it was invulnerable to attack from the air. Only an enemy surface fleet could possibly launch an attack against the United States. And the most effective counter to such an attack was a strong U.S. Navy. Given this presumed geographical insulation from air attack, Congressmen voted for naval rather than aerial armaments.

But while Mitchell and the General Staff may have stood in wonderment at the complacency bred by isolation, they were divided in their conception of the airplane as an implement of war. The General Staff saw the airplane as merely one more weapon at the disposal of the Army. In the words of Secretary Weeks, aviation was a "combatant branch" of the Army, "the same as the Field Artillery, Infantry, [and] Coast Artillery . . . ." The airplane was, in their view, species, not genus. Mitchell, his followers, and, indeed, the majority of Air Service officers saw the airplane as genus. It was an independent member of a three-membered military family composed of land, sea, and air forces.[13]

Given this philosophical clash, it followed that views on how the military establishment should be organized would differ. Unlike the General Staff, which wished to maintain the status quo, Mitchell pressed for an organizational solution patterned after the British Air Ministry. "What we want to see and all airmen want to see," he said in an address before the NAA, in October 1924, "is a Department of Air" — a department equal in status to the War and Navy Departments and with cognizance over all aspects of aviation, military, civil, and R. & D. "Practically every big air service in the world is organized along those lines," he said on another occasion.[14]

Mitchell was making a tactical error in insisting on the inclusion of civil aviation. Important segments of the civil aviation community held views on the airplane's place in the military scheme of things that were similar to Mitchell's. Yet they did not support Mitchell's solution because they believed civil aviation should not be entangled with the fortunes of the military. MacCracken, for example, believed that either the Air Service should be given a separate portfolio in the Cabinet or else the War and Navy Departments should be consolidated into a new department with three separate subdivisions — Air, Navy, and Army — existing in total parity with each other. But to mix military with civilian affairs was beyond his understanding. "Water transportation for commercial purposes is not under the Navy Department and I have never known of anyone wanting it put there," he argued. So why should commercial aviation be under an air arm. Godfrey Cabot agreed. Any scheme such as that proposed by Mitchell, Cabot wrote to MacCracken, would "have the effect of placing civil aeronautics under military control . . . ." He believed this to be undesirable.[15]

The General Staff exploited Mitchell's tactical error. "There seems to be a tendency to make the development of [civil] aviation dependent on the organization and development of military aviation," Brig. Gen. Hugh A. Drum, the Assistant Chief of Staff for Operations and Training, argued before a congressional committee. "This is wrong in principle and contrary to our national customs and experiences." Drum restated the matter on a subsequent occasion. Commercial aviation, he said, "is a business problem and belongs to the business sphere of our national life . . . ." Patrick, Weeks, and Edwin Denby, the Secretary of the Navy, advanced the idea of a bureau of aeronautics in the Department of Commerce at every opportunity. And they advanced it not merely as a civil or commercial proposition. Promoting civil aviation, which such a bureau would do, had important military implications. "The growth and development of civil aviation constitutes an invaluable adjunct to military preparation in time of peace," General Patrick stated. To Secretary Weeks, it was "apparent . . . that commercial aviation is an essential factor in modern national defense." A viable civil aviation industry, according to these people, would advance the state of the art, provide civil airways that could be used by the Army both in peace and war, and produce a civilian pilot corps that could be tapped in an emergency. All this, the argument went, would relieve the Army of the expense of maintaining a large peacetime Air Service and of making large capital investments in airways.[16]

With the United States presumably insulated from air attack, Mitchell and his followers appeared to have the worse of the argument over expanding U.S. air power. This, in turn, weakened their advocacy for a department of air. But in 1924 an event occurred that bolstered Mitchell's stock. Two U.S. Army biplanes successfully circumnavigated the earth, making the first round-the-world flight in history. The United States' geographic insulation from air attack was immediately brought into question.[17]

Before too long, this and other issues were being debated before a special committee of the House of Representatives. The work of this committee was a matter of concern among highly placed administration officials — a concern partially stemming from the circumstances that led to the committee's appointment. As the election of 1924 neared, the Coolidge administration came under increasing attack not only from Democrats, but also from Republicans of the Robert M. La Follette stripe. One progressive Republican, Congressman John M. Nelson of Wisconsin, launched an all-out assault on the administration's aviation policies, charging, among other things, that the true sponsor of the Winslow bill was a pernicious "aircraft trust" bent on monopolizing commercial aviation. The proposed bureau of aeronautics, Nelson held, was the aircraft trust's intended instrument for taking over this industry. Nelson went on to charge gross irregularities in the letting of Army and Navy contracts. In March 1924, the House passed a resolution introduced by Congressman Bertrand H. Snell (R-N.Y.), who would help manage La Follette's third-party presidential campaign, calling for an investigation of Nelson's charges. Coolidge handed insurgent Republicans a sound drubbing in the November elections. But in engineering the passage of this resolution, insurgents had wreaked their vengeance on the President. The committee selected to carry out the House resolution would survive months after the demise of the 68th Congress and live into the 69th. Coolidge may have won the election, but he could not simultaneously wipe out the insurgent legacy of the 68th Congress.[18]

Most of the five Republicans and four Democrats picked to serve on the committee of inquiry were selected from the House Committee on Patents because of the belief that the investigation would largely involve patent and other technical matters; nevertheless, the composition of the committee gave the administration pause. The committee chairman, Florian Lampert (R-Wisc.) had a progressive voting record. Frank L. Reid (R-Ill.) was known to be a friend of Billy Mitchell. These two Republicans, allied to the four Democrats, could very well control the committee's proceedings. Lampert indicated from the start that his committee would not be satisfied with merely investigating contract irregularities. The committee would conduct a full review of the entire field of aviation. Lampert went about this job in an effective, businesslike manner, free of emotional outbursts, inquisitorial tactics, or scandalmongering. The reasoned approach and professional demeanor of other committee members, especially Randolph Perkins (R-N.J.), who acted in effect as committee counsel, and Clarence F. Lea (D-Calif.), who had served on the Frear Committee, impressed most observers outside of the administration and helped bring the aviation issue to the fore.[19]

A small, outspoken group of Congressmen supporting Billy Mitchell's organizational scheme for aviation was encouraged. Time and again Charles F. Curry had introduced legislation establishing a department of aviation, only to be studiously ignored by his colleagues. No amount of inducement by Curry could bring the House Military Affairs Committee to hold hearings or take action on his bill.[20] But in January 1925, during the closing weeks of the lameduck 68th Congress, John C. McKenzie (R-Ill.) swung the House Military Affairs Committee into action. The committee took up Curry's bill and called Billy Mitchell as its first witness.

Mitchell, who had been out of town and was actually delayed in appearing before McKenzie's committee, was also called to appear before the Lampert Committee. Frustration had been welling up in aviation's stormy petrel. The Navy's opposition to the Lassiter Board recommendations had infuriated him, as had its resistance to making the bombing test results public. Thus, in January and February 1925, Mitchell used these committees as a forum from which to attack the Navy brass and the General Staff, who, he charged, were deliberately obstructing aerial development.

Mitchell's attack could not be overlooked by the administration. Weeks, for one, decided that he had had enough. General Patrick, who had protected Mitchell in the past, now found it impossible to defend him with any semblance of conviction. In March, the administration took a decisive step: it would replace Mitchell as assistant chief. It was at this point that Coolidge dashed off his curt message to Morrow. In April, Mitchell was reduced to his permanent rank of colonel and transferred to the Eighth Corps in San Antonio, Texas. [21]

Coolidge probably had no fixed idea of when he would act on the suggestion that he had made to Morrow. He simply sensed a distant danger in the political wind and decided on what course to take if and when that danger became imminent. He realized that the Lampert Committee would have to be dealt with in time. And he must have known that while Mitchell could be packed off to the hinterlands, there was no guarantee that he would remain silent. Events ultimately dictated Coolidge's timing.

On August 31, 1925, three Navy seaplanes left San Francisco bound for Hawaii. The following day one of the seaplanes, a PN-9 with a crew of five, was reported lost. Three days later, while the search for the missing flying boat was proceeding, the Navy's rigid airship *Shenandoah* was destroyed in a storm over Ava, Ohio. Fourteen of its crew of 43, including its commander, Zachary Lansdowne, perished. Though a Navy submarine would, on September 10, find the PN-9 floating on the Pacific Ocean, its crew none the worse for wear, everyone believed during the space of a week that the nation had suffered twin disasters. Reaction was immediate, calling into question military air policy. *Aviation*, in an editorial entitled "Take Aircraft Out of Politics," charged that the *Shenandoah*'s trip had been planned to generate publicity for the Navy and "bring out the crowds" while Coolidge was visiting the Midwest. "The Army and Navy are publicity mad, and no risk is too great to take to spread propaganda that may have a favorable effect on appropriations," the editorial charged. Some congressional critics sounded an even shriller note. But the biggest blast of all was fired by Billy Mitchell. [22]

The luckless Landsdowne was his friend, and Mitchell, smarting from his enforced exile, reacted with a scathing denunciation of the administration's policies. "These accidents," he charged in a blistering nine-page statement released to the press on September 5, "are the direct results of the incompetency, criminal negligence and almost treasonable administration of the National Defense by the Navy and War Departments." The lives of airmen, he asserted, were being used as so many pawns by nonflying Army and Navy officers who "knew practically nothing" about aviation.[23]

Coolidge acted swiftly and decisively. He appointed the nine-man Morrow Board to study "the best means of developing and applying aircraft in national defense" and directed it to lay a report "before me for information and also for the use of the incoming Congress." He also determined to court-martial Billy Mitchell.[24]

To Coolidge's mind, his administration had been impugned. His military and economic policies had been brought into question. More importantly, the *Shenandoah* disaster had given his detractors the upper hand and had raised the prospect of their imposing a solution to the aviation question that ran counter to his wishes. Coolidge was committed to the same solution of the aviation question as his two immediate predecessors. Considering the origin and makeup of the Lampert Committee, which, along with Mitchell, was the center of attention in the unfolding aviation drama, it was unlikely that it would recommend such a solution. Indeed, the tide was running particularly strong for a British-type air ministry. Congressman William A. Oldfield (D-Minn.), chairman of the Democratic Congressional Committee, announced that the Democratic party would support Mitchell in the Congress. James M. Curley, the Mayor of Boston, received loud and sustained applause in defending Mitchell before an American Legion convention. Fiorello La Guardia declared that he would "back Colonel Mitchell to the limit." Even Senator Borah, who had previously fought the creation of a department of aviation, expressed qualified support for a united air service. Coolidge needed something that would steal the opposition's thunder. The purpose of the Morrow Board was to upstage the Lampert Committee and, at the same time, turn back the onrushing tide toward unification.[25]

IV

The makeup of the Morrow Board assured in advance that it would recommend an aviation policy the President could accept. Of the nine members, eight were Republicans; the sole Democrat, Congressman Carl Vinson, was both conservative and safe on unification. Two were retired military officers — Maj. Gen. James G. Harbord and Rear Adm. Frank F. Fletcher. Neither was a flier, and thus they could be expected to support the views of the military establishment. Two other members came from Congress — Hiram Bingham and James S. Parker. Bingham, a freshman Senator and the only flier in the group, had already proposed a civil air regulation bill that had received Coolidge's endorsement. Parker sat on the House Interstate and Foreign Commerce Committee and had been in general agreement with the approach advocated by Winslow, whom he expected to succeed as committee chairman in the 69th Congress. Three men, in addition to Morrow, had been drawn from private life — Judge Arthur C. Denison, William F. Durand, and Howard E. Coffin. Coffin's views on unification were public knowledge, as were those of Durand, who sat on the National Advisory Committee for Aeronautics. Denison lacked a track record, but so did Morrow, and no one ever doubted where he stood.

Morrow had to work against time. The Lampert Committee had already held five-month-long hearings, between October 1924 and March 1925, amassing thousands of pages of testimony. It was expected to file its report in mid-December. Morrow had to conclude his work before that deadline. The Board sat for eight weeks, devoting the first four to taking testimony from 99 witnesses, none of whom had anything new to say. Indeed, virtually to a man, these 99 witnesses had already testified before the Lampert Committee.

Mitchell's appearance before the Board was easily the highlight of the hearings. Mitchell had arrived in Washington on the evening of September 25 and was met at Union Station by a large, noisy crowd of supporters, including two American Legion posts, that carried him from the train on its shoulders. He took the witness stand on September 29. Everyone expected sparks to fly. But this wily antagonist, who had hitherto exhibited an unerring flair for dramatizing his cause, suddenly and unaccountably lost his touch. The fire had gone out of him. He delivered a long, discursive monologue in a singsong voice, repeating old arguments and stale facts until he had his audience in distinct discomfort. "Betty [Mitchell's wife] got fidgety," recorded Mrs. H. H. ("Hap") Arnold. "Everybody got nervous. You could feel the coldness go through the board. We were sunk." Mitchell, too, sensed his ineffectiveness. After two hours of reading from his prepared text, which he had extracted from a recent publication, he asked Morrow whether he was taking up too much time. Morrow was not about to come to Mitchell's rescue.

Dwight Morrow

"No; go right ahead, Colonel," he replied. Mitchell read for another half hour or so and then asked whether the Board was not "getting tired of all this stuff?" Morrow, a model of politeness, replied that Mitchell's testimony was very interesting and that he could continue. He let Mitchell ramble on for more than four hours and had him back the next day for another hour and a half, by which time Mitchell, his voice nearly gone, was visibly embarrassed. Morrow had let Mitchell hoist himself by the petard of his own prolix harangue. He had said nothing new, save that he was now willing to accept a department of defense in place of an air ministry.[26]

Events now followed in quick succession. Morrow wound up his hearings on October 15. Mitchell's court-martial began October 25. Coolidge released the Morrow Board report on December 2. The 69th Congress convened on December 7. The Lampert Committee report appeared on December 14. Mitchell's trial ended in conviction on December 17.

If anything characterized Morrow's report to the President it was a lack of originality. In its recommended approach, the report was a direct philosophical descendant of the thesis set down by NACA and Newton D. Baker in 1918-1919. This was the kind of report Coolidge wanted and this was the kind of report he got. "The peace-time activities of the United States have never been governed by military considerations," the report declared. Hence, a department of aeronautics, with control over both military and civilian aviation, was rejected because it was "contrary to the principles under which the country has attained its present moral and material power." The Board recommended, therefore, that a bureau of air navigation be established in the Department of Commerce under an Assistant Secretary for Aeronautics. The Federal Government, the report declared, "should progressively extend the air mail service" and "meet the manifest need for airways and air-navigation facilities . . . ."[27]

As to the military question, the Board conceded that aircraft played more than an auxiliary role in warfare. The Air Service, the Board said, could function as "an air force acting alone on a separate mission." Though this position was not as advanced as Mitchell's conception of the airplane, it was clearly more advanced than the General Staff's. Thus, in order to point up the distinctiveness of the airplane's military mission, the Board recommended that the name of the Air Service be changed to Air Corps. There was a superficial similarity here to an idea advanced by a number of people — General Patrick and Godfrey Cabot among them — that the Air Service be given the same status as the Marine Corps; the Morrow recommendation, however, was no more than a weak parody of this idea. Air Corps officers, the Board continued, should be given representation on the General Staff and an Assistant Secretary of War for Aeronautics should be created by the Congress. The Board also recommended the creation of a similar Assistant Secretary post for the Navy. The Board's recommendations were unanimous.[28]

The Lampert Committee report, released 12 days later, was not so radical as Coolidge had feared. To begin with, it found no substance in Nelson's charges of the existence of an aviation trust or of irregularities in military contracting. More importantly, the committee rejected the idea of an air ministry. Indeed, its prescription for organizing civil aviation was the same as the Morrow Board's. Finding commercial aviation handicapped "by the lack of congressional legislation for its regulation and encouragement," the committee recommended that Congress create "a bureau of air navigation in the Department of Commerce." With both Morrow and Lampert in such close agreement, the civil aviation issue appeared all but settled.[29]

But on the question of military aviation, Morrow and Lampert parted company. To the Lampert Committee, the military services as then organized performed similar and overlapping functions — functions that were often uncoordinated. These shortcomings, the committee said, could be overcome by the creation of a single department of defense, which, through its unity of command, "would harmonize our national defense system, reduce expenditures . . ., and prevent needless duplications . . . ." It was an idea 20 years ahead of its time.[30]

Virtually lost sight of in the shuffle was a joint study undertaken by the Department of Commerce and the American Engineering Council — a study that Hoover made much of but which had little influence on events. Like the Morrow report, which preceded it in print by a couple of weeks, this study contributed nothing new in the way of ideas or proposals. But it did accumulate a vast store of useful information. And it did recommend, like its more publicized predecessors, the establishment of a bureau of civil aeronautics in the Department of Commerce. Considering that some of the most respected men in aviation circles — W. F. Durand, Alexander Klemin, C. T. Ludington, Edward P. Warner — sat on the joint committee, the recommendation, though scarcely packing the authority of the Morrow Board, threw additional weight into the scale against an air ministry solution.[31]

Coolidge had achieved his purpose. He had successfully blanketed the recommendations of the Lampert Committee with his own aircraft board report, which presented a moderate alternative to Mitchell's extremist prescription. "If . . . the public had only been given the Lampert Report," *Aviation* commented, "the effect would have been embarrassing to the Administration." The result was that the Lampert Committee recommendations, particularly those advocating a department of defense, did not receive the attention they might otherwise have gotten; nor, in the opinion of some observers, the attention they deserved. "Somebody in Washington is getting careless," Frank A. Tichenor wrote in *Aero Digest*. "Actual thought protrudes in many places from the Lampert Report." He found the recommendation for a department of defense both "constructive and refreshingly wise." In contrast, the Morrow report was a political whitewash. But Tichenor was clearly in the minority. "Our [New York] papers as well as those in Washington have received the published report of the President's Aircraft Board with a great deal of sympathy and in many [instances] with real enthusiasm," Samuel Bradley told Bill MacCracken. The *New Republic*, which had supported Mitchell in the past, abruptly switched its support to Coolidge. The *Nation* threw in its endorsement, thus making it unanimous among the country's two leading liberal periodicals. To a writer in *U.S. Air Services*, "The appointment of the Morrow Air Board was the most statesmanlike act of the present Administration." And though there were dissenters, one thing, as the *Philadelphia Record* remarked, was now generally held as settled: "That is the necessity for the immediate creation of a Bureau of Civil Aeronautics."[32]

V

Coolidge transmitted the Morrow report to Congress with an unqualified endorsement and asked that the Board's recommendations be implemented. Legislators scurried to get into the act. No fewer than 21 bills and resolutions dealing with aviation were introduced in the first session of the 69th Congress.[33]

Hiram Bingham and James Parker, having sat on the Morrow Board, not unexpectedly spearheaded the administration's legislative efforts. As early as October 1925, Hoover and Bingham had agreed that Stephen B. Davis, Lamb's successor as Commerce's solicitor, would draft a bill that Bingham would introduce in the Senate. "I trust [Davis] would draft a bill that would suit you — and let me read it," Bingham said on the occasion. On December 8, Bingham introduced the product of Davis's labor — S.41, a bill to encourage and regulate the use of aircraft in commerce. The bill was referred to the Senate Commerce Committee. Two days later, Parker introduced the same bill in the House, which was sent to Winslow's old committee, now chaired by Parker himself. Not to be outdone, Charles Curry reintroduced his old unification bill.[34]

In broad outline, S.41 followed the recommendations of the Morrow report, which made it, in effect, a warmed-over version of the Wadsworth bill. This was safe enough since Wadsworth's measure had cleared the Senate on two occasions. The bill, in brief, limited Federal authority to aircraft and airmen engaged in interstate or foreign commerce. But it did differ from the Wadsworth bill in at least three important respects: (1) It made no provision for an aviation bureau in the Department of Commerce; (2) it created a new assistant secretary, as recommended by Morrow; (3) it provided that the Federal Government establish and operate aids to air navigation.

The decision not to provide for the creation of a new bureau, largely dictated by Hoover, arose out of a concern for economy. Much of the work for establishing airways and providing other services, Hoover held, "can be undertaken by the extension of existing bureaus in the Department of Commerce which have already an overhead and directing staff . . . in all parts of the country." For example, the Bureau of Lighthouses would undertake airway lighting; the Bureau of Standards, aviation research and development; the Coast and Geodedic Survey, airway mapping. Thus, Hoover argued, the Government would avoid the expense of establishing a complete bureau, with a whole new hierarchy of bureau heads and chiefs superimposed on new field installations and supply shops. It was an argument that an economy-minded Congress would understand and appreciate.[35]

The Bingham bill avoided the political pitfalls inherent in the Winslow bill by limiting Federal authority to interstate and foreign commerce. As the Senate Commerce Committee noted in favorably reporting out the bill, S.41 avoided "constitutional entanglements" by reserving intrastate flying to the states. And like the Wadsworth bill, it was a simple measure; it granted general powers and resisted the temptation to plunge into minutiae. It therefore avoided the contentious questions engendered by the much more comprehensive Winslow bill. This, at least, was what the bill's supporters believed.[36]

True to past performance, the Senate completed its work before the House. The floor debate in the Senate was brief. Few amendments were offered and only a single section — one calling for the transfer of NACA to the Department of Commerce — was stricken from the bill. The Senate passed the measure by a voice vote on December 16.[37]

When the bill got to the House, Parker's committee had not even begun action on its own measure. It set its bill aside, therefore, and turned its attention to Bingham's. The forces that had stifled the Wadsworth bill in the past now began to undermine the Bingham bill. Just before Christmas a subcommittee composed of Parker, Schuyler Merritt (R-Conn.), Clarence Lea (D-Calif.), and Carl E. Mapes (R-Mich.) met to consider the Senate's handiwork. "Save for Mr. Parker," Frederic P. Lee reported to MacCracken, "the subcommittee did not take kindly to the proposal that it adopt the Bingham bill." Parker was in something of a quandary. In late September, he had promised Godfrey Cabot that he would introduce a bill similar to Winslow's, probably not realizing at the time that the administration would turn around and opt for a Wadsworth-like measure. But he had gone along with the administration, cooperating to the extent of introducing its measure in the House. He could not reverse himself again very easily, even though he was more attuned to a stronger regulatory measure. What he now did, in effect, was temporarily abdicate his committee leadership and allow Schuyler Merritt, a close friend of Winslow, to step into the vacuum.[38]

MacCracken had been keeping a close watch on events. As early as November he perceived that the Senate would "leave open a considerable field of regulatory jurisdiction for the states to occupy." Cabot advised MacCracken not to meddle ("Sit tight and say nothing, and see what happens"). He proceeded to outline a cautious strategy. If the bill passed Congress substantially as passed by the Senate, "We will hail it as a step in advance"; but the NAA would insist that it was an inadequate step, point out its most glaring deficiencies, and consider how most effectively to organize a campaign to cure them. "Does this plan seem all right to you?" he asked. It did not seem all right to MacCracken. The time to act was before the bill passed, not after. The NAA would not be doing its duty if it sat back and said nothing. It should insist that the bill be amended in the House "so as to give the Government exclusive regulatory jurisdiction over all aeronautics." It was the Wadsworth-Winslow controversy over again.[39]

Cabot's advice deterred MacCracken not in the least. He and Howard Coffin sought out Merritt and found him both a sympathetic listener and willing ally. Thus, what ultimately emerged from Parker's committee unmistakably bore MacCracken's stamp. By no means, however, was it another Winslow bill. The House measure was a hybrid. It possessed both the simplicity of Wadsworth's approach and the power of Winslow's, but without incorporating the excesses of the latter. Though approving of the amended bill's provisions, Cabot was incensed that Coffin and MacCracken would lobby for an amended bill without consulting the NAA's board of governors. They had now jeopardized the bill's passage, Coffin scolded. Lester Gardner, Cabot reported, felt that the bill would now attract the opposition of "all the small fliers in the country . . . ." This was playing into the enemy's hands. With the Bingham bill imperiled, the Curry bill's chances improved. Both Senator Bingham and Representative Parker were now "afraid of the Curry bill and of the man that is behind it, meaning Mitchell," he told MacCracken. So why not accept the Bingham bill, rather than throwing "the fat in the fire because we can't get at first everything exactly as we could wish."[40]

Cabot had misjudged the mood in the House. As expected, the opposition focused on the state rights issue, but to little effect. George Huddleston carried the brunt of the debate, warning of the dangers to individual and state rights posed by the grant of so much power to a central authority. "Perhaps even a disembodied spirit will not be permitted to wing its way upward into a better world," he said, "without petitioning Mr. Hoover and getting a pilot's license before he starts." Hyperbole was great fun, but it swung no votes. Thomas L. Blanton (D-Tex.) rose in opposition to the measure because it did not adopt the unified service solution, but here, apparently, not because of ideology, but for reasons of economy. The bill passed the House on April 12, 1926, by a margin of 229 to 80.[41]

The House-Senate Conference met a few days later. It was clear from the beginning that the House managers would have to yield on a number of issues. An analysis of the House vote revealed a clear North-South division. Of the 80 votes cast against the measure, 63 came from Southerners, and 12 more from representatives of border states. While the Southern bloc could be overwhelmed in the House, it did not suffer from the same debility of numbers in the Senate.[42]

The House measure differed from the Senate's in six major provisions (and a number of lesser ones) — *viz.*:

- *Aircraft registration.* Required the compulsory registration of all aircraft in the navigable airspace. (The Senate restricted registration to aircraft engaged in interstate or foreign commerce.)
- *Aircraft certification.* Authorized the Secretary of Commerce to determine the airworthiness of all registered aircraft. (Again the Senate's provision was limited to interstate and foreign commerce.)
- *Airmen certification.* Provided for the periodic examination of any airman flying a registered aircraft. (The Senate bill omitted the element of periodicity.)
- *Air traffic rules.* Extended Federal air traffic rules throughout the navigable airspace. (The Senate provided that such rules apply only to airmen and aircraft in interstate or foreign commerce.)
- *Airports.* Included airports among the air navigation facilities that could be established by the Secretary of Commerce. (The Senate bill excluded airports.)
- *Penalties.* Provided for a system of criminal penalties to help enforce Federal air regulations. (The Senate provided only for civil penalties and liens.)[43]

Four of the six major issues involved state rights. One issue, airports, raised the specter of runaway Federal spending. The sixth issue, criminal vs. civil penalties, was resolved in favor of the Senate, though the Senate's provision was strengthened by providing for additional administrative machinery for enforcement.[44] The other issues were more difficult to resolve and required an assist from NACA.

On April 15, Bingham wrote Charles D. Walcott asking that NACA examine the issues separating the House and Senate managers and make "a full report embodying such constructive criticisms and recommendations as your committee may deem advisable and necessary." Bingham knew what he was doing, for NACA had invariably taken a conservative approach to all civil aviation issues. NACA's full committee was holding its semiannual conference at Langley Field, Va., when Bingham's request came. A special subcommittee headed by William F. Durand was quickly organized. The subcommittee dealt essentially with two questions: Federal aid to airports and Federal control over intrastate air commerce. Federal policy toward airports, the subcommittee decided, should be analogous to Federal policy toward seaports. The Federal Government established and maintained lighthouses, dredged channels, and furnished weather forecasts; it left to municipalities, however, the establishment and control of port facilities. It followed, therefore, that while the Government should chart airways, provide airway lights for night flying, maintain emergency fields, and furnish weather reports to pilots, it should "leave to municipal authorities the control of airports." In other words, airways were like channels or harbors; airports, like docks. And docks, traditionally, were provided by local governments. Herbert Hoover and Paul Henderson had made similar arguments applying the same reasoning before the Morrow Board in September 1925.[45]

The NACA subcommittee made another argument against Federal airport development that would carry even greater weight with legislators. If airport development became a Federal responsibility, the subcommittee argued, local initiative in airport development would be destroyed. It would also bring pressure to bear on Congress to make large appropriations for airport land acquisitions. "The financial burden on the Federal Treasury would be so tremendous," the subcommittee said, "that it would take a great many years to carry the policy into effect, if, indeed, the responsibility thus assumed would ever be discharged." The result would be, the subcommittee predicted, that airports would not be established in the numbers needed, and "the primary object of the bill — the encouragement of commercial aviation — would be defeated."[46]

If the subcommittee used some convoluted reasoning in arguing against Federal involvement in airport development, it really took some winding twists and turns in deciding against Federal control of intrastate commerce:

> Assuming for the sake of argument that the regulation of intrastate air commerce and of all private flying is constitutional, is it advisable? The primary purpose of the whole bill is, or should be, to encourage commercial aviation, and as an incident to that encouragement to provide reasonable and needful regulations. The regulation of private flying is not necessary at this

time to encourage air commerce necessary to the major purpose
of the bill — the encouragement of commercial aviation . . . . It
is therefore recommended that the regulatory provisions of the
bill be limited to the regulation of aircraft engaged in interstate of
foreign commerce.[47]

Whether the subcommittee knew it or not, it was saying that safety was
of no concern unless it affected commerce. Walcott approved the
subcommittee's work and sent it off to Bingham.

The conferees agreed with NACA's stand on airports. They knew
Congress would not open the Federal coffers for this purpose; they also
knew that everyone of consequence in the administration, from Hoover
to the Budget Director to the President, opposed the provision. On the
question of Federal jurisdiction, the conferees compromised. Federal
licensing, or certification, authority was restricted in all cases to aircraft
and airmen in interstate commerce; Federal air traffic rules, however,
would apply to everyone using the airways.[48] MacCracken, in explaining
the compromise to a correspondent, stated that the law would apply —

. . . to everyone to the extent that they must have an identification number and obey the air traffic rules. Pilots and machines
used for non-commercial purposes are not required to get certificates or licenses. If the plane is used only to transport the owner
from his residence to his place of business, it is not considered a
business use. If, however, the plane is used for calling upon
customers or to advertise the business or in delivering merchandise, it is used in furtherance of the business and must have a
certificate of airworthiness and be operated by licensed personnel, if the business engages in interstate commerce.[49]

The states were thus left with a measure of authority over intrastate
aviation. But MacCracken and Merritt had decidedly shaped a stronger
measure than the original Bingham-Parker bill.

Both Senate and House agreed to the conference report on the same
day, May 13, 1926. On May 20, Calvin Coolidge signed the Air
Commerce Act into law.[50]

Coolidge also had his way in the settlement of the military question.
An Air Corps was created as prescribed by the Morrow Board, and the
War and Navy Departments got assistant secretaries for aeronautics.
The Navy job went to Edward P. Warner; the Army job, to F. Trubee
Davison.[51]

Hoover offered the position of Assistant Secretary of Commerce to Paul Henderson, the man who had made the U.S. Air Mail Service a going concern. Henderson refused it. He preferred to stay with National Air Transport, where he was making money for the first time in his life. Hoover turned to a tinplate manufacturer from Philadelphia, one Hollinshead N. Taylor, who had managed the flying activities connected with the Sesquicentennial Celebration. Taylor was the kind of man Hoover liked, a sober businessman. The problem with Taylor was that he wanted to remain a businessman while running the Government's civil aviation activities. Washington was not far from Philadelphia, and he saw no reason why he could not commute back and forth rolling tinplate and regulating flying. He would take the position under no other conditions. Taylor would not do. Failing to find any other businessman to take the job, Hoover finally turned to an obvious choice, MacCracken. He would have turned to him earlier had he known what to make of so ingenuous a man. So he kept him in reserve to use only when other possibilities were exhausted.[52]

News of MacCracken's impending nomination brought out Hiram Bingham's fighting spirit. This was a slap in the face. MacCracken had been the chief opponent of his bill; now he was being asked to become the top civil aviation official in the Federal Government. "Very doubtful of advisability of suggested appointment on account of many reasons," Bingham cabled Hoover from his vacation retreat in Puerto Rico. Hoover radioed back that MacCracken would be kept in line. "I propose to give a large proportion of my own time to [aviation affairs]," he assured Bingham. Could he therefore have the Senator's support? Other forces were now at work. The organized elements of the aviation community backed MacCracken. But even more important was the backing of Martin Madden, chairman of the powerful House Committee on Appropriations. Madden was from Chicago; he was also Paul Henderson's father-in-law. Since Henderson could not be persuaded to make the financial sacrifice to land this Federal plum for Chicago, Madden determined that another Chicagoan must have it. He took the matter to Coolidge. The rest of the Illinois delegation was not inactive. Meanwhile, Hoover sought out Bingham on the latter's return from Puerto Rico and managed to persuade the Senator not to oppose the nomination. Bingham had "some prejudice against Mr. MacCracken," Hoover told Coolidge, "[but] he doesn't make any point of it." Mac-Cracken's nomination was assured.[53]

VI

The long legislative struggle was over. Civil aviation had what it wanted — a cornerstone on which to erect a commercial air transport system. "The first great step for genuine advancement of commercial aeronautics in America has been taken," remarked a writer in *U.S. Air Services*. "The Air Commerce Act will be the agency through which air transport will come into its own." *The New York Times* talked of the legislation "blazing the way" to a U.S. commercial aviation system.[54] Nearly everyone who expressed an opinion in the matter discerned that U.S. civil aviation had come to a crucial dividing line in its history.

Calvin Coolidge said nothing. If he thought in terms of filling the air with commerce, he kept it to himself. To the President, the important thing was that he had prevented an egregious piece of mischief from being perpetrated. And he had, with the help of Dwight Morrow, stilled the agitation and restored calm. He must have been pleased with Morrow's performance, as others were. Indeed, his old Amherst classmate had become a particular object of praise. Even Morrow seemed pleased with himself. "I fear," he wrote to Jean Monnet, "that I am in danger of getting out of the class of which my son considers you one of the most conspicuous members — that small group which tries to get things done for which other people get the credit." In this case, Morrow continued, he was being praised for what a board of nine men had achieved.[55] Absorbed in paying himself a backdoor compliment, Morrow had overlooked the President's role in the whole affair. This was no small oversight, for if the Air Commerce Act was enacted in 1926, it was due in large measure to the political skill of Calvin Coolidge. The act itself was perhaps the only genuine legislative achievement of the Coolidge Presidency.

II

The Republican Era

1926–1932

4. Regulating Air Commerce

In 1924, William P. MacCracken, Jr., had tried to allay the fears of a group of fliers fretting over the prospect of Federal air regulation by pointing to the first two lines of the Winslow bill, which contained the following charge: "The Secretary [of Commerce] shall encourage, foster and promote civil aeronautics." Moreover, MacCracken continued, the powers granted by the bill would be exercised by "the head of the Department of Commerce, which is now and always should be under the direction of a successful and able business executive." In 1926, Herbert Hoover, the successful businessman MacCracken had alluded to, was still at the helm of the Department of Commerce. And the Air Commerce Act, in slightly different language, had entrusted him with the selfsame charge contained in the Winslow bill. "The purpose of this bill," Hiram Bingham had explained in introducing what eventually became the Air Commerce Act, "is not so much to regulate as to promote." Later, while the bill was being amended in conference, NACA had advised the House and Senate managers that "the wisest policy to pursue at this time is to provide a maximum of encouragement with a minimum of regulation."[1]

Clearly, then, the intention of the framers of the Air Commerce Act was not to insure aviation safety as an end in itself. Safety in the air had as its chief goal the promotion of aeronautics. Attaining this goal required a careful balancing of interests. "Regulations should not be so strict that the growth of the industry will be retarded," a Department of Commerce official wrote. "Yet at the same time, they must be strict enough to protect both the industry and the public consumer of aeronautical products and services." In the years to come, it would be no easy task to keep the broad interests of the public and the parochial interests of the aviation industry in balance. The two interests, though not wholly incompatible, often clashed. In short, the framers of the Air Commerce

Act, by entrusting to a single agency both promotional and regulatory powers, had created a potential and permanent source of conflict.[2]

Whether MacCracken gave thought to this potential source of conflict is problematical. Even if so inclined, he had little time to draw fine distinctions or fret over where the public interest began and the private interest ended. He had a job before him — an organization to build, regulations to draw up, airways to construct. Besides, who was to say whether the public interest in aviation did not precisely coincide with the private interest of the industry. His principal responsibility, he believed, was to foster the development of the industry. If he weighed his acts at all, it was to determine whether they furthered that end. Furthering that end was in itself in the public interest, for only a healthy, viable air transportation industry could be of ultimate value and service to the public.

II

Putting together a working organization was MacCracken's first task. Matters had been delayed somewhat by the protracted search for an Assistant Secretary for Aeronautics and by Hiram Bingham's opposition to Hoover's ultimate choice. The fact that there was little money to operate with also helped slow down the pace. But an operating agency, named the Aeronautics Branch, did take shape rapidly when Mac-Cracken officially took office in August.

The speed with which the Aeronautics Branch was put together once a start was made was a direct result of Hoover's decision to utilize existing Department of Commerce bureaus in aeronautical work. Accordingly, airway development and maintenance was assigned to the Bureau of Lighthouses, aeronautical research to the Bureau of Standards, and airway mapping to the Coast and Geodetic Survey. It was a relatively easy matter for these bureaus to absorb their new functions and create new divisions to carry them out. The Bureau of Standards was already engaged in some aeronautical research, mainly radio aids; the people involved in this work were simply moved into a new Aeronautics Research Division. The Bureau of Lighthouses had an extensive field organization upon which the activities of an Airways Division could be superimposed. And the Coast and Geodetic Survey could take in stride the establishment of an Airways Mapping Section. Hence, only the Air Regulations and Information Divisions among major organizational units had to be established from scratch.[3]

To run the day-to-day affairs of the Aeronautics Branch, Mac-Cracken eventually established the position of Director of Aeronautics and selected Clarence M. Young, a 37-year-old attorney and former combat pilot, to fill it. Young, a crisp, quiet man whose manner gave a hint of repressed energy, was the perfect counterpoise to the flashier and less inhibited MacCracken. Young would be involved in one way or another with nearly all the affairs of the Aeronautics Branch. He had supervisory responsibility, however, only over those elements directly under the Branch — regulation, information, and administration. His involvement with functions entrusted to other bureaus was primarily in an advisory capacity.[4]

MacCracken's authority, of course, reached all functions, though in places it flowed downward through intervening administrative layers. In theory, he could reach the divisions lodged in bureaus other than the Aeronautics Branch through their respective bureau heads. In actual practice, the chiefs of these divisions ran their own shops under the scrutiny, if not the supervision, of Young, while MacCracken concentrated primarily on political and policy matters. The work of these divisions was approved by MacCracken and financed out of funds from the Aeronautics Branch budget. Establishing this kind of loosely knit organization had certain short-term advantages, but it did not make for a well-integrated unit. The Aeronautics Branch lacked structural integrity — a shortcoming that could be lived with over the short term in order to attain as rapid a start-up as possible.[5]

Next to putting together a working organization, the task of devising rules regulating aviation activity loomed uppermost in MacCracken's mind. "The first thing we needed," he later recalled, "was a system of Air Commerce regulations." The Department of Commerce has always had strong ties to the American business community. These ties were never stronger than during Herbert Hoover's tenure as Secretary of Commerce. Hoover succeeded in cultivating the trust and confidence of business to an unparalleled degree. Much of his success was due to his methods. "The Department has followed the policy of seeking the advice and assistance of those best qualified to interpret the needs of industry and business in general," declared J. Walter Drake, the Assistant

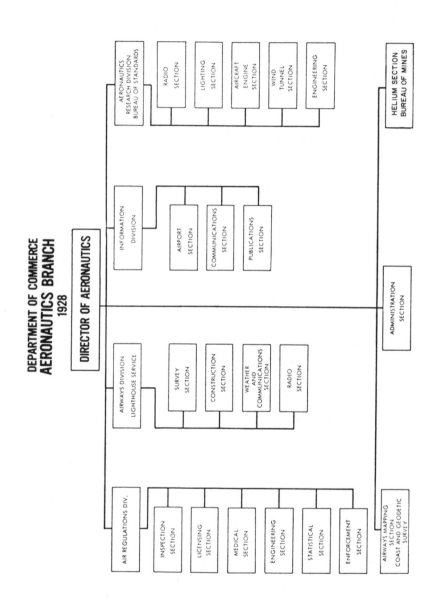

DEPARTMENT OF COMMERCE
AERONAUTICS BRANCH
1928

DIRECTOR OF AERONAUTICS

AIR REGULATIONS DIV.

INSPECTION SECTION

LICENSING SECTION

MEDICAL SECTION

ENGINEERING SECTION

STATISTICAL SECTION

ENFORCEMENT SECTION

AIRWAYS MAPPING SECTION
COAST AND GEODETIC SURVEY

AIRWAYS DIVISION
LIGHTHOUSE SERVICE

SURVEY SECTION

CONSTRUCTION SECTION

WEATHER AND COMMUNICATIONS SECTION

RADIO SECTION

ADMINISTRATION SECTION

INFORMATION DIVISION

AIRPORT SECTION

COMMUNICATIONS SECTION

PUBLICATIONS SECTION

AERONAUTICS RESEARCH DIVISION
BUREAU OF STANDARDS

RADIO SECTION

LIGHTING SECTION

AIRCRAFT ENGINE SECTION

WIND TUNNEL SECTION

ENGINEERING SECTION

HELIUM SECTION
BUREAU OF MINES

Secretary of Commerce, "and has endeavored to direct its policy to meet such needs when so interpreted." Policy was never established as if it were the Secretary's personal preserve. It was established in consultation with business leaders. The same methods would be followed in regulating aviation. "It has always been the policy of this department . . . to carry on such regulatory functions as it has in cooperation with the industry itself," Hoover told a gathering of 300 members of the aviation community. "We have no desire to impose a thing . . . ." The industry, in other words, would help write the rules that it would live by. As Charles L. Lawrance, president of the Aeronautical Chamber of Commerce later remarked, "The industry to a large degree has had the privilege of self-regulation."[6]

The first set of rules were drafted by Aeronautics Branch personnel with the assistance of staff members in the Department's Solicitor's office who had experience in rulemaking. When this draft was completed, in October 1926, MacCracken called in representatives of the War, Navy, and Post Office Departments and went over the draft with them personally. These meetings resulted in the first round of revisions. The second round resulted when several hundred mimeographed copies of the revised draft were circulated among members of the aviation community, primarily airframe builders, engine manufacturers, and air transport operators. These people were then invited to a series of conferences, at which they criticized the draft and offered suggested changes. For the most part, those invited were on the business end of aviation, though pilots and aircraft mechanics did attend as individuals rather than group representatives. Two conferences were held with airframe manufacturers, two with operators, one with engine manufacturers. Representatives of the insurance industry were also brought in; MacCracken wanted to make certain that underwriters were ready and willing to write reasonable insurance policies once the regulations were promulgated. A separate conference was even set aside for aviation editors. At these conferences, MacCracken listened to one and all, "sorting the sane from the silly," according to one observer, "and generally doing quite as well as any mere human being could do on a job in which nobody but an Angel of the Lord could please everybody." Everyone wasn't pleased, but the procedure proved so satisfactory that, in the coming years, every major revision of the regulations was preceded by similar conferences. More importantly, nearly everyone was pleased with the attitude of the new regulatory agency. As *Aviation* noted, the Department of Commerce had made its bow in the aeronautical field with "a spirit of cooperation and helpfulness that gives great promise."

A third draft, based on the input gathered at these meetings, was mailed to everyone who had attended a conference. When written criticisms came back, the rules were again revised. This draft, the fourth, was submitted to a committee of the Aeronautical Chamber of Commerce, which met with Department officials in Washington, for final comment. Then followed the fifth (and final) draft, which was promulgated as the Air Commerce Regulations on December 31, 1926. All provisions did not become effective immediately, however. Aircraft owners, pilots, and mechanics subject to the regulations were permitted to operate without a license until July 1, 1927, if they applied for a license prior to March 1, a deadline later extended to May 1.[7]

To handle the nationwide licensing and inspection activities contemplated by these regulations, the Inspection Service of the Air Regulations Division established nine district offices in the United States. These offices were manned by people who possessed a variety of technical skills and performed a variety of services — they inspected factories, tested aircraft, and examined pilots and mechanics. Each inspector was responsible for particular centers of aviation activity within his district, traveling from one center to another according to an itinerary drawn up by the district's supervising inspector. Itineraries were mailed out each month to airports, local aviation authorities, and to all parties for whom the district office had an application for a license. In this way, anyone who required the services of a Commerce Department inspector knew on which day and at what location he would be available during the ensuing month.[8]

In an understandable gesture, MacCracken offered Pilot's License No. 1 to Orville Wright. Wright declined the offer. He no longer flew, he told MacCracken; besides, he did not think that he needed a Federal pilot's license to show that he had been the first man to fly. At Hoover's suggestion, Pilot's License No. 1 went to MacCracken; No. 2, to Clarence Young. Charles Lindbergh, then an airmail pilot for the Robertson Aircraft Corporation, secured Pilot's License No. 69.[9]

The original Air Commerce Regulations were distinguished by their brevity, simplicity, and directness. The regulations laid down a set of commonsense air traffic rules and provided for the registration, certification, and inspection of aircraft and the licensing of pilots and aviation mechanics. All aircraft were required to be registered with the Department, which would assign them an identification mark for permanent display on the fuselage. Only aircraft engaged in interstate or foreign commerce, however, required a Federal license — that is, a certificate attesting to their airworthiness. Aircraft used for pleasure or other noncommercial purposes, even if crossing state lines, did not need a license, though they could be licensed at the option of the owner. All pilots operating certificated aircraft required a license, as did mechanics repairing such aircraft.

The technical requirements to qualify for any of the three categories of pilot's licenses — transport, industrial, and private — were disarmingly simple. Transport and industrial pilots needed only to pass a written and flight test and to have logged a prescribed minimum of solo flying hours — 100 hours for the first category, 50 for the second. Private pilots needed no specified number of solo flying hours. (A minimum of 10 hours would subsequently be established.) Expertise in particular types of aircraft was not specified. Underlying this simplicity — and indeed, seeming inadequacy — was the belief that refinements should come with experience, even if it meant that in the beginning regulations would not meet many exigencies.[10]

There were requirements other than flying skills that an applicant had to meet before qualifying for a license, among them age (16 for a private license, 18 for all other) and citizenship (U.S. for all except private pilots, who could be any nationality). Applicants also had to be of "good moral character," though what standard the Department used as a yardstick for morality and how it went about applying it is uncertain. The suspicion is that the standard was indeterminate, and its application in the great majority of cases was merely a matter of form. More specific and far more important to aviation safety was the requirement that applicants pass a physical examination. MacCracken made one of his happiest choices when he selected Dr. Louis Hopewell Bauer as Medical Director of the Aeronautics Branch. Bauer had spent seven years in the Army Air Service, six of which had been devoted to organizing and directing the Army's first flight surgeon school. He had written a book on aviation medicine and was one of the foremost experts of his time in this infant field.[11]

"There is no occupation in which physical condition is of such paramount importance as flying," Bauer believed. He also believed that "a pilot physically fit today may not be so next week." Hence transport pilots were required to submit to a physical every six months in order to retain their license, industrial and private pilots once a year. Bauer personally drew up a set of physical standards for each pilot category and outlined an examination procedure to be followed by examining physicians.

Though every pilot applicant would be flight tested by a Department of Commerce official, he would not be examined by a Department doctor. Hiring the required force of physicians for this task was considered next to impossible — and, even if possible, wasteful. The scheme decided upon was to designate a select number of doctors in private practice as aviation medical examiners. These physicians would receive no pay from the Government; they would collect a fixed fee from each applicant they examined. Bauer wanted a medical examiner in at least every principal city in the United States. He set out to select each man personally. By February 1927, he had collected a widely scattered force of 57 physicians. Among them was Dr. William P. MacCracken, Sr., who accepted the appointment only after Bauer, casually disregarding his boss' explicit instructions to appoint any qualified physician but his father, indicated that he would not take no for an answer. By the end of June, the Department had designated approximately 125 physicians as aviation medical examiners — a roster that would expand sixfold by the turn of the decade.[12]

Certificating aircraft required a different system. MacCracken wanted the certification process to begin at the aircraft factory, where, technically, the Aeronautics Branch did not have the legal authority to intrude. But the manufacturing plant was the place where the Branch had to begin unless it intended to pick apart every airplane that the manufacturer sold into interstate commerce. "We've got certain safety factors, and we'll have our engineers check your plans with respect to them," MacCracken told the manufacturers. "But mainly we'll rely on you to comply voluntarily." The manufacturers accepted the proposition. The result was the institution of the approved type certificate.[13]

This device was — and still is — of incalculable value in facilitating and simplifying the licensing of aircraft of identical design and construction. Aircraft designers were required to meet the minimum engineering standards set forth in detail in a Department of Commerce handbook, first issued in October 1927. Blueprints and engineering data were sent to the Aeronautics Branch for examination by its Engineering Section. If the data conformed with the Government's standards, an Aeronautics Branch inspector would visit the manufacturing plant to determine whether the manufacturer was following the approved design and specifications. This was followed by the flight testing of one aircraft of the type being manufactured — first by a company test pilot, then by a Federal inspector. When these tests were passed, the aircraft was issued an approved type certificate, which authorized the manufacturer to produce aircraft of "an exact similarity of type, structure, materials, assembly, and workmanship" to the test model. Individual airplanes of the approved type received an airworthiness certificate (or license, as it was then called) after the manufacturer certified in an affidavit that he had followed the specifications of the type certificate and the aircraft was flight tested by an Aeronautics Branch inspector. If a manufacturer chose not to secure a type certificate for an aircraft type he was building in quantity, he was forced to subject each and every aircraft he produced to the same analysis and tests undergone by a type-certificated model before he could obtain airworthiness certificates for them. Aircraft constructed prior to October 1927 were exempted from this kind of detailed analysis, though they had to be flight tested.[14]

Engines were also type-certificated; here, however, the Department adopted the cumbersome procedure of requiring the manufacturer to deliver an engine to the Aeronautics Branch for testing. Among other things, the engine was given an endurance block test by engineers in the Bureau of Standards. The test consisted of a 50-hour endurance run in 10 five-hour periods. Immediately following the block test, the engine was torn down and a detailed inspection was made of its parts. Failure of a major component during the block test meant the denial of a type certificate.[15]

Type certification proved such a felicitous procedure that it was soon expanded into other areas — first to propellers and then to other aircraft components. Today, as in the late 1920's, it is at the core of Federal procedures for certificating aeronautical products.

III

The Aeronautics Branch had all it could do to keep up with its regulatory activities during its first two years of operations. "I have been busier than a top sargeant [*sic*] trying to get a gang of Waco cadets hauling lumber," MacCracken wrote to a friend in the summer of 1926. The frenzied pace continued for many months; yet, despite long hours and extraordinary exertion, the Air Regulations Division was unable to stay abreast of its workload.[16]

The first 12 months of operation were made especially difficult by a general shortage of funds. Hoover had grossly underestimated the cost of the new undertaking. Reasoning that start-up costs would be minimized by utilizing existing bureaus in the endeavor, and that this organizational scheme would also cut on-going administrative costs, he calculated that airway development would require "perhaps $400,000 a year" and other services, including regulation, "something additional." Thus, the administration asked Congress for a mere $550,000 for fiscal 1927 — $300,000 for airways, $250,000 for regulatory and other activities.[17]

MacCracken could not get one cent more. The Coolidge administration was perhaps as tightfisted as any in American history. Its economic text, nominally based on the political economy of Adam Smith, often came straight out of *Poor Richard's Almanac*. MacCracken despaired of ever receiving a realistic budget after attending his first Presidential economy conference, an affair held annually by Coolidge before an official gathering of Cabinet and subcabinet officers. The President, in attendance merely to point up the importance of the proceedings, got things started with a short talk on the virtues of economy. But the meeting did not begin in earnest until William Mayhew Lord, the Budget Director, took the floor to review the budget. Lord, a careful man of very precise manner, had risen to the rank of brigadier general watching over the U.S. Army's disbursements. He believed in being thorough. Not one item was overlooked or unaccounted for by the good general. That done, Lord gave his own talk on the sins of profligacy. "One of the things he wanted you to be careful about was paper clips," MacCracken recalled. "Don't waste paper clips." It was that kind of economy talk. Indeed, it was that kind of an administration.[18]

The paltry $250,000 for safety and regulatory activities was patently inadequate. By the end of June 1927, the Inspection Section had only 15 aeronautical inspectors in the field to examine applicants for pilots' and mechanics' licenses and inspect aircraft and engines. The Licensing Section, which handled all the paperwork, had only 10 people. Inevitably, corners had to be cut. "With our funds so short and our staff so small

[we] stipulated that everyone who applied for a license could fly until we had the opportunity to pass on him," MacCracken explained. The same procedure was followed for aircraft; they were allowed to operate under a temporary letter of authority until the Branch could get around to inspecting them. Some activities were simply ignored. The work of inspecting and rating airports, which the Air Commerce Act required the Department to perform at the request of airport operators, was put on the back burner. Not a single airport was rated in fiscal year 1927. At the end of that year, the Branch's backlog was enormous. Approximately 1,800 pilots, 1,600 mechanics, and 1,100 airplane owners had filed licensing applications. At year's end, the Branch had managed to license 110 pilots, 100 mechanics, and 140 airplanes, and to issue 9 type certificates. Some inspection districts reported that their work was six months in arrears.[19]

The pace had to quicken, and did, over the next 12 months. Fortunately, the fiscal year 1927 budget proved nothing more than an aberration. Both the administration and the Congress came to grips with reality, and the Aeronautics Branch budget rose to $3.8 million during fiscal year 1928. Of this amount, $700,000 went for regulatory activities. This permitted expanding the field inspector force to 40 and the Licensing Section to 25. The output of the Air Regulations Division increased dramatically. Licenses were issued for 2,632 pilots, 2,806 mechanics, and 1,728 aircraft; in addition, 38 aircraft and 4 engines were type certificated.[20]

This was an incredible amount of work to have been performed by a force of less than 100 men and women. Yet there must have been times when many of these people felt they were engaged in the labors of Sisyphus, for, do what they might, the backlog got progressively worse. Standing at approximately 4,500 applications of all types on June 30, 1927, it shot up to 9,400 by mid-1928. A number of factors contributed to the surge in applications, among them the falling due of the first block of license renewals and an improvement in the fortunes of aircraft manufacturers, who were now producing new aircraft at a rate of 150 per week. But nothing affected the workload of the Branch as dramatically as Lindbergh's crossing the Atlantic. Following that flight, thousands of Americans decided they wanted to learn to fly. The Aeronautics Branch was swamped with a flood of applications that exceeded its wildest expectations. "Over 17,000 young men and women have now applied for

Federal air-pilot's licenses or permits," Coolidge reported in his state of the Union message in December 1928. "More than 80 percent of them applied during the past year." Thus, Clarence Young noted, the most serious problem of the Aeronautics Branch "was and still is to keep licenses current."[21]

Not all the lag in processing pilot licenses was due to the dramatic surge in applications. A contributing factor was the centralized structure of the Licensing Section, which meant that most of the processing had to be performed in Washington. For example, a pilot applicant living in Dallas, Tex., would secure his application at the Dallas district office (Inspection District No. 7), fill it out, take a physical, and send his application and medical record to Washington. There the application was checked for errors and forwarded to District No. 7. The applicant then took his written and flight examinations, the results of which, along with the original application, were sent back to Washington. If everything was in order, Washington would mail the applicant his pilot's license.[22]

Mailing forms back and forth from the district offices to Washington was a time-consuming process that could have been eliminated if the work of the Licensing Section had not been wholly centralized in Washington. The Aeronautics Branch was not unmindful of this fact, but could do little to improve matters. With only 25 people processing licenses, it was impossible to distribute them over nine field offices without spreading them too thin. At the root of the problem was the small amount of money allocated for safety and regulatory purposes. Both the Congress and the administration, excited by the possibilities of round-the-clock commercial flying, gave the lion's share of aviation funds to airway development, which, in fiscal 1928, made off with 82 percent of the Aeronautics Branch budget. Thus, the Licensing Section staff put in an average 21 hours overtime per day, while individual inspectors in the field regularly worked 10- to 15-hour shifts — only to keep falling steadily behind.[23]

Delay in securing a license may have been no more than a minor inconvenience for a prospective pilot; delay in securing a type certificate was a very serious matter for an aircraft or engine manufacturer. He might be forced to halt operations in his factory, which would increase his start-up costs; or worse still, he might lose prospective customers. The Aeronautics Branch caused manufacturers no end of headaches during the first two or three years of its existence. Most of these headaches stemmed from an inordinately long type-certification cycle.

In a 30-month period, the Branch received 227 applications for approved type certificates from aircraft manufacturers; at the end of that period, it had 133 applications, or more than half the total, still pending. This is not to say that the Government was solely responsible for this slow processing rate — more than one manufacturer submitted inadequate or hastily drawn data that had to be shipped back for further work — but it was primarily responsible. Some manufacturers had to wait months to secure approval of a minor change in an aircraft that already possessed an approved type certificate. Shuttling engines between Washington and California, which was rapidly becoming a center of aeronautical manufacturing, proved both time-consuming and irritating. Engines were sometimes damaged during their trek across country, necessitating more delay until replacement parts arrived from the manufacturer. Only slightly less irritating was the long distance that many industry engineers were forced to travel in order to come in personal contact with Government engineers. As in the case of the Licensing Section, decentralization would have worked wonders.[24]

Like other sections in the Air Regulations Division, the Engineering Section was understaffed. Here the problem was not only the general paucity of funds for regulatory activities, but the Federal salary scale. Aeronautical engineers, in short supply and capable of earning more in private industry, were very difficult to come by. And those that did take Federal employment were being lured away by higher salaries. The result was a high turnover rate not only among Engineering Section personnel, but also among aeronautical engineering inspectors in the Inspection Section. In 1928, the Branch hit upon the expedient of giving summer employment to aeronautical engineers on university faculties. By fall, this infusion of people and talent had reduced the Engineering Section's work to a current status. By the following summer, however, the section had fallen behind again. But when the Branch attempted to hire another batch of summer help, it was unavailable; private industry, not slow in recognizing a good thing, had snapped up all available talent for itself. In the same year, nine Aeronautics Branch engineers resigned to take jobs with industry. Turnover among engineers continued very high, even into the Great Depression. That the Engineering Section managed at all during these early years was due primarily to the wide acceptance of type certification among manufacturers. By 1930, 80 percent of all U.S. airplane production was covered by type certificates; had this not been the case, the Government's aircraft certification effort would have collapsed.[25]

For all these difficulties, some activities began to turn the corner in 1929. In June of that year, Young could report that "the inspection section is in the unique position of being current with its work regarding the handling of new applications." Inspectors, however, were still forced to work long hours "under a high nervous tension." Yearly budget increases, which continued through fiscal 1932, also helped close the gap somewhat in other areas. But the Air Regulations Division as a whole never really caught up with its workload until 1930 and 1931, when a severely depressed economy began slowing down the pace of aviation activity.[26]

                                        IV

One of MacCracken's principal objectives during these formative years was "to convince people that airplanes were a safe means of transportation." Without the public's acceptance, aviation would be relegated to moving the mails. The key to public acceptance, he believed, lay in the ability of the Aeronautics Branch to gain the public's confidence. But before this could be done, the Aeronautics Branch "would have to ride herd on a lot of this barnstorming going on around the country." Aviation would have to replace its colorful, but reckless, image with one more staid.[27]

On the other hand, there was danger that in the process of riding herd on wrongdoers MacCracken would retard flying and, in the end, stifle the very activity that he was charged with fostering. He could not be a hardnosed regulator in pursuit of an ultimate standard of safety; but neither could he be a permissive guardian. He had to steer a middle course. All of which meant that the standard of safety that he set would be influenced, if not wholly dictated, by the need to maintain a growing and prosperous aviation industry. "The manifest intent of the [Aeronautics Branch] under Hon. William P. MacCracken, Jr. . . . " remarked a contemporary observer, "has been to give the industry a maximum of encouragement and a minimum of regulation."[28] Others, who had run afoul of Federal regulations, may have felt differently. On balance, however, MacCracken and the people he gathered around him succeeded in the difficult task of steering a middle course. In so doing, they set an example that would be followed with but few and brief exceptions by their successors.

"True enforcement . . . is accomplished through . . . diplomacy and tact," asserted Elmer McD. Kintz, chief of the Legal Section of the Aeronautics Branch. In the beginning, at least, a gentle slap on the wrist made do for penalties prescribed by law. MacCracken had decided that the aviation community should have a brief period in which to familiarize itself with Federal regulations. Thus, until mid-1927, violators as a general rule were not subjected to fines, suspensions, or license revocations; rather, they were let off with a reprimand on the theory that ignorance or misunderstanding, not willfulness, was the principal offender.[29]

This was only the general rule. Crackdowns did occur. One thing MacCracken would not tolerate was mixing flying with drinking, which was, needless to say, prohibited by the Air Commerce Regulations under penalty of license revocation or suspension. "When it came to liquor and aviation," he asserted, "I was a rabid prohibitionist." The first rule he set for his field inspectors was that if they expected to work for him they would have to abstain from alcohol 365 days of the year. And though he admitted to not having complied with the Eighteenth Amendment in the past, he decided to set an example and swear off for the duration of his tenure as Assistant Secretary — no easy thing to do in Washington even during Prohibition. He had scarcely set down the rule when he was obliged to apply it. A young Department of Commerce pilot wrecked his aircraft while buzzing Bolling Field, in Washington, D.C. A half gallon of bathtub gin turned up in the wreckage. Matters were complicated by the fact that the errant pilot happened to be the son of a U.S. Senator, and MacCracken was still serving on a recess appointment. He nevertheless demanded and received the young man's resignation. The prohibition against drinking was one provision of the Air Commerce Regulations that was enforced to the letter.[30]

Recklessness on the part of those who knew better was also dealt with severely. On one occasion a test pilot of high repute, probably feeling full of himself, decided to buzz a number of Connecticut towns. When he landed, the local police threw him in jail and reported the

William P. MacCracken, Jr. (left), poses with Herbert Hoover and Assistant Secretary of Commerce J. Walter Drake on the day of his swearing-in as Assistant Secretary for Aeronautics

incident to the Aeronautics Branch. MacCracken personally took a hand in the matter and suspended the test pilot's license for 60 days. In some quarters the penalty was considered too severe, for the pilot had been deprived of his usual means of livelihood for the duration of his suspension. But MacCracken reasoned that his action "may have indicated to other lesser lights that I was not going to show favortism, and that I was going to enforce these rules." Even Charles Lindbergh, at this time an obscure airmail pilot for the Robertson Aircraft Corporation, nearly had his license suspended. Lindbergh had come to MacCracken's attention by parachuting from his airplane on two separate occasions within the space of a few weeks. Though both jumps had been clearly warranted, MacCracken wondered whether Lindbergh might not have avoided his brushes with disaster if he had exercised more caution during earlier phases of his flights. His second jump, moreover, had resulted in his airplane crashing within yards of a barn. "He's not going to help commercial aviation if he keeps dropping these airplanes around the countryside," MacCracken reasoned. Only the intervention of William B. Robertson, the airmail line's president, saved Lindbergh's license.[31]

The familiarization period over, the Aeronautics Branch began meting out other forms of punishment in addition to reprimands — fines, suspensions, and revocations. The reprimand, however, remained the principal enforcement tool throughout MacCracken's tenure. In fiscal 1928, some 54 percent of violators were let off with a talking to, either oral or written; 29 percent were fined, and 22 percent had their licenses suspended. The usual fine was $25, though many ran considerably higher. Revocations were rare — only two during fiscal 1928, or less than 1 percent of the total number of penalties levied. Fiscal 1929 showed the same tendency towards leniency. Though reprimands dropped to 39 percent of all penalties assessed, they were still the most widely used form of disciplinary action. Fines climbed to 26 percent, however, and suspensions to 15 percent. Moreover, the number of revocations jumped to 21. But on balance, as one observer noted in 1930, the Aeronautics Branch was still "exceptionally lenient with violators."[32]

The Aeronautics Branch was also exceptionally liberal in granting waivers to private fliers. Through December 1928, the Branch had failed approximately 10 percent of pilot applicants. Another 10 percent, though they did not meet all the required medical standards, were permitted to fly on waivers. "We have tried to be a little lenient," MacCracken explained to a congressional committee. "We did not want to be too severe, because a great many of these student pilots indicated that they did not intend to engage in aviation as a business. They simply wanted to fly their own planes, and where they have given that indication, we have been more apt to sign the waiver." Tabs were kept on a group of 9,000 pilots to determine how the safety record of those flying with waivers compared with that of those flying without. The results did not speak well for the liberal policy of granting waivers. Slightly over 9 percent of pilots in the test group with no physical abnormalities were involved in accidents during one 12-month period; on the other hand, 34 percent with a physical abnormality met with an accident. Over a 3-year period, 1.5 percent of the normal group and 2.4 percent of the abnormal group were killed. But the results did speak well of the Branch's medical standards; they showed a definite correlation between safety and physical fitness.[33]

When Young succeeded MacCracken as Assistant Secretary in October 1929, the Branch gradually began to deal more severely with violators; indeed, it began to enforce all regulations more stringently. The real crackdown began with fiscal 1931, when only 15 percent of total violators were handed a reprimand. The following year, though the number of violations climbed, still fewer reprimands were handed out. Nor was the tendency to substitute a nominal fine for a reprimand, particularly prevalent during 1929 and 1930, continued. Instead, the Aeronautics Branch turned to suspensions as a primary enforcement tool. At the same time, revocations were being handed out with greater frequency — 63 in fiscal 1931, 101 in fiscal 1932. By now, 8 out of 100 violators were having their licenses revoked, up from less than 1 out of 100 in 1928. The Aeronautics Branch was finally riding herd on aviation's irresponsible and incompetent elements.[34]

V

Industry had sought and looked forward to Federal regulation. Whether it knew it or not, it would now pay a price, for safety did not come free of charge. Its costs could be calculated in dollars and cents. And though in the long run, investing in safety paid dividends, operators and manufacturers unaccustomed to making outlays for meeting Federal standards and specifications sometimes took a shortsighted view of things.

Lindbergh's two emergency parachute jumps in 1927 were due as much to weather conditions as to the fact that he was flying old war-surplus equipment. Aeronautics Branch personnel spent a good deal of time thinking of what to do with these war-vintage machines, particularly those in commercial service. Many operators picked up war-surplus equipment for a nominal price, patched it up, and pressed it into service either on airmail routes or on their fixed-base operations. The Robertson Aircraft Corporation, for example, bought 450 surplus Standards and, as William B. Robertson related, put them "through our factory . . . in such a way that they became perfectly airworthy," and sold them on the open market. Though these aircraft had never been intended for passenger operations, some operators were packing as many as five passengers into a Standard. The result was that many an operator was doing a brisk business in these dilapidated machines, as were spare-part suppliers.

MacCracken had serious reservations about the safety of this equipment. "The ten years which have elapsed since those ships were constructed has meant that there has been a good deal of deterioration in the material itself," he pointed out to a group of industry representatives. "The rebuilding that has been done has been done without any supervision, and without much means of checking on it." Accident statistics bore out MacCracken's suspicions. Over a 10-month period, war-surplus equipment experienced structural failures at twice the rate of postwar equipment.[35]

In October 1927, a Department of Commerce information bulletin announced the intention of the Aeronautics Branch to take war-surplus aircraft out of interstate commerce, beginning on January 1, 1928. A few people in the industry saw merit in the proposal. "I believe that the fellows that are using those ships today," declared J. G. ("Tex") Rankin, a flying school operator, "if [they] put them all out into the field and put a match to them, they would be better off at the end of the next year." Even Robertson, who had a big stake in the old machines, had to admit that "it would be much better for aviation in general to have the old surplus machines . . . washed out." But as to his case in particular, Robertson pleaded with MacCracken that such an action would cripple "the sales of our rebuilt Standards." The planned washout, therefore, was "wholly unfair and ill-timed." Even now, Robertson wired Mac-Cracken, supply houses were "feeling tremendous reaction on spare parts and operators predict a move of this kind would seriously cripple commercial aviation progress." Floyd J. Logan, a fixed-base operator, took a different tack. "This government sold these war surplus ships and accepted the purchasers' money knowing full well that they were going to be sold and resold for flying purposes," he told Department of Commerce officials. "They received this money without any time limit as to flying . . . . If this government now should break faith with those purchasers, it would be very unfair indeed." MacCracken backed off. The information bulletin had been in error. "I assure you," he told Robertson, "that no definite policy will be formulated until after the forthcoming Aviation Conference to be held in the early part of December."[36]

At the conference, which had been scheduled to discuss proposed changes to the Air Commerce Regulations, MacCracken made it clear to the industry that he had no intention of grounding all war-surplus equipment; his intention was to prohibit its use in passenger carriage.

Out of the 300 or so attendees, not one spoke in favor of the proposed prohibition. "If the aeroplane is unsafe to carry passengers, why is it safe to carry [student pilots] in it?" asked a Fairchild Company representative. The only true test of whether an aircraft should be flying was whether it "is now airworthy and fit," asserted one operator. To ground an entire class of aircraft because of age and without regard to their airworthiness would be taking property without due process of law. William B. Stout, representing the Ford Motor Company, believed the question would be settled in time by "the natural gravitation of the industry." The industry was going to get nowhere "running a peanut stand" — i.e., putting patches on old equipment and posing as a transportation mode. The industry would — indeed, it had to to survive — acquire "a whole new suit of clothes," and the question of war surplus equipment would resolve itself. A fixed-base operator expressed the same thought. "We were forced into new production ships much against our wishes and with a good deal of gnashing of teeth . . .," he explained. But now that his company had the new ships, it would never consider going back to Standards and Jennies. The new ships cost less to operate, they were faster, and they produced larger profits. Competition would drive the old ships off the commercial airways.[37]

A ban was never imposed. Whether these aircraft were airworthy would be determined case by case. And the Department did maintain the upper hand by requiring rebuilt aircraft to be "of original specifications and design" and that they pass the same flight test required of new aircraft. In the end, the Aeronautics Branch licensed only a fraction of existing war-surplus equipment. The rest were left to the individual states to contend with.[38]

Some new equipment fared no better, especially engines being tested for type certification. Engines repeatedly broke down during the first few hours on the endurance block. By the end of 1928, the Engineering Section had rejected more than 50 percent of the engines tested. Half of these rejects, according to an Aeronautics Branch official, "would not have stayed in the air four hours." This proved costly to engine manufacturers. It meant that they had to improve their quality control and testing procedures or else go out of business.[39]

It was difficult on occasion, particularly in the beginning, to tell a manufacturer that he might as well stop production because his aircraft was not airworthy. In some cases, stopping production would have put him out of business. The pressure on Federal officials in such cases was enormous. In more than one instance, the Aeronautics Branch granted manufacturers temporary certificates in order that they could continue building while correcting their deficiencies as they went along. The result was a number of "curious accidents" during 1927 in the light commercial planes class — wings flew off, fuselages failed, aircraft suddenly lost stability. "I know what your department has been up against in attempting to control some of the haywire development without being accused of trying to strangle the infant industry," wrote a *New York Times* reporter to MacCracken. The reporter proposed to write an article on the subject. Without explicitly affirming or denying the reporter's contention, Mac-Cracken wrote back that an article could be written "along the lines you suggest." He only asked that no names be mentioned and that "the facts or statements . . . be so guarded that they could not be interpreted by others as referring to any particular instance . . . ." MacCracken then admitted that "we have not been able to accomplish all that might be desired . . . ." Exercising both promotional and regulatory powers was no easy cross to bear. "You have been confronted with an appalling job," the *Times* correspondent remarked in sympathizing with MacCracken.*[40]

Experimental aircraft presented special problems. MacCracken, and Young after him, realized that the industry should be given the greatest latitude in developing new equipment, otherwise aviation would stagnate. They resolved, therefore, not to tamper with development on the experimental level. Licenses for experimental aircraft were handed out more or less on a pro forma basis. The only restriction placed on such aircraft was the use they could be put to. Problems arose, however, not so much with established firms with sizable capitalization, but with backyard tinkerers, whose knowledge and workmanship were often exceeded by their ignorance and incompetence. The problem was pointed up when a fixed-base operator and long-time MacCracken acquaintance, E. B. Heath, went down in an experimental aircraft. Heath, who was not an

---

*But MacCracken was not always forced to compromise. Everyone did not possess the political muscle of the established operators and manufacturers. Hence, those on the fringes of aviation activity paid a disproportionate price for Federal regulation. The Gates Flying Circus, for example, was driven out of business in 1928 by MacCracken's crack down on surplus war equipment and Federal regulations banning stunting and wingwalking without parachutes. Bill Rhode, *Baling Wire, Chewing Gum and Guts: The Story of the Gates Flying Circus* (New York, 1970), 140.

engineer, had nevertheless performed the engineering work for this aircraft; a high school graduate had done the drafting. Not surprisingly, the aircraft ripped off a wing during a test flight, and Heath was killed. "It seems a miserable shame that proper engineering analysis is not required before experimental airplanes leave the ground," argued a concerned correspondent in a letter to Young. But the Aeronautics Branch believed its policy was sound. Government should not intervene in the creative process; besides, as Gilbert G. Budwig, the Director of Air Regulation pointed out, "It would obviously burden the manufacturer with a tremendous amount of useless work if he were obliged to obtain our approval on airplanes before they were developed to the point of production." No change was instituted. But in giving the established developer the freedom he required at the experimental stage, the Branch was at the same time leaving the tinkerer at the mercy of his own uncertain devices. All this could be rationalized, of course, as part of the price paid for progress. In any event, the tinkerer would not have wanted it otherwise.[41]

A companion problem was the rapid growth of demonstration flights following Lindbergh's Atlantic crossing, again testing MacCracken's determination to convince the American public that flying was safe. Of particular concern was the sudden rash of transoceanic flights by ill-equipped daredevils attempting to repeat Lindbergh's feat. During the spring and summer of 1927, 40 people (including Europeans trying to reach American shores) attempted transoceanic flights; 21 lost their lives. In the course of a single air race between San Francisco and Hawaii, seven people perished, including one woman. Before the year was out, 24 Americans had died in transoceanic and other types of stunt or demonstration flights. Americans may have been enraptured by Lindbergh, but all of them did not accept this toll in human life as part of the price of progress. The result, as the *Literary Digest* noted, was a public outcry "to stop these death flights." Some people went so far as to call for a complete ban on demonstration flights.[42]

The Aeronautics Branch had left transoceanic flight totally unregulated. MacCracken, jolted by the public outcry, retreated to a legalistic line of defense. The Aeronautics Branch, he explained, was powerless to regulate transoceanic demonstration flights because they were noncommercial in character. Linking this want to the general lack of power to regulate intrastate flying, he declared publicly that Congress should authorize the Department of Commerce to license every pilot and every airplane that took to the air. He was immediately shot down by Hoover and by a sizable portion of the press. What was needed was more common sense, not more regulation, the Secretary declared. "I do not believe we should attempt to stifle the spirit of youth or the pioneer work which must precede all development," he said. Besides, governmental regulation would be too inflexible. While the *New York Times* felt that some regulation of overseas demonstration flights might be practical, it observed that "aviation would not have reached its advanced stage if risks had not been taken in feats of adventure." To the *Outlook*, "The quickest way to make aviation as safe as possible is to encourage experiment and trial." Progress should be everyone's main concern; it was not in the interest of progress to debar airmen from undertaking "everything that an official might consider dangerous." The *Nation* editorialized that the public, by making heroes out of fliers, was responsible for the activity that it now sought to ban. But to ban this activity, the journal contended, would be "one of the most ridiculous excrescences of a law ridden age." Above all, Fiorello La Guardia said, the Government should not interfere with such flights. Finally, Charles Lindbergh himself came out in opposition to Federal restrictions.[43]

In the midst of the controversy, Coolidge appointed a committee of three — MacCracken and his two counterparts in the War and Navy Departments, F. Trubee Davison and Edward P. Warner — to study the question. Even before this committee had finished its work, Coolidge announced his belief that further regulation would be harmful to the advance of aviation. Two days later the three-man committee stated an identical belief.[44]

Much of the problem had been caused by a failure in communication. No one, with the possible exception of MacCracken, tried to find common ground on which the issue could be reasonably resolved. Instead, both sides in the controversy talked in absolute terms. Those concerned most with the loss of human life advocated a total ban; those concerned most with aviation progress insisted on total laissez-faire. The obvious solution was some measure of regulation, which, MacCracken's publicly stated opinion to the contrary, was attainable without Congressional action. The controversy gradually faded when the rash of transoceanic demonstration flights ran its natural course and the number of fatal accidents was thereby reduced. When the issue had long been forgotten, the Department banned the flight of all aircraft bearing unlicensed identification numbers to foreign countries. Not one word was raised in protest.[45]

VI

The first set of Air Commerce Regulations had been drawn up without benefit of experience. "[They] were made up practically out of whole cloth," Clarence Young asserted. "There was no precedent to go upon." But the Aeronautics Branch fully intended to learn from experience and amend its rules accordingly. The Air Commerce Regulations were to be a set of living rules — rules that would go through a continuing evolution.[46]

Everyone lobbied for changes. Pilots believed medical standards were too rigorous and fees charged by aviation medical examiners, which were set by the Aeronautics Branch, too high. Medical examiners complained of the size of the outlay they had to make for special diagnostic equipment and even questioned the necessity for the equipment. Flying-school operators in search of more students proposed that physicals be deferred for all student pilots until they flew solo, unabashedly admitting that this would permit schools "to sell more student courses." At the same time, they urged that the solo-hours requirement be raised from 10 to 20 hours "in order that the student would be better equipped to fly." Worthwhile suggestions did emerge, even though they had been made for the wrong reasons. For example, the minimum flying time required to qualify for a private pilot's license was eventually raised, but not because flying school operators wished to improve their business. It took a fatal accident to get the requirement stiffened.[47]

Anyone 16 years of age or older was eligible to qualify for a pilot's license; minors were not required to secure parental consent. Thus, one Edward Mallinckrodt, a minor, secured a private pilot's license. Not long thereafter, he took a friend up for a spin, and, in the course of performing some ill-advised aerial maneuvers, cracked up — killing himself and his passenger. Young Mallinckrodt's parents first learned their son was a licensed pilot on hearing of his death. The elder Mallinckrodt and his attorneys waged a protracted debate with the Aeronautics Branch to raise the minimum solo time to 50 hours, the minimum age to 18, and to require minors to secure parental consent. The Branch would not budge on either the age question or the issue of parental consent. It did, however, raise the minimum solo time to 50 hours.[48]

Other lobbying efforts proved less successful. The flap over trans-oceanic demonstration flights had been something of a rare incident in that it subjected the Aeronautics Branch to pressure from the general public. Aviation issues rarely troubled the American public between 1926 and 1932; aviation was the exclusive concern of a very small minority of the population. Pressure of any significance came chiefly from this minority, which, in effect, constituted the Branch's constituency. Demands for action coming outside of this constituency could usually be politely ignored.

A case in point was the question of requiring air transports to carry parachutes. Some people, including many air transport users, believed that such a requirement was a reasonable safety measure. They saw no difference between airliners carrying parachutes and ocean liners carrying life preservers. Moreover, they argued, segments of aviation routinely carried these contrivances. Military aviators were required to wear them, and many fixed-base operators, private fliers, and airmail pilots carried them voluntarily. "In all my cross-country flights I use a parachute," wrote a private pilot, "so why should I do any differently when flying as a passenger."[49]

Air transport lines opposed the idea. Placing parachutes in the passenger cabin, the operators argued, would only call to the attention of air travelers the possibility of an accident. Thus, far from giving them a feeling of security, it would discourage their use of air transportation. The operators had unsuccessfully used the same argument against requiring the installation of seat belts. They had a more solid argument, however, when they claimed that many an air traveler could never be persuaded to jump and that an order to don parachutes could very well lead to mass panic. The Aeronautics Branch agreed, though some of its officials believed they could see the day when parachutes would be standard equipment on all air transports. The position of the Branch was that most fatal accidents took place under circumstances that precluded the use of these devices, and it offered an analysis of accident statistics to support this conclusion.

The death of Knute Rockne in an air transport crash in 1931 brought what few parachute advocates there were into the open. "To me it seems a tragedy that Mr. Rockne did not even have a chance to save himself," said an official of the Norwich Pharmacal Company. Enough people held the same sentiment to prompt Maurice H. Thatcher, a Congressman from Kentucky, to introduce a bill making parachutes compulsory on air carriers. Nothing came of the measure, or of a similar one introduced by Representative Emanuel Celler, a New York City Democrat. With the industry solidly against any action and the public largely unconcerned, the Department easily fought off this attempted congressional intrusion into its regulatory function.[50]

Suggested rule changes made by the industry itself usually fared better. An early source of industry complaint was the ease with which apparently incompetent mechanics could secure a Federal license. So the Branch stiffened its requirements, with the result that complaints began coming in that "examinations are getting so tough that even the very best mechanics have a tough job in passing." The problem lay in the fact that in revising its rules the Branch had adopted as its standard the level of competence required to service air carrier aircraft. It had, in other words, gone from one extreme to the other. The logical solution would have been to establish a system that rated mechanics according to the type of aircraft or engine they were capable of servicing. Needless to say, such a solution had occurred to Young and other Aeronautics Branch officials. But the Branch pleaded that it did not have the resources to handle the additional examinations that such a program required. Meanwhile, Young nursed a vague hope that "conditions in the industry would gradually work out so that this matter would take care of itself."[51]

The solution that the Aeronautics Branch rejected for mechanics it adopted for transport pilots. Prior to December 1929, an applicant for a transport license could demonstrate his skills in any aircraft, even in a small 100-horsepower plane designed to carry one or two people. Thus qualifying, the pilot was authorized to fly any airplane, including Ford or Fokker trimotors. This policy was illogical on its face, yet it was abandoned only after a three-year accumulation of accident statistics underlined its shortcomings. Henceforth, transport pilots were required to demonstrate their ability to fly each type of aircraft in which they carried passengers for hire.[52]

The number, and the qualifications, of crew members required to ride the cockpit of air carrier aircraft was — and still is — a much discussed topic between the airline industry and the Federal Government. Many Aeronautics Branch personnel believed that the trimotored

Fords and Fokkers, standard equipment on passenger routes of that day, could not be safely handled by a single transport pilot. Indeed, in the late 1920's, a rule was promulgated that required both a pilot and copilot possessing a transport license to man these aircraft. The rule was ambiguously worded, however, and more than one airline interpreted it to suit itself, some airlines putting a mechanic in the copilot's seat. When field inspectors cracked down, air carrier complaints began to reach the upper echelons of the Aeronautics Branch. "It would prove a great hardship on the commercial operators," wrote the general manager of an independent carrier, "if a regulation stipulated two licensed [transport] pilots be assigned to a ship . . . ." The operator had a point. The ratio of crewmembers to paying passengers was extremely high in the aircraft of that day, which, at best, could accommodate no more than 10 to 12 passengers. "Now then, with a pilot, co-pilot, courier (or steward), and lastly, a radio operator, the result is an economic absurdity," another operator complained. And this absurdity would be perpetuated "unless a policy is developed which will enable operators to cut down on the cost based upon such employees."[53]

The industry found the Aeronautics Branch both understanding and accommodating. It eased the burden of the airlines by requiring a copilot only on aircraft that (1) had a capacity of 15 passengers or more, or (2) a gross weight of 15,000 pounds or more. In 1929, only a small minority of trimotors or other aircraft met or exceeded these specifications. The Branch also allowed the holder of a limited commercial license to serve as copilot; moreover, he was not required to possess a rating for the particular aircraft he flew. At the same time, the Branch resisted the efforts of radio operators to have one of their number permanently installed in the cockpit. The pilot in command, the copilot, or any other member of the crew could serve in the capacity of radio operator. The copilot, moreover, could serve as steward.[54]

The standards in the cockpit were not raised until May 1932, when the Branch established a new pilot category, scheduled air transport. This rating, which called for greater experience and skills than the transport rating, was made mandatory in January 1933 for all first pilots flying aircraft in scheduled interstate air passenger service. At the same time, the amended regulations specified "that where a copilot is required in scheduled interstate air passenger services by Department of Commerce Regulations, such a copilot shall hold a Transport Pilot license . . . ." As in other instances, the Branch had bent to the industry's wishes at a time when more rigorous standards would have clearly constituted a heavy economic burden. But the growing complexity of air navigation and the impending introduction of a new generation of air carrier aircraft ultimately forced the Branch to raise its standards, if for no other reason than the good of the industry. Maintaining a high standard of safety was itself a sure means of fostering air commerce.[55]

Other important reforms were adopted. Only pilots, mechanics, and aircraft were certificated under the first set of Air Commerce Regulations. This list was gradually expanded during the late twenties and early thirties to include, most importantly, interstate air passenger lines and flying schools. Though airline certification was probably inevitable, it came mainly as a reaction to a series of nasty accidents — accidents that caused rumblings in the Congress and gave rise to sentiment in some quarters that the responsibility for airline safety might be advantageously transferred to the Interstate Commerce Commission.

Clarence Young got the hint. Thus, beginning in May 1930, no "person, firm, copartnership or corporation" could conduct scheduled air passenger operations in interstate commerce without acquiring a certificate of authority from the Department of Commerce. To qualify for such a certificate, an interstate carrier had to meet certain minimum standards. It had to demonstrate that it possessed an adequate ground organization, adequate maintenance procedures, and a sufficient number of qualified personnel to handle the service it intended to provide. Aircraft were required to carry equipment and instruments specified by the Aeronautics Branch. This certificate was, in a sense, a license to operate and resembled the certificate of convenience and necessity, which had been in general use by local and state governments for many years. It differed from the certificate of convenience and necessity, however, in that it did not grant the holder a route monopoly. It also differed in that it was issued without an inquiry into the financial responsibility of the carrier, save for the fact that the equipment and facilities that the carrier possessed did provide at least an indirect clue to its financial resources. In the final analysis, however, airline finances could not be ignored entirely, though the Aeronautics Branch was looking at the other side of the coin. "We of course recognize the fact that our requirements are apt to cost money," wrote a Department of Commerce official, "and in that way influence finances, and for that reason have kept them down to the minimum which we consider consistent with safety."[56]

Flying schools could not be dealt with so readily as airlines because the Air Commerce Act had failed to give the Secretary authority over this area. The Air Mail Act of 1925, the Air Commerce Act of 1926, and Lindbergh's flight of 1927 helped create increased activity in all branches of civil aviation, including the instructional field. Hundreds of flying schools cropped up virtually over night. Curriculums and the quality of instruction varied widely from one school to another, as did the going rate for a standard beginner's course. It was the kind of thing that could be expected in the absence of either Federal or state regulation. Especially troubling was that some school operators were only interested in how much money they could make, and how fast. They attracted pupils by underpricing the competition and making up the difference by skimping on instruction. Some of the more unsavory operators "guaranteed" a license to their pupils, pocketed their money in advance, and then graduated them knowing full well that they were ill-prepared to pass the Federal examination. The unwary, as always, made up the largest number of victims. But even someone wishing to select his school carefully had little to work with in order to make a considered choice.

Meanwhile, accidents began to pile up. A study by the Aeronautics Branch revealed that 20 percent of fatal accidents involved students on solo flights. Another analysis revealed that out of a total of 147 accidents, nearly 50 percent involved pilots with less than 50 hours flying time — a clear reflection on the quality of instruction. By late 1927, both the Aeronautics Branch and the Aeronautical Chamber of Commerce viewed the situation as extremely serious. Rather than take a more direct form of action, however, which would have involved seeking Federal legislation, Department of Commerce and industry representatives decided to give flying-school operators one year in which to put their house in order. Meanwhile, the ACC sought to work through better business bureaus, trade journals, and other private bodies in an effort to focus public attention on the shadier operators.[57]

A year later, the same trouble spots existed; indeed, if anything, matters had deteriorated. Fed up, a number of states decided to take matters into their own hands by legislating flying-school standards. This gave the Aeronautics Branch additional concern, for state standards would inevitably vary from jurisdiction to jurisdiction, creating even more chaos. Young had little choice but to turn to Congress for new powers. Hiram Bingham, who had made peace with MacCracken and was also on excellent terms with Young, introduced a bill amending the Air Commerce Act, which was duly passed in February 1929.[58]

By no stretch of the imagination did the new powers granted by this amendment prove entirely sufficient. According to the constitutional wisdom of that day, since flying schools were engaged in intrastate commerce, they could not come directly under Federal control. Bingham's amendment, however, permitted the Secretary of Commerce to examine and rate schools that voluntarily sought a Department of Commerce certificate. Even this small increment in Federal responsibility was helpful. Reputable operators tended to seek Federal certification. This meant that the discriminating, if not the unwary, had a standard by which to select a school. But as an American Bar Association official pointed out in 1930, "When it comes to stopping the fellow who will not comply, there is not any direct power to do it, because it is intrastate commerce." The Air Commerce Act was not without its flaws.[59]

VII

Leaving the regulation of intrastate aviation to the states created problems not only with flying schools, but in other areas vital to aviation safety. What could and did go on came close to making a mockery of Congress' stated resolve to promote safety in the air. In 1928, for example, one Mary A. Ashburn, an aspiring pilot, failed the Department of Commerce physical. The young woman had a congenital eye defect that seriously contracted her field of vision. In explaining the reasons for her rejection to a Senator from her home state, Herbert Hoover pointed out that failing the Federal medical examination "does not prevent Miss Ashburn from receiving instruction from an intrastate operator of aircraft, if both the airplane and pilot are unlicensed." Whether Miss Ashburn decided to exercise this alternative — which, because of its inherent danger, was scarcely an alternative at all — is unknown; but others in similar circumstances did.[60]

One such man, having failed his Federal pilot's test, continued to fly his own private plane out of a small local airport. The airport manager, seeing the aircraft unlicensed and in a state of disrepair, ordered it and its owner off his field. Undaunted, the unlicensed pilot moved to a vacant field, took a passenger up for a joy ride, and ended up killing himself and his passenger. Protecting people from themselves had not been contemplated by the Air Commerce Act. The responsibility for this incident lay with the state in which it occurred.[61]

Jurisdictional responsibility was not always so clear. One man possessing a Federal pilot's license had repeatedly been warned by aviation officials in Massachusetts not to fly a particular airplane, which they believed was not airworthy. Because he disregarded these warnings, Massachusetts suspended his license. But he continued to fly and ultimately cracked up. He was promptly arrested and charged with flying without a license. The pilot, however, challenged the state's contention in court; Massachusetts, he maintained through his attorney, had no authority to suspend a Federal license. The man had a point. Logically, his case was a matter for Federal authorities, yet they were powerless under the circumstances. Federal jurisdiction did not cover unlicensed aircraft employed in intrastate commerce. Such cases, a direct result of giving the states control over intrastate flying, would continue to bedevil the system for years to come.[62]

The Commissioners on Uniform State Laws had had considerable success in persuading state legislatures to adopt the uniform state aviation law. But this measure had been stripped of all regulatory provisions at the behest of MacCracken and others at a time when these men still nurtured the hope that Federal authority would extend over all flying activity. Since Congress decided to limit Federal authority to interstate commerce, however, except in the vital area of air traffic control, a sizable regulatory void was left for states to fill. Few states jumped into the void (by March 1928, only 10 states had made an attempt to regulate flying); those that did, did so with little or no regard to what their sister states were doing. Accordingly, confusion reigned.

One fact clearly emerged amidst the confusion: unlicensed pilots had appreciably higher accident and fatality rates than licensed pilots. "The assertion of the Department of Commerce that the lack of adequate regulatory laws in many of the States accounts, in large measure, for fatal casualties in flying cannot be challenged," commented the *New York Times* in September 1929. The solution, according to the *Times*, was "uniformity of regulatory laws throughout the country."[63]

MacCracken and Young had long advocated the same solution. "The enactment and enforcement of State and local laws to govern the licensing of pilots of aircraft is impeding the progress of the industry," Young said before a regional transportation conference. "The only solution is for the States to relinquish all rights to regulate flying and entrust the Federal Government with the development of the industry." This was strong talk, and Young may have been encouraged by the fact that some Congressmen, most notably William B. Oliver (D-Ala.), a member of the influential House Appropriations Committee, had begun to feel "that sooner or later Congress and the States must recognize the importance of giving central control to a matter of this kind." But Young was probably speaking more out of a sense of frustration than a conviction that Congress was prepared to adopt such a solution any time soon. A less satisfactory but attainable solution would have to be found.[64]

Some states had already suggested the logical course to pursue. Pennsylvania, for example, rather than draw up an aviation code of its own, provided that state licensing and inspection requirements would be identical to Federal requirements. It also provided that the holder of a Federal license did not require a state license, shrewdly anticipating that everyone would apply for a Federal license. Michigan went a step further; it made it mandatory for anyone flying within its borders to possess a Federal license. In January 1930, the Department of Commerce issued a statement proposing in so many words that all states follow Michigan's example. The aviation committee of the U.S. Chamber of Commerce stood foursquare for the proposal. So did Charles Lindbergh, who added that "non-uniform local regulations are sure to prove the greatest hindrance to the progress of flying."[65]

At the end of 1930, Young called a much-publicized conference of state officials and other interested parties. Prodded by the Department of Commerce, the Aeronautical Chamber of Commerce, and notable figures from the aviation community, the state officials went home and began to get results. The states, it developed, were not so diligent in exercising their rights as Congress was vigilant in preserving them. Within two years, 29 states required Federal licensing for all intrastate flying operations, seven for intrastate commercial operations. Six states accepted either a state or Federal license. Four others stubbornly stuck to a state licensing requirement, while only two, Georgia and Louisiana, had no aviation law whatever. All of this meant that the Air Commerce Regulations now applied, to one degree or another, to intrastate flying activities in 42 of the 48 states. For all practical purposes, Federal control over intrastate air commerce was now a moot question.[66]

VIII

The aviation industry may have asked for Federal regulation, but it also had some anxious moments wondering whether regulation would further rather than deter industry progress. "No man," remarked *Aviation*, "ever had a chance to make himself more thoroughly unpopular than the Assistant Secretary of Commerce [for Aeronautics]." MacCracken did not make big waves. By the time he left his post for a Washington, D.C., law practice, industry's doubts had been put to rest. "What is it that has wrought this change in feeling, and this increase in the habit of looking to the Aeronautics Branch for assistance and advice, regarding it as a mentor rather than as a policeman?" *Aviation* asked. The answer lay in "a growing confidence in the Department's aeronautical personnel, and specifically in the men who have had charge of the work and shaped the policies."[67]

These policies — the initial leniency in enforcing regulations, the granting of waivers to private pilots, the issuance of temporary certificates to less than airworthy aircraft — may have taken their toll in accidents, and they certainly did not further MacCracken's expressed desire to convince the American public that aviation was safe, but they eased the transition from nonregulation to regulation and helped bring the Aeronautics Branch into close rapport with the aviation community. No doubt, too, people remained in business who could not have survived an initially more rigorous regulatory policy, which was, perhaps, to the good. The Aeronautics Branch thus earned a reputation for fairness and reasonableness and for having the best interests of the industry at heart. Such a reputation gave the Branch a measure of leverage with the industry that it would otherwise not have possessed. This leverage was used to advantage when it came time to stiffen up on enforcement, to institute such important reforms as airline certification, or to clamp down on intrastate flying, a move made infinitely easier with the support of such industry organizations as the Aeronautical Chamber of Commerce.

The policy of the Aeronautics Branch may have been "a maximum of encouragement with a minimum of regulation" throughout MacCracken's and Young's tenures, but regulation did bear results. "The demand now being made by various states for federal licenses on all airplanes means plain, simple, outright prohibition — prohibition of private construction and flying," complained a private airplane builder.

This, he inaccurately predicted, was "the end of private flying." What it did signal was the end of the kind of operation that this man was running; unlicensed pilots and less than airworthy aircraft had been grounded. It also meant improved safety in the air. The number of fatalities in private flying dropped 20 percent in 1931 and another 20 percent in 1932. No doubt, part of this drop was accounted for by the falling off of private flying activity during the depression — but not all. Aircraft miles flown per fatal accident rose steadily during the early thirties; indeed, they achieved a year-to-year rise throughout the decade.[68]

Air carrier safety showed even greater improvement. Between 1930 and 1932, when the full force of the new safety rules were first felt, the air carrier passenger fatality rate per 100 million passenger miles flown was cut in half. More importantly, this was only the beginning. The policies adopted during the early thirties, when combined with the introduction of the Boeing 247 and the DC-2 — the first airliners of modern design — ushered in a new era in air carrier safety. The difference between the pre-1933 period and the post-1932 period was so dramatic that it is no exaggeration to say that 1933 marked a watershed in airline safety.[69]

If anything suffered from all this, it was aviation's reputation as a reckless, adventurous, rip-roaring enterprise. Not that this reputation died immediately; and certainly the airplane continued to suggest romance. But the airplane was slowly but surely being stripped of its heroic trappings. As early as 1929, *Commonweal* felt certain that "the airplane should some day be safer than any form of land travel . . . ." Writers in the *Scientific American* and *Forum*, after reviewing accident statistics, proclaimed air carrier travel safe and assured the public that the Aeronautics Branch was as solicitous for the welfare of the air traveler "as a broody hen over her chicks." Still, as a writer in the *Nation* noted, with railroads many times safer than airplanes, not all the adventure had gone out of air travel, which helps explain why a Department of Commerce official could observe in 1932 that aviation "does not yet affect the daily routine of any considerable percent of our population . . . ." But MacCracken and Young, in their fashion, had gone a long way toward taking the risk and the thrill out of flying.[70]

5. Lighting the Airways

"Long chained, like Prometheus, to the earth, we have freed ourselves at last, and now can look the skylark in the face," Will Durant
wrote in celebration of the airplane. Durant was only partially correct. A
modern airliner streaking across the sky appears to be as free as a bird in
flight — a thing emancipated, for the brief period that it remains aloft,
from earthly dependence; in reality, that airliner is as dependent on
terrestrial devices as the most earthbound of creatures, tethered to the
ground, as it were, by an invisible umbilical cord. Indeed, the pilot of a jet
transport flying by instruments is in closer contact with people on the
ground than the lone occupant of an automobile driving along a
highway. And he is infinitely more dependent on them. Air traffic
control specialists, electronic technicians, weathermen — some 35,000
strong — are engaged in helping to make his journey aloft possible by
manning an intricate and farflung air navigation and air traffic control
network.[1]

The invention of the airplane was only the essential first step in
aviation's development; it alone could not have ushered in commercial
air transportation as we know it today — a safe, reliable, and efficient
means of moving people and goods. The essential second step was the
development of the ground-based airway. This was well understood at an
early stage in the evolution of air commerce. "Experience has shown that
the airplane is far from independent of the ground over which it flies,"
observed an aeronautical engineer in 1925. "In fact the efficiency of its
performance is quite dependent on the thoroughness of the organization
on the ground along its course." Paul Henderson put the same idea in the
form of a paradox. "An airway exists on the ground, not in the air," he
said. It was this characteristic of commercial aviation — its dependence
on ground organization — that prompted Congress to authorize the
Secretary of Commerce to designate and chart civil airways and estab-

125

lish, operate, and maintain along them "all necessary air navigation facilities except airports."[2]

II

The modern commercial airway, like the airplane, is an American invention. Specifically, it was conceived, with an assist from the U.S. Army, by the U.S. Air Mail Service in the early 1920's. But unlike the airplane, the airway was invented out of necessity. From the beginning — indeed, on the very first day that it inaugurated airmail service, between Washington and New York, in May 1918 — the Post Office Department felt the lack of ground organization.

The navigational problems encountered in initiating this service were instructive. The pilot chosen to fly the first leg (Washington to Philadelphia) of the inaugural run on the Washington-New York route was a young Army lieutenant fresh out of flying school, one George L. Boyle. Boyle had two things going against him: he was green, and he had an atrocious sense of direction. Hence, when he took off (amidst a great deal of fanfare that had even brought President Woodrow Wilson to the scene) he promptly got lost and eventually ended up landing in Waldorf, Md., some 25 miles south of Washington. The mail was put on a train. Two days later, Lt. Boyle was given a second chance. This time matters were not left entirely to his uncertain navigational skills. Another aircraft escorted Boyle to Baltimore and pointed him in the direction of Philadelphia. Boyle was instructed, moreover, to keep the water — that is, Chesapeake Bay — always on his right. Boyle followed instructions sedulously. He flew along the water's edge to Elkton, Md., crossed the narrow strip of land between Chesapeake Bay and the Delaware River, and passed over Wilmington, Del., into New Jersey, only to realize that the water — now the Delaware River — was on his left. Mindful of his instructions, he made a prompt aboutface, followed the river south into Delaware Bay, and scooted all the way around the Jersey Shore to Cape May, whereupon he made the dual discovery that he was out of gas and the water was now not only on his right, but on his left and in front of him as well. He executed a dead-stick landing, foiled only by a lack of fuel and the immensity of the Atlantic Ocean.[3]

Admittedly, inexperience was largely to blame for these early misadventures, and fortunately for the Air Mail Service, it had pilots with a better sense of direction than Lt. Boyle. But navigational problems continued to present difficulties for the Post Office, particularly with the inauguration of a transcontinental service between New York and San Francisco, and inexperience was not at their root. The trouble was a near-total lack of reliable airborne or ground-based navigation aids. Light beacons, radio ranges, radio markers — aids that would later become basic to air navigation — nowhere existed in the early 1920's.

Of course, a pilot could get along without such aids. Indeed, the birdman and other early fliers would have found navaids superfluous. A man sailing in a small lake without ever losing sight of land does not need navigational aids. Nor does the man who takes his airplane up on a sunny day for a short spin. But his problems multiply when he decides to go from one location to another some appreciable distance away, particularly if he intends to depart and land according to a regular schedule.

By 1921, airmail planes were equipped with, among other things, a compass, a turn-and-bank indicator, and an altimeter. The compass and the turn-and-bank indicator were only marginally reliable (in the words of one pilot, his compass "made like a merry-go-round in slow motion"); the altimeter, often more sensitive to weather conditions than to changes in elevation, gave only a rough idea of altitude. Under the circumstances, an airmail pilot had to supplement these instruments with his own sensory aids — the feel and sound of the wind or the sight of the ground.

A pilot's ability to recognize towns, railroads, rivers, farms, prominent structures, and other landmarks along his route was critical. Aerial maps did not exist during the first two years of the service. "There were no maps from Bellefonte to Cleveland, so that [the pilot] had to make the trip trusting to his compass and a general sense of direction," complained the manager of the Bellefonte airmail station in explaining the tardiness of a particular airmail flight in December 1919. "The matter of the maps has been reported several times but no action appears to have been taken." The Post Office did make road maps available, but they were maps of individual states, each with a different scale of distances. The only towns listed on these maps were those with post offices. Nor did the maps show altitudes or mountains. "The only contour map I ever saw before 1921 was the one in Union Train Station in Washington," recalled one veteran airmail pilot. "We had no idea how high the mountains we crossed were, unless we measured them ourselves." Such vital data as a pilot had not put to memory, he put in a little black book, which might contain anything from the height of church steeples to the names and locations of farmers with telephones. Finally, a pilot had to rely on his own innate sense of direction. It did no harm, therefore, if a few drops of homing pigeon ran in his veins.[4]

Airmail pilots, then, navigated by visual reference to known landmarks. They rarely flew at night, and then only for short distances. During bad weather, pilots could do one of two things: they could fly above the weather ceiling and get down through it somehow at the end of the flight, or they could fly beneath the weather, always keeping visual contact with the ground. Contact flying was far and away more popular. But it was pushed to lengths that would fill pilots of today with horror. In 1919, the General Superintendent of the Air Mail Service, in the course of stating that a 200-foot ceiling was the limit for practical flying, noted that "a number of runs had been made with the mail during which a part of the trip was flown at an altitude of 50 ft." Hedge-hopping pilots often flew so low and found themselves in so dangerous a proximity to land obstacles that they had a choice of either turning back (if the weather had not closed behind them) or attempting a crashlanding.[5]

The airmail pilot did benefit from the existence of an extensive, if rudimentary, system of radio stations, which helped govern flights by the weather information they disseminated. On August 20, 1920, the Department issued orders for the establishment of radio stations at each airmail landing field that could not be served by U.S. Navy stations. A total of 17 stations were eventually deployed, including a large station in the Post Office Department headquarters building in Washington, D.C. These early radio stations, forerunners of the modern flight service station system, were primitive by today's standards. The radiotelegraph transmitter, usually a two-kilowatt arc (spark transmitters were used initially), was normally housed in a small wooden structure some distance from the airfield so that the station's high antenna would not interfere with low-flying aircraft groping for a landing in bad weather. Neither ground-to-air nor voice communication existed. Messages were sent by code at a rate of about 30 words a minute and were strictly between stations. Radio, then, was employed solely for ground-to-ground communication, not for navigational assistance.[6]

Messages contained information on aircraft arrivals and departures, and on weather conditions prevailing in the vicinity. One operator was normally sufficient to man a single station; only two aircraft a day — one in each direction — landed at or overflew any field along the route.

Stations were operated, therefore, on a schedule designed to coincide
with arrivals or overflights. In the case of overflights, pilots reported
their position by buzzing the station low enough for the operator to
identify the aircraft visually. This left the operator with time enough to
maintain his equipment, which was part of his job, and relay all manner
of other messages transmitted by the Post Office or other Federal
agencies. The Department of Agriculture in particular made extensive
use of the Post Office's network, transmitting weather forecasts and
market quotations for grains, livestock, and other commodities.[7]

In brief, the airmail pilot, having neither navaids nor radio communication with the ground, could fly only by day. Consequently, the early
operations on the transcontinental airmail route did not provide true
airmail service. Mail planes worked in conjunction with the regular
trains. From each of several points along the route each morning a load
of mail chosen at random would be taken off a train and given a leap
forward by air, traveling to a point that could be reached before dark.
That evening, if the mail thus airlifted had farther to travel, it would be
put on another train. Hence, no mail traveled more than a minor part of
the transcontinental distance by air. The result of each day's operations
under this system was that a small fraction of the mail was given a slight
kick forward.[8]

The effort scarcely seemed worthwhile. Flying the mail cost a great
deal of money — a great deal more than transporting it by rail. Yet the
airmail rendered only a minute commercial advantage. Even with all the
elaborate shifting from train to plane to train, the time saved was
insignificant. Paul Henderson's first impression of the airmail when he
became Second Assistant Postmaster General in the spring of 1922 "was
that it was an impractical sort of fad, and that it had no place in the
serious job of postal transportation." It became clear to Henderson that if
the airplane was ever to attain a permanent place in the general scheme of
postal transportation it "must be used for continuous flight of mail over
relatively long routes." This meant flying at night, something that had
never been undertaken on a regular schedule or over a long route.
Without night flying, the airmail was a mere frill — an expensive
plaything to be discarded once its novelty wore off.[9]

Henderson's predecessors in office had come to the same conclusion
and had, on February 22, 1921, conducted a daring night-flying experiment in order to demonstrate the practicality of night flying and thus

induce Congress to fund the lighting of the transcontinental route. On that day, the Post Office dispatched two plane loads of mail from New York to San Francisco and another two from San Francisco to New York. For navigational guidance, pilots flying the night segments had to depend totally on their primitive airborne equipment, bonfires lit along the route by accommodating citizens, and dead reckoning. Only one plane made it through, and that because of the courage and remarkable flying skills of James H. ("Jack") Knight, a youthful veteran of the North Platte-Omaha mail run. Knight, undaunted by the failure of relief pilots to show up at Omaha or Iowa City, flew three segments of the route himself, pushing on through a raging snowstorm and a treacherous Mississippi Valley fog until he arrived to a hero's welcome in Chicago. Congress approved the lighting project, only to see it fall victim to the Harding administration's cost cutting.

In 1923, Henderson managed to secure funds for lighting a portion of the transcontinental, though he found many a man who doubted that the project would ever succeed. "Over 90 percent of the advice which came to me was to the effect that it could not be done," he recalled. He got contrary advice from two young Army lieutenants, Donald L. Bruner and Harold R. Harris, who had begun experimenting with night flying at McCook Field, near Dayton, Ohio, in 1921. The Army was an old hand at night flying; it had conducted night bombing missions during the war and had continued night-time experiments after the Armistice. But, like the Post Office's February 1921 experiment, the Army's wartime techniques depended too much on pilot skill and too little on ground organization.* Bruner and Harris depended on ground organization. They equipped a 72-mile stretch of airway between Dayton and Columbus with rotating light beacons, field floodlights, and flashing markers that enabled pilots to fly from one beacon to another, determine

---

*An AEF veteran described one of the Army's early experimental airways: "After the armistice our squadron was moved to the north coast of France near Boulogne and we were formed into a mail squadron. Mail was flown over the channel by one squadron of machines and we carried it from there to Cologne a distance of about 280 miles. We had ballon [sic] stations along the route where they had numbered ballons to let up on days when the clouds were dense but as the ballons could only go 4000 ft. high and the clouds were usually from 500 to 6000 ft. thick we seldom saw them and we depended entirely on navigation by dead reckoning in poor weather and in good weather by both navigation and land marks." William L. Carroll to Otto Praeger, November 24, 1919, RG 28, AMS.

precisely where they were along the airway, and land safely at their destination. Between July 2 and August 13, 1923, the Army attempted 29 scheduled night flights along this airway and managed to complete 25 without incident. With this example before him, Henderson could confidently proceed with his own project.[10]

The stretch of land between Chicago and Cheyenne was chosen as the logical place to begin night operations. The land was flat, with no natural barriers to contact flying and few obstacles to light emplacement. Emergency fields could be conveniently sited. But this sector was also a logical selection because of its strategic location on the transcontinental. Daylight flights from either coast could reach Chicago or Cheyenne before nightfall. Hence, the Chicago-Cheyenne segment became the middle one of three, and mail flown by day from New York to Chicago was transported during the night to Cheyenne, continuing the following day to San Francisco. For eastbound mail, the process was reversed.[11]

Regular night service began July 1, 1924, though, as Henderson explained to MacCracken, "The first thirty days of operation will be announced as a 30-day trial so that if we get into difficulty we will be able to take a little recess to square away." The trial went off without a serious hitch. In the fall of 1924, anticipating the long nights of the winter months, the Post Office extended the lighted airway westward to Rock Springs, Wyo., and eastward to Cleveland. The next step was to connect Cleveland and New York, thereby establishing an overnight service between New York and Chicago. This work, begun in the winter of 1924–1925, was completed more than six months later, with overnight service beginning on July 1, 1925.[12]

The terrain between New York and Cleveland, which included the Allegheny Mountain Range, presented formidable problems. In the prairie and plains regions, lights could be installed more or less on a straight line; pilots could follow the lights just as one would follow a highway or a picket fence. In the east, a new system of airways was dictated by the terrain. Flat land for emergency fields was insufficient. Locating beacons on mountain tops that were both accessible from the ground and visible from the air was extremely difficult. Hence, though beacons were placed along the most direct air route, they were not spaced at regular distances as in the west. They were located instead atop the highest peaks. This forced pilots flying the route to rely on their compass for navigation and to use the lights as a check rather than a picket fence.

Later, when the airway between Rock Springs and Salt Lake City, which traversed the Laramie and Wasatch Ranges of the Rocky Mountains, was lighted, similar problems were encountered.[13]

The airmail was no longer a fad. Westbound coast-to-coast flights were being regularly completed in 34 hours 20 minutes; eastbound flights, because of favorable prevailing winds, in 29 hours 15 minutes. Railroads required in excess of three days to make the same trip. Thus, the transcontinental airmail operation was providing a measurable saving in time. In the process, the airplane was given a truly utilitarian function. None of this could have been accomplished without the lighted airway. When C. G. Grey, an English aviation journalist, visited the United States in 1924, he found that "the U.S. Post Office runs what is far and away the most efficiently organized and efficiently managed Civil Aviation undertaking in the World." The secret of the Post Office's success, he declared, "is that the real work is done on the ground." Thus, with its heavy emphasis on ground organization, the U.S. Air Mail Service had laid the foundation for commercial air carrier operating techniques. And though the Kelly Act and the Air Commerce Act ended the Post Office's roles of airmail carrier and builder of airways, for years to come the airmail remained the pulse of America's commercial air transport system. The airmail contracts let under the Kelly Act provided the economic base on which today's great trunk lines were built. But if in the ensuing years the Post Office Department provided the financial incentives for commercial aviation's development, the Department of Commerce provided the critical ground organization without which a viable air transportation system could not exist.[14]

III

The Air Commerce Act gave the Secretary of Commerce broad powers for providing civil aviation with the ground organization required for its development. The Secretary could provide light or other signal structures, radio directional finding facilities, radio or other electrical communication facilities, and any other structures or facilities used as aids to air navigation. And though airport development was prohibited, the Secretary could establish and maintain emergency landing fields. An emergency landing field, according to the act, was any locality adapted for the landing and taking off of aircraft that was located along an airway and was intermediate to airports connected by the airway. An emergency field, however, could not be equipped with facilities for shelter, supply, and repair of aircraft and could not be used regularly for the receipt or discharge of passengers or cargo.[15]

The act distinguished between civil and military airways, but made no provision, as the Federal Aviation Act of 1958 would do, for the establishment of a common air navigation system for both civil and military aviation. The Secretary of War was permitted to designate military airways, prescribe regulations for their use, and establish navaids on them. But a military airway could be designated a civil airway by the Secretary of Commerce; in such a case, the Secretary of War would continue to operate the facilities on the airway until such time as the Secretary of Commerce could provide for their operation.[16]

The task of establishing and maintaining airways was the job of the Airways Division in the Bureau of Lighthouses. The division's principal activities were reflected in its internal structure, which included four key sections — Survey, Construction, Radio, and Weather and Communications. The Survey Section surveyed and laid out new airways, selected beacon and emergency landing field sites, and concluded negotiations for licensing these sites and conditioning the fields. The Construction Section arranged for the purchase of lighting equipment and structures and supervised their installation. The Radio Section designed, procured, and supervised the installation of equipment for radio communication stations and radio range beacons. Finally, the Weather and Communications Section supervised the weather-reporting and communications service. As far as was practical, the activities of the Airways Division in the field were administered through the district offices of the Lighthouse Bureau.[17]

MacCracken selected a district superintendent from the Bureau of Lighthouses, Fred C. ("Cap") Hingsburg, to run the Airways Division. Hingsburg knew next to nothing about flying. MacCracken had resolved that "I wasn't going to have any ground people trying to do these jobs," but he hired Hingsburg because "he knew lighting," though, at this stage, nothing about lighting airways. People who did know about airway lighting were at a premium. They existed only in the Army Air Corps and the Air Mail Service. Former Air Mail Service personnel were quickly grabbed up, among them Charles I. Stanton, who had helped build the transcontinental airway. Civilian personnel in the War Department were also induced to join the Aeronautics Branch. This, naturally, tended to strain relations between the Air Corps and the Department of Commerce, not only because the Air Corps was losing hard-to-replace personnel, but also because the salary for such people was being steadily pushed up. Hoover finally agreed not to hire any airway specialists from the War Department until he had secured a clearance from the Air Corps.[18]

By the end of June 1927, the Airways Division had a complement of 134 people on board. On July 1, 1927, the Post Office Department let a contract to the Boeing Airplane Company to fly the mail between San Francisco and Chicago; on the same day, the transcontinental airway was transferred to the Department of Commerce. With this transfer came, along with 17 radio communication stations, 95 emergency landing fields, and other facilities, a contingent of 146 former Air Mail Service employees — people with a long experience in lighting and maintaining airways. Thus, the Department of Commerce inherited with the transcontinental airway the Post Office Department's expertise in ground organization.[19]

IV

The basic idea of aerial lighting came from marine lighting, which partially explains why the Airways Division was placed in the Lighthouse Bureau. But the two lighting systems could not — and did not — develop along precisely analogous lines because the navigational problems confronting ocean-going craft were not precisely analogous to those confronting airborne craft. A ship travels on a surface; an airplane, in three-dimensional space. A seaman, equipped with time-tested navigational instruments, places only occasional reliance on lights. An airman flying at night in the 1920's was forced to rely almost exclusively on light beacons. The seaman encounters relatively few lights at sea and has no difficulty identifying a navigational beacon. An airman flying over a city at night sees a confusion of lights.

These and other differences were recognized in the United States, and appropriate concessions were made to them. In contrast, Europeans applied virtually the same principles to aerial lighting as they did to marine. They thought in terms of widely spaced aerial lighthouses of great power and constructed either shielded lights throwing a beam in an approximately vertical line or simple spotlights radiating in all directions. No intermediate fields were provided or contemplated. The scheme did not work.[20]

The American plan involved the deployment of two classes of lights — rotating beacons and course lights — as well as the provision of intermediate landing fields at strategic points along the route. The rotating electric beacons, each projecting an intense and concentrated beam, were placed about 10 miles apart. The earliest standard airway beacon employed by the Aeronautics Branch was mounted on a 51-foot skeleton steel tower and consisted of a 110-volt, 1,000-watt Mazda lamp and a 24-inch parabolic mirror. The tower stood in the center of a concrete slab, approximately 70 feet in length, that was shaped in the form of an arrow. The arrow, black along its edges and yellow in the center, pointed in the direction of the next higher-numbered beacon. On the feather end of the arrow stood a small shed containing either a generator or emergency equipment. The beacon's number was painted in large black numerals on the roof of the shed. The facility produced a beam of 1,000,000 candlepower.[21]

Deciding on a standard maximum candlepower and a standard flash length was a tricky proposition. The beam had to possess a high maximum candlepower, otherwise it would be quickly absorbed or scattered, particularly on hazy days. Moreover, if the flash length was too short, the effect on the eye would be the same as a reduction in candlepower. Flash length could be increased by increasing the beam's horizontal spread, but this would also have meant a reduction in candlepower unless the luminous flux was increased. Increasing the luminous flux would have required using more power, which would have meant, in turn, a more costly system. Slowing down the beacon's rotation was another way of increasing flash length. This would have resulted, however, in increasing the interval between flashes, which also had its drawbacks.[22]

The Air Mail Service first thought in terms of directing the beacon's beam straight up in the air, believing that the beam by "wiggling around up there would attract the attention of the pilot." It did not work. The Army, on the other hand, had directed the beam at an angle of 2.5° above the horizon, and rotated the beacon at a rate of 10 revolutions per minute. The Air Mail Service finally settled on a beam of very high intensity directed at a 1° angle above the horizon and making three revolutions per minute. All this was further refined and perfected by the Aeronautics Branch. Its one-million-candlepower beam was directed at a point 1.5° above the horizon and rotated so that it struck the pilot in the eye at 10-second intervals. Though the pilot could not see the beam itself until he was relatively close to the beacon, he could see a clear flash of light from a distance of up to 40 miles each time the beacon turned towards him.[23]

Two course lights were mounted on the platform of the beacon's tower, one pointing forward and the other backward along the airway. These were 500-watt searchlights that projected a beam of 100,000 candlepower when fitted with either red or green lenses. Every third beacon had green course lights, indicating that the beacon was on an intermediate landing field; all other beacons had red course lights. As the mechanism revolved and the clear flash of the beacon passed from the pilot's vision, the red or green flash of the course light came into view. Course lights flashed coded dot-dash signals that indicated the beacon's position on the airway. Code signals ran from 0 to 9; thus, if a pilot received a signal for the number 4, he knew he was flying over the fourth beacon of a particular 100-mile stretch of airway. But he could not determine his precise position merely by receiving a course-light signal if he did not know independently over which 100-mile stretch he was flying.[24]

It was the regularity of these flashing lights and the distinctiveness and brilliance of the beacon's beam that enabled pilots to distinguish them from competing stray lights and even pick them out from vast clusters of lights in and around metropolitan areas.

In 1931, the Aeronautics Branch adopted a new standard beacon that dispensed with the two course lights. This beacon featured a single 1,000-watt incandescent lamp and a doublet lens system at each end of a 36-inch drum. The beacon projected two beams 180° apart. Each optical system consisted of an inner and outer prismic lens. The outer lens of each doublet was clear; one inner lens was clear and the other was either red or green, depending on the beacon's location on the airway. The beacon, making six revolutions per minute, flashed alternate white and colored light every five seconds. The clear lens projected a beam of approximately 1,600,000 candlepower; the code-flashing colored lens, about 400,000 candlepower. This system, more economical in its use of electrical power than the older system, was originally designed for the Southwest, where commercial current was scarce, but ultimately became the standard beacon on the airways. Moreover, since these beacons were more powerful than the 24-inch variety, they could be placed along an airway at 15- rather than 10-mile intervals.[25]

The Airways Division also employed a variety of auxiliary lights. When the Post Office Department first installed lighting on the transcontinental, it used both electric and gas beacons. The Department of Commerce discontinued the use of the gas beacons, except as auxiliary lights or as alternatives to electric beacons in areas where electricity was not available. Dioptric lanterns of 300 or 375 millimeters in diameter were used with single acetylene burners or with a cluster of three burners. Another widely used auxiliary unit had a double-ended range lantern fitted with two 18-inch doublet lenses similar to those employed in course lights and used a double acetylene burner as its light source. These beacons, which could be left unattended for as long as six months, were installed in desert and other uninhabited or difficult-to-reach areas. They were also used as auxiliary beacons in areas where the ground elevation between adjacent standard beacons was such that it blocked the pilot's view from one beacon to the next. In such cases, the auxiliary lights were placed on high elevations between standard beacons so that the pilot could maintain light-to-light contact at all times.[26]

Before the introduction of lighting on the transcontinental, an airmail pilot encountering either mechanical difficulties or bad weather was compelled to seek out a natural landing place — a grain field, pasture, or farm — and hope that no holes, stumps, or other hazards were hidden beneath its growth. With the inauguration of night flying, the Post Office Department established and maintained intermediate, or emergency, landing fields at approximately 30-mile intervals along the transcontinental airway. The Department of Commerce continued the practice. Because the Air Commerce Act specifically prohibited the Secretary of Commerce from establishing or maintaining airports, these fields could be used only for emergency landings, not for regular operations.[27]

The usual intermediate field was a square or triangular affair spread over some 50 acres. In lower altitudes, each field had two landing strips between 2,600 and 3,000 feet in length and between 400 and 600 feet in width; at altitudes above 4,000 feet, the length was increased to about 3,500 feet. The two landing strips formed either an "L", "T", or "+". The inner angles at the junctions of the strips were usually beveled off to provide additional diagonal landing space that could be used during strong crosswinds.

Fields were graded and sodded according to specification. For easy identification from the air, they were marked at the intersections of the runway centerlines by circles measuring 50 feet in diameter. Inside the circle was a central disk 12 feet in diameter that shared a common center with the circle. Panels 40 feet in length ran from the circle's outer border along the runway centerline to indicate landing direction. The circle, disk, and panels were constructed of crushed rock tamped flush with the field's surface and painted yellow.

A variety of lights, including an airway beacon, lit the field. Boundary lights marked the field's borders. These were installed at intervals of approximately 300 feet around the perimeter of the field and consisted of waterproof prismatic globes and fittings mounted on iron pipe-like standards that stood 30 inches above the ground. In areas with heavy snowfall, the standards stood higher. The globes were clear and usually held a 10-watt bulb. Approach lights were installed within the boundary-light system at each end of the runway. These lights were similar in every respect to the boundary lights, except that they had a higher wattage lamp and green rather than clear globes. Obstructions lying along or around the approach path were marked by red lights.[28]

Fields were leased by the Government from private owners or municipalities. The average rent ran between $400 and $500 per year. Individual rates, however, varied dramatically. In the heavily populated Northeast, rent ran as high as $1,200 for some fields. On the other hand, some communities were so eager to have intermediate fields established within or near their jurisdictions that they furnished land to the Department of Commerce for a token charge of $1.00 per year. In 1932, the Airways Division was leasing some 70 fields on favorable terms such as these. The average cost of establishing a field, including surveying and site selection, grading, and lighting, came to $5,500.[29]

Airway construction costs, however, varied widely from location to location, depending on the ease or difficulty of establishing fields or emplacing lights at particular sites. The continental United States has as varied a terrain as can be found anywhere in the world. Vast mountain ranges, flat prairie land, gently rolling countryside, swamp, desert, dense virgin timberland — all make up its rich topography. Crisscrossing this land with a system of lighted airways and intermediate fields was no easy task. Swamps, snow and sand drifts, precipitous mountains, and rocky gorges presented severe obstacles to the airway engineer.

Laying the airway between Portland, Ore., and Spokane, Wash., was a case in point. Between Portland and Umatilla, Ore., the most practicable flying route east was along the Columbia River, which had carved a huge notch through the Cascade Mountains — the Columbia Gorge. But this gorge, particularly along a 50-mile stretch between Cape Horn and Lyle, Wash., was extremely susceptible to dense fog, which frequently lowered ceilings to 250 feet. When such conditions prevailed, regular rotating light beacons located at altitudes above 250 feet were virtually valueless to pilots. To deal with this situation, the Airways Division decided to install a system of low-altitude lights along the walls of the gorge between Cape Horn and Lyle. Twenty-three sites were established, 12 on the Washington side of the gorge, 11 on the Oregon side. Of these 23 sites, 19 were clustered over a 30-mile distance between Beacon Rock and Hood River, a stretch that included the narrowest and most hazardous portion of the gorge. Transporting equipment to, and establishing installations on, this sector was fraught with difficulties. The site of the 55-mile beacon station on the Washington side of the gorge could only be reached by way of a flume, which had been constructed by a lumber company for floating logs down a timbered mountainside to a sawmill standing at river level. A sled was constructed, fitted to the sides of the flume, and tower, beacon, control cabinet, and other accessories were sent sliding more than half a mile down to the site. The flume, which was supported by a trestle, was as much as 250 feet above the mountainside in places. Workmen stood on an unguarded 12-inch catwalk that paralleled the flume to guide the sled down.[30]

At other hard-to-get sites, pack animals were used to transport beacons and other equipment. Burros carried all the equipment used to establish a beacon site and radio communication station atop Sexton Mountain, in Oregon. Some slopes, however, were so precipitous that even these surefooted animals could not negotiate them. At one site in the Southwest — Desert Peak, Ariz. — a trolley line, consisting of cables stretched between two poles and a hook suspended from a carrying pulley, was constructed. A block and tackle connected to the pulley and to a truck at the bottom of the peak provided the lifting power. Since ascending and descending the site each day would have been both dangerous and time consuming, the construction crew camped at the site for the six days that it took to erect the beacon.[31]

Swamps also presented special problems. At a site along the New Orleans-Atlanta airway, the foundations for several beacon sites had to be built on piles driven deep through swampland and mud to hard stratum. Another site, near Mobile, Ala., had to be established on a swampy island at the confluence of the Tensaw and Blakely Rivers. Equipment was transported from Mobile down the Mobile ship channel into the Tensaw. For a mile or so from this point, the river was extremely shallow. But going aground was only one of the hazards that had to be reckoned with. During the Civil War, piles had been placed in the river to block traffic from the ship channel. Many of the piles had not been removed, and the boat transporting the equipment ran the risk of ramming into these obstructions.[32]

Perhaps the greatest hardships endured by airway engineers were those incident to extending the transcontinental airway across Great Salt Desert. When the area between Beowawe and Parran, Nev., was first surveyed, Airways Division engineers decided to avoid a desolate 150-mile stretch immediately west of Beowawe by bending the airway to the north of Battle Mountain and approaching Parran by way of the Humboldt River Valley, which offered a much more congenial terrain. This made for such a circuitous route that it was soon dubbed "the Great Circle." It was therefore decided to provide a shorter, alternate route directly across Great Salt Desert. The area was so remote and barren — the nearest settlement was 75 miles away — that the Airways Division was forced to bring in complete camping equipment and enough supplies, including water, to maintain a force of 32 men for the 102 days required to emplace the 27 acetylene light units, which had to be used instead of electric lamps because of the unavailability of power in the area.

Construction began on October 9, 1928; on October 13, the first of a series of blizzards struck the camp. From that day forward work was performed under almost impossible weather conditions. The terrain presented other difficulties. At some sites, towers, lanterns, and acetylene tanks had to be transported by tractors — and, when they failed, by men — to locations from 4,000 to 6,000 feet above road level. The yielding nature of the alkali beds found in the area forced the crews to construct special caissons for tower mountings. When the deep snow came, the problem of transportation was compounded. Motor vehicles were useless, so the crews, adapting to their environment, used sleds, snowshoes, and even skis for transporting materials and for just getting about. Before the project was completed, on January 18, 1929, these men had regularly endured snow five feet deep and temperatures 18° below zero.[33]

Construction at sites such as these cost the Department appreciably more than, say, in the Plains States; but it also cost more in the physical demands it made on the airway engineer. "I want the record to show," MacCracken said years later in describing the hazards faced by airway construction crews, "that the airway superintendents who went up there, and the construction crews and gangs who went along with them to erect the beacons, were the real American heroes." It was as much in recognition of the work of these people as anything else that the Aeronautics Branch was awarded the Collier Trophy for 1928.[34]

V

The first airways constructed by the Department of Commerce followed the mails. "It would be of great advantage to us if you would indicate to what extent you believe the air mail routes now under contract and in contemplation during the ensuing year should be furnished with lighting equipment and other navigational aids," J. Walter Drake, the Assistant Secretary of Commerce, wrote to W. Irving Glover, the Assistant Postmaster General, on June 19, 1926, a day before the Air Commerce Act became law. With scheduled air passenger service nonexistent in 1926, the immediate purpose of lighting airways was to permit airmail contractors to carry the mail by night. But even after passenger carriers began scheduled runs off regular airmail routes, the Department did not light or otherwise develop these nonairmail airways. "It is the policy of the Department, in regard to lighting," declared MacCracken in September 1927, "to give first consideration to those routes already in operation or under [airmail] contract." He would have stated the case more accurately had he said that the Department

President Calvin Coolidge presents the Collier Trophy for 1928 to the Aeronautics Branch. Left to right: *Coolidge, Clarence M. Young, Senator Hiram Bingham, unidentified, and William P. MacCracken*

developed only airways along which the mail was flown. Hence, throughout this early period, the Department of Commerce lit no airway that was not already a daytime airmail route or a route that the Post Office had determined to let a mail contract for.[35]

In a few cases airmail contractors themselves lit portions of airways, particularly during 1926 and 1927, when the Aeronautics Branch found it impossible to provide at once the night-flying facilities required by contractors. Three airmail operators proposed to MacCracken that they erect and operate lighting facilities at critical points along their respective routes, with the understanding that the Department would buy these facilities when its budget allowed. Though this agreement was informal, the Department did eventually make good on its promise. Other contractors constructed airways without prior agreement with the Department. As a result, in 1933, two lighted non-Federal airways existed, one between San Antonio and Big Spring, Tex., the other between Phoenix, Ariz., and Los Angeles. By far the more significant of the two was the 360-mile-long Phoenix-Los Angeles airway, which had been established by American Airlines with facilities similar to those employed by the Department of Commerce. This carrier flew the mail along the southern transcontinental, which stretched along Atlanta, Dallas, Fort Worth, El Paso, and Phoenix before terminating in San Diego. American used the Federal airway up to Phoenix, and then switched to its own airway for the Phoenix-Los Angeles leg. This airway, too, eventually became part of the Federal system.[36]

If the mail determined routes, it followed that it also determined who flew them on a regularly scheduled basis. "Every route we operate is an airmail route," explained an airline executive. "The Post Office Department comes along and says, 'We want mail carried from here to here,' we bid on it . . . . We operate entirely where the Post Office Department wants us to operate." Few airmail contractors ventured off established airmail routes in search of passengers during the late twenties and early thirties.[37]

In 1929, when Herbert Hoover became President, he formalized the procedure for determining routes by ordering the creation of the Interdepartmental Committee on Airways. Composed of six members — three from Commerce, three from Post Office — the committee passed on all proposals, whether from the Post Office or private interests, for extending the civil airways.[38]

The first airway light beacon put in operation by the Airways Division was installed some 15 miles northeast of Moline, Ill., on December 7, 1926. By July 1, 1927, the Aeronautics Branch had lit 2,080 miles of airway, including routes between New York and Boston, Chicago and St. Louis, and Chicago and Dallas. This, together with the

2,041 lighted miles (New York-Salt Lake City) on the transcontinental, which were turned over to the Department of Commerce on that date, came to 4,121 miles of lighted airway. Nearly 1,800 miles along eight airways (including New York-Atlanta, Los Angeles-San Francisco, and a portion of Los Angeles-Salt Lake City) were added in fiscal 1928.[39]

The following fiscal year, the airways construction program went into high gear. Thirteen lighted airways were added, bringing the total number of lighted airways to 27 and the total number of miles lighted to 10,183 — nearly double the mileage available at the end of the preceding year. Operating facilities included 881 revolving light beacons, 263 intermediate landing fields, and 27 radio communication stations.[40]

On January 29, 1929, in what *Domestic Air News* called "a red letter event in the history of the Airways Division of the Department of Commerce," beacon No. 25, at Miriam, Nev., on the San Francisco-Salt Lake City route was turned on, thus closing the final 20-mile unlighted gap on the transcontinental airway. The east and west coasts had finally been linked with a system of airway beacons. By February 1933, two more transcontinental routes had been lighted. One route, the central transcontinental, ran between New York and Los Angeles; the other, the southern transcontinental, extended from New York to San Diego by way of Atlanta and Dallas.[41]

By 1933, the Federal Airway system comprised 18,000 miles of lighted airways on which were installed 1,550 rotating light beacons and 263 intermediate landing fields. And though this fell somewhat short of the goal set by MacCracken and Young to light 25,000 miles of airway, the administration felt justly proud of its achievement. "I know of no satisfaction equal to the growth under one's own hand of a great economic and human agency . . .," Hoover said in recalling this achievement years later. "I felt a personal triumph with every mile of service we added."[42] It was perhaps the only triumph that came out of the ruins of his administration; but it was a triumph whose edge had been blunted by Hoover's inability to deal effectively with the nation's economic travail.

"Of all American contributions to the technique of air transport operations," Edward P. Warner noted, "[flying at night by beacons] was the greatest." How great it was, and how far it put the United States ahead of the rest of the world, was attested to by the fact that, as late as the early 1930's, when Americans were flying more or less routinely at night, Europeans "were still but fingering the hem of the idea of night flying." But the revolving light beacon was only one of a number of navigation aids contributing to the emergence of commercial air transportation in the United States. Indeed, though the light beacon survived many decades on the nation's airways, its life in the mainstream of American aviation was brief.[43]

6. The Emergence of Radio

The lighted airway solved the problem of flying, or navigating, at night. But this technique of following a lighted course was merely an extension of contact flying. It required the pilot to maintain visual contact with a ground-based facility. It was, in short, a fair-weather flying technique.

Hence, though the lighted airway proved a tremendous stimulus to aviation growth, it alone was not enough to insure aviation's development into a reliable transport system. Air transport companies sold transportation in competition with other established carriers — railroads, steamships, buses. If they were to compete successfully, they had to offer the same safety, comfort, and regularity of service as competing modes. But they could not insure regularity of service if their schedules were at the mercy of the weather. An economically viable air transport system demanded flying by night as well as by day, and in nearly all vicissitudes of weather; flying in all vicissitudes of weather demanded an extensive communications system, including two-way voice communication, and an all-weather navigation system. Radio was the medium turned to by the Aeronautics Branch to provide these devices and permit the airplane to operate reliably on a scheduled basis, carrying mail, passengers, and express over fixed routes at regular intervals.[1]

II

The 17 radio stations inherited by the Aeronautics Branch from the U.S. Air Mail Service were capable only of point-to-point transmission via radiotelegraph. Radio navigation did not exist. Nor did voice communication. Pilot and radio operator could not communicate with each other.

Actually, at its inception, the Air Mail Service did have intentions of making a much wider use of radio. The thinking at the time was to employ radio for air navigation and for two-way air-ground communication. Leased wire service would be employed for point-to-point communication, just as it is today. Accordingly, in 1919, a number of spark transmitters were installed at locations along the eastern sector of the transcontinental airway. Radio-navigation experiments were conducted up to mid-1920 and then abruptly abandoned, as was the notion of using radio for anything but point-to-point communication. (Experiments were revived in 1925, but abandoned again after a few months.) The facilities were converted to radio broadcast stations. But with the creation of the Aeronautics Branch, the idea of making a broad-gauge use of radio was revived in earnest.[2]

Two-way communication between the air and the ground was considered imperative by the Aeronautics Branch and by the emerging air carrier operators.[3] Safety and schedule reliability demanded it. Weather broadcasts, emergency messages, and airport landing instructions could be relayed to the pilot. But as matters stood in 1926, a pilot was fed information concerning weather, wind velocity, the position of other aircraft, and other pertinent details just prior to takeoff. This information was accurate enough insofar as it reflected conditions at departure time. But if weather conditions changed while the pilot was en route, the ground organization was powerless to warn him of this fact. Thus, instead of avoiding a newly developing storm area, he would unknowingly head into it. Conversely, a pilot experiencing unexpected conditions could not pass on this information, which would have been of interest to other pilots, to the ground organization.[4]

The first intensive experimental work in the United States on two-way communication between aircraft and the ground was done by the military services in collaboration with the Bureau of Standards during World War I. This work yielded radio devices that were used by the military for relatively short-range communication; they were inadequate, however, for civil air operations in the 1920's.[5]

Practically all development work in ground-to-air communication ceased at the end of the war and was not begun again until the Aeronautics Branch enlisted the aid of the Bureau of Standards in 1926. By no means, however, did Bureau of Standards engineers have to begin where they had left off in 1918. The intervening period had seen great advances in a number of other areas, particularly in broadcast transmission and reception.[6]

The decision to abandon the old arc transmitters and go to more sophisticated devices was made immediately after the creation of the Aeronautics Branch. At the time, only the transcontinental airway was served by radio, and the Branch had to decide whether to extend the same system on the feeder routes or introduce something better. The Branch opted for something better. Until the new system was developed and in place, weather information and other messages on routes other than the transcontinental were transmitted over telephone lines.[7]

The Bureau of Standards began its development efforts in December 1926 at its experimental station at College Park, Md. By the end of the following April, the Bureau was operating an experimental ground-to-air radiotelephone system. Two-way conversations were successfully carried on over distances of up to 50 miles. Shortly thereafter, a 1,000-watt radiotelephone transmitter was installed at Bellefonte, Pa., on the transcontinental airway, for service tests. In August 1927, this station successfully communicated with an airmail plane over a distance of 150 miles. In March 1928, the Department of Commerce announced the award of contracts for the manufacture of 12 new radio stations. The Department also announced that same month its intention to establish radiotelephone stations throughout the Federal airway system. The first seven stations were installed in October 1928.[8]

The new standard radio communication stations had a 2-kilowatt radiotelephone and radiotelegraph transmitter (with motor generator), line amplifier, and two microphones. This transmitter operated on frequencies between 190 and 500 kilocycles when broadcasting by voice or code to aircraft. Each station also included two receivers and a 400-watt crystal-controlled radiotelegraph transmitter for point-to-point communication; the transmitter operated on frequencies between 3,000 and 6,000 kilocycles.[9]

Concurrently with its work on two-way communication stations, the Bureau of Standards devoted its attention to the development of an airborne receiver. Among other things, the set had to be rugged, light in weight and of small physical dimensions, capable of receiving both radio beacon signals and voice communication, and free from ignition system interference. In addition, the equipment had to possess uniform volume control from zero to maximum signal strength, a high sensitivity to permit the use of short vertical pole antennas (thus eliminating the dangers inherent in the use of weighted trailing-wire antennas), and a high selectivity to allow close spacing of frequency channels.[10]

The receiving set ultimately designed by the Bureau of Standards, largely the work of two radio engineers, Haraden Pratt and Harry Diamond, had a total weight (including power supply) of approximately 30 pounds. A simple airborne transmitter was also developed for voice transmission on a single frequency. In May 1927, in a public demonstration, this equipment was put aboard an aircraft and flown over Washington, D.C. Aeronautics Branch officials in the aircraft held two-way conversations with MacCracken and Dr. George K. Burgess, the Director of the Bureau of Standards, while both men sat at their office desks. One of the two-way conversations was broadcast live over a local radio station. "I believe it is safe to say that this means a new type of flying," noted a Boeing Air Transport official in contemplating the implications of air-ground communication. "[It] will involve 'camping on the heels' of bad weather, getting right up under the storms, sitting down at emergency fields, maintaining communication at all times with terminals, receiving weather information and short-period forecasts . . ." — all of which would increase both safety and regularity of service. The set went into production in 1928.[11]

As a way of inducing operators to equip their aircraft with two-way radios, the Watres Air Mail Act of 1930 provided that a premium be paid to airmail contractors carrying mail in aircraft capable of two-way communications. Earlier, the Federal Radio Commission had cleared the way for air transport companies to develop a communications network of their own by allocating radiofrequencies for their exclusive use. A national airport and landing-field frequency of 278 kilocycles was established for ground-to-air communications. Airport and landing-field transmitters operating on this frequency were limited to 10 watts of power. The commission also set aside the single frequency of 3,106 kilocycles as a national calling frequency for aircraft. All air-to-ground communications were transmitted exclusively on that frequency.[12]

The first group of new stations had scarcely been in place on the airways before leased teletypewriter circuits were introduced, beginning in 1928, as a weather-collecting system. A number of reasons dictated going to land lines. For one thing, even at this early date, the radiofrequency spectrum set aside for aviation by the Federal Radio Commission was showing signs of congestion. For another, teletype promised a faster and more reliable service. Lines and machines were leased from the American Telephone and Telegraph Co. at a cost of $70 per mile per year. Later, in 1932, the Aeronautics Branch, urged on by Congress, began purchasing teletypewriter machines as a cost-cutting measure.[13]

Some 700 miles of land lines went into operation initially, on the New York-Chicago route, which served as a proving ground for the new system. After one year's experience with this 700-mile system, Cap Hingsburg explained, "We found that the transport companies [operating on the route] have decreased their delays and defaulted schedules by better than 30 percent . . . and all the commercial aircraft operators . . . are anxious to have it extended to other airways." Also eager was the Interdepartmental Committee on Civil Airways, which urged the Aeronautics Branch in 1929 to strengthen its weather-reporting services by adding more teletype circuits. Circuits were added at a rapid pace in the ensuing three years. Thus, though radio was being put to more and more uses on the airways, it steadily yielded its point-to-point communications function, particularly its role in weather collecting, to land lines. But radio remained the sole means of disseminating weather information to the user.[14]

The Weather Bureau, then a part of the Department of Agriculture, played a key role in the weather-collecting system. Its role had been defined in the Air Commerce Act, which directed the Chief of the Weather Bureau "to furnish such weather reports, forecasts, warnings, and advices as may be required to promote the safety and efficiency of air navigation . . ., particularly upon civil airways . . ., and . . . to observe, measure and investigate atmospheric phenomena, and establish meteorological offices and stations" for this purpose.[15]

The Weather Bureau had been providing the U.S. Air Mail Service and private pilots with a measure of meteorological services, but nothing on the scale and variety contemplated by the Air Commerce Act. Thus, beginning with 1926, pilot balloon stations were established to conduct upper-air soundings and ascertain direction and velocity of winds aloft. These observations were made by following the flight of a small hydrogen-filled free balloon through a theodolite. The information gathered by these units, as well as information collected by so-called first-order Weather Bureau stations, was transmitted to collecting centers and ultimately used in making weather forecasts. Other Weather Bureau stations made local weather observations.[16]

In August 1931, the Weather Bureau intiated an experimental

weather-map service along six key points between Kansas City and New York. The experiment proved a decided success, and the service was adopted on a permanent basis nationwide in December 1932. At its inception, the service provided 78 air terminals around the country with a complete weather map of the United States six times a day, thus enabling airmen and operators to plan their flights with the reasonable expectation that weather encountered en route would be substantially as forecast.

The map service, later reduced to four times a day, was based on four comprehensive weather reports sent over Federal teletype circuits at 2 a.m., 8 a.m., 2 p.m., and 8 p.m. daily. Less comprehensive reports, based on local weather observations, were transmitted along the airways hourly. [17]

Point-to-point communications were conducted sequentially. Weather reports came into a Department of Commerce airway communications station by teletype (or, at some locations, by radiotelegraph). At a prescribed time, a teletype operator at a station along a particular airway — say, Hadley Field on the New York-Chicago airway — started the sequence by typing the current weather report for his area on the teletype. This report appeared on all the machines in the hook-up. When the Hadley operator finished typing his report, he rang a bell, signaling the next operator down the line (Bellefonte) that the circuit was clear for his report. Without further ado, the Bellefonte operator began typing his report, to be followed by the next station operator down the line. When the last station in the sequence had sent its report, all stations on the circuit had a detailed account of current weather conditions along the New York-Chicago airway. This information was then relayed to aircraft in flight. [18]

Weather broadcasts to aircraft in flight were at first broadcast by radio communications stations on individually assigned schedules at various times during the hour. This did not prove a very satisfactory procedure, for it required a pilot to refer to a printed schedule to determine the broadcasting time for a station he wished to listen to. Later, weather broadcasts were arranged and timed so that a pilot flying a route with which he was at all familiar knew what time these broadcasts were made and on what frequency. This was accomplished by grouping all airways radio stations into three networks, or chains — blue, brown, and red — and timing their broadcasts so that overlapping or conflict within chains was eliminated. Thus, the pilot only had to know which chain covered the airway he was flying and the broadcasting time of that chain.[19]

Radio communications stations were also engaged in position, or progress, reporting — that is, they followed the progress of aircraft filing flight plans. When an aircraft took off on the first leg of its journey, its departure time and destination, among other things, were sent by teletype to all radio stations along its route. Thus alerted, these stations kept a lookout for the aircraft. When a pilot passed over the first station, he would call in and identify himself if his aircraft was equipped with a two-way radio; otherwise, he would give the station operator some unmistakable signal — perhaps he would flash his navigation lights on and off, or close and open his throttle — that established his identity. The operator would now send on the teletype the time the aircraft passed over his station. This information was received automatically at the aircraft's point of departure, point of destination, and all points yet to be over-flown. The process would be repeated until the flight terminated.[20]

By mid-1933, 68 radio communications stations, placed at intervals of approximately 200 miles from each other, served the Federal airways. This system was supported by 13,000 miles of leased teletype circuits. By the end of the following year, 775 radio-equipped aircraft were flying the airways (326 with two-way radios, 449 with one-way installations capable only of receiving). Of these, 345 were air carrier aircraft flying scheduled routes.[21]

III

During the late 1920's, the Aeronautics Branch began installing another type of radio facility along the Federal airways — the four-course radio range. This facility became, and remained until after World War II, the standard civil air-navigation aid on the U.S. airways. In the process, it revolutionized the flying technique of commercial air carriers.

The U.S. Air Mail Service had experimented briefly with radio navigation devices. In mid-1919, the Post Office borrowed a spark transmitter from the U.S. Navy, installed it at an airfield in College Park, Md., and used it as a directive beacon. By March 1920, spark transmitters had been installed and used for the same purpose at five sites along the transcontinental airway — Chicago, Cleveland, Bellefonte, New York, and Newark. A Navy station at Philadelphia was similarly used. Of the flying experiments conducted with these stations, the most notable was a flight on May 20, 1920. On this occasion, Wesley L. Smith, an airmail pilot, flew an airplane equipped with a radio receiver and a fixed loop antenna from College Park to Philadelphia without regard to compass or landmarks. In mid-1920, the Air Mail Service abruptly abandoned these experiments, as well as the thought of employing radio as a navigational device. But the idea of employing radio for air navigation was by no means abandoned in all aviation circles; the U.S. Army kept the idea alive.[22]

The Army was no stranger to radio direction finding. Homing devices had been developed during World War I by winding large loops between the wings of biplanes carrying sensitive receiving sets. Crude though it was, the method worked reasonably well; it possessed, however, certain inherent disadvantages. While only the simplest of transmitting equipment was required on the ground, complicated receiving equipment, with which there were certain difficulties, had to be carried aboard the airplane. Moreover, the system was a homing device, no more. It was no help in the presence of a side wind, which could force an aircraft to drift off its course. Though a pilot could eventually bring his aircraft to its destination, it was usually by way of a circuitous route. The device did not enable a pilot to fly a chosen course.[23]

The reverse procedure — that is, placing the direction-finding equipment on the ground rather than aboard ship — had been used with a measure of success in Europe. With this system, aircraft equipped with both transmitting and receiving equipment would request ground stations for directional assistance. Two or more direction-finding stations would locate the aircraft by triangulation and radio the information back to the aircraft. A similar procedure had been used in the United States to guide merchant marine vessels into port. But as an aeronautical navaid, the procedure had nearly all the shortcomings of the airborne direction finder, and others in the bargain.[24] Thus, in 1920, the Army enlisted the services of the Bureau of Standards to develop a distinctly different device — one that would guide aircraft along a chosen course and require only the simplest of airborne equipment. Out of this work emerged the four-course radio range.[25]

Many hands went into making the final product. Physicists and radio engineers at the Bureau of Standards, borrowing heavily from European workers, conceived the basic system between 1920 and 1922. U.S. Army Signal Corps engineers made key improvements to the system in the ensuing four years. Bureau of Standards engineers added further refinements between 1926 and 1928. Percival D. Lowell, a Bureau of Standards radio engineer, contributed the basic suggestion, which was in turn derived from the old Telefunken compass, a device the Germans had employed during World War I to guide Zeppelins on bombing raids over England. This compass employed a number of similar directional antennas that could be switched into an electrical circuit in succession. Working from this idea, two Bureau of Standards physicists, F. H. Engle and Francis W. Dunmore, devised a system consisting of two separate coil antennas crossed at an angle of about 135° with respect to each other. The antennas were approximately 50 by 120 feet and were supported by three masts. Signals were transmitted alternately from each coil. A receiving set located anywhere on the line bisecting the angle between the two coils would receive signals first from one coil and then the other. At this location, the intensity of the two signals was the same. At any point not on the bisector of the angle between the coils, signals of unequal intensity were received. The difference of the intensity depended on the location of the receiving set.[26]

Tests of the system on the ground showed that the area of equal intensity effectively marked out a course that could be followed without reference to landmarks, compass, or other navigation devices. The apparatus was then taken to Dayton, Ohio, and flight-tested by the Army.[27]

The chief shortcoming of this system, as with the Telefunken compass, was the difficulty of keeping it in balance. The Signal Corps overcame this by adopting an antenna system composed of two directional antennas set at right angles to each other, and by devising a signal-switching arrangement that caused the signals from the two antennas to merge into a steady dash at the zone of equal intensity. The antennas were independently energized by a rotatable coupling device, or goniometer. The goniometer permitted orienting the course in any desired direction without moving the antennas. This arrangement was both simpler and more stable than the Telefunken antenna system. The

Bureau of Standards spent approximately two years, between 1926 and 1928, refining and testing this system before it was ready for airway use.*[28]

The range that ultimately came into general use along the Federal airways consisted of a 1,500-watt tone-modulated transmitter with motor generator, goniometer, loop-tuning equipment, and an automatic keying device. This apparatus was housed in a single-room frame building, 18 by 21 feet, and usually operated by remote control from radio communication stations. The range operated over a frequency band of 190 to 565 kilocycles.[29]

The antenna system featured two single-wire vertical loops strung on five wooden masts — four at the corners of a square and one in the middle. A single vertically disposed loop radiated energy in a figure 8 pattern. Two such loops placed at right angles to each other produced a pair of overlapping figure 8 patterns. One figure 8 pattern was keyed with the Morse character "A" (dot-dash), the other with the character "N" (dash-dot). At the four intersections of the two figure 8 patterns, the "A" and "N" signals were of equal strength, forming four zones of equal intensity. When the transmission of the "A" and "N" signals was properly timed and both had the same tone, they interlocked, or meshed, at the zone of equal intensity, just like the teeth of a gear. Thus, within the zone of equal intensity, neither letter could be distinguished from the other. All that could be heard was a steady monotone signal, or long dash. This was the on-course signal, or beam.[30] A pilot flying the range in an aircraft equipped with a simple receiver and a nondirective antenna could follow the equisignal line — i.e., the on-course signal — passing through one of the intersections of the field patterns by listening for the long dash produced in his earphones. If he happened to drift to one side of the course or the other, the "A" or "N" signal would become audible, warning him to correct his course in one direction or the other.[31]

Beacons had a range of 100 miles and were located 200 miles apart. When the pilot reached the limits of one range, he tuned his receiver to the station located 100 miles due ahead on his course. The on-course signal was interrupted every 24 seconds for station identification. It was

<hr>

*In the meantime, the U.S. Air Mail Service again became interested in radio navigation, beginning experimental work on a similar system early in 1925. The effort, however, did not live out the year — a victim of budget trimming. Paul Henderson to Mr. Egge, February 28, 1925, Harry G. Smith to S. A. Cisler, November 28, 1925, RG 28, AMS.

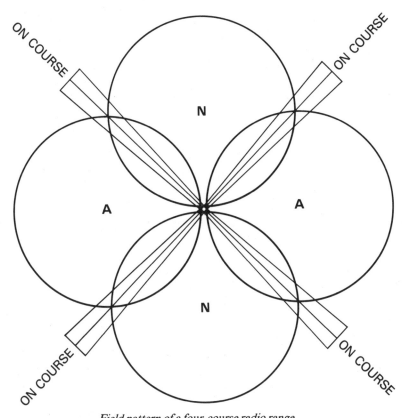

Field pattern of a four-course radio range

also interrupted at fixed intervals (every 15 minutes) for regular weather broadcasts and at irregular intervals for special weather broadcasts.[32]

It was this facility, then, that opened up the real possibilities of regularly scheduled flying. With a radio beacon, aircraft could navigate in nearly all weather without visual reference to the ground. They could climb above fog or low-hanging clouds and ride the beam to their intended destination. A scant 18 months after radio navigation was introduced on the airways, an ad hoc committee of radio and aviation experts pronounced the four-course range "indispensable" to aviation.[33]

The four-course radio range gave the pilot his line of position; it did not, however, fix his position in space, except at long intervals when he passed over the beacon station itself. Again with the cooperation of the

Bureau of Standards, the Aeronautics Branch was able to come up with another radio device, one that enabled a pilot to determine his "fix," or position along the airway. This device, the radio marker beacon, was a simple low-power radio transmitter with a single wire antenna on a single mast that emitted a characteristic signal that could be detected and identified by a pilot as he passed over the vicinity of the marker. The earliest versions of this device were nondirectional and had an effective range of three to four miles. A chain of these markers served the same purpose for instrument, or blind, flying as course lights did for contact flying at night — each link in the chain represented a milestone, indicating to a pilot how far he had progressed along his chosen course.[34]

The Bureau of Standards completed its development and testing of the aural radio range in 1928 (though it did continue to work on a visual type beacon — i.e., one that employed two or three reeds on the instrument panel to indicate the aircraft's on-course position — for some time to come). Most of the flight testing had been conducted at two stations, College Park and Bellefonte. College Park was and continued to serve as a development laboratory and demonstration station. Bellefonte was chosen, however, because of its strategic location on the New York-Cleveland airway, a hazardous mountainous route that could not be lighted as ideally as one might wish. In due course, the Airways Division established beacon stations at Hadley Field, N.J., and Cleveland, Ohio. Beginning in December 1927 and running through February 1928, National Air Transport, Inc., in cooperation with the Aeronautics Branch, made a number of demonstration instrument flights over the New York-Cleveland airway. With the successful completion of these demonstrations, the Bellefonte station was transferred from the Bureau of Standards to the Airways Division, becoming the first radio range beacon to be commissioned on the Federal airways.[35]

The program to equip the airways with radio range and marker beacons did not gather a full head of steam until fiscal year 1931, or some three years after the Bellefonte station went into operation. For one thing, the Airways Division was giving priority to lighting the airways; for another, establishing radio beacon stations was not an inexpensive proposition. In 1928, a fully equipped beacon station cost $24,000, a tidy sum for that day. Moreover, the annual maintenance cost per station came to $12,000. The Aeronautics Branch budget, though steadily rising, could not accommodate a faster installation rate. Then, too, flying by instruments, unlike the contact flying required on lighted airways, was virtually an unknown technique. Pilots had to undergo long hours of training (though scheduled air transport pilots did not have to be certificated for instrument flying until 1933). This took time. And air carriers had to equip their aircraft with the necessary airborne devices. Thus, though MacCracken and Young had early determined to equip all airways with radio, as well as light, beacons, radio-beacon construction did not catch up with light-beacon construction until fiscal year 1933.[36]

The first airway of any distance to have a continuous radio-marked course was New York-Cleveland, which went into full-time radio operation in November 1928, with stations at New Brunswick, N.J. (Hadley Field), Bellefonte, and Cleveland. In August 1929, range stations went into operation at Goshen, Ind., Sterling, Ill., and Des Moines, Iowa. In October, two more stations, Chicago and Boston, were opened, making continuous instrument flight possible from Boston as far west as Omaha via New York and Chicago. Before fiscal year 1930 was out, a station was also opened at Key West, Fla., permitting instrument flights from the U.S. mainland to Havana, Cuba.[37]

Nine radio markers — the first to be placed on the airways — went into operation the same fiscal year. Fifteen were added in fiscal 1931, 39 in fiscal 1932, and seven in fiscal 1933, for a grand total of 70.[38]

By the end of this period, a new type of radio marker had been developed and was ready for installation on the airways. Experience had proven the nondirectional marker of limited value at or near intermediate fields. What was required was a low-powered directive marker that could also function as a localizer range. The new markers had 50-watt transmitters (compared to 7.5 watts for the old) and loop antennas and possessed a range of up to 30 miles. They were installed so that one of their courses coincided with the centerline of the best runway on the intermediate field. Since they were essentially miniature radio ranges, they were also used to fill gaps along an airway that was too short to warrant the installation of a large beacon station.[39]

To the nine radio range stations in place at the end of fiscal 1930 were added 41 more the following fiscal year. In February 1931, with the commissioning of the Medicine Bow, Wyo., range, radio-beacon service became available over the entire course of the New York-San Francisco airway. In the next two fiscal years, 40 more range stations went into operation, bringing the total to 90 stations by mid-1933. These 90 stations covered an airway expanse of some 18,000 miles — nearly equal to the expanse covered by light beacons. Radio had come into its own on the airways.[40]

IV

Thus, in the six years between 1926 and 1932, the character of the Federal airways had been dramatically transformed. In 1932, more than 18,000 miles could be traversed at night or in bad weather. Moreover, compared to the airways of 1926, those of 1932 were equipped with a great diversity of navigational aids.

A typical 1,000-mile segment of airway had 30 intermediate fields, 60 electric light beacons, 20 gas beacons, 5 radio stations, 5 radio range beacons, and a number of strategically placed radio marker beacons. The cost of constructing a 1,000-mile segment came to approximately $450,000. But this was only the beginning. It cost the Department of Commerce in the neighborhood of $250,000 a year to operate and maintain each 1,000-mile segment, which meant that, by the end of 1932, the Aeronautics Branch required a minimum of $4.5 million a year just to maintain existing airways — a sum equal to approximately 50 percent of its budget.[41]

A small army of men was required to operate this farflung system; in consequence, salaries, though low, took a sizable portion of the airway budget. Airway mechanicians and radio operators earned, on the average, $2,400 a year; airway keepers, who were charged with maintaining intermediate fields, between $1,200 and $1,500. The Branch also employed a large number of part-time employees who did not fall under the classified civil service. These people, drawn from the communities and farms surrounding intermediate fields and other sites, served as weather observers or caretakers. Part-time weather observers made $600 a year; caretakers, between $60 and $480, depending on the type of beacon they serviced. A caretaker often owned the land on which the beacon was located and collected, in addition to his salary, a small rental for the Government-used site. Beacon sites in rural areas cost the Aeronautics Branch virtually nothing — between $10 and $25 a year. For some of the more prosperous farmers, this small rental was not worth the trouble of having a facility emplaced on their land. Other landowners, feeling they were being shortchanged, held out for more money. When negotiations failed, MacCracken appealed to the property owners' sense of patriotism. "Having received such patriotic cooperation in this national airway project from the good citizens along the airways," he wrote to a California farmer in 1928, "I feel sure that it is only necessary to explain the situation to you in order to secure your willing cooperation." But he was not above buttressing his appeal with a threat: "I think neither of us wishes to contemplate the only other alternative, which is condemnation of the land in question, the value to be fixed by the courts." In general, however, rural residents were only too happy to see the airways — and the additional income that they brought to their communities — come their way.[42]

Airway mechanicians covered an extensive area. Each mechanician was responsible for the working condition of 12 rotating beacons, 4 flashing beacons, and the electrical equipment and control apparatus on 3 intermediate fields — all strung over a sector 175 miles in length. He traveled from site to site in a half-ton truck well stocked with tools, wire, and spare parts and usually performed his repair work on the spot, tracing short circuits, replacing electrical wiring and underground cables, grinding valves, or overhauling electric motors and generators. Though his schedule called for visiting each site only twice a month, he was the troubleshooter on the airways and, as such, was on call at any hour of the day or night.

Airway keepers led a more leisurely existence. They were located at major intermediate fields where they made weather observations, operated teletype machines, and performed light maintenance. At fields with little traffic and at all outlying beacon sites, light maintenance was performed by part-time caretakers. These people visited beacons under their care once a day and did little more than clean dirty lenses, replace burned out bulbs, keep gas beacons supplied with fuel, and alert airway mechanicians to an equipment breakdown. Rarely did a caretaker devote more than two hours a day to this job, which allowed him to engage in farming or other economic activity on a full-time basis. Caretakers and airway keepers located on emergency fields, however, were expected to provide pilots with transportation to and from town, furnish them with meals, and, if necessary, assist them in repairing their aircraft — services for which they were reimbursed by the Government.

Caretakers and airway keepers also had to act as watchmen. This involved anything from guarding against theft to keeping farmers' cows off runways. Vandalism was a problem, and caretakers had to keep "general supervision" over their light beacon "to make sure that boys in the neighborhood do not molest it." Wandering animals were decidedly a danger to landing aircraft; the airways, in turn, posed a threat to animals. In 1932, the Secretary of Commerce was presented with a claim of $112.50 by an Illinois farmer who alleged that one of his prize Guernsey cows had died from lead poisoning after licking wet paint from a directional arrow on a beacon site. Theft was common along the airways, and armed robbery was not unknown. In 1925, a team of postal inspectors judged that the airmail field near Bryan, Ohio, was in "danger of a hold-up," and recommended that the caretaker be furnished with the necessary firearms to ward off any such attempt. The Post Office Department approved the step. In 1929, a powershed along the New York-Atlanta airway was burglarized three times within a period of four months, the thief making off with oil, gasoline, tools, and other equipment on each occasion. The local sheriff appeared incapable of dealing with the situation, which forced the Department of Commerce to call in Federal agents. "Thefts of kerosene, gasoline and oil at airway sites are quite frequent . . ., and local authorities apparently have been unable to render effective assistance in attempts to apprehend those guilty of the thefts," Cap Hingsburg reported to the Secretary of Commerce in January 1931 as the Aeronautics Branch prepared once again to enlist the services of Federal agents. Searching for a more permanent solution, Hingsburg toyed with the idea of permitting airway personnel to obtain commissions as deputy sheriffs.[43]

Life on the airways was rarely as exciting as chasing thieves. High points on the Allegheny, Rocky, and Sierra Nevada Mountains abounded with desolate sites that required airway keepers and radio operators to tolerate long spells of isolation and boredom. It was not the kind of life everyone could endure. One newly hired radio operator, assigned to the Elko, Nev., radio station, "got off the train, looked around, and climbed right back aboard for parts unknown," recalled Art Johnson, a veteran radio operator who had helped establish the Elko station under the U.S. Air Mail Service. But Elko was a beehive of activity compared to such places as Bitter Creek, Wyo., Locomotive Springs, Utah, Buffalo Valley, Nev., or Donner Summit, Calif., which were located in wilderness country or on high mountain passes that could be reached only by mule train. Radio operators at such locations spent three or more months in isolation, emerging from their hibernation only after the spring sun had melted the heavy winter snows. Some winter sieges were so long that operators depleted their supplies before they could end their isolation, thus necessitating food drops from the air. Their shelter, a drab prefabricated hut furnished strictly for utility, housed from one to four men, who could do little more for recreation than hunt or tramp in the snow. "They gave me snowshoes and told me they went with the job," recalled a radio operator assigned to a one-man station at Blue Canyon, Calif. "I can remember having to tunnel out of the keeper's house through the snow to get to the station." Airway keepers with a wife and children were provided with family quarters — a white wooden building of approximately 600 square feet with two bedrooms, living room, kitchen, and bath. The Department of Commerce charged the keeper $20 a month for these quarters during the late twenties and early thirties.[44]

The introduction of vacuum-tube radio transmitters eliminated one source of entertainment available to the more enterprising radio men. The old arc transmitters ran on a mixture of alcohol and air. The alcohol was laced with potassium permanganate, rendering it unfit for human consumption. Radio operators soon learned, however, that by taking a copper radiator line, wrapping it with asbestos and safety wire to form a coil, and heating it with a blow torch, they could distill the potassium out of the alcohol. "That stuff was really potent," related an Elko radio operator. A coke bottle full was enough to "get the whole town drunk."[45]

It was these people — radio operators, mechanicians, airway keepers, weather observers, caretakers — who, as much as the mail that fed the traffic, transformed U.S. commercial air transportation from a marginal activity to a going concern — these people, and the introduction of radio on a wide scale. "I would go so far as to say that without [radio navigation aids] genuine air passenger service is impossible," asserted Dr. J.H. Dellinger, chief of the radio section of the Bureau of Standards, in 1929. "[Real] service is not available until the air traveler can count on a scheduled service as regular as the railway trains, independent of weather or other contingencies." More than any other device, radio — and all its uses — made scheduled service possible. It became, and remains today, an indispensable element in aviation's ground organization.[46]

7. Fostering Civil Aviation

Licensing pilots, inspecting and certificating aircraft, setting down traffic rules, laying out and equipping airways with navigational aids — all this was calculated, in the final analysis, to further the development of civil aviation. But when the Air Commerce Act stated, "It shall be the duty of the Secretary of Commerce to foster air commerce . . .," it contemplated something more than regulatory and airway-building activities. The act, in short, made the Aeronautics Branch a booster of civil aviation, just as the Department of Commerce as a whole was a booster of American business in general. Hoover, MacCracken, and Young believed it their duty to nurture the infant industry and do what they could to protect and promote its interests. Their promotional activities took a variety of forms and a substantial percentage of their time and energy. But when all was said and done, it was the Aeronautics Branch as regulator, not as promoter, that truly furthered civil aviation's development.

II

Americans had bread during the Coolidge era, Frederick Lewis Allen observed, but they wanted circuses. Everything was ballyhooed — sports, books, table games, automobiles — as millions of people turned their fickle attentions from one trifle to another. Aviation was no trifle (though many an aviation event was); but it could be — and was — ballyhooed.[1]

MacCracken had a message he wanted to get out, a message that would awaken the American public to the exciting prospects of aviation as a mode of transportation. Hundreds of news releases carried it, explicitly or implicitly. Between 30,000 to 50,000 aeronautical bulletins

165

were mailed out to the public by the Branch each month. A newsy, informative official periodical, the *Air Commerce Bulletin*, had a monthly circulation of 30,000. A platoon of Aeronautics Branch officials regularly made the rounds as afterdinner speakers. In the spring of 1927, one official, H. H. Blee, was sent on a tour of 59 U.S. cities in an effort to stimulate greater interest in airmail use. "Mr. Blee will give talks of a popular nature completely illustrated with stereoptican slides and devoted to the commercial and industrial application of aeronautics," *Domestic Air News* announced.

MacCracken himself carried the message around the country, appealing to local pride, the profit motive, or the desire of many to see a new enterprise succeed. He traveled extensively, sometimes riding in an open cockpit for hours ("Made the trip in 5 hours and 10 minutes," he related after returning to Washington from Atlanta. "It was cold and I looked like a boiled lobster . . ."). It was not necessary to make a direct plea on all occasions. He was tall, attractive, and personable, and his mere presence at a ceremony or banquet could be testimonial enough to civil aviation. His schedule was packed with public appearances and private engagements. "I have been on the go every minute," he wrote his father after a particularly hectic week, in 1928, in which he attended a dinner with a foreign dignitary, went to the theater, entertained guests at his home on two separate evenings, delivered an out-of-town speech, gave a radio talk, appeared and spoke at the christening of a Pan American aircraft, lectured before a class of New York University students, and went to dinner given by the Chief of the Air Corps. All the while, he could look forward to a succeeding week that would require him to be in Detroit on Sunday, Pittsburgh on Tuesday, Washington on Thursday, Chicago on Friday. His efforts did not go for naught; MacCracken had a knack for getting in the news. "I had the pleasure of seeing you crash into the talking movies the other night . . .," wrote an admiring advertising executive. "From reports which appear in the newspapers quite frequently, I gather you are doing a wonderful job. I don't know who your publicity agent is, but he must be good." MacCracken did not need an agent; he was a born booster.[2]

Not everyone was convinced by what MacCracken had to say. "It is hard for aeronautical enthusiasts to put themselves in the places of the general public who do not regard flying as a 'cause,'" *Aviation* observed in July 1929. The plain fact was that aviation had an unpleasant side.

"About once in two or three weeks an airplane . . . flys [*sic*] over my place so low," complained the owner of the Cackle Corner Poultry Farm near Garrettsville, Ohio, "that the hens become so frightened that they pile up, thus injuring each other and my egg yield drops one or two hundred eggs per day and by the time I get them back to normal along comes another low flying machine and sends the egg yield down again . . . . The loss to me is so great that I fear it may put me out of business . . . ." The offending airmail carrier, National Air Transport, was ordered to fly higher when passing over Garrettsville.[3]

All noise problems could not be solved so easily. Most complainants lived in the proximity of airports, where low-flying aircraft performing landing or takeoff operations passed over their residences. "The Department can take no action to prevent such flights," explained Elmer McD. Kintz, Chief of the Legal Section of the Aeronautics Branch. Local authorities, prodded by their constituents, sometimes stepped into the breach. Roosevelt Field ran afoul of the Nassau County, N.Y., district attorney's office when it permitted pilots logging flying time for transport licenses to drone over the rooftops of nearby residents all night long. In this case, the district attorney and the airport operator came to terms amicably by agreeing to a curfew on night operations. Other cases landed in court. In 1931, a Federal appeals court temporarily enjoined the Curtiss Airports Corporation from operating its Cleveland airport on the grounds that it constituted a nuisance. "These instances are proof of a problem that will become more acute as the airplane becomes more universally used," *Aviation* warned. Aeronautics Branch officials were fully cognizant of this fact; they were also aware that there was no easy, short-term solution in sight. They turned therefore, to long-range R & D efforts that looked to the reduction of propeller flutter and the development of engine-muffling devices.[4]

Meanwhile, rulemaking and enforcement made do for the absence of on-the-shelf technology. Strict enforcement of flying minimums was of some help, and new rules could cover a variety of nuisances and abuses in the noise area and elsewhere. When the Wilmington, Del., Chamber of Commerce complained of aircraft "throwing out masses of advertising matter" over the city, the Aeronautics Branch put a stop to the practice.[5] The citizens of Wilmington and other cities were no doubt appreciative; do what it might, however, the Aeronautics Branch could not hope to satisfy everyone. All people did not see aviation as Federal officials did.

In March 1930, a *New York World* editorial writer approached the subject of light beacons in a way that left little room for further argument:

> We have heard that these are air beacons, designed to help aviators, just as lighthouses aid mariners . . . . We doubt all this . . . . For the plain truth is that aviators could lose a bass drum more easily than they could miss New York. If it is well supplied with anything, it is supplied with light; standing on the ground you can see the glare from fifty miles away . . . . Thus we cannot escape the suspicion that the aeronautical function of these lights is the excuse for their presence rather than the reason for it . . . . So far as we are concerned they are not desirable at all. They can be extremely annoying. If you are seated by an open window, it is enough to give you the heeby-jeebies to have these long fingers of light constantly crossing your vision . . . . How can you concentrate on anything with that merry-go-round in front of you?[6]

Clearly, many Americans did not understand aviation or grasp its significance. "I wonder if many industries are as misunderstood by the general public as aviation?" Amelia Earhart asked in a letter to Clarence Young. "I suppose anything which has movement . . . has a romantic appeal." But, said Miss Earhart, tossing out a strange statement for someone who had a share in romanticizing flight, romantics had "no sense of values."[7] Be that as it may, the romantics did have their day when, on an overcast morning in late May 1927, a 25-year-old aviator from Minnesota took off from an airfield in New York City and headed across the Atlantic for Paris. No aviation event, before or since, so stirred the public imagination.

III

It was not merely what Charles Lindbergh did, but the way he did it and, more importantly, how he deported himself in the aftermath of his flight that had such an instant and enduring impact on the public. There is no denying the heroic proportions of the deed; yet other men could have performed it, enjoyed a few weeks of public adulation, and faded into obscurity. Lindbergh marked his feat with a touch of nobility. He thereby filled an emotional void for a generation of Americans starved for genuine public heroes. Here was a generation with lackluster political leaders, a generation so bereft of inspirational public figures that it had to choose its heroes from among men and women with feet of clay. So the public embraced this young, shy, handsome aviator, whose modesty, sincerity, and simplicity so sharply distinguised him from the spiritually frail images on the silver screen, in the sports arena, or at the helm of industry.[8]

Everyone seemed to be taken by him. Coolidge made Lindbergh a colonel in the Air Corps Reserve and dispatched a cruiser to Europe to bring him and his aircraft back to the United States. On June 11, when the cruiser docked at the Washington Navy Yard, the President, the rest of Washington officialdom, and thousands more were at hand to meet it. Coolidge pinned the Distinguished Flying Cross on the young pilot and, roused from his usual taciturnity, delivered a long speech singing the honoree's praises. From there Lindbergh was driven to the temporary White House on Dupont Circle to dine with the Cabinet. Two days later came the triumphal parade up Broadway, where an estimated 4.5 million New Yorkers turned out to see him and shower 1,800 tons of paper along his path.[9]

The exploiters set upon him in droves. Movie contracts, speaking engagements, endorsements — all manner of lucrative offers were thrown his way. Dwight Morrow, who had met Lindbergh at the Cabinet dinner and taken a liking to him, was concerned. He asked Harry Guggenheim if the Daniel Guggenheim Foundation could not save Lindbergh "from the wolves" by giving him something to do. The upshot was that Lindbergh, Guggenheim, and MacCracken got together and decided that Lindbergh would tour the country in the *Spirit of St. Louis*, making at least one stop in each of the 48 States. The Department of Commerce would provide the tour with an escort aircraft, a pilot, and an advance man; the Foundation would be the official sponsor and pick up the tab for Lindbergh's expenses.[10]

The purpose of the tour was to promote aviation. Lindbergh would urge local citizens to build airports and patronize the airmail. Not that words were really necessary. MacCracken counted on Lindbergh's "very presence to excite enthusiasm for aviation." The tour, launched in July, would see Lindbergh log 20,000 miles in three months. He had been saved from "the wolves," it appears, in order to be exploited by MacCracken and Guggenheim — but exploited in the benignest sense of the word, for Lindbergh wholeheartedly believed in aviation.[11]

The tour over, MacCracken concocted yet another promotional campaign: Lindbergh would take members of Congress, the Supreme

Court, and foreign ambassadors and their families for a brief spin over Washington. Two trimotored aircraft borrowed from the military services, were placed at Lindbergh's disposal. For a solid week, in March 1928, Lindbergh was at Bolling Field from sunup to sundown flying people who, only a short time before, would not have dreamed of venturing into an airplane. "After the first brave planeloads went up, and people saw they survived, the idea caught on like wildfire," recalled MacCracken, who, as host, greeted prospective passengers and escorted them to a waiting plane. "Soon it seemed that half of Washington was calling our office and negotiating for a ride." Women appeared particularly eager to ride with the famous aviator. "Will you kindly permit the bearer, Mrs. Donald Primrose, to occupy one of the places assigned to me in the flights with Colonel Lindbergh?" inquired Senator Hugo L. Black in a letter to MacCracken. Some people even came from out of town to seek an opportunity to ride in an airplane piloted by Lindbergh. One woman, her husband, and their young son, acquaintances of MacCracken, journeyed from New York, drove directly to Bolling Field, and managed to get on the day's last flight. "Henry, Henry, Jr., and I join in thanking you for giving us the supreme thrill of our lives!" the woman wrote MacCracken. A ride with "Lindy" was "more than we had dared to hope could happen. [Now] I can die happy."[12]

Staging the flights was a shrewd public relations move. Influential people, some of whom would be voting on Aeronautics Branch appropriations, had been introduced to flying. As Lindbergh later explained, "The Washington flights . . . were for the purpose of bringing political attention to aviation, and demonstrating its potentialities to men and women who were in a position to exert great effect on its development." The ease with which Aeronautics Branch appropriations sailed through Congress over the next few years can no doubt be explained in part by the successful staging of these flights.[13]

Lindbergh's brief, unofficial connection with the Aeronautics Branch linked the flier with the agency in the public mind. The result was that the Branch was soon serving as a conduit for his mail, handling requests for autographs, speaking engagements, and endorsements. "Several bond issues for municipal airports will be submitted to the electors [in November]," MacCracken wrote Lindbergh in October 1927. "I have been besieged by several cities . . . to have you speak before that date in their community in support of the bond issue." That same month, Paul Henderson wired MacCracken: "Illinois Manufacturers Dinner . . . will

Lindbergh was Time *Magazine's first man of the year*

be a flop if we don't get Lindbergh. Will you . . . help all you can?" An advertising firm wrote MacCracken asking him to persuade Lindbergh to advertise the wares of a clothing manufacturer. Copies of Lindbergh's autobiography, *We*, were regularly left at the Department for Lindbergh to autograph. One Congressman delivered six copies. Lindbergh's autograph was in such demand that on his occasional visits to the Department Lindbergh would sit down and sign a stack of postcards. As late as October 1930, the Department was still mailing out these cards on request. No one seemed to tire of making over the young hero, no one except Calvin Coolidge, who appeared to have had enough early on. Asked to pin a medal on Lindbergh in December 1927, the President said no; he had already pinned one on him and had not meant to establish a precedent.[14]

Lindbergh's exploit lacked intrinsic technical significance and contributed little or nothing to the evolution of the airplane as a transport vehicle. One man crossing the Atlantic alone scarcely suggested the practical advantages of aviation. Lindbergh had not even been the first to make a nonstop crossing of the Atlantic by airplane; two Royal Air Force officers, John Alcock and Arthur Whitten Brown, had performed the feat in 1919 by flying a Vickers-Vimy bomber from Newfoundland to Ireland. And only two weeks after the Lindbergh flight, Clarence Chamberlin flew nonstop with one passenger from Roosevelt Field, N.Y., to Eisleben, Germany. But by going alone, Lindbergh captured the public's imagination, and therein lies the significance of his achievement to aviation. The public's attention was riveted on an aviator and an aerial event, with the result that thousands of Americans suddenly became air-minded. Many a young man, inspired by Lindbergh, excitedly turned to aviation as a profession. And the remarkable aviation boom that followed, though it had been in the making prior to May 1927, had undoubtedly been accelerated and intensified by Lindbergh's flight. Aircraft sales soared, new capital poured into the industry, airline stocks hit record levels. Aeronautics Branch officials could have doubled or tripled their promotional efforts and could not have come close to having the galvanizing effect on aviation activity produced by this single event.[15]

IV

If there was one area of aviation that MacCracken hoped Lindbergh's 48-State tour would stimulate above all others it was airport development. Encouraging airport construction was perhaps the most important promotional activity undertaken by the Aeronautics Branch. The Air Commerce Act prohibited the Secretary of Commerce from establishing, operating, or maintaining airports; the act did call upon him, however, to "encourage" the establishment of these facilities. Thus, save for his airport-rating function, which was exercised only at the request of airport operators, the Secretary's responsibilities in this area were wholly promotional in character.

MacCracken did not take this responsibility lightly. The airport was as critical to aviation as the airway; indeed, in the view of many, an airport runway was simply an extension of an airway. But while airway development, because it was the responsibility of a single central agency, proceeded in a planned, systematic way, airport development, being the responsibility of hundreds of municipalities, was largely a hit or miss proposition — haphazard, uneven, and uncoordinated. Widely dispersed local authorities could not do a job requiring a large measure of central planning and direction.

The problem quickly came home to the Coolidge administration when airport development failed to keep pace with Federal airway construction, thus putting a severe strain on many airports to accommodate the increase in aviation activity. "The actual thing immediately necessary in the development of commercial aviation is airports . . .," Herbert Hoover asserted in June 1927. Joseph S. Ames, former chairman of the National Advisory Committee for Aeronautics, expressed the same thought in different words. MacCracken told the annual convention of the National Aeronatics Association in September 1926 that "commercial flying will be hampered as long as we are limited to Army, Navy, and a few private flying fields." Two years later, Frederick L. Hoffman, dean of the advanced research department of Babson Institute, declared, "The outstanding defect of our air transport development is the want of adequate airport facilities. We have not a single airport at the present time [to compare] with European airports . . . ."[16]

The Aeronautics Branch strove within the limited confines of its charter to alleviate the situation. The dissemination of technical and statistical information constituted an important part of its work in this area. A technical aeronautical bulletin dealing with airport design and construction was published, as was a bulletin on airport management. Another bulletin, listing all airports and landing fields in the United States, was issued and updated periodically. In addition, Aeronautics Branch personnel were placed at the disposal of municipalities requiring expert opinion on airport site selection and other technical matters. Beyond these activities, however, the Department of Commerce had to confine itself to employing its powers of persuasion. Aeronautics Branch personnel took to the speakers circuit, addressing chambers of commerce, citizen groups, and aviation clubs in an effort to stimulate interest in airport development. As always, MacCracken carried the major burden on the circuit.[17]

This promotional campaign, combined with the enthusiasm generated by the passage of the Air Commerce Act and Lindbergh's Atlantic crossing, moved some city fathers to action. Buffalo, Detroit, Baltimore, Los Angeles, San Francisco, and Atlanta voted airport bond issues of between $1 million and $4 million. Others did nothing. New York, for example, tried to make do with a small field (Hadley) in New Brunswick, N.J. "Frankly," wrote MacCracken to a New York City banker who complained about the poor service out of Hadley Field, "it is rather a disgrace to conceive of a city of the size of New York without an adequate airport." When the Aeronautics Branch drew up a plan for a $5 million airport project for New York, the city came up with only $500,000 for a secondary site. "The City of New York has been extremely generous in the wonderful reception it has accorded our famous aviators . . .," MacCracken pointed out, "but I think the City should be equally generous in providing the actual facilities which will make [aviation's] development possible." A decade would pass before a modern air carrier airport was built in New York City proper.[18]

A theme running through MacCracken's promotional efforts was that airport development was a public function. Private ownership of airports, though it enjoyed a vogue in the late 1920's, was not encouraged. City planners tended to agree. H. M. Olmsted pointed out that the monopolistic character of airports made public ownership necessary "in order that fairness to all users may result." "Private flying fields will continue to be established in all sections," commented a writer in *American City*, "but not until a city has built a municipal airport can it be said to have fulfilled its primary obligation in encouraging thoroughly competent air service." MacCracken phrased the matter in stronger terms: "It is the duty of every municipality to own an airport, just as much as it is its duty to own and maintain the streets, parks, and harbor facilities within its limits."[19]

It was one thing to call attention to a municipality's duty, and quite another to persuade a municipality to assume it. As a matter of fact, not all local or state officials believed airport development was entirely a municipal responsibility. In 1930, John M. Vorys, the Director of Aeronautics for the State of Ohio, argued:

> Neither private, commercial, nor municipal airports can be depended upon to give us an adequate airway system. The highway analogy of federal aid to the states for airports on federal airways, and state aid to municipalities and counties for the intercounty airways, can be followed with profit. After all, a modern airplane is a motor vehicle running with a gasoline engine, on rubber tires, at the start and the end of every flight; and the providing of this type of 'highway' is as much a state function as the providing of other types of highway.

Vorys saw no long-term difficulties with funding. As with the highway program, most airport development funds would come initially from general revenues; eventually, however, "you will . . . receive most of the money from the aeronautical industry by way of gasoline tax."[20]

Vorys' statement was prophetic, but, for the time being, unpersuasive. Hoover continued to reiterate his "dock" concept of airports, which held that all terminal facilities "should be provided by the principal municipalities of the country in the same way coast cities provide docking facilities for home and foreign ocean trade." When a proposal was made to build with Federal funds a badly needed modern airport for Washington, D.C., Coolidge dismissed the idea, holding that the airport should be built with private funds. Joseph A. Ames, in discussing whether Congress should lift the ban on Federal airport development, stated: "I know of no additional legislation that is necessary or desirable." Chester W. Cuthell, an American Bar Association official, told a legislative air conference in 1930, "So far as putting through a federal aid scheme is concerned, as the automobile men did with the Good Roads Movement, . . . I entertain no hope whatever of getting such legislation as that through." States and cities wanting airports would have to get out and raise their own money.[21]

As an airport development policy, the "dock" concept was scarcely a policy at all. It was a way of muddling through. For the needs of the twenties, however, it proved adequate enough. If nothing else, the airports of that period were within the means of private investors and local communities; they could be afforded because the aircraft of that day made relatively modest demands on landing-area preparation and development. In the early 1930's, however, larger and faster airliners were introduced that required longer and harder-surfaced landing and takeoff strips — strips that were costlier to construct. At the same time, the Great Depression dried up both private and local government funds. In these circumstances, the dock concept would become an argument for doing nothing. The airport policy of the 1920's would prove inadequate for the 1930's.[22]

V

Concern over aviation insurance rates had at least as much immediacy for the Aeronautics Branch in the 1920's as airport development. "Next to wives not letting their husbands fly," wrote the secretary of a local chamber of commerce in July 1926, "I believe the attitude of the insurance companies toward aviation is holding it back more than any other thing." The attitude of the insurance companies was that travel by air was "extra-hazardous." Accordingly, in 1926, regular life policies specifically denied protection in case of death in an air accident. Moreover, few insurance companies offered options to regular policies (at extra cost) insuring pilots or air passengers. "In our opinion," wrote the head of a law firm to an airline client, "efforts of your organization to secure wider interest in passenger flying are being handicapped under antiquated provisions of life and accident [insurance] policies . . . ."[23]

In 1927, a sprinkling of insurance companies made a cautious entry into aviation coverage. John Hancock offered pilots holding regular policies aviation accident insurance of up to $10,000 at an extra premium of $10 per thousand. No sooner had these rates been announced than the company began reasoning that "the tremendous impetus given to flying recently has greatly emphasized the risk." The extra cost per thousand was upped to $25. Barber & Baldwin, Inc., an underwriter, offered $100,000 accident policies that included coverage for death or injury in an air mishap for an annual premium of $4,000; the same policy without aviation coverage could be had for $400. Even people who conceded that "travel by aircraft is without question a hazardous method of getting about" believed these premiums were outrageously high.[24]

The aviation industry hatched a variety of schemes to bring rates down. These ranged from securing group insurance for aviation clubs meeting certain minimum safety standards to having the Daniel Guggenheim Foundation for Aeronautics help meet losses incurred by underwriters in insuring any airline from among an "Honor Safety Roll" established by the Foundation. In the final analysis, however, the only thing that could have an appreciable impact on rates was aviation's safety performance.[25]

Rates were unreasonably high in the 1920's for two reasons: a general fear of flying, which was apparently shared by the underwriters themselves, and the lack of a documented aviation safety record. Of the two, the absence of a track record was by far the more important. No one, including insurance companies, kept systematic air accident statistics prior to 1926; those that made an effort, such as the Aeronautical Chamber of Commerce, collected data in a catch-as-catch-can manner. This is where the Aeronautics Branch came in. It collected and analyzed a wide variety of statistics; and what it did not collect and analyze it could cull from its records. In May 1927, MacCracken made arrangements for Barker & Baldwin, which specialized in aviation insurance, to receive duplicates of all aircraft inspection reports and data on the flying records of individual pilots. Young continued the practice. "The files of the Aeronautics Branch of the Department of Commerce pertaining to safety and accidents in aeronautics . . . have been opened to the Actuarial Society of America . . . ," he announced in May 1930. That same month, both Metropolitan Life and the Travelers Insurance Company got access to the same files. The following year, the Branch granted Travelers request "to get a record of those pilots appearing on [our] list who . . . had a record of warnings, reprimands, fines, suspensions, or revocations, or other action taken against them together with the number of each types of record and the date of each offense."[26]

Providing the insurance industry with this kind of information undoubtedly helped reduce rates. Between May 1926 and January 1929, rates dropped an average of 40 percent. Even more encouraging, as *Domestic Air News* observed, "out of fifty leading accident insurance companies in the United States and Canada, 42 do not have an anti-air-travel clause . . . ." By 1932, premiums were still high, but no longer unbearably high.[27]

The Aeronautics Branch was as open with other segments of the aviation industry as it was with aviation insurers. The charge to promote civil aviation bred a spirit of accommodation within the Branch; it also

bred a close, sometimes all-too-cozy, relationship between Federal aviation officials and the various segments of the industry — a relationship
that worked to narrow the distance normally separating the regulator
and the regulated. MacCracken moved freely and casually in and out of
aviation circles and felt at ease entertaining airline officials at his home.
Some Federal officials accepted cut-rate fares from airlines. Others went
a step further. "I shall be more than glad to take advantage of your
kindness . . .," wrote Gilbert G. Budwig, the Chief of the Air Regulations Division, in accepting an "annual pass good over the line of the
Kohler Aviation Corporation." Cap Hingsburg, the Chief of the Airways
Division, saw no impropriety in having Paul Henderson, an airline
official, help him secure a loan for a stock transaction. In 1931, when the
Aeronautical Chamber of Commerce found that it could no longer
maintain a Washington office, Clarence Young thought nothing of
furnishing two ACC employees with "desk space in our . . . Information
Division" for a period of weeks and allowing them the use of Government telephones "in contacting their clientele in Washington."[28]

This is not to suggest that these instances represented the general
state of affairs (or that Hingsburg's conduct, had it been known by high
Department officials, would have been condoned); they were sympto-
matic, however, of an attitude of mind that led Federal officials to be
overly solicitous and protective of the aviation industry, occasionally at
the expense of the public. The position taken by the Department of
Commerce on the question of making accident reports public was
illustrative of this attitude.

VI

Under the Air Commerce Act it was the duty of the Secretary of
Commerce "to investigate, record, and make public the causes of
accidents in civil air navigation in the United States." The act said
nothing else concerning the matter. There was no elaboration on what
the Secretary should or should not make public, whether he should issue
a detailed report on each accident, assign individual or company error, or
just present a periodic statistical analysis. The Secretary, therefore, had a
great deal of latitude in selecting the kind of information to make public.

In 1926 and 1927, the Branch issued a few full-scale reports on major
air disasters. Pilots, aircraft, and air carriers were identified and the

probable cause of the accident was attributed in each case. The industry's reaction was pained. In consequence, the Department discontinued the practice. It now fulfilled its responsibility to "make public the causes of accidents" by periodically issuing a table of statistics showing that so many accidents were caused by pilot error, so many by mechanical failure, so many by sundry other reasons. A tight lid of secrecy was placed on all other particulars. In this way, the cause of a specific accident could never be traced by the public, the Congress, or interested parties.[29]

On September 3, 1929, a Transcontinental Air Transport (TAT) airliner, the "City of San Francisco," crashed near Mount Taylor, N.M. Eight people perished in the wreck. Senator Sam D. Bratton (D-N.M) asked the Department to furnish him with a copy of the accident report. The Department refused. Bratton countered by introducing a Senate resolution directing the Committee on Interstate Commerce to obtain and make available to the Senate all the facts relating to the accident "and all other accidents and wrecks of airplanes engaged in interstate air commerce in which lives have been lost." Bratton's resolution also directed the committee to investigate "the feasibility or advisability of placing those engaged in [interstate air] commerce under the supervision of the Interstate Commerce Commission."[30]

The resolution hit an immediate snag in the person of Hiram Bingham. Besides raising a jurisdictional issue — Bingham maintained that the question belonged in the Committee of Commerce, which "always" had jurisdiction over matters concerning the Department of Commerce — he argued that the timing of the resolution was extremely unfortunate. MacCracken, who had conducted the affairs of the Aeronautics Branch in such a way "as to win praise from all those who are interested in aeronautics," was just preparing to step down as Assistant Secretary for Aeronautics, Bingham pointed out; yet Bratton was asking the Congress to detract from the achievements of this man.

Bingham, though he succeeded in bottling up Bratton's resolution, was quickly outflanked by Kenneth McKellar (D-Tenn.), who entered the fray in the wake of a fatal air accident that occurred near Memphis. On October 16, McKellar introduced a resolution directing the Secretary of Commerce to furnish the Senate with the accident report of this crash. Two days later, he accepted an amendment to his resolution by Bratton broadening the request to include the accident report of the New Mexico crash. Under McKellar's guidance, the resolution cleared committee and passed the Senate within a week of its introduction. "A precedent has been created," *Aviation* observed, when the Department turned its findings over to the Senate, "and inevitably there will be repeated attempts to secure the same public exposure of the results of the Department's inquiries in other cases."[31]

Aviation had prophesied correctly. In late January 1930, a TAT Ford Trimotor crashed in Oceanside, Calif., killing 15 people. Bratton was back with another resolution requesting the Secretary of Commerce to furnish the Senate with "complete findings" on each aircraft accident since May 20, 1926. This time Bratton precipitated a full-scale debate that spread to the press. It was Bratton's contention that all information gathered by the Department of Commerce in the course of an accident investigation "belongs to the public." This information was also a matter of vital concern to injured parties. "Suppose the company was negligent," Bratton said. "Suppose women were made widows and children orphans by this accident. The department seals its findings and leaves the widows and orphans in each case to get along the best way they can."[32]

Bratton was not alone in demanding disclosure. "Louder grows the protest in the Senate and the press against the policy of the Department of Commerce not to make public its detailed findings in such disasters," *Literary Digest* noted. Even Bingham had to admit that the secrecy surrounding accident investigation was not in the public interest; nor was it, he believed, in aviation's interest. "There is a reason for every crash," he told the Senate, "and public confidence can only be inspired by giving this reason, and putting the blame where it should be." "The aeronautical interests do not demand an ostrich-like policy of secrecy when an accident occurs," asserted Charles C. Rohlfing, a contemporary student of aviation regulation. "They are entitled to full candor and freedom from exaggerated press stories." The press would be less prone to invent sensational causes for accidents, Rohlfing argued, if it had access to the real causes. To the *New York Herald Tribune*, "The semi-annual accident reports which the department [publishes] are not very illuminating, and the public confidence may well be shaken if the agitation in Congress and elsewhere about 'secrecy' continues." "Nothing does more to inspire public confidence than a frank facing of the facts," *Aviation* declared.[33]

Young, backed by Secretary of Commerce Robert P. Lamont, fought the resolution tooth and nail. A frank facing of the facts in public was precisely what he did not want. Nor would he admit that the public had a right to know the facts. In making their case, he and other members of the Aeronautics Branch exploited a weakness in the Air Commerce Act, which made no provision for subpoenaing witnesses or taking testimony under oath. "We cannot compel persons to come forward with [information]," Young argued. "Our information at the present time is wholly voluntary," pointed out Elmer Kintz. If witnesses suspected that the testimony they gave would be publicly divulged, the Department's sources of information would dry up. Few pilots would testify against their employers; those that did, Kintz maintained, "would be fired." Moreover, since the Air Commerce Act did not prohibit the use of accident reports in legal proceedings, making reports public would permit their use in civil suits; the reports, therefore, would become instruments for collecting damages from airline companies and aircraft manufacturers. These suits could so injure some companies that they would be forced out of business. Accident investigation, said Pendleton Edgar, chairman of the Accident Board of the Aeronautics Branch, "is not for the purpose of affixing blame or liability on any particular individual." "The purpose of the Air Commerce Act was to foster aviation," Young said in an address before the National Exchange Clubs, "and the sole purpose in investigating accidents is to determine the causes and promote aviation by what we learn." The Department secured an opinion from the Attorney General stating that "the statistical method . . . adopted to make public the causes of accidents in civil air navigation . . . seems to be a reasonable compliance with the requirements of the [Air Commerce Act], having in mind its expressed purpose to foster air commerce."[34]

The Department's arguments would have been more convincing had they been more consistent with past policy. Divulging the testimony of air carrier pilots may have put these men's jobs in jeopardy; yet the Aeronautics Branch turned over sensitive pilot records to insurance companies, which could use them to cancel pilots' policies — an outcome nearly as damaging to a professional pilot as losing his job. On more than one occasion in the past, moreover, the Aeronautics Branch had released a complete accident report to a carrier involved in an accident. It was difficult to maintain convincingly that the public was not entitled to the same information given special interests. The inconsistency of the Department in initially interpreting the Air Commerce Act as compelling a public airing of its accident findings and then interpreting the act to better suit the presumed interests of the operators was not lost on its critics. "In other words," Kenneth McKellar charged, "when [airline] owners protested, the Department simply disregarded the law absolutely and undertook to repeal [sic] it and did repeal it." Young's position, Bratton suggested, was that only "ambulance-chasing lawyers" would benefit if the Aeronautics Branch complied "with the plain mandate" of the law; this demonstrated that "the sympathy of the Bureau is with aviation, and they utterly disregarded the public in connection with the whole subject."[35]

A less inclusive version of Bratton's resolution was passed by the Senate in May 1930. But this resolution, like McKellar's, did nothing to resolve the basic issue. Indeed, since the Senate and the Department still held diametrically opposed views on the question, a tug of war between them was bound to erupt and re-erupt each time an aircraft fell out of the sky. Hiram Bingham worked toward a permanent solution. He introduced a bill that required the Secretary of Commerce to release a report on the probable cause of all fatal air accidents in interstate commerce. At the same time, the bill empowered the Secretary to subpoena witnesses, hold public hearings, receive testimony under oath, and compel the production of evidence. The bill protected negligent parties by prohibiting the use of any data gathered in these proceedings in court. With this protection afforded the operators, the Department supported the measure. Nevertheless, Bingham encountered great difficulty in trying to steer the bill to passage. "It is possible," he speculated, "that some of the aviation companies are blocking . . . passage . . . and do not want to have a full investigation of accidents and the results immediately made public, because they fear its effect on their business . . . ." It required four years before a bill similar to Bingham's could be enacted, thereby ending the threat of a periodic tug of war between Congress and the Executive over the public disclosure of probable cause.[36]

But the point of all this is that the charge to foster civil aviation did assume undesirable aspects. It was used as a cloak to hide industry deficiencies from public view — deficiencies that were of more than passing concern to the air transport user. This was all part and parcel of the overly protective attitude of the Aeronautics Branch toward the industry. Fortunately, this attitude never progressed to the point where it redounded to the serious detriment of either the industry or the Branch.

The saving element in this attitude was that it usually prevailed when side issues were at stake. It never prevailed when safety was directly at stake. The Branch recognized that playing fast and loose with public safety meant playing fast and loose with the industry itself. (And for the most part, the industry recognized this fact, too.) This the Branch demonstrated during the investigation of a fatal air accident in the spring of 1931.

VII

The airline crash that killed Knute Rockne and seven others near Bazaar, Kans., on March 31, 1931, was the most sensational air accident that the Aeronautics Branch dealt with in its brief history. Rockne, the Notre Dame University football coach, was a legendary sports figure, and the news of his death was emblazoned across the front page of every major newspaper in the country. This was not an accident that the Branch could treat as just one more statistic.

Rockne was flying in a trimotored Fokker F-10A operated by Transcontinental Air Transport. By the standards of that day the F-10A had a good safety record. The aircraft, designed by Anthony Fokker, a Dutch-born aircraft manufacturer who had worked for the Germans during the First World War and eventually immigrated to the United

A Fokker F-10A

States, was a high-wing monoplane constructed of a composite of materials. The fuselage was built of welded steel tubes and covered with fabric; the wings were of an all-wood cantilever design with a load-bearing plywood skin. Features of Fokker's design had been borrowed by other manufacturers. The trend by the late 1920's, however, was clearly away from Fokker's composite construction to an all-metal structure.[37]

The craft bearing Rockne had been flying in turbulent weather. Eyewitnesses on the ground, hearing the sputter of engines, turned up to see the aircraft appear out of a cloud bank and rip off a wing before hitting the ground. Aeronautics Branch investigators rushed to the scene. Their initial conclusion, after talking to eyewitnesses, was that the pilot put undue stress on the aircraft's wings by pulling out of a dive too precipitously. The tentative finding was pilot error. But when the investigators discovered ice near the wreckage and an engine with a missing propeller, they changed their minds. They concluded that a piece of ice had worked loose from the aircraft's hub and struck and broke a propeller blade. This caused severe vibration, putting a load in excess of 100,000 pounds on the engine and engine mount. The load had snapped the wing. On April 2, only two days after the crash, the Aeronautics Branch reversed its long-standing and long-defended policy of silence and issued a statement presenting this broken-prop theory as the probable cause of the accident.[38]

Five days later this theory was discarded. Excavations at the accident site turned up the missing propeller in one piece, despite the fact that it had been driven deep into the ground by the force of the engine. Embarrassed, the Department came forth with a new explanation. Ice had collected on the aircraft and "rendered inoperative certain of its instruments." This caused the aircraft to go into a steep glide. "The result seems to indicate," the Department declared in a public statement, "that when coming out of this maneuver, the change of direction occurred at such unusual rapidity as to build up an enormous load on the wing, which in return brought about the wing failure." The primary cause of the accident was attributed to weather. This explanation, too, was soon discarded.[39]

The desire of the Aeronautics Branch to clear up the mystery of this accident as soon as possible and thereby get the story off the front pages is understandable. But the headlong rush to announce half-baked conclusions is — and would be under any circumstances — puzzling; in light of what Aeronautics Branch officials knew about the Fokker F-10A, it is inexplicable. As early as December 1930, an inspector for National Parks Airways, Dillard Hamilton, wrote Gilbert G. Budwig, the Director of Air Regulation, expressing some concerns he was having about the F-10A. His chief worry was the Fokker's wings. "The plywood covering checks in very good shape but I always worry about the spars and internal bracing. That is covered up where one cannot check," Hamilton wrote. He then proceeded to tell Budwig of a recent visit by "a Fokker factory man." The factory representative had advised the operator to adjust the airplane's ailerons an inch above the trailing edge of the wing "to relieve tail heaviness." With this rigging, Hamilton argued, "the ship goes into a bank easy"; but bringing it back out of a turn required overcontrol: "I am afraid someone will get into trouble in bad weather with controls so slow."[40]

Budwig was puzzled by the factory representative's recommendation since he did not believe it would correct tail heaviness; he advised that the ailerons be rigged in the usual manner. As to the wings, Budwig thought Hamilton did not have to worry about their internal structure as long as the plywood skin stayed glued to the spars. If the internal joints tore loose "the wing would probably deflect badly enough to tear the covering loose. . . ."[41]

A month later, Hamilton's concern about the aircraft's rigging was reinforced by the Navy. The airplane had been tested, found unstable, and ultimately rejected for naval use. The Aeronautics Branch decided to take a closer look at the F-10A, particulary inside its wings, where no maintenance could be performed without ripping off the plywood skin. By the eve of the Rockne crash, the Branch felt it had found enough evidence to justify grounding the aircraft immediately. "We missed the boat by one day," Clarence Young recalled, which makes the departmental speculations about ice, broken props, and weather even more inexplicable.[42]

Missing the boat by one day, Clarence Young waited five weeks — until May 4 — before taking the aircraft out of passenger service. The ban, which covered all F-10's and F-10A's built in 1929, was not total; the aircraft could still be used in mail carriage provided pilots wore parachutes. Thirty-five aircraft in all were affected, 15 belonging to American Airways, 10 to Pan Am, 7 to TAT, and 3 to United. Nothing like it had ever hit the American aviation industry. And nothing has

FIFTEEN CENTS (IN CANADA, 20¢)   March 14, 1932

TIME

The Weekly Newsmagazine

COL. CLARENCE MARSHALL YOUNG
Volume XIX   "The Air Commerce Act says 'No.'"   Number 11
                         (See AERONAUTICS)

Circulation Office, 350 East 22nd Street, Chicago.   (Reg. U. S. Pat. Off.)   Editorial and Advertising Offices, 135 East 42nd Street, New York.

Clarence M. Young

FIFTEEN CENTS

TIME

The Weekly News-Magazine

VOL. II   NO. 18

ANTHONY H. G. FOKKER
"Once an enemy—"
(See Page 24)

DEC. 31, 1923

Anthony Fokker

since. There would be other bans, but none would strike an aircraft, an aircraft designer, and an airframe manufacturer with so devastating a force.[43]

Immediately after announcing the ban, Young called in representatives of the affected airlines to explain his decision. Neither Fokker nor anyone from General Motors, which had controlling interest in the Fokker Aircraft Corporation, was invited. Fokker stormed into Washington and demanded admittance to the meeting. Turned away, he ranted and raged and generally made a nuisance of himself, upbraiding every Commerce official in sight. Young tried to let Fokker down easy. Precisely why the aircraft was grounded was not revealed publicly. The official announcement merely stated that inspection and maintenance would be performed on the aircraft and that structural problems had played no part in imposing the restriction. This implied that TAT had improperly maintained its F-10's, and that the Government wanted to insure that other operators did not make the same mistake. "The United States will not see Fokker airplanes blown from the sky merely by the error of maintenance of one operator," Fokker fumed after finally getting access to Young.[44]

But maintenance, though a contributing factor, was far from being at the root of the problem. When Federal inspectors peeled the skin off the aircraft's wings, they found that moisture, accumulating in the interior of the wings, had "caused deterioration of the glue, materially decreasing the strength of the wing, since this type construction is to a great extent dependent on the glue." With evidence that the spruce and birch spars were coming unstuck, Young had no choice but to order the inspection of the internal wing trussing on all 35 Fokkers. And he required that this inspection be conducted periodically. He further ordered the installation of a counterbalance weight on the ailerons.[45]

In late June, 20 of the banned aircraft were cleared to return to passenger service; five others were reinstated later. Some never returned. Those that did remained in passenger service only a short time. The periodic inspection ordered by the Government was a difficult and costly procedure. More importantly, confidence in Fokker's wood-and-glue wing construction had been lost, never to be restored. Talk of dry rot made the rounds among industry officials. TAT assembled a number of its F-10's, stripped them of their engines, and set fire to the lot. And Young eventually proscribed the Fokker-type wing construction. The F-

10 had been driven from the U.S. commercial transport field. So was Fokker. Though he continued to manufacture airplanes in Holland, the brilliant "Flying Dutchman," whose aircraft had been the envy of his competitors for more than a decade, was eased out by General Motors. In the summer of 1931, the Fokker Aircraft Corporation was renamed the General Aviation Manufacturing Corporation. The automotive giant built only 20 more aircraft of Fokker design, and those only to fulfill previous contractual commitments. Its investment in one of aviation's most famous talents had been lost.[46]

But while Fokker and General Motors had been decided losers, "the public," as the *New York Times* observed in summing up the episode, "has been the gainer."[47] So, too, on balance, was U.S. civil aviation. It is noteworthy that criticism of Young or the Aeronautics Branch remained at a bare minimum throughout the spring of 1931, and this despite the fact that the early phase of the accident investigation had been badly botched. Indeed, Young's reputation in the industry remained solid throughout the rest of his tenure. Clarence Young had demonstrated that there were ways of fostering civil aviation other than ballyhooing its merits or throwing a cloak of secrecy over its deficiencies.

8. Reshaping the Airway Map

When Herbert Hoover resigned his Commerce post in the summer of 1928 to seek the Presidency, he left behind a piece of unfinished aviation business — the development of a vigorous air passenger service. Airway construction had proved a tremendous stimulus to airmail carriage. But its effect on passenger carriage, always considered the backbone of an air transport system by Federal aviation officials, was a disappointment. Air transport companies were reluctant to offer the service. In consequence, the Government's multimillion dollar investment in airways and navaids was only supporting a relatively minor activity of the U.S. Post Office Department. As Secretary of Commerce, Hoover could do little to remedy the situation; as President, he could — and did — do a great deal. By the time he left office, the nucleus of what eventually became the greatest air passenger system in the world was in place. This was unquestionably an accomplishment of a high order; but the manner in which Hoover and his associates achieved their ends would redound to their discredit. More importantly, their acts helped usher in the most tumultuous period in the history of U.S. air transportation — a period that ultimately produced a sharp, decisive turn in Federal civil aviation policy.

II

The air transport companies that had successfully bid for airmail contracts in 1925 and 1926 saw themselves primarily as mail carriers. After all, the Air Mail Act of 1925 had been the spur to their creation. "The main job of the National Air Transport . . . is to carry the mail over its route with the greatest possible regularity," wrote an NAT executive in June 1928. "Its second job is to carry such express matter as

191

is handed to it. No passenger business has been sought . . . ." What passenger business did come its way was not always given an unqualified welcome. "Imagine our surprise when we were informed that we would not be allowed to go on as the space allotted to me would be taken up by the mail," wrote an enraged traveler who had made reservations on an NAT flight. Not all air travelers received such shabby treatment; but neither were they accorded a red-carpet reception. Flying, particularly over long distances, was not the most comfortable way to get from place to place. Few carriers purchased aircraft specifically designed for passenger service. Boeing Air Transport, for example, which ran between San Francisco and Chicago, flew single-motored biplanes with space for two passengers. The company thus informed its customers of the availability of "comfort rooms" at all stations, and warned them that "long flights may be disagreeable unless precautions are taken." In 1929, United Aircraft & Transport, Boeing's parent company, operated 31 airplanes, 21 of which were equipped to carry passengers; none offered any accommodations beyond a seat.[1]

But air transport companies were in the business of making money, and had they believed that they could increase their profits by expanding passenger operations, they would have. The fact of the matter was that the economics of airmail carriage was a deterrent to the development of an air passenger business. The Air Mail Act of 1925 (i.e., the Kelly Act) had set airmail postage rates at 10¢ an ounce or a fraction thereof; it also provided that airmail contractors be compensated at a rate not to exceed 80 percent of the revenues derived from this postage. An ordinary airmail stamp was good within any of three airmail zones; mail crossing from one zone into another required additional postage. The system proved cumbersome and virtually unworkable because it required counting every piece of mail in order to compute what an operator had earned. And though the rate of compensation appeared generous, carrier profits were practically nil because the zone system kept volume down. This system was quickly discarded. In June 1926, Congress authorized the Postmaster General to compensate carriers at a rate not exceeding $3 per pound of mail over the first 1,000 miles (or fraction thereof) and 30¢ per pound for each additional 100 miles. In February 1927, the Post Office abandoned its complex zone system; the 10¢-per-ounce postage was now good between any two points in the United States. Finally, in May 1928,

Congress amended the Kelly Act a second time by, among other things, dropping the postage rate to 5¢ an ounce.[2]

The 1926 and 1928 amendments and the abandonment of zones transformed the airmail from a service that had been intended to be self-supporting to a federally subsidized operation. At the same time, these measures ushered in a major boom in airmail carriage. "The result . . . without the slightest doubt will be marked by the vastly increased use of the air mail by both business houses and private individuals throughout the entire country," *Aviation* predicted in welcoming the postage rate adopted in February 1927.[3] What the magazine failed to predict was that carriers themselves would soon rank among the biggest air mail users. Any fool could find a way to take undue advantage of the system. At 5¢ per ounce, a pound of mail or freight cost 80¢ to ship 1,000 miles or less; for this the carrier received up to $3 in compensation. Hence, a carrier could send its own mail by air and pocket $2.20 per pound, minus operating costs. Indeed, under this system, some airlines could pay the postage on all the mail on their route and still make a handsome profit.

It did not take long for talk to make the rounds that contractors were sending blank letters to themselves and that they had, indeed, approached large business concerns and offered to pay the postage on their airmail, provided each letter weighed a full ounce. "One Christmas during that period I received from an airline a Christmas card, sent by air mail over their own route, which had been thriftily padded out by enclosing five blank sheets of paper in the envelope," Edward P. Warner recalled. "The postage was five cents; the airline was paid approximately 18 cents for transporting its own card in an airplane that would not have a full load in any case; the card, envelope, and addressing cost perhaps four cents, leaving a net profit of about nine cents on each card sent out; a nice combination of good will to man and business sense." Another carrier printed and freely distributed along the territory it served airmail postcards made of cardboard so thick that each weighed in at one ounce. Some contractors took full advantage of the postal regulations requiring the padlocking of all sacks containing registered mail. If, for example, a carrier was transporting 10 registered letters on a particular trip, each letter would be placed in a separate sack — thus affording the carrier the opportunity to weigh in nine extra padlocks. Some operators chose less subtle ways to increase their take; they threw aboard telephone directories, bricks, lead bars, iron stoves, and spare engine-parts — postage paid — to round out a trip's load.[4]

The economics of airmail carriage being what it was, contractors could scarcely be faulted for ignoring the air traveler. In 1929, established air transport lines charged air passengers an average rate of 10.6 cents per mile, or approximately $300 to fly from New York to San Francisco. If passenger fares corresponded to the maximum per-pound postal rate, a one-way ticket for a passenger weighing 200 pounds and traveling 3,000 miles across country would have come to $1,800. From this reckoning alone, airmail carriage was six times more profitable than passenger carriage. In reality, it was even more lucrative. Mail handling entailed small overhead costs. Passengers required waiting rooms, ticket booths, reservation services, and larger and more expensive aircraft, complete with pilot, copilot, steward, and some of the comforts of home.[5]

Not all carriers were eligible to receive the maximum rate. The June 1926 amendment to the Kelly Act provided for converting to the per-pound rate by multiplying $3 by a fraction — "the numerator of which is the per centum of revenues derived from air mail to which the contractor was previously entitled under the contract, and the denominator of which is eighty." Thus, a contractor receiving the maximum 80 percent return from airmail postage sales generated by his route was automatically entitled to the maximum $3 per pound. But a carrier that had won its contract with a bid of, say, 50 percent of gross postage sales was now entitled to only $1.88.* Rates varied, therefore, and in some cases over a wide range. These inequalities were compounded by the fact that distance, unless it exceeded 1,000 miles, did not affect the rate. A carrier receiving the maximum rate could make more money transporting 100 pounds of mail 100 miles than a carrier flying the same load 10 times the distance but commanding less than this maximum rate. Accordingly, the rate per pound between New York and Chicago (718 miles) was $0.86; New York and Boston (192 miles), $3; Chicago and Atlanta (768 miles), $0.78; Cleveland and Pittsburgh (123 miles), $3. When distance is inserted into the equation, the rate paid the Cleveland-Pittsburgh contractor was approximately 25 times greater than the rate paid the Chicago-Atlanta contractor. The existence of these inequalities was alone reason enough to revamp the system.[6]

---

*50/80 [i.e., 0.625] x 3 = 1.875.

The Post Office Department under Coolidge turned its head to these inequalities and to all but the most flagrant of contractor abuses. Its principal concerns were that the airmail take hold and that these pioneer commercial operators succeed as airmail carriers. The airmail did, indeed, take hold. Between 1927 and 1929, the annual airmail poundage increased nearly sevenfold, from 1.1 million to 7.1 million. Carrier revenues took a corresponding jump. In fiscal 1927, the airmail revenues of domestic carriers came to $1.4 million; in fiscal 1929, to $11.2 million. At the same time, revenues from airmail postage, which amounted to something over $5 million during fiscal 1929, did not come close to paying the fare. The Federal Government was indulging in an informal subsidy.[7]

Investors and speculators alike could be forgiven if they saw the airline business as a no-lose proposition. Aviation stocks, in line with the general craze of optimism that swept Wall Street in the late 1920's, were bid up to fantastic heights. One speculator parlayed a $40 investment in a small engine manufacturer into a $3.4 million fortune inside of two years. In 1929, the value of all aeronautical products produced came to $91 million; yet the aggregate value of listed aviation securities amounted to $1 billion. "It is only natural that many of those who have been actively in the aviation business for many years should rub their eyes and pinch themselves and occasionally wonder whether what they see and hear is really true," *Aviation* remarked in February 1929, warning at the same time that many aeronautical stocks "have been bid up to a point . . . which discounts far ahead the growth which the companies may make in the future."[8]

When the sell-off finally came, it drove prices down even more swiftly than the speculative madness had driven them up. Within two years, the aggregate value of listed aviation stocks had plunged to a mere $50 million. But even as holders of aviation stocks were taking a bath, even as a convulsive economic crisis was shaking the nation to its foundations, airmail carriers continued to bask in prosperity. The Kelly Act, as amended, guaranteed the flow of Federal largess.[9]

With few of the airmail contractors making a serious effort to entice the air traveler, the bulk of passenger traffic went by default to a growing number of independent operators who did not possess Federal contracts. These lines were, by and large, shoestring operations doing business off the primary airmail routes. Most of them were operating in the red. Even the more substantial independents, who had invested in the latest passenger equipment, had difficulty balancing their ledgers. The passenger airliners of that day — the trimotored Fords and Fokkers — could not make a profit carrying passengers alone. "It is no secret from anyone who follows American aeronautics that passenger carrying has so far proved to be something less than El Dorado," commented *Aviation* in 1930. The independents knew that this would be the case. Their objective, however, was not so much to develop a profitable air passenger business as to establish an "equity" over their chosen routes in the hope that they would someday be awarded the privilege of flying mail over them.[10]

The original airmail contracts ran for a period of four years and were due to expire in 1929. Thus, as Hoover prepared for his inauguration, the independents were lining up their political support in the Congress and elsewhere, eagerly awaiting the opportunity to bid for contracts on both the old mail routes and the passenger routes they had developed themselves.

The mail operators were feeling more than a mite skittish. If their routes were thrown open to bids, they could lose everything. They did have, however, a great deal more economic and political muscle than the independents. The corporate structure of the mail carriers had changed drastically since the first domestic airmail contracts were let under the Kelly Act. The steady growth in airmail income had convinced a powerful segment of the nation's banking community that aviation was a profitable proposition. Aided by the stock boom, which made it easy to refinance and float new issues, these interests set out to gain control of both the transportation and manufacturing sides of the industry.

"There is an entirely new [aviation] line-up in which high finance plays the leading role," commented one observer in 1929. "The pioneers of the industry have cashed in their hard earned profits, and . . . have relinquished complete control [to bankers]." Three giant holding companies — United Aircraft & Transport, North American Aviation, and Aviation Corporation (AVCO) — now controlled a vast proportion of the nation's aviation firms. In 1928, United Aircraft had swallowed up Pratt & Whitney, Hamilton Propeller, Standard Steel Propeller, Stearman, Sikorsky, Northrop, and four airmail operators — National Air Transport, Boeing Air Transport, Varney Air Lines, and Pacific Air Transport — which formed its air transport subsidiary, United Air Lines. Late that same year, General Motors, Haydon, Stone & Co., and

Bancamerica-Blair organized North American Aviation and quickly gained control of Eastern Air Transport, Transcontinental Air Transport, Curtiss Aeroplane and Motor, Wright Aeronautical Corp., and a score of lesser companies. AVCO, the third largest combine, was formed in 1929. Its air transport subsidiary, American Airways, included such pioneer lines as Colonial Airways, Southern Air Transport, Robertson Aircraft Corp., and Continental. When the Hoover administration began reconstructing the airway map, these new combines proved more than a match for the independents in the competition for routes.[11]

III

Walter Folger Brown, Hoover's Postmaster General, was an intelligent, hard-driving, dynamic administrator. He was also a man with a vision. He wanted to create a stable, efficient air transport system that served both passengers and the mail and linked the United States through a network of serviceable airways — a system that would "encourage the habit and practice by the public of using aviation in the ordinary affairs of life."

The new Postmaster General was in an excellent position to have his way. He was the most gifted and most experienced political operator in the administration. And he had a direct line to the White House, where he enjoyed the confidence and respect of the occupant. It had been Brown, from his post as Assistant Secretary of Commerce, who lined up the party regulars behind Hoover's candidacy. It had also been Brown, once Hoover secured the nomination, who helped direct the successful Republican campaign against Al Smith. Postmaster General seemed a natural post for a man of Brown's political attainments. Brown, said Hoover, had "a greater knowledge of the Federal machinery and its functions than any other man in the United States." He had, too, some unfortunate traits. He could be ruthless, arrogant, and overbearing, and he was single-minded to a fault in pursuing his ends. These qualities, as much as his better side, would influence the course of events in the coming months.[12]

Brown and Hoover could plainly see that the nation's air transport system lacked order. Out of 53 established airline routes, 43 were less than 500 miles in length; 8 ran over distances between 500 and 1,000 miles. Besides being uneconomic in length, these routes were poorly situated to serve the transportation needs of the nation. Only the transcontinental airway, stretching from San Francisco to New York and served by United Air Lines, made any kind of sense. American Airways, though a vast operation, had such a chaotic route structure that it was said that it went "from nowhere to nowhere." Unless one wished to travel from New York to San Francisco or points in between, one could scarcely find a continuous service for any considerable stretch of the country. The obvious remedy was to reshape the airways — and the lines flying over them. "We laid out as a preliminary ideal four major east-west transcontinental lines," Herbert Hoover explained, "and eight major north-south continental lines with secondary adjuncts." These lines would be created through mergers and the judicious dispensing of airmail contracts. Hoover and Brown also resolved to reduce the outrageously high airmail rates and, at the same time, induce carriers to undertake passenger service in earnest.[13]

Two interrelated factors complicated matters: one was the independents; the other, the imminent expiration of the original contracts. Dealing with the independents individually was out of the question. The Government was not buying "peanuts and pencils and pig iron"; it was buying a highly specialized service. Therefore, Brown explained, "there was no sense in taking this Government's money and dishing it out, giving it out as a handout to every little fellow that was flying around the map and was not going to do anything . . . to develop aviation in the broad sense." Mail subsidies would go to well-financed lines capable of providing a first-rate passenger service over long, continuous routes. The worthier independents would either be absorbed by these trunk lines or given contracts for necessary feeder routes. The rest would be left to fend for themselves.[14]

Opening the old mail routes to competitive bidding was unthinkable. It was the surest way to perpetuate — indeed, compound — the existing chaos. "Irresponsible, unproven companies might bid low to get into the picture, and then find themselves unable to do the job . . .," Mac-Cracken said.[15] Brown elaborated:

> If we throw these matters all open to competitive bidding you will find promoters coming in and wanting to bid off the contract, having no knowledge of the costs, having no knowledge of the factor of obsolescence, the amount of equipment they have to throw away each year because of improvements in the art, having no knowledge of the bad luck, the usual losses that are

not directly incident to the operation. They will come in and bid
a price that will be lower than the experienced man who has had
his fingers burned, and then we would be obliged to let the
contract to the promoter who will pick up flying personnel and
such equipment as he can get by the Department of Commerce,
and he will start out and have the same accidents and the same
bad luck . . . that the men who have been through this whole
thing have had, and we will be doing the most unbusinesslike
thing of throwing away an invaluable industry.[16]

Competitive bidding of any kind would frustrate — or, at the very least,
make more difficult — the creation of a truly national air transport
system. It was to be avoided at all costs.

The 1928 amendment to the Kelly Act appeared to offer a solution.
It stipulated that mail operators could convert their contracts into 10-
year route certificates. In September 1929, Brown called in the operators
to negotiate the terms of the new route certificates.

Events now took an ironic twist. The established operators had
actually spearheaded the drive to get the Kelly Act amendment passed.
And in 1928 they were looking forward to the day when they could
surrender their contracts in exchange for route certificates, which, they
believed, offered long-term security. A year later, the route certificate
appeared to be a different kettle of fish; it promised little more security
than short-term, competitive contracts. This change of heart came when
the operators learned of Brown's determination to lower rates, and they
took a second look at a provision in the amendment stipulating that the
rate of compensation for certificate holders would be determined by
"periodical negotiation" between the holder and the Postmaster General.
The law set down no standards of fairness or reasonableness. It established no impartial rate-setting mechanism. Instead, it gave the Postmaster General, an interested party, virtually dictatorial power in setting
rates. Even if the Postmaster General was himself fair and reasonable, he
was potentially subject to a variety of political pressures — from within
the administration, the Congress, and the public at large. Exigencies
could make it necessary for him to show certain financial results. It was
conceivable, then, that he might set rates that had no relationship to the
carriers' operating costs and their need for a fair return on their
investment. There was no way to guard against such arbitrary, politically
motivated rate reductions.[17]

The negotiations got nowhere, forcing Brown to call a halt to the
proceedings in mid-October. He now asked the operators to meet as a
group and decide among themselves upon a standard formula for

determining rates. This, too, proved impossible of attainment. Carriers, operating under the crazy-quilt rate structure, had formed widely divergent views on the worth of their services. Brown now determined that he required new powers from Congress to achieve his ends. Meanwhile, with contracts due to expire on November 7, he had to insure that the old routes would not be opened to competitive bidding while he was awaiting congressional action. Accordingly, one day before expiration, he used the authority he believed granted him by an 1878 statute to extend the contracts for six months.[18]

Brown, with the help of MacCracken (now in private law practice in Washington), Paul Henderson, and other airline lobbyists, drafted a bill that contained two key provisions. One provision scrapped the per-pound mail rate in favor of a space-mile rate. Under this formula, the Post Office paid contractors up to $1.25 a mile for a specified number of cubic feet of cargo space. The contractor would receive this payment whether all, part, or none of the space was taken up by mail. Thus, the more space the contractor had available — that is, the larger the aircraft he used on mail runs — the greater his compensation. It was an ingenious provision, for it gave operators a strong incentive to buy large modern transports and make space unused by the mail available for passengers. Like the old formula, Brown's contemplated a subsidy; Brown's formula, however, subsidized passenger, not mail, carriage. A contractor employing small aircraft with space sufficient only for mail received no subsidy — just a fair payment for his services. The second key provision — and the one that would prove controversial — provided that the Postmaster General, at his discretion, could award airmail contracts "by negotiation and without advertising for or considering bids."[19]

His bill drafted, Brown now proceeded to commit a costly blunder. The provision allowing the Postmaster General to bypass competitive bidding was bound to stir controversy. It placed an enormous amount of power in the hands of a single official. On the other hand, Congress was as eager to bring order to the confused aviation picture as the administration. Most importantly, Clyde Kelly, the author of the Air Mail Act of 1925, was on record as favoring the same provisions that Brown had now incorporated in his proposal — and Kelly usually got what he wanted in the way of airmail legislation. With Kelly in harness, the administration could expect only scattered opposition outside of the minority party. Brown and Kelly were old acquaintances; they had known each other since the Bull Moose campaign, when they fought the good fight supporting Teddy Roosevelt. By the time the two men landed in Washington, however, they had begun to drift apart, politically and personally. Relations had become so strained that Brown wanted nothing to do with his old political associate. Given Kelly's legislative record, however, common courtesy and good sense dictated that Brown either ask Kelly to introduce his bill or, at the very least, take him into his confidence. Brown could not bring himself to do either. He rationalized that Kelly, because he was now chairman of the House Civil Service Committee, was not an appropriate channel for his legislation. He therefore ignored the Pennsylvania Congressman and sent his bill directly to the House Post Office Committee, where it fell into the hands of Congressman Laurence Hawley Watres, who ended up introducing the measure.

Predictably, Kelly took umbrage; indeed, as MacCracken recalled, he was "fit to be tied." He was widely known as the "father of the airmail," and was proud of the title. With the help of James M. Mead, the ranking Democrat on the Post Office Committee, Kelly succeeded in bringing proceedings on the bill to a halt. This forced Brown to swallow his pride and send MacCracken, hat in hand, to plead with Kelly. The outcome was that Kelly agreed to allow the bill to progress to passage in return for certain concessions. The section granting the Postmaster General the power to award contracts without competitive bidding would go. Brown had paid dearly for allowing his personal feelings to get the better of him.[20]

The Watres Act, signed into law by Hoover in April 1930, still represented an improvement over the old law. It adopted the mile-space rate formula, and permitted established airmail operators to exchange their contracts for long-term route certificates under conditions that provided for congressional review of periodic changes in the rate of compensation imposed by the Postmaster General. It vested, moreover, powers in the Postmaster General that he did not possess before. Namely, it authorized him, when he believed it was in the public interest, to "make any extensions or consolidations of routes which are now or may hereafter be established." Clyde Kelly and his allies, while concentrating on denying the Postmaster General the power to negotiate contracts, had overlooked the potential of this provision for the exercise of arbitrary power. Walter Folger Brown had not.[21]

IV

"We have been watching with great interest the progress of the Watres Bill," wrote C. E. Woolman, vice president of Delta Air Service, an independent carrier, ". . . and hope that this bill . . . will at an early date permit the Post Office Department to contract with the various [passenger] lines" now operating without mail carriage. Delta was not the only independent eager for a mail route. All independents wanted, and were in desperate need of, such routes. "Unless our Government . . . makes it possible for regular schedule air passenger lines to receive some revenue from the transportation of mail," stated Erle P. Halliburton, president of Southwest Air Fast Express (Safeway), another independent, ". . . the very life of transportation of passengers by air [will be] in the balance." Halliburton, a shrewd Oklahoma businessman who had made a fortune in oil drilling, estimated that independents required "a revenue of not less than 50¢ per mile from some source other than . . . passengers" in order to remain solvent.[22] Passage of the Watres Act without the provision for negotiated contracts had raised the independents' hopes that they would soon be earning this additional revenue.

The Postmaster General, though under intense pressure from the independents, had other ideas. On May 19, 1930, he met at the Post Office Department headquarters in Washington, D.C., with officials of 16 airlines and airline holding companies. His purpose for calling the meeting was twofold: to reconstruct the airway map in some meaningful fashion and to work out "some method . . . of aiding the passenger transport operators who had no mail contracts . . . ." He did not intend, however, to assist all independents — only those that fitted into his overall scheme. The majority of passenger carriers were missing from the meeting; they had not been invited.[23]

On the wall of the conference room hung a map on which Brown had reconstructed the airways. Referring to the map, Brown told the conferees that the hodgepodge fashion in which the airways had grown was unacceptable. Only United's service over the transcontinental airway made economic sense. He had no intention, however, of giving United a monopoly in transcontinental airmail carriage. He wanted to create two more transcontinental lines — a central and a southern — to compete with United and with each other. He also envisioned a number of north-south and feeder lines. "He stated that he wanted to work it out so that on any route there would be just one operator flying both mail and passengers, day and night . . .," recalled F. G. Coburn, the president of AVCO. On the other hand, Brown wanted to protect the pioneering investments of both the mail operators and the independents. To do this, he would have to avoid competitive bidding; and competitive bidding could only be avoided if all the elements in the business agreed on some equitable distribution of routes and services. Route swaps and mergers would have to be effected. He had the power to do this, Brown stated, under the provision of the Watres Act permitting him to extend and consolidate existing mail routes. As for the independents, "mail pay could be given to [them] by subletting operations from the mail contractors without competitive bidding . . . ." With that, Brown left the operators to themselves to work out who got what. William Mac-Cracken, at the meeting to look after the interests of his airline clients, was elected chairman of the conference.[24]

Paul Henderson, now representing United, was incredulous. The whole thing "seemed to me so contrary to the spirit of the law, from what I heard in the hearings . . . preceeding the passage of the [Watres Act] that I personally took the thing as a joke." At the first opportunity, Henderson approached MacCracken and told him that the meeting should be adjourned "until we had some more definite information about the legality of the plan that we were supposed to consider . . . ." MacCracken thought Henderson was "crazier than hell"; he would not adjourn the meeting. Henderson now called Chester W. Cuthell, a New York attorney representing TAT, an independent, into the corridor and told him of his misgivings. Cuthell's response was ingenious. If the same meeting were being held across the street at the Raleigh Hotel, Cuthell said, it would be improper; however, since it was being held at the request and under the auspices of Federal officials, it was perfectly all right.

Henderson was still not satisfied. That night he asked a friend whose legal opinion he trusted, Judge John Edwards, whether he believed Brown's plan to reconstruct the airmail map by extensions was contemplated by the Watres Act. To Edwards, there was a great deal of difference between "extension" and "elongation." "'Extension' might be thought of in terms of the tail of a dog," Edwards said, according to Henderson, "but it certainly would not be longer than the dog . . . ." But if the legislation had used the word elongation, "it might be extension to any length compared to the thing that it was an extension to." What Brown had in mind definitely required making the tail longer than the dog.[25]

Henderson was not the only man with nagging doubts about the proceedings. Two days after talking to Henderson, Cuthell was no longer so certain that the cloak of Federal sponsorship guaranteed their legality. "I am very sure that the P.M.G. will go the full limit to avoid competitive bidding," he wrote to his boss, C. M. Keys, "but the dangers to his own situation of overstepping his authority are obvious. Unless everyone is taken care of, there may be an attack on the whole program in the courts . . . ." Others, less concerned with legality, still looked at the proceedings with a jaundiced eye. "The Postmaster General was not able to get the necessary legislation . . . to enable him to grant airmail contracts . . . without competitive bids," wrote Colonel L. H. Brittin of Northwest Airways. "He has made up his mind to do this anyway and has hit upon a plan . . . ." The plan, Brittin believed, was probably conceived "in iniquity."[26]

Years later, in maintaining there was no collusion at the conference, MacCracken asserted that all officials present "represented companies which wanted to receive air mail contracts, but our biases tended to cancel each other out." He could have added that the operators' biases tended to cancel everything out. "The air mail contractors are having a desperate session in Washington," Colonel Brittin reported; the Postmaster General's plan was causing them "no end of trouble." The carriers simply could not agree on how to divide the spoils. In trying to work out their pioneering rights, Brown explained, they "started out with the notion that the mere touching of a line gave them a pioneer's claim to the equity. If, for example, Eastern Air touched the line from Atlanta to Los Angeles, as it did touch it at Savannah, Eastern Air said they were pioneers to that extent, and they made claims, and I think everyone of them . . . made claims wherever they touched any of the routes."[27]

On June 4, the operators delivered a memorandum to Brown stating that they could reach agreement on only seven relatively minor routes — routes in which there was only one party in interest. The upshot was that the operators agreed to allow Brown to act as an umpire in resolving the outstanding issues. Such an outcome had not been altogether unanticipated by Brown. He could now proceed in his own way and select the companies he believed were the most suitable.[28]

Chester Cuthell left Brown with something to think about at the last session of the conference. "What would happen if the Comptroller

General ruled against a particular extension?" Cuthell asked. "What will happen," Cuthell said, answering his own question, "is that the Comptroller General will not pay the bills . . . ." The operators had served notice on Brown that, before going to the expense of buying equipment for a new route, they wanted a Comptroller General ruling on the scope of the Postmaster General's extension powers. Early in July, Brown requested Comptroller General John R. McCarl to rule on extending Northwest Airways' Chicago-Minneapolis route into Winnipeg, effectively doubling the length of the route. The case was purely bogus. The Postmaster General had no desire to run a line between Minneapolis and Winnipeg; he merely wanted a ruling to guide him in developing the two new transcontinental routes. McCarl, a crusty bookkeeper who, in opposing the original Watres Bill, had charged that it would open the door to "fraud, favoritism, waste, and extravagance," was not about to let Brown have his way. Within five days he ruled that extensions of airmail routes must be extensions in fact and not major additions. Brown had suffered another setback. His cherished transcontinental routes would now have to be opened up to competitive bidding. But he could still have his way if he eliminated the competition before the bidding. This he set out to do in systematic fashion.[29]

Brown had determined that the southern transcontinental route should go to American Airways; the central transcontinental, to a new company formed by the merger of Transcontinental Air Transport and Western Air Express. Brown had proposed the merger at the spoils conference, and the principals had agreed, provided they were awarded the route. Western was a profitable, well-managed operation — one of the few airlines to pay a dividend. TAT, an independent that had made a name for itself by hiring Charles Lindbergh and advertising itself as the "Lindbergh Line," had never turned a profit; it was, however an experienced carrier and had the strong financial backing of North American Aviation. Harris M. Hanshue, Western's president, had resisted the merger at first; but when it was made abundantly clear to him that he could either merge or be squeezed out entirely, he capitulated. All three of these lines were the kind of substantial, well-financed companies that Brown preferred.

There was little or no chance that other mail carriers would attempt to bid on these two routes. Though these operators had no formal agreement not to bid against each other, they did have a general understanding. "Everybody knew that my company was going to bid on the southern transcontinental and it was common knowledge amongst all of us that TAT and Western Air would bid on the middle one," stated F. G. Coburn of American Airways. ". . . I did not fear that the United would come down there and bid for the southern transcontinental, because the Postmaster General had said that he wanted the three independents competitive lines." The problem was to keep the small, shoestring operators, or "wildcatters," which in Brown's estimation were incapable of operating these transcontinental routes, from bidding on the contracts. William P. MacCracken came up with a solution. He proposed that the advertisement for bids require all bidders to possess at least six months' experience in operating aircraft on regular night schedules over a route of 250 miles or more. Since only mail carriers had this kind of night flying experience, this requirement would automatically disqualify all independents. Brown inserted this provision into the Post Office's advertisements for the two routes, which appeared on August 2, 1930.[30]

N. A. Letson, president of United States Airways, had attended the spoils conference and had known of the Postmaster General's desire to award the central route to TAT and Western Air. His line ran between Kansas City and Denver, and he had directed much of his energies to acquiring an airmail contract for this route. Brown had promised Letson a contract as early as 1929. When the August advertisements appeared, Letson became disturbed because his own route had not also been advertised. He immediately went to Washington, saw W. Irving Glover, the Second Assistant Postmaster General, and was told that the Kansas City-Denver route was no longer essential to the airway map. Alarmed, Letson sought assistance — the kind of financial assistance required to qualify as a bidder on the central route. "I found a group of men in the East who had been looking for me just as diligently as I was looking for them," Letson related. Letson's new-found allies were two ragtag lines, Pittsburgh Airways and Ohio Air Transport. Despite the fact that none had night flying experience, they resolved to merge and submit a bid for the central route under their new guise, the United Avigation Company.[31]

Meanwhile, the night flying provision had raised more than a few eyebrows. Clyde Kelly publicly announced that the requirement, since it was not set down in the Watres Act, was in violation of the law. Kelly expressed the same sentiments privately to McCarl. Officials in the

Justice Department also had doubts. "If . . . the requirement of 6 months night flying experience in the Postmaster General's advertisement is intended as limiting the bids which he is willing to consider, it seems clearly invalid . . .," said one Justice Department attorney. "In my opinion," said another, ". . . the Postmaster General [does not have the authority] to limit bids to those who have had [night flying experience]."[32]

When the bids were opened, on August 24, United Avigation emerged as the low bidder. Brown disallowed its bid; United Avigation did not meet the night flying requirement. But before the award was formally made to TAT and Western Air, which were still in the process of merging into Transcontinental and Western Air (TWA), a Pittsburgh newspaper carried a story that Letson was preparing to sue the Government. Some Post Office Department officials began to get cold feet. Chase Gove and Earl B. Wadsworth, assistants to Glover and Brown, felt that the Department "should fill out all the bids." Glover shot back: "We had better all stick together, or we will all hang together."[33]

Kelly intruded once again. He urged United Avigation to "fight to the limit to get the low bid . . . to the Comptroller General." Letson and a New York broker who was helping back United Avigation appealed to McCarl. Again the Comptroller General knocked a prop from under Brown. "I feel compelled to state," he informed Brown, "that the stipulation for night flying experience is not supported by law . . . ." Brown had additional props to lean on. He charged that United Avigation lacked the financial resources to undertake the operation of the route and was, therefore, not a responsible bidder. McCarl, when he asked United Avigation to answer this charge, found to his surprise that the company was no longer interested in pursuing the matter. Left only with Brown's representations and findings of fact, McCarl had no choice but to allow the contract to go to TWA.

Months later, on May 29, 1931, McCarl learned the reason for Letson's sudden change of heart. On that day, American Airways sublet to United States Airways an airmail route running from Kansas City to Denver. Brown, using his extension powers, had granted the route to American one day earlier. It was relatively easy to put two and two together. In the midst of the hassle over the night flying provision, Brown got word to Letson that he could have his long-cherished Kansas City-Denver mail route — provided Letson withdrew from the contest over the central transcontinental. Letson agreed, and Brown was as good as his word. But since he could not grant United States Airways a route without competitive bidding, he persuaded American Airways to take the route as an extension and then sublet it to Letson. Letson's pullout rendered United Avigation impotent, too weak to challenge the TWA award.[34]

No interloper appeared in the bidding for the southern route. Brown, however, had to strain to guarantee that American Airways would have no competition. Five lines, in addition to American, were interested in the southern route — Standard, Safeway, Eastern, Delta, and Wedell-Williams. The last mentioned, a small carrier based in New Orleans, had been putting up a losing struggle to enter the airmail business. One of its representatives had crashed the spoils conference, only to be shown the door by MacCracken. When the advertisement for bids appeared with the night flying specification, the company gave up. "That was the joker in the qualification for bidders," remarked one of its former employees. Turning down a takeover bid by American, Wedell-Williams went out of business in 1931. Delta, too, was put off by the night flying provision. In Delta's case, however, the line's investors did not suffer a complete financial drubbing. "Mr. Brown laid down the premise that we had to buy [Delta] out . . .," said Hainer Hinshaw, an American Airways executive. So American absorbed Delta in a cash transaction. Standard Air Lines, which flew between Los Angeles and El Paso, met the same fate. As for Eastern, it served notice that it was not entirely satisfied with the arrangements. The line ran a route between Savannah and Tulsa and felt qualified to bid on the southern route. Brown, according to Hinshaw, told Captain Thomas B. Doe, Eastern's president, that if he bid on the southern route, his own route would belong to American within a year. Doe backed off. This left Safeway to contend with.[35]

Erle Halliburton was nobody's fool. He had money and talent and he knew his way around Washington's power structure. He had attended the spoils conference and had agreed to have the Postmaster General act as route arbiter. No more than a month after the breakup of the conference, however, Halliburton informed MacCracken that, unless his line was immediately awarded an airmail route, he would withdraw his consent to this agreement and demand the privilege of bidding on any route he pleased. Brown knew Halliburton was going to present a problem and tried to eliminate him before putting the southern route up for bids. Some of Safeway's routes ran into the territory of United Air Lines. Brown proposed that United buy Halliburton out and thus eliminate this competitor for its passenger service. United turned the proposition down. In consequence, when the Post Office advertised for bids, Halliburton was still around to ruffle Brown's feathers over the night flying requirement.[36]

Halliburton's lawyers set him on a different course from that followed by United Avigation. They advised him not to bid. His bid would be turned down, which would leave him with only one alternative — lengthy and costly litigation. Instead, he should seek an injunction to stop the bidding. This Halliburton was prepared to do, if necessary. In the meantime, he decided to "just sit tight and not let them know what I intended doing and have them come to me . . . ." The press carried unsubstantiated reports, however, that the Oklahoma entrepreneur was prepared to go to court. Halliburton got his first feeler two days after the advertisements appeared. A Republican national committeeman from Oklahoma, who had a small interest in Safeway, wired Halliburton that "it would be for best interest of you and your associates . . . to work out consolidation with TAT." Halliburton wired back: "I do not intend to merge, or become connected with, or associated with TAT who prostituted names of Lindbergh and Earhart to general public and then asked the taxpayers to pay for such prostitution."

Hainer Hinshaw, given to understand by Brown that the situation had to be cleared up, finally appeared at Halliburton's rooms in the Mayflower Hotel in Washington. The two men worked out the sale of Safeway to American for $1.4 million. At the time, Safeway's total assets consisted of 13 aircraft and a hangar in Tulsa, all of which had an estimated market value of between $700,000 and $800,000. Safeway's name was worth nothing to American, and without a mail contract, nor was its route.

The deal was complex and depended on a number of pieces falling into place. Halliburton and Robertson Aircraft, an American subsidiary, would bid jointly on the southern route. If successful, the two bidders agreed to merge into a new corporation. American had the option of picking up Halliburton's stock in the new company for $1.4 million. Whether this money would be available, however, depended on TWA winning the central route. American Airways owned a large interest in

Western Air Express. Brown had made it clear at the spoils conference that he wanted true competition between the three transcontinental lines. He insisted that American divest itself of its interest in Western. TWA, therefore, agreed to pay American $1,115,500 for its shares in Western Air and, to make an even $1.4 million, $284,500 for Safeway's Tulsa hangar. Everything fell precisely in place, and Brown had his three transcontinental lines.[37]

Brown reshaped the rest of the airway map by using his route-extension powers. In May 1930, at the time of the spoils conference, there were approximately 14,700 miles of airmail routes in the United States. By the end of the Hoover administration, Brown had doubled this mileage. The two new transcontinental routes had accounted for 5,750 miles. The rest — 8,900 miles — Brown added by extensions. The beneficiaries were United (411 miles), American (4,156), North American's twins, TWA and Eastern (2,516), Northwest Airways (1,621), and Pittsburgh Aviation Industries (195). McCarl's ruling in the Winnipeg case had not deterred the determined Postmaster General. Thus, he managed to accomplish his purpose without the powers he sought in the original Watres Bill. "Here was a public official who had a certain idea about how a certain matter should be carried out . . .," Senator Pat McCarran (D-Nev.) said of Brown. "That idea was so impelling that . . . he sought to carry [it out] even in the face of the law as it was written."[38]

V

Brown's vision of a national air passenger system was now a reality. Air carriers reached most of the great population centers of the United States. American, TWA, and United each connected the East and West Coasts. Northwest Airways, which was on its way to becoming a fourth transcontinental line, ran along the nation's northern tier. Eastern Air Transport cut the country transversely along the east coast. United operated two transverse routes, one along the west coast, another from Chicago to Dallas. These lines, though they enjoyed a monopoly in mail carriage on their routes, competed vigorously for passengers and express at important terminals.[39]

Despite the depression, passenger traffic increased significantly. In 1929, domestic airlines carried 160,000 passengers; in 1932, 474,000.

Between 1930 and 1932, the number of passenger-miles flown jumped from 84 million to 127 million. During the same period, scheduled aircraft miles increased from 16.2 million to 34.5 million.[40]

The future promised a continuation of this accelerated growth trend. Just as airlines were beginning to take a keen interest in passenger carriage, aircraft manufacturers were on the verge of making significant improvements in passenger-carrying aircraft. Soon to be on the manufacturers' drawing boards were the B-247 and DC-2 — aircraft that would revolutionize airliner design. Featuring an aluminum-alloy stressed skin, a low cantilever single-wing, retractable undercarriage, variable-pitch propellers, and two engines housed in a NACA cowling and arranged in front of the leading edge of the wings, these aircraft were faster, more commodious, and more profitable to operate than the high-winged trimotors they would soon replace. The modern airliner, as much as the restructured airway map and the built-in incentives of the Watres Act, was responsible for the continued growth in air passenger travel during the first half of the 1930's.[41]

Meanwhile, with airmail operators exchanging their contracts for route certificates, Brown reduced the mail rates paid carriers. In 1929, the average rate per mile had stood at $1.09. Through periodic renegotiation, Brown succeeded in hacking the rate to $0.54, or to half of what it was when he took office.[42]

The Hoover administration was justly proud of Brown's achievements. (Many years later, Hoover would still talk of the nation being rescued from a tangle of ill-conceived airway routes.)[43] At the same time, however, discerning observers suspected that Brown may have paid too high a price — how high had not yet been reckoned — to achieve his ends. That a final reckoning would come was evident from the growing number of questions being asked about the system Brown had created.

With depression upon the land, Congress began focusing on the continuing deficits run up by the airmail service. These deficits, declared Senator Carter Glass (D-Va.), were "a wicked expenditure of the taxpayers' money in these times of dreadful necessity." Though Brown had reduced rates sharply, he had also stimulated traffic, which caused gross payments to carriers to rise yearly. In 1930, carriers collected $14.6 million from the Post Office. Of this amount, $9.3 million was not covered by postal revenues — that is, it represented a subsidy to the carriers. By 1932, this subsidy was running at an annual level of $13.9

million. In February 1933, the House Post Office Committee, now under the control of a Democratic majority, recommended, "in the interests of justice and economy," a complete change in the method of payment to airmail contractors. "Whatever justification there may be for a large subsidy as a means of establishing the new aviation industry," the committee said, "it is time now to look forward to a cessation of such payments and the establishment of the air mail service on a self-sustaining basis." The committee viewed with alarm the rate-making powers vested in the Postmaster General and recommended that they be curbed. A system based on "accepted rate-making principles" and free of political influences was "absolutely essential."[44]

Senator Sam Bratton had been thinking along these lines as early as 1929 and had introduced legislation placing all Federal civil aviation functions, including those performed by the Aeronautics Branch, under the Interstate Commerce Commission. The measure provided for the issuance of certificates of convenience and necessity and the economic regulation of air carriers. All interstate commerce, Bratton declared, "whether it be by rail, express, air, or otherwise," should be under the ICC: "The whole [transportation] industry should be governed as one . . . ." When first introduced, Bratton's bill encountered nearly universal opposition, both within Congress and the aviation industry. At a national air traffic conference in 1929, Erle Halliburton stood virtually alone in support of the measure. He urged the convention to pass a resolution asking Congress to empower the ICC to set both passenger and airmail rates and to require the Post Office to route airmail over any responsible line, just as it did with surface mail. At MacCracken's urging, the convention not only voted Halliburton's proposition down, but also refused to study the question.[45]

But the debate continued outside the airline industry. An aircraft transporting passengers or goods was in the same business as a bus or a railroad. "It is inconceivable that different sets of rules . . . will be set up for the airline . . . merely because a different instrumentality is used in carrying out the purpose of the business," declared Thomas H. Kennedy, a member of the California bar. Yet the Congress had set up different rules for airlines when it declared in the Air Commerce Act that "the Secretary of Commerce shall grant no exclusive right for the use of any civil airway, airport, emergency landing field, or other air navigation facility under his jurisdiction." This was in direct opposition to its policy toward railroads, and the general policy of the states toward transport carriers and utilities. Congress, of course, had its reasons; it wished to give free rein to the development of a new industry. And critics of Bratton's proposal could accurately point out that Congress had initially given the railroads the same free rein and did not step in to regulate them until "pernicious practices made it necessary." As for issuing certificates of convenience and necessity, Congress had not required their possession by interstate railroads until 1920 and had not yet moved to establish the same requirement for interstate motor carriers.[46]

A number of states saw matters differently. Transportation possessed the characteristics of a public utility; that being the case, competition was wasteful and self-defeating. By 1932, 11 states required intrastate air transport lines to possess certificates of convenience and necessity.[47]

By this time, some members of the airline industry were having second thoughts. The Postmaster General's airmail-rate-setting powers constituted a form of regulation. Was it better, some airline executives began asking themselves, to come under the control of a disinterested independent commission that set rates under established standards of fairness and reasonableness, or under the control of one man acting arbitrarily? Brown's rate-cutting over the past two years had led to such questions. The scramble for passengers posed still more. During one summer, for example, no fewer than five passenger-carrying lines flew between Los Angeles and San Francisco. Competition drove down the one-way fare between these two points from $50 to $22. Of the five carriers, one was an established airmail operator; the rest were upstarts. No wonder that, in March 1932, Paul Henderson advocated Federal regulation of routes and fares in order to protect United's routes from intruders. There were now like-minded men in the airline industry. "They see a measure of protection in [ICC regulation], a measure of control whereby, through certificates of convenience and necessity, they may have assurance against infringements by other operators on territory that their lines serve," observed the *New York Times*.[48]

Even the Air Line Pilots Association believed that cutthroat competition had no place in the industry. In June 1932, David L. Behncke, the president of ALPA, wrote Clarence Young:

> It seems that Braniff Airways charges $49.00 and some odd cents
> to fly a passenger from Dallas to Chicago. United Air Lines

charges $54.00. Braniff no doubt has inferior equipment and
pays its pilots $200.00 a month . . . . United pays from $500.00
to $700.00 a month and tries to do the right thing.

Yet, when a passenger comes into the passenger station at
Dallas, he is confronted with the price of $54.00 to go by way of
United while immediately opposite huge Neon signs inform him
he can go by Braniff for $49.00. To the average air traveller,
United and Braniff are about the same, merely two air lines.

This is a good example of how interstate commerce control
is constantly forced to the front.[49]

"There is going to come a time, and I do not think it is far off, when rates
and revenues established by the various lines will have to be regulated,"
Behncke said in another letter to Young. "It may be said confidently,"
asserted Thomas Kennedy, "that the public interest demands [economic]
regulation of air transportation seeking to eliminate wasteful competition." Two young Illinois lawyers, Fred D. Fagg, Jr.,and Abraham
Fishman, after reviewing the question of certificates of convenience and
necessity for air transport, concluded that Federal economic regulation
of the industry was a certainty. The only thing in doubt was precisely
when such control would come.[50]

Other matters were also coming under attack. "Within the past four
months," noted *Aviation* in December 1931, "two of the greatest
newspaper chains have independently waged campaigns of a similar
order, each in a series of articles designed to prove undue concentration
of contract awards and the existence of a sinister octopus in the air
transport field . . . ." In *Aviation's* opinion, the airmail route awards
made under the Watres Act constituted "a frank subvention to a limited
group of companies." That route awards went to a limited number of
operators there was no denying. Four operators — TWA, United,
American, and Eastern — all of which were controlled by giant holding
companies — carried 89 percent of the airmail. Only six other operators
carried mail. The independents were as desperate as ever; indeed, they
were beating a trail to the bankruptcy courts.[51]

Independents that were still in business in 1931 and 1932 tried
desperately to get their case before the public and the Congress. Alfred
Anderson, president of Continental Airways, informed Secretary of
Commerce Robert P. Lamont that his line stood ready "to submit a bid
to carry air mail between any points throughout the United States" at
half the prevailing average rate. "We believe present conditions warrant
Congress making a change in the law so that there can be re-letting of air

mail contracts and thereby bring about a large savings to the government
. . . ," Anderson said. Eugene Vidal, an executive with the Ludington
Lines, which ran an hourly shuttle between New York and Washington,
relentlessly sought an airmail contract, and untiringly issued public
complaints when he failed. "For your information," Brown wrote to the
president of Eastern Air Transport, "I have another letter from Mr.
Vidal . . . protesting against the extension of your service to Atlantic
City and again offering to carry the air mail from New York to
Richmond at a saving of a thousand dollars a day over the compensation
paid to Eastern . . . ." Ludington was no ordinary interloper. When the
line inaugurated its shuttle, *Aviation* hailed the event as "one of the
boldest recent developments in the entire field of transportation." The
line, moreover, was making a profit — demonstrating that it had the skill
and wherewithal to run an efficient operation. The press reported the
Ludington-Brown feud in detail, a fact that would later lead to some
interesting developments.[52]

In July 1931, when the Post Office Department announced 16
contract extensions, none of which went to independents, "dissatisfaction [among independents] broke out into organized protest . . .,"
Aviation reported. Disgruntled passenger carriers founded the Independent Air Passenger Association, an organization with the express goal of
throwing open all new airmail routes to competitive bidding. Meanwhile,
Clyde Kelly threatened to open a congressional investigation into the
Post Office's handling of contracts under the Watres Act. Congressman
Mead did get an investigation going. Struck by the heavy concentration
of aviation activity in a few large combines, Mead's committee sounded a
warning to these companies: "Interlocking financial interests and di-
rectorates between air mail operating lines and between such lines and
manufacturers of aircraft, aircraft motors, and accessories should be
prohibited so long as such air mail operating lines are supported by a
Federal subsidy."[53]

Through all this, Walter Brown was unperturbed. He expected the
independents to die a swift death. Those that did not die would be bought
out by their large competitors, as Ludington was by Eastern in March
1933. With these interlopers gone, the whole matter would blow over.
Brown was only half right. As expected, the majority of independents
failed to survive; the issue, however, would not go away. Paul Henderson, apprehensive about the growing number of complaints going to

Congress over Brown's wholesale use of his extension powers, sought John McCarl's counsel. The Comptroller General ventured a prediction. Long before United Air Line's route certificates had expired, he said, United would not be carrying any mail.[54]

III

The New Deal

1933–1938

9. Of Hope and Disenchantment

Political forecasters had an easy time of it in 1932. After 12 years of Republican rule, the country had gone to pot, and it was a dead certainty that the Democratic Party would sweep the election in November and place one of its own in the White House. When Herbert Hoover was inaugurated, in 1929, the United States was enjoying its greatest period of prosperity. For many people, the American economic dream was about to be realized; the United States appeared to be on the verge of reaching a permanent plateau of economic plenty. Then things went awry. In October 1929, prices on the New York Stock Exchange collapsed; after that, with only a rise here and there to engender false hope, it was all down hill for the American economy. In three years the country had gone, in Dixon Wecter's phrase, "From Riches to Rags."

The gross national product, which had stood at $103.1 billion in 1929, dropped to $58 billion in 1932, declining at an annual rate of 10.8 percent. During the same period, annual disposable per capita income sank from $683 to $390; the aggregate value of U.S. farm products was sliced in half; new investment dwindled from an annual rate of $7.8 billion to a mere $100 million.

Every segment of the economy was affected. The nation's steel plants operated at 12 percent of capacity. In three years, close to 86,000 businesses failed; more than 5,000 banks suspended operations, nearly equaling the total of the entire decade of the twenties, and wiping out in the process some 9 million savings accounts. Farms were being fore-closed at a rate of 20,000 per month. Investors and speculators alike took an unmerciful pounding. In all, some $74 billion went down the drain as New York Stock Exchange securities lost 89 percent of their 1929 value.*

---

*General Motors plunged from a bull market high of 72 3/4 to 7 5/8; Montgomery Ward, from 138 to 4; Radio Corporation of America, from 101 to 2 1/2; AT & T, from 304 to 72; U.S. Steel, from 261 3/4 to 21 1/4.

As might be expected, the suicide rate per 100,000 of population shot up dramatically — from 12.8 in 1926 (the peak year of Republican-era prosperity) to 17.4 in 1932.

The price of everything dropped precipitously. The wholesale price index dipped from 49.1 in 1929 to 33.6 in 1932; the index for industrial commodities, from 48.6 to 37.3; the index for farm products, from 64.1 to 29.5. Eggs in Chicago had commanded a wholesale price of 35 cents a dozen in 1929; they went for 15 cents in 1932. The wholesale price for butter in New York City stood at 45 cents a pound in 1929; it fell to 21 cents. During the 1932 harvest, farmers did well to sell their corn for 23 cents a bushel or their wheat for 53 cents. Agricultural prices had been depressed throughout the 1920's; nevertheless, they fell further and faster than the average price of all goods. The general indexes, moreover, gave scarcely a hint of the depth of the depression in some localities. In Wisconsin, farmers sold their milk for less than 2 cents a quart; in Oklahoma, their eggs for 5 cents a dozen. Some farmers, rather than accept such ruinous prices, which represented only a fraction of the cost of producing their products, set fire to their fields, left their fruit to rot on trees, or slit the throats of their livestock and dumped them into canyons.

If the product of man's labor went for virtually nothing, so did the labor that produced it. The average annual wage (after deducting for periods of unemployment) in 1929 was $1,356; in 1932, this figure dropped to $754. The average farm laborer — always among the lowest paid in the American economy — saw his monthly wages drop from $49 in 1929 to just under $27 in 1932. But it was a fortunate man who drew wages of any sort. Beginning with 1,550,000 unemployed in 1929 (or 3.2 percent of the work force), the nation saw its unemployment rolls skyrocket to 12,060,000 (or 23.6 percent) in 1932 — and these rolls would get longer still.

Every city in the United States had its soup kitchens, where hungry men and women queued up for a daily handout. A million or more men took to the road, jumping aboard gondolas or cattle cars, in a bootless search for employment. When they tired of their fruitless quest, they pitched shacks of tar paper and scrap metal on the outskirts of town and dug in for the long haul. Hundreds of these makeshift communities — soon to be dubbed Hoovervilles — sprouted like weeds over the American urban landscape.

There was irony in all this. No war or plague or natural disaster had hit the United States. Its industrial plant was modern, efficient, and intact; its people were industrious and eager for work; its lands were fertile and its crops abundant. As Franklin Roosevelt said in his inaugural, "Plenty is at our doorstep, but a generous use of it languishes in the very sight of the supply." The economic system had simply gone askew, and try what it might, the Hoover administration could not right it.

But there was more to this frightening experience than dormant factories, rotting crops, and woeful want. The Great Depression had affected the American psyche. As the weeks stretched into months and the months into years, Americans seemed to lose confidence in their ability to recover. Economic depression bred a deep emotional despondency, accompanied by pessimism and fear — even terror. If the underlying crisis was economic, the immediate crisis was a crisis of morale. And if the causes of the economic collapse were complex, the causes of the collapse of morale were simpler; they could be traced directly to the occupant of the White House. Herbert Hoover, an intelligent, compassionate, and, in many ways, an able man, was nevertheless out of his depth. The nation needed inspired leadership to pull it out of its mental depression, and Hoover was not equipped by temperament to provide it. Indeed, his temperament seemed to exacerbate the nation's anguish. Hoover, said William Allen White, was "constitutionally gloomy, a congenital pessimist who always saw the doleful side of any situation." Henry L. Stimson, Hoover's Secretary of State, likened being in a room with the President to "sitting in a bath of ink." Hoover's gloom rubbed off on the American people.

Roosevelt prepared for his inaugural at the most critical point of the depression; the nation's entire banking system, stunned by a run on deposits of unprecedented proportions, was about to go under. More ominously, violence flared among the deprived and discontented — violence that seemed to lend plausibility to ugly talk of revolution. What followed is a familiar enough story: Roosevelt's sober, but dramatic, inaugural address; the bank holiday; the reassuring fireside chat announcing the reopening of banks; the whirlwind special session of Congress, during which Roosevelt secured 15 pieces of legislation in an electrifying "Hundred Days." The legislation itself was a hastily improvised jumble of deflationary and inflationary measures, much of it working at cross-purposes. But no matter; substance was of secondary importance. Far more important than what Roosevelt and his New Dealers did was that they were doing something and that they conveyed a firm determination to do more. They had given the country a sense of movement; this, combined with Roosevelt's contagious, cheery self-assurance, lifted the nation's spirits. The crisis of morale was over. Charles Edison, president of Thomas A. Edison, Inc., posted a notice on his company's walls: "This old world is starting to move." Roosevelt, a cripple confined to a wheelchair after a bout with polio, had, as one of his contemporaries put it, taught a generation of Americans to walk.

But if the nation's spirits had been lifted, its economy had not; it would remain more or less depressed for a long time to come. Hence, perforce, economic issues — the trilogy of relief, recovery, and reform — would absorb most of the energy of the President and his administration. In the coming four years, Roosevelt took little time to deal directly with subsidiary matters — aviation policy among them — unless they were thrust before him by events.[1]

II

The Great Depression did not affect all segments of aviation activity alike. Manufacturers of aeronautical goods were hardest hit. Civil aircraft production dropped from 5,414 units in 1929 to a mere 896 in 1932; the total value of all aeronautical products produced, from $91 million to $34.8 million. General aviation activity was hard hit. Total aircraft-hours flown sank to 69 percent of their 1929 level; total aircraft-miles flown, to 71 percent. Not until 1938 would general aviation again attain its 1929 level of activity. With everyone's pocketbook pinched, the number of student pilot certificates issued by the Aeronautics Branch declined markedly, from 20,400 in 1929 to 11,325 in 1932 — all of which put flying school operators under a severe strain.[2]

Air carrier operations were another story; they bucked the trend. "Strangely enough," Clarence Young told a congressional committee in December 1930, "[the depression] has not been felt [by] the air transport [industry]." Nearly three years later, General Hugh S. Johnson, the head of the National Recovery Administration, reported to Roosevelt that air transport "represents an exception in the present depression in that it has added to its personnel and expanded steadily from year to year." Starting from virtually nothing in 1929, passenger-miles flown increased to 85,125,000 in 1930 and jumped to 127,433,000 two years later; over the same period, the number of passengers carried tripled. Revenues earned in mail carriage nearly doubled. While other industries were letting off employees, scheduled domestic and international air carriers increased their work force by 254 percent in three years. "Air transport has won fame as a depression-proof industry," *Aviation* observed with satisfaction in March 1931. "Of how many other industries can that be said?" asked the same journal 17 months later, after noting that air transport companies were enjoying another record year.[3]

Had Clarence Young, or anyone else, thought about it, he would not have found the performance of the air carriers so surprising. Their main source of revenue was the mail, and the Post Office, thanks to Congress, had plenty of funds to dispense. The Watres Act had been designed to stimulate air passenger traffic, and it was working. Moreover, with air fares becoming competitive with Pullman fares, an increasing number of people were finding the airplane a convenient way to travel. But to put all this in perspective, it should again be emphasized that air passenger traffic began from a very low base. And while 1932 was a banner year for air carriers, fewer than half a million passengers were transported during the entire year. Air transport was still for the affluent, or what remained of them.

The ability of the air transport industry to grow and prosper during the depression was a tribute to Hoover and Walter Folger Brown. They had built the industry from scratch, and, from all indications, they had built well. Nevertheless, there was a growing disaffection among established mail carriers with Republican policy. Brown's high-handedness in awarding routes did not sit well with all industry members. The Postmaster General's vast power was a cause for considerable concern; the industry could never feel secure as long as one man had such enormous control over its destiny.

In 1932, Brown and the mail operators came close to an open break. In that year, with the airmail continuing to run up large deficits for the Post Office, airmail postage was increased from 5 to 8 cents. Realizing that this increase would adversely affect their volume, the operators protested, though only mildly; they could never afford to forget that the Postmaster General had the power to reduce their rate of compensation. The operators eventually countered with what they believed was a reasonable proposal to increase both their and the Government's airmail revenues. They proposed introducing an air lettergram — a single lightweight sheet that folded into an envelope and sold for 3 cents. Brown rejected the idea. The 3-cent lettergram would have cut heavily into surface mail, and Brown, according to Eddie Rickenbacker, did not wish to antagonize the railroads. The airmail operators took this disappointment with bitterness and looked forward to Roosevelt's inauguration. Indeed, they appeared to take an immediate liking to the new administration.[4]

Particularly to those on the operating side of aviation, New Dealers appeared to be more airminded than their predecessors. The Republicans, after all, had left the Air Corps to muddle through with second-rate equipment. And where within the Republican administration (with the singular exception of the Aeronautics Branch) was to be found a cabinet or subcabinet official who was of the civil aviation community, who was really one of them? Hoover, for example, had never been aboard an airplane. Brown flew occasionally; the rest of the Cabinet, rarely if ever. New Dealers, on the other hand, took to the air readily. The President's official family was loaded with veteran air travelers. The airways leading into Washington, observed one scribe, "were black with . . . briefcases." Then there was the President's wife, who used air transport as a matter of course, and his son, Elliott, who was a licensed pilot and a genuine aviation enthusiast. All this appeared to bode well for the future. "In the industry's struggle of recent years," said Frank A. Tichenor in *Aero Digest,* "not the least formidable of the obstacles in the path to progress was the necessity of dealing individually and in the mass with a great many people who had never flown . . . ."[5]

The new administration appeared to be made up of a different breed of men, particularly the men immediately around the President — the "Brain Trust" — and the people on the subcabinet level. They reflected an image that was more in keeping with aviation's own. Younger and more vigorous than their predecessors, New Dealers were also progressive and thoroughly modern. This was precisely the kind of image that aviation itself wished to project. To many in the aeronautical industry, according to one observer, aviation "stood to older and more commonplace transportation somewhat as the [New Deal] brain trust stood to [the old-line] politics . . . ."[6]

It was around the President himself, however, that the industry's enthusiasm for the new administration was centered. Roosevelt's precedent-shattering flight from Albany to Chicago in June 1932 to deliver his acceptance speech before the National Democratic Convention was the kind of dramatic gesture that endeared him to the aviation community and made him appear airminded. Roosevelt was the first Presidential candidate to fly and would become the first President to fly while holding office. (Theodore Roosevelt once took a short spin around an airport, but only after being out of office two years.) "The aviation industry is proud, Mr. President, in the knowledge that in you America has achieved its first flying Chief Executive," Frank Tichenor enthusiastically declared in an open letter to Roosevelt. Edward P. Warner, editor of *Aviation,* also made over Roosevelt's inclination to use whatever transportation mode suited his need. "You enter the White House as the first American president ever to have flown either prior to or during his term in office," Warner remarked. "We need not extol the utility of aviation to you. You know. You have seen for yourself." Tichenor, Warner, and others fondly recalled Roosevelt's strong advocacy of naval air power as Assistant Secretary of the Navy in the Wilson administration and proclaimed the new President, with some exaggeration, "a charter member of the group of those who have contributed 'firsts' to aviation history." There was, then, a clear and general expectation among the established air transport industry that Roosevelt's election meant a new deal for aviation.[7]

So much for first impressions. A great deal of this was mere illusion — the illusion created by an attractive, energetic leader promising new and better things to an action-starved nation. The New Deal was no more airminded in 1933 than the previous administration. Indeed, Roosevelt had not directly addressed himself to aviation problems throughout his Presidential campaign. Industry spokesmen were correct, however, when they concluded, as did Edward P. Warner, that "great events impend in Washington. With the change of administration, a fundamental change in air mail policy has become inevitable." But this change would be the product not so much of deliberate intent as the force of unexpected events.

This is not to say that Roosevelt did not have an aviation policy, vague though it might have been at this early stage. His policy, however, could not be discerned directly; one had to read between the lines. It seemed clear that Roosevelt, unlike his predecessor, preferred to think of aviation in a broad context — that is, as an integral part of a complex national transportation system. A campaign speech on railway policy delivered in Salt Lake City gave some clues to his thinking. In this address, Roosevelt declared his intention to coordinate "all carrier service in a great national transport policy . . . ." He made it clear, at the same time, that he did not favor unbridled competition. "We have not only permitted but frequently required [railroads] to compete unnecessarily with each other," he said. Each railroad, he continued, "should have a recognized field of operation and a definite part to play in the entire national scheme of transportation." Roosevelt was addressing himself directly to railroads, but his views applied equally to other interstate transport modes. "I advocate," he said, expanding the focus of his speech, "the regulation by the Interstate Commerce Commission of competing motor carriers."

Once in office Roosevelt acted quickly to formulate a national transportation policy. In May 1933, he sent Congress a message declaring that "our problem is so to coordinate all agencies of transportation as to maintain adequate service." Not yet ready to submit a comprehensive plan for permanent legislation, he asked the Congress, as a temporary measure, to create a Federal Coordinator of Transportation. Congress responded the following month by passing a measure establishing such a coordinator, who, among other things, was charged with providing "for the immediate study of . . . means of improving conditions surrounding transportation in all its forms . . . ." Roosevelt was indeed planning changes. But what ensued was neither in line with his original plans nor with the optimistic expectations of the air carriers. Events, not policies, would be the prime movers in civil aviation affairs for years to come.[8]

III

Politics, too, had their influence. Unfortunately, it was not the adept politics for which Franklin Roosevelt came to be noted. The President blundered both in the choice of men to run the administration's civil aviation interests and in the manner in which he chose them. Things were botched so badly that no explanation or series of explanations offers a very plausible theory for what he did. The most generous thing that can be said of his actions is that he was so engrossed in other matters that he had no time to attend to aviation affairs.

Roosevelt's appointment of Daniel C. Roper as Secretary of Commerce was acceptable to the aviation community, as it was to other business interests. Not that Roper had a consuming interest in aviation, or for that matter any experience; but the views and associations of this old-line Wilsonian made him a welcome choice to businessmen. The choice of a replacement for Clarence Young was another matter. Perhaps out of political naivete many people in the aviation community clung to the hope that Young would be retained by the new administration. Young, true enough, was a Republican, but he had never been politically active; besides, presiding over the Aeronautics Branch was the job of a technician. Why, ran this sentiment, replace a technician who was doing a good job and had never meddled in politics? Of course, Roosevelt could be excused for seeing matters differently. He had no intention of retaining Presidential appointees from the previous administration without compelling reason. As it was, any number of deserving Democrats could fill Young's shoes.[9]

Young would go; but, more importantly, so would the position of Assistant Secretary for Aeronautics. Shortly after taking office, Roper appointed a committee to study the organizational structure of the Department. This committee recommended, among other things, the restructuring of the responsibilities of the Assistant Secretaries. There were only two Assistant Secretaries in the Department; one had cognizance over aviation, the other over all other forms of transportation and all other activities of the Department. The committee believed that transportation matters "could be better coordinated and at the same time handled more expeditiously" if they came under the cognizance of a single Assistant Secretary. Roper liked the idea and sent it on to the President for approval. There was little question that the recommendation would appeal to Roosevelt. The existing setup concentrated disproportionately on aviation affairs; it was a good bet, therefore, that Roosevelt would see this imbalance working at cross-purposes with his intention to institute a coordinated transportation policy. Thus, using his reorganization powers, he issued an Executive order in June 1933 abolishing the position of Assistant Secretary for Aeronautics and creating in its place an Assistant Secretary for Transportation, with oversight over all transportation matters in the Department of Commerce. This structural shuffle did not sit well with the industry. As *U.S. Air Services* expressed the matter, "No man is expected to perform the impossible, and it would seem humanly impossible for any one man to take care of all of the other transportation agencies under the new arrangement, and give to aeronautics the individual and undivided effort that has brought American aviation to the point it holds today." What really hurt was that the aviation function had been downgraded in status, and that the Aeronautics Branch now had an additional echelon to hurdle to get to the Secretary of Commerce.[10]

Had Roosevelt filled the new transportation post with someone from the aviation community he would have gone a long way toward dispelling the industry's misgivings. Instead, he reached down and picked an obscure Missouri lawyer, one Ewing Y. Mitchell, for the job. Mitchell had no administrative experience and no discernible previous interest in either aviation or transportation in general. (Mitchell, said MacCracken, "had no more interest in aviation than he had in Sanskrit, and he knew less about it.") As a matter of fact, he did not even want the job; he hankered instead for a diplomatic portfolio. To his credit, when approached by Roper, Mitchell told the Secretary that he had "scant qualifications" for the post; Roper persisted, however, and Mitchell, probably assuming that it was useless to hold out for the job he really wanted, gave in. He would prove a misfit in the Department of Commerce.[11]

When Clarence Young succeeded MacCracken as Assistant Secretary of Commerce, he abolished the position of Director of Aeronautics, which he had vacated, preferring to direct the Branch himself. But now, with the position of Assistant Secretary for Aeronautics itself abolished, the Department was forced to reactivate the position of Director, which now became the highest civil aviation post in the Federal Government and encompassed many of the line responsibilities previously exercised by the Assistant Secretary.

To say that there was a mad scramble for this job among aviation experts of Democratic persuasion would be an understatement. By May, no fewer than 43 people, each backed by his various supporters within the Democratic Party, had made a bid for the post. Of these, no more than half a dozen were serious contenders: Eugene L. Vidal, James C. Edgerton, J. Carroll Cone, Rex Martin, John H. Geisse, and George Nalle. All had substantial political backing. Vidal, a former airline executive, was the son-in-law of Senator Thomas P. Gore, a blind Populist-turned-Democrat from Oklahoma. Edgerton, who, in 1918, had flown one of the legs of the inaugural run of the U.S. airmail, was backed by Senator William G. McAdoo (D-Calif.), the former Secretary of the Treasury under Wilson. Martin, who had written a book on aviation, hailed from Illinois and, naturally enough, had the support of the most important Illinoisan in the Congress, Speaker of the House Henry T. Rainey. He also had the endorsement of Congressman Kent E. Keller; orphaned early in life, Martin had been virtually adopted by Keller and eventually given employment on the Congressman's staff. Geisse was the nephew of Senator Thomas T. Walsh. The Montana Democrat had himself been slated for a Cabinet post; however, he died two days prior to Roosevelt's inauguration — but not before pushing his nephew's candidacy. "The Senator was very much interested in this young man and considered him unusually qualified for the air service," Roper wrote. "John Walsh, the Senator's brother, and Mrs. Gudger, the Senator's daughter, are urging that Mr. Geisse be appointed Director . . . ." Walsh's death undoubtedly weakened Geisse's candidacy. Cone, a state aviation official from Arkansas and veteran Army aviator, appeared to have more political clout — the support of Joe Robinson, the Senate Democratic leader ("Robinson . . . is very much interested in his appointment," Roper noted). Finally, the Vice President, John Nance Garner, put in a good word for his candidate, George Nalle.[12]

Their maneuvering for office notwithstanding, these men were not political hacks. None of them, with the exception of Cone, had been involved in local or state politics; all had experience in aviation and all happened to be young, talented, and on the make. They just happened to have on top of all this good political connections — connections, as MacCracken remarked, that were good enough "for a Cabinet post, much less a 'baby' Cabinet position."[13]

Confronted by these contenders and their supporters, Roper was at a loss for what to do. It was, he wrote, "one of the most difficult appointment situations with which I have to deal . . . ." All appeared qualified. But were he to choose from among them he would make a dozen enemies and one ingrate. He decided to pass the buck. "Under the circumstances," he wrote in a memorandum for the record in May 1933, "I would like to have the President designate his own choice from this group . . ., or, if he pleases, find someone outside of the group and I will then endeavor to take care of the remainder of the gentlemen in some connection with the air transportation."[14]

Roosevelt, for reasons known only to himself, decided to postpone a decision. (It is doubtful that the President, like his Secretary of Commerce, had no stomach for this sort of thing.) Thus, on the same day that he named Mitchell Assistant Secretary for Transportation, he appointed Cone Chief of the Aeronautical Development Division, Vidal Chief of the Air Regulation Division, Martin Chief of the Airways Division, and Edgerton executive assistant to Mitchell. Geisse was eventually placed in an inferior post. No one was named Director.[15]

Leaving the top position open was widely interpreted as an open invitation to the three major contenders — Cone, Vidal, and Martin — "to compete with each other for the position . . . ." The contenders got the same impression; thus, the race for favor was on between these three men. It was not the healthiest form of competition. "Unquestionably," observed a Department of Commerce official who had witnessed the jockeying for position from a ringside seat, "the candidates were not satisfied with making a good record for themselves in their assigned capacity, but endeavored to disparage their competition by interfering in matters outside their own assigned jurisdiction." All seemed to be full of suggestions on how to improve the others' operations. At the same time, they neglected their own responsibilities. "[None] felt like setting out to make a careful investigation of the functioning of their particular divisions, fearing something which might place them at a disadvantage might occur in Washington while they were out of town." Allowing matters to drift in the field and meddling across jurisdictional lines had, according to the same official, "a very damaging result on the efficacy of the [Aeronautics Branch]." Vidal himself understated the case years later when he said, "We had a rather unpleasant time all summer . . . ." On top of all this, with no director and with Mitchell ill-equipped to exercise administrative control, the Aeronautics Branch found itself rudderless. A feuding triumvirate could scarcely exercise leadership. "It was a ruinous, nightmarish situation," MacCracken declared.[16]

The suspense was finally broken in September, when Roper announced that Vidal had been selected to head the Aeronautics Branch. Vidal probably had had the inside track all along. He was a friend of one of the President's sons, Elliott, and a close acquaintance of Amelia Earhart, who was a particular favorite of Mrs. Roosevelt. It appears that both Elliott Roosevelt and Miss Earhart played key roles in tilting the balance in Vidal's favor. Elliott, for example, invited Vidal to Warm Springs to meet his father. None of the other contenders had entree to the President. Nor, it is fair to say, did they possess Vidal's credentials.[17]

The 38-year-old Vidal had come a long way from the South Dakota farming town of his birth. A small man, but possessing the lean,

Eugene L. Vidal flanked by Franklin D. Roosevelt and Secretary of Agriculture Henry A. Wallace, Warm Springs, Ga., 1933

muscular body of an athlete, he had gone to the University of South Dakota on an athletic scholarship. By the time he graduated in 1916 with a degree in civil engineering he had given the university its money's worth; he earned letters in football, baseball, basketball, and track. But he was not the usual college athlete; he also earned the distinction of finishing at the head of his class. In the fall of 1916, he entered West Point and stood out once again on the athletic field and in the classroom before graduating two years later. There followed eight years of Army service that was divided between athletic and aviation activities. Shortly after securing his wings, he was assigned to West Point as an instructor — the first airman to serve in that capacity at that institution. He spent the rest of his Army service at the Military Academy — teaching, placing second in the pentathlon competition in the 1920 Olympic Games at Antwerp, coaching the American pentathlon entries in the 1924 Olympics, and serving as a volunteer backfield coach for the Cadets. In 1922, he married Nina Gore in a ceremony, according to the *Washington Post,* "attended by most of official and social Washington."

He left West Point and the Army in 1926 to pursue a career in civil aviation. Four years later Vidal came to the attention of the aviation community when, as general manager of the Ludington Lines, he inaugurated an every-hour-on-the-hour air shuttle between New York and Washington, an event termed at the time as "one of the boldest recent developments in the entire field of aviation." In the process, he gave Postmaster General Brown some pause with his persistent, though unsuccessful, badgering for airmail contracts and his well-publicized statements that Ludington could carry the mail for a fraction of the cost then being incurred by the Post Office. Ludington, though it made a profit at first, could not survive the competition of its mail-rich rivals and was ultimately absorbed by Eastern Air Transport. Vidal, however, by trying to disrupt Brown's cozy system, had earned the emnity of the mail operators. Now this same man — an independent upstart — was in the saddle at the Aeronautics Branch. This was something for the operators to ponder. Was there symbolism here? Was Roosevelt trying to tell them something? Was this a signal for the independents to take heart and the established operators to run for cover? Only time would tell.[18]

Meanwhile, the operators could look with some annoyance at the goings-on within the Aeronautics Branch. Vidal's appointment did nothing to improve relations between the triumvirate; indeed, in some respects, it strained matters further. Roper may have anticipated that Cone and Martin would not take their loss gracefully; thus, perhaps as a way of easing the blow, he elevated the two men from division chiefs to assistant directors. Cone was given cognizance over air regulation; Martin, over airway development and maintenance. This was a mistake. Raising the status of these two men tended to perpetuate the impression that the triumvirate, though somewhat altered, would continue — all of which helped diminish Vidal's authority. To make matters worse, it failed to assuage the losers. "The knives were drawn from the beginning," Edward P. Warner noted, "and even after the directorship was filled, ancient rivalries could not be forgotten . . . ." The bureaucratic jockeying continued. Cone, for example, tried to get the Branch's aircraft fleet transferred from Martin's control to his. Martin returned the favor by attempting to have Cone's position abolished. The friction between these men often took the form of petty sniping — trying to palm off undesirable employees on one another or embarrassing each other at conferences. Cone, on balance, was more of a problem than Martin, for neither he nor his more ardent supporters really reconciled themselves to Vidal's appointment. Whenever the going got tough for the Aeronautics Branch, Cone's supporters in the press made pests of themselves calling for Vidal's resignation. Cone, moreover, was quicker than Martin to dispute Vidal's authority, to question his judgment, or to appeal over his head. Roper tried at one point to ease Cone out of the Aeronautics Branch by offering to appoint him Commissioner of Lighthouses. The Arkansan did not take the bait. So the disputatious Cone and Martin remained to hang like a millstone around Vidal's neck. Vidal, observed *U.S. Air Services,* had two assistants, "but damn little assistance."[19]

Matters might have worked out better if Ewing Y. Mitchell had been an effective administrator. Mitchell administered nothing and meddled in everything. No trifle escaped his attention. Personnel appointments on all levels, the use of Government aircraft, the spending of public funds on seeming frills ("The wanton waste of public funds indulged by my immediate predecessor, Colonel Clarence Young, . . . is appalling"), the acceptance of gratuities by Department officials — these were the things that occupied his time. He twisted Roosevelt's inaugural statement that the "money changers have fled from their high seats in the temple of our civilization" to mean that "the money changers were to be driven from the temple" — and, in his own way, attempted to do just that, but apparently with little success. "Almost from the beginning of my term of office . . .," he complained to Roosevelt, "I was met with the active hostility of the entrenched special interests, who fattened at the public crib during the past Administrations and who have marked me for slaughter because I have consistently opposed their efforts to continue their predatory tactics under your Administration." He possessed the mind and temperament of an inspector general, not of a policymaking official. Policy matters either went by the board or were left to be wrestled with by Vidal. As a result, something of a power vacuum formed at the top, into which stepped the Secretary's administrative assistant, Malcolm Kerlin, an old-line Department official who had served in the same capacity under the Hoover administration. Kerlin, a skilled bureaucratic infighter, quickly established his authority over budgetary matters. This, needless to say, gave him a great deal of leverage. Mitchell, in sizing up Vidal, said that his "greatest weakness was the frequent surrender of his well-conceived plans to the dictation of Mr. Kerlin and others." The fact was, however, that with a weak Assistant Secretary, Vidal could do little to protect the Aeronautics Branch's flanks — a weakness that was exploited by other bureaus during the annual struggle for funds.[20]

Mitchell had the old-fashioned idea that the spoils belonged to the victor. "I have repeatedly urged Secretary Roper, orally and by written memorandum, to appoint some New Dealers to key positions in those Bureaus [that come under my jurisdiction]," he wrote to the President, "but up to date . . . not one single member of our party has been appointed to a key position [except in the Aeronautics Branch]." Why the Aeronautics Branch proved an exception is difficult to say; but it was certainly true that Mitchell and others of similar persuasion had been eminently successful in staffing its ranks with members "of our party." With only one exception, all division chiefs that had served under Young were swept away. A number of section chiefs met the same fate. Prominent casualties were Gilbert Budwig, long-time chief of the Air Regulations Division, F. G. Hingsburg, the man who had supervised the construction of the first Department of Commerce airways (though it should be stated that he would have been removed eventually for personal indiscretions), Harry H. Blee, Chief of the Development Section, and Stanley Crosthwait, Chief of the Administrative Division. Even the rolls of aviation medical examiners were tampered with. "Mr. Mitchell's assumption that the recommendation of a national Democratic committeeman was the prime requisite for qualification as a medical examiner . . . would have wreaked havoc if it had been enforced," related Dr. Wade Hampton Miller, who survived Mitchell's purge. "I owe my remaining with the Department of Commerce to the fact that my name is an indication of my politics."[21]

This minipurge of aviation officials added another distressing element to the Aeronautics Branch's picture. "From various quarters disturbing reports and rumors are reaching us to the effect that the Aeronautics Branch . . . is showing the evil results of too much politics," noted *U.S. Air Services* in September 1933. "No one at this date imagines that the spoils system can be eliminated from American politics," wrote Frank Tichenor that same month. It had seemed logical to him, however, that the Aeronautics Branch would not be tampered with because "the work of guaranteeing government safety and control to civilian aeronautics was a technical job for scientifically trained men . . . ." Hence, Tichenor found it "shocking to see the speed with which positions in the Aeronautics Branch have been used for political patronage . . . ." Yet Tichenor had to admit that the new men were capable. Referring to Vidal, Martin, and Cone, he said: "Their records as competent workers in the field of aviation cannot be questioned . . . ." He could have added that such New Deal recruits as Denis Mulligan, a talented young attorney, R. W. ("Shorty") Schroeder, who had spent his life in aviation, and John Geisse were at least as gifted as the people that departed. Doubts persisted, nevertheless, and the Department was forced into the position of having to defend its actions. "I can assure you," Roper wrote to the president of the California chapter of the National Aeronautic Association, "that the men now occupying the administrative positions in the Aeronautics Branch have had long and varied experience in aviation activities and are fully and well qualified to hold these positions, and I feel sure that when you are fully informed as to what has been done by these men, you will realize that such reference as you have made to 'political patronage' is not justified." Roper could put the qualifications of the new men on public display; but he could still not entirely dispel the impression, held by Tichenor and others, that some New Dealers looked upon the Federal civil aviation bureau as "just one more branch with a lot of juicy plums on it."[22]

IV

Impressions counted for much during the early days of the New Deal. "If [Roosevelt] burned down the Capitol we would cheer and say 'well, we at least got a fire started anyhow,'" Will Rogers cracked, sensing, as others did, that, in 1933, action in and of itself mattered more than its precise character. But specific acts have their specific consequences, and the New Deal's acts were no exception; they had a widespread effect, on industry, labor, agriculture, governmental operations, and businesses large and small. They also had a profound impact on the Aeronautics Branch.[23]

In a campaign speech in Pittsburgh, Roosevelt had foolishly promised to balance the budget and cut the cost of running the Federal Government by 25 percent. Though he sensed that economic conditions demanded an inflationary policy, he decided to keep his campaign pledge and pursue a deflationary course, if only temporarily. Besides, budget-balancing and cost-cutting would serve to pacify and reassure bankers, businessmen, and other adherents of classical economics. The result was the Economy Act of March 20, 1933, which reduced veterans' benefits and empowered the President to cut Federal civilian and military salaries up to 15 percent. At the same time, using his Executive powers, Roosevelt wielded the economy ax on the fiscal 1934 budget, which he had inherited from the Hoover administration. The weight of the President's austerity drive fell heavily on the Aeronautics Branch.[24]

The Aeronautics Branch budget had held up surprisingly well under the strain of depression. Indeed, in fiscal 1932, it hit an all-time high of $10.4 million. The following year, however, neither the Budget Director nor the Congress was in a generous mood. Congressmen picked over items they would not have given so much as a glance in the past. Thomas L. Blanton (D-Tex.) was incensed, for example, when told that the Aeronautics Branch had lowered its per diem rate by only 20 percent (from $5.00 to $4.00); the price of food and lodging in Texas, he maintained, had fallen 50 percent, and he saw no reason why per diem could not be cut by the same percentage. "You take hotels like the Baker Hotel in Dallas, Tex., for instance," he lectured Young, "the Texas Hotel in Fort Worth, and the Baker Hotel at Mineral Wells, Tex., which are all first-class hotels — you can go in there now and get a real good meal, a regular dinner, for 50 cents. It used to cost a dollar and a half." The Branch took an overall cut of 17.3 percent, bringing its budget down to $8.6 million.[25]

"The decrease eliminates all items of new airway construction,"

Young explained. In other words, it was a no-growth budget, despite the fact that air transport activity was growing at an unimpeded rate. Before the year was out, Young found he could not maintain the entire 18,000-mile airway system. Three airways were shut down — Norfolk-Washington, Phoenix-San Diego, Kingsville-Houston — and the rest of the system went on a part-time schedule; lights were turned on and off to conform with scheduled airmail and passenger operations. Nonscheduled operations would simply have to make the best of it.[26]

Fiscal 1934 produced a repeat performance. This time the Branch absorbed a 10-percent slash, to $7.7 million. It was this austere budget that Roosevelt began to hack away at in the spring of 1933. In late March, the President ordered all Federal Departments to "cease obligating all or any part of . . . unobligated funds . . . for public works projects . . . ." This put a temporary halt to new airway construction, though, admittedly, the Aeronautics Branch was planning precious little construction at this time. A few weeks later Roosevelt struck again: he impounded a whopping 32 percent of the Aeronautics Branch budget. This left the organization with a mere $5.17 million, or half the funds that it had had available two years earlier.[27]

Clearly, there was no way the Branch could continue to maintain its usual level of service. Rummaging for solutions, F. C. Hingsburg suggested to Edgerton that the situation could be met by placing "on an inoperative status 6,000 miles of lighted airways, 15 radio communication stations, 15 radio beacons, 30 radio marker beacons, and 1,000 miles of teletype system." In addition, Hingsburg foresaw the necessity of "dropping 321 employees with a total annual salary of $318,855 . . . ." This was not the prescription followed, though the level of the eventual cutback exceeded that proposed by Hingsburg.[28]

Big savings were achieved by eliminating a large number of intermediate fields and reducing the wattage of beacon lamps. The intermediate field system was a ripe area for economy. The new twin-engine transports were faster and more reliable and possessed a longer range than their predecessors. The standard 25- to 30-mile spacing between fields, therefore, appeared to be overly conservative for the needs of modern transports (though not necessarily for general aviation aircraft). Hence, the Branch adopted a 50-mile spacing between fields and thereby eliminated 74 fields at the end of fiscal 1933 and another 21 the following

year. Branch officials recognized that this step would cause consternation among communities losing their fields — and they were right — but
they had no choice but to move as they did and worry about local
repercussions later.[29]

Additional savings were achieved by reducing land rentals. The
Branch became a tough bargainer in renegotiating expiring leases.
"There was nothing very difficult about it," Vidal explained with some
satisfaction, "we simply offered the landowners about half what formerly
had been paid them. This worked out very nicely." Undoubtedly it did
for the Branch, though decidedly not for the cash-short farmers who
owned the land.[30]

Cutting down the number of intermediate fields was accepted as a
tolerable expedient by most of the aviation community. Tampering with
the light-beacon wattage, however, became — and remained for years to
come — a sore point with many airway users. The Branch's new regime
had never been entirely satisfied with Young's attempt to trim costs by
lighting the airways only when scheduled flights were in the air. The
practice worked a hardship on private and nonscheduled flying. Rex
Martin, collaborating closely with lighting experts in the Bureau of
Standards, came up with what appeared to be a far preferable solution.
By replacing the standard prismatic lens with a clear glass cover, he
could cut wattage in half (from 1,000 to 500 watts) without appreciably
affecting the beacons' candlepower. Bureau of Standards tests supported
this claim, but many a pilot never became reconciled to "Rex's 'Scotch'
beacon." "I will never believe that we can see a light just as well with less
intensity than with more . . .," said David L. Behncke, president of the
Air Line Pilots' Association. Others claimed that the low wattage beacon
was fine during clear weather, but that it shone "just about half as far as
the higher powered light" during hazy or rainy weather. On balance,
however, Martin's solution was less disruptive to the system than
Young's. And the new light could penetrate the elements satisfactorily;
what it could not penetrate was the psychological barrier in some pilots'
minds.[31]

In trying to make ends meet, the Aeronautics Branch had, up to this
point, come up with solutions that cut away fat and left the airways
virtually unimpaired. But there was only so much fat to trim. Roosevelt's
budget was so austere that essential services and activities had to be

abandoned. Accordingly, between the end of fiscal 1933 and the end of fiscal 1934, the work force was cut by 17 percent (at one point it was down as much as 33 percent from the peak of the employment level of the previous year). Prominent among personnel casualties in the field were all associate and junior airway engineers, all junior civil engineers, all radio and junior radio engineers, all but six assistant airway engineers, all patrol pilots, and all but six communication supervisors. The flight checking of navigation aids was cut back drastically. The scale of regulatory and inspection activities was reduced. In-house engine testing for type certification was eliminated. Research and development activities came to a virtual standstill ("At the present time . . .," wrote E. Y. Mitchell in August 1933, "the Department of Commerce finds it impossible to undertake any new research activities whatever"); indeed, the Aeronautics Research Division was abolished. The Airport Section met the same fate, while the Radio Section was reduced to a skeleton force.[32]

Service in the field inevitably suffered. Working a particular hardship on pilots and aircraft owners around the country was the abandonment of the itinerant inspector system. No longer would inspectors travel on a publicized schedule from airport to airport to inspect aircraft or examine and license pilots. Instead, inspectors were permanently assigned to 45 locations around the country. In this way the Branch could both reduce the inspector force (air regulations personnel were cut by 15 percent) and save travel expenses. "The new plan of the Department of Commerce to require students and pilots going for examination for license, to make their own way to the nearest inspector, may be a fine idea insofar as economy for the Department is concerned," noted a *Western Flying* editorial, "but it makes it hard on the candidates who live a long way from the inspector's base. It means the expenditure of considerable time and money . . . ."[33]

It proved impossible to facilitate the economy program and to effect these changes without completely reorganizing the Branch. The first major organizational change was made in June 1933 when the Airways Division was transferred from the Bureau of Lighthouses to the Aeronautics Branch. With this division no longer tied to the Lighthouse Bureau's field structure, it could now be reorganized to conform with available resources. The last major step came a year later with the abolishment of the Aeronautics Research Division and the absorption of

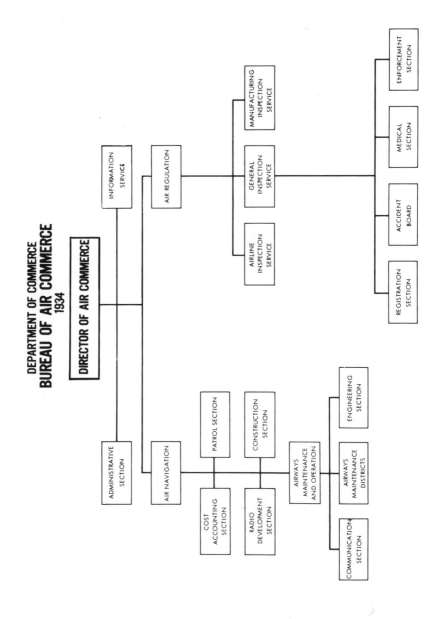

DEPARTMENT OF COMMERCE
BUREAU OF AIR COMMERCE
1934

DIRECTOR OF AIR COMMERCE

INFORMATION SERVICE

AIR REGULATION

MANUFACTURING INSPECTION SERVICE

GENERAL INSPECTION SERVICE

AIRLINE INSPECTION SERVICE

REGISTRATION SECTION

ACCIDENT BOARD

MEDICAL SECTION

ENFORCEMENT SECTION

ADMINISTRATIVE SECTION

AIR NAVIGATION

PATROL SECTION

CONSTRUCTION SECTION

COST ACCOUNTING SECTION

RADIO DEVELOPMENT SECTION

AIRWAYS MAINTENANCE AND OPERATION

AIRWAYS MAINTENANCE DISTRICTS

ENGINEERING SECTION

COMMUNICATION SECTION

other aeronautical activities scattered throughout the Department's
bureaus into the Branch. Hoover's disjointed organizational scheme had
thus been abandoned. On July 1, 1934, Roper capped the reorganization
by renaming the Aeronautics Branch the Bureau of Air Commerce.[34]

What Roosevelt took with one hand he gave back, at least in part,
with the other. Austerity was not a way of life with him. "I realize well
that thus far we have actually given more of deflation than inflation
. . .," he wrote to Colonel E. M. House in April 1933. "[But] it is simply
inevitable that we must inflate . . . ." It was an odd piece of business,
this simultaneous pursuit of deflationary and inflationary policies; but
Roosevelt's mind did not run in neatly defined channels. He was
determined to cut back the cost of traditional Federal activities; at the
same time, he was equally determined to spend lavishly on new programs
to deal with the economic emergency. He saw nothing paradoxical in
pursuing both policies simultaneously.[35]

The Economy Act had served his cost-cutting objectives; the National Industrial Recovery Act (NIRA), enacted in June 1933, would
serve his inflationary policy. Among other things, NIRA created the
Public Works Administration (PWA), which was designed to put the
unemployed to work on national projects of permanent value. By
December 1933, PWA had funneled some $952,000 into the Aeronautics
Branch's empty coffers. The bulk of this money went for airway
development, which had been at a virtual standstill for more than a year.
By the end of fiscal 1934, 2,681 miles of airway had been lighted with
PWA funds. Public works funds would remain an important source of
airway financing during Roosevelt's first term.

Additional funds were pumped into aviation projects by the Civil
Works Administration, a temporary agency created by Executive order
in November 1933 to provide work relief to millions of unemployed. One
of the major programs of this organization was the building of airports.
Between November 1933 and March 1934, CWA poured $11.5 million
into airport construction. CWA dispensed these funds directly rather
than channeling them through the Department of Commerce, as PWA
did with airway construction funds. The Aeronautics Branch, however,
did receive some CWA funds (approximately $100,000 in fiscal 1934) to
help defray the cost of planning these airport projects. At the request of

CWA, the Branch selected an aviation supervisor for each state and appointed two or more engineers in each state to supervise the development work.

Little of permanent value to aviation came out of the CWA effort. CWA had no time to plan substantial projects. Its overriding concern was to put people to work quickly; what the projects accomplished was of secondary importance. Consequently, CWA's airport program was an airport program in name only. "These are not really airports," Vidal explained. "They are landing strips, two perpendicular strips, up to 3,000 feet in length and at least 300 feet wide, with well-defined boundaries. They will simply be leveled off with whatever clearing is to be done, and seeded." Whether a particular community needed such a field or whether a field could accommodate the aviation activity serving a community did not matter. "I am telling you," asserted a prominent member of the aviation community a couple of years later, "that . . . one dollar of relief money does not get as far as one dollar of regular appropriation." Later, when the most acute phase of the work-relief emergency had abated, PWA and the Works Progress Administration would spend airport development funds more wisely than CWA had done.[36]

The New Deal, then, spent huge sums on marginal aviation programs while economizing on such vital Department of Commerce activities as air regulation and airway development. All this came at a time when the air transport industry was beginning to order in large numbers modern high-performance aircraft — DC-2's and B-247D's — aircraft that were more dependent on ground-based radio aids than their predecessors. Though air transport operators kept a public silence for the moment, they wondered about the wisdom of this policy and, if continued, about its long-term effect on their operations. Word of their private doubts had a tendency to surface. "There have been some rumors to the effect that your inspection service . . . and the checking of pilots, and the medical examination of pilots, has been curtailed to the detriment of safety in commercial flying," Congressman Robert L. Bacon (R-N.Y.) told Vidal in December 1933. William D. Oliver (D-Ala.), chairman of the House subcommittee handling Department of Commerce appropriations, had gone directly to Vidal on first hearing of Roosevelt's economy drive and was "agreeably surprised" on being assured that the Aeronautics Branch could live with the cuts; he was surprised "because our committee had been admonished against any cut in this appropriation, for the reason that apprehension was voiced . . . that any cut would seriously endanger the safety of passengers." Vidal stuck by his guns: the reduced budget would not impair safety. Doubters — and there were many — kept their own counsel for the moment; they would have their say later.[37]

Meanwhile, Roosevelt's economic programs were having an effect on the air transport industry. First to feel the pinch were the airmail operators. In September 1933, Postmaster General James A. Farley called the operators together and told them the bad news: because of budgetary exigencies, airmail rates were being cut by 28 percent. Though the mail operators were prospering, this news came as a real blow at a time when most carriers were making long-term investments in new equipment. From this point on, airmail carriage ceased to be a bonanza. Indeed, 1933 was the last year in which mail revenues exceeded passenger revenues.[38]

Having reduced the revenues of transport lines, the New Deal set about increasing the industry's cost of doing business. Air transport was thus caught in the jaws of the New Deal's economic vice; it was perhaps the only industry to feel the effects of both the deflationary and inflationary policies of the New Deal. Roosevelt's principal instrument for inflating the economy — raising prices and wages above their ruinous 1933 levels — was the NIRA, specifically that portion of the act which established a National Recovery Administration to draw up, administer, and enforce codes of fair competition among the nation's industries. Under the air transport code, approved by the President effective November 27, 1933, the industry assumed increased payroll costs of approximately 20 percent. This rise in costs, *Aviation* estimated, "taken together with increases in material and other costs under NRA conditions, [means that] the airlines will face a gross increase in annual expenses of some two to three million dollars for present amount of operation." When the code was being hammered together, Lester D. Seymour, chairman of the air transport committee of the Aeronautical Chamber of Commerce, reminded NRA Administrator Hugh S. Johnson that "air mail payments are the backbone of this industry." With these revenues decreasing and costs due to rise under NRA, Seymour warned, many lines could be facing hard times ahead. "That is something for the Post Office Department and the Bureau of the Budget to bear in mind when the estimates for next year's air mail appropriations are being

laid out . . .," *Aviation* commented. Little did the air transport companies suspect that things would get worse before they got better.[39]

                                        V

The CWA airport development program contributed its share to
alleviating the nation's unemployment problem. Picking up momentum
rapidly, it had, during the winter of 1933-34, 70,000 men working at 700
locations constructing new airports or improving existing sites. It gave
the economy in general a shot in the arm, and, to a degree, it probably
stimulated flying. But it was scarcely the kind of program that could
bring the heavily depressed aeronautical manufacturing industry out of
its economic doldrums. Something more direct and more substantial was
needed for that, and, at least in the view of Eugene Vidal, that something
should be undertaken by the Federal Government, which, under the Air
Commerce Act, had the responsibility of fostering aviation's
development.[40]

"If there is such a thing as a New Deal for aviation," Vidal told the
Society of Automotive Engineers, "it is the recognition of the Government's additional duty to aid the development of a sound aviation
industry, which means above all other things, the development of greater
markets for products of that industry."[41] At the same time, Vidal wanted
to do something for private flying, which he believed had been neglected
by a Federal Government preoccupied with commercial aviation:

> The forgotten man of aviation is the private flyer, and his
> brothers are legion. They work at manual training branches in
> high schools and at engineering tables in colleges, and each
> dreams of the day when his inspired design will revolutionize
> aeronautics. They build model planes by the millions and trudge
> out to local airports each week-end to worship their idols from
> the ground and long for the day when they will have saved
> enough . . . to buy a hop. They are the young business women
> and men who travel by air and would like to fly for recreation or
> sport or pleasure but cannot afford to. They are the older folks,
> who would like to include air travel in their daily social and
> business lives but have not yet met it within the ken of their
> experiences. They are the multitudes who admire Lindbergh
> . . . and all others to whom the air is as commonplace as Sunday
> roads, [but] stand on the edge longingly — physically and
> mentally worthy of the kingdom of flight, but financially
> unprepared.[42]

Vidal, then, would democratize aviation — bring it to the multitudes. His hope was that "the New Deal may do for the airplane what the pioneers of mass production did for the automobile; convert it from a rich man's hobby to a daily utility or inexpensive pleasure for the average American citizen." All this could be attained by the development of a "low-priced, easily operated and maintained airplane" that could be mass-produced. ("[If] the price is to be within the reach of the average person," Vidal said, "[the aircraft] must be produced and sold in large numbers.") Thus, the American aircraft manufacturing industry would get back on the road to economic recovery by allowing the American people to enter "the kingdom of flight." The program, moreover, would dovetail with the airport building program, permitting "future owners of these [low-cost] aircraft [to] reap [its] benefits. . . ."[43]

The basic idea was not really new. "As soon as we know as much about [airplanes] as we do about automobiles — and that will not be long — then they can be built by the thousands or by the millions," Henry Ford had said in 1924. Unquestionably, by 1933, airplanes could have been mass-produced. The big hitch was unit price. Vidal believed that the price could not exceed the average price of a new automobile, which, in 1933, ran between $500 and $1,000. There was no question in his mind that "an airplane for that price, sold on the installment plan, would have a popular appeal" — provided, like the modern automobile, it was easy to handle and inexpensive to operate and maintain. The same people who bought automobiles would buy his flying flivver ("The automobile driver . . . he is our customer . . . ").[44]

After going "into price . . . very carefully," Vidal settled on a $700 price tag for a two-seat single-engine all-metal aircraft capable of a top speed of 100 m.p.h. He visited Henry Ford in Dearborn; Ford engineers, who "spent a bit of time on us," according to Vidal, estimated that they could produce an automobile engine for the aircraft at $65 a unit "if we would take a full day's production, which at that time was 3,500 units." The low unit price for the engine, when combined with a subsidy to airframe manufacturers for tooling costs and an early initial airplane production run of 10,000 units, Vidal believed, made his $700 estimate reasonably attainable.[45]

In securing Roosevelt's approval for the program, Vidal also got a promise of $1 million in PWA funds to take care of industry's start-up costs. In negotiating with PWA officials, however, Vidal managed to secure an allotment of only $500,000. He believed, nevertheless, that this fund was sufficient.[46]

Shortly after announcing the program, in November 1933, Vidal conducted a survey to demonstrate that a market existed for his machine. Thousands of questionnaires were mailed to prospective buyers. By February about "18,000 replied, and 13,000 said they would purchase," Vidal announced. "The 13,000 affirmative replies included nearly 10,000 saying yes without reservations and about 3,000 making final decision upon future financial status . . . ." Survey participants had also been asked to list "the number of their friends or acquaintances who would be probable purchasers"; they listed 57,000 names. "Surely one in ten of this group is an assured purchaser," Vidal concluded.*[47]

Vidal was heartened by these results. And it did appear that private fliers, on balance, were enthusiastic about the program. One Illinois town, for example, inspired by Vidal's proposal, resolved that an air reserve corps of one million members be established and that the Federal Government grant the members of this corps "aid in purchase of . . . airplanes by a 40% grant of the purchase price . . . ." "What do you think of this [resolution]?" Vidal asked Maj. Gen. Benjamin D. Foulois, the Air Corps Chief. "We are at least stirring up interest throughout the country."[48]

Vidal had indeed stirred up interest. His proposal had "set the high-water mark in news excitement not only for November but for a much longer period," *Aviation* observed. But the reaction was by no means uniform: "There are those who cheer the scheme, those who denounce it, and those who ridicule it . . . ." Aircraft manufacturers did not do much cheering; instead, in the words of one observer, they met the

---

*It seems unlikely that an aircraft sales program of this magnitude could have been successful in the winter of 1933-34, or, indeed, at any time during the Great Depression, which ran into 1940-41. Vidal assumed that the average buyer of a new automobile would become the primary customer for his flivver; in doing so, he was banking on a breed that had been in rapid decline since 1929. New auto sales were depressed nearly as much as new aircraft sales, dropping from an all-time high of 4,455,100 units in 1929, to 1,103,500 units in 1932. But while new auto sales were on the wane, the desire or need to own a new car, it seems fair to say, was not; demand was being pent up by economic conditions. It would have been a rare man, indeed, who had $700 to spend on a new transportation vehicle in 1934 and chose to put it into an airplane; people would have bought the vehicle they had been waiting to buy all along — the motor car, which had a great deal more utility than a two-seat airplane. If Vidal was right, however, in assuming the existence of a large pent-up market for his airplane, then he was proposing a program that would have worked havoc on the nation's airways. In November 1933, there were fewer than 10,000 certificated civil aviation aircraft; Vidal proposed to double that number by the spring of 1934. It is doubtful that the airways were capable of accepting such a large increase in traffic in one increment.

scheme with "a shower of dead cats and brickbats." "Automobile engines will never be used for practical aircraft of any type until aircraft engines become standard for automobiles," said William B. Stout, skeptical of the performance of Ford's $65 engine. Grover Loening suggested that the aircraft manufacturing industry was perfectly capable of taking care of its business, and the Department of Commerce might do well to mind its own — developing airways and intermediate landing fields. "There have been sneers and skepticism . . . . There have been groans and complaints . . .," noted Robert J. Pritchard, editor of *Western Flying*. Aviation editors joined in, what must have appeared to Vidal, a conspiracy to kill his proposal with ridicule.[49] Even Pritchard, who was not ill-disposed toward the project, could not resist poking fun:

> At last some one is willing to adopt the child!
>
> What a chance for a scenario writer!
>
> Poor little Private Flying — a waif, homeless and neglected, shoved hither and kicked thither, forlorn and forgotten, while her beautiful sister, Transport Flying, rolls in prosperity and popular favor, lauded in the public prints, and basking in the adulation of the multitudes.
>
> Poor little P. F. — rummaging in the ash-can for the scraps from T. F.'s table, and slowly starving to death.
>
> And then the happy climax. As the despairing orphan sinks to the gutter with exhaustion, enters the benign and wealthy old gentleman (played by Mr. Eugene Vidal), and with a shriek of delight, ragged little P. F. flies to his arms, crying 'Daddy!'[50]

Aviation conducted a survey of the industry; among those questioned, 64 percent of the airframe manufacturers and more than 50 percent of the engine manufacturers were categorically opposed to the scheme. But the most revealing statistic was that 70 percent of those surveyed expressed concern that potential customers, led to believe that a $700 airplane was in prospect, would put off purchasing existing aircraft costing three to four times as much. Far from helping their business, Vidal was destroying it. As *Aviation* commented, when Vidal announced his project "a considerable segment of the aircraft industry thought it a joke — and not a particularly funny one."[51]

Industry opposition killed the project. By the winter of 1934, the New Deal was already locked in battle with the air transport industry over airmail contracts; it did not want another aviation hassle with manufacturers. In March 1934, PWA withdrew its promised allotment. "Now in order to keep going," Vidal recalled years later, "we shifted our

[emphasis] to the development of a safer, more easily flown airplane
. . . ." But it was a low-key program with no grand design. The idea of a
"Poor Man's Airplane" was dead.[52]

It had been a disappointing year for aviation. The air fraternity's
hope for an attentive, airminded administration, though not completely
shattered, had been seriously diminished. The ability of the Aeronautics
Branch to carry out its responsibilities had been impaired by ill-
conceived economies and the appointment of incompatible officials.
Airmail payments had been cut back while the cost of operating an air
transport line had been deliberately run up. Money going to airport
projects appeared to be misspent. To top it all off, when the administration came forth with a new aviation program, it rankled; it appeared to be
no more than a gratuitous attempt to tell aircraft manufacturers how to
run their business. But all of this was the stuff of disenchantment, not
alienation. That would come later; that would come with stunning
suddenness in the winter of 1934.

10. "The Crack of Doom"

The flivver, the budget cuts, the NRA, the appointment of Vidal, the persistent internal squabbles — all these matters were a source of irritation and disappointment to the aviation community; but neither individually nor collectively were they of surpassing importance. Indeed, much if not all of the unpleasantness that had transpired in 1933 could be attributed to a passing phase; it could be rationalized away as part of the process of a new administration settling into office. Of greater concern to aviation were some ominous activities on Capitol Hill, activities that had actually commenced before Roosevelt's inauguration. These proceedings were intimately connected with the Hoover administration's handling of airmail contracts.

II

On February 25, 1933, during the dying days of the lameduck 72d Congress, the Senate passed a resolution establishing a special committee to conduct an investigation of airmail and ocean-mail contracts. On the surface, it seemed a curious action for the Senate to take. Only four days earlier, the House Post Office Committee had issued a seemingly exhaustive report on the U.S. airmail service. The Senate, however, had matters in mind that the House report had not begun to touch on.

Joseph T. Robinson, the Senate Democratic Leader, who was not known for his interest in aviation or postal affairs, had fathered the investigation. He, like other Senators, had been besieged by independent carriers complaining of the treatment accorded them by the Post Office. Early in 1933, a complaint came from an unexpected source — Paul Henderson, who was furious over Brown's running a route extension into United Air Line's territory and granting it to a competitor, Northwest

249

Airways. Henderson was so upset by this intrusion that he volunteered all he knew about Brown's route awards. Henderson's story was corroborated by a Hearst newspaper reporter, Fulton Lewis, Jr., who had collected a sheaf of information on the maladministration of postal contracts. Lewis, his curiosity aroused by Ludington's inability to secure an airmail contract, had dug deep into all airmail route awards under the Watres Act. He pieced together the events before, during, and after the spoils conference, only to find that Hearst would not print the story. So he dumped the information he had collected on Capitol Hill.[1]

Robinson handpicked Hugo L. Black, an Alabama populist who had been advocating radical measures to deal with the economic crisis, to head the investigation. Black was not certain that he wanted the assignment. "That's hardly in my line down in Alabama," he told Robinson. But when he talked to one of Robinson's sources, who related "a story that was almost beyond belief," he decided to take the job on.* Given a free hand to select the members of his committee, Black chose William H. King (D-Utah), who had been instrumental in getting Henderson to talk, Pat McCarran (D-Nev.), Warren R. Austin (R-Vt.), and Wallace H. White, Jr. (R-Maine). Black and King had voted against the last airmail appropriation, Austin and White for. McCarran, a freshman, had an unmarked aviation slate.[2]

The investigation moved methodically and unspectacularly. The better part of 1933 was spent in gathering documentary evidence, which came principally from Lewis and the mail carriers themselves. The bulk of Post Office Department records dealing with contract matters had been destroyed on Brown's orders during the closing days of the Hoover administration; filing cabinet after filing cabinet had been emptied and its contents burned. What was not burned was packed up and carted off by Brown in a crate the size of a coffin. The carriers had not taken the same precaution; hence, their files became a primary source of information for Black committee investigators.

Black did not rush to go public. When he finally opened his hearings, on September 26, 1933, he concentrated on ocean-mail contracts. He called steamship company witnesses exclusively through December 8, at which point the committee broke off for the yearend holidays. Not until

---

*In an interview in May 1968, Black would not say who this source was. It seems likely, however, that it was either Henderson or Lewis.

January 9, 1934, did Black shift gears. On that day, he called two Post Office Department civil servants (who told of the destruction of postal records) and, in succession, Thomas H. McKee (the Wedell-Williams official who had tried to crash the spoils conference), Paul Henderson, and Erle Halliburton. In the ensuing days came a long procession of industry witnesses, many of whom had attended the spoils conference. Led on by Black, who phrased his questions much like a prosecuting attorney and bolstered testimony with reams of documents, the witnesses told all. What they had to say made headlines daily. The smell of scandal was in the air.[3]

III

The hearings had barely gotten on track before they were derailed by Bill MacCracken. Early in January, committee investigators had determined that MacCracken's office files contained correspondence relating to airmail matters — a not too startling discovery since MacCracken's clients read like a who's who in aviation. Black anticipated no problems. He and the former Commerce official had been friends since their first meeting at an ABA convention in 1926. Their wives were also particularly close and were daily companions when the scandal began to unfold. Black approached MacCracken and asked that the files be turned over to the committee. MacCracken refused; to turn over these confidential communications to the committee would violate the privileged relationship between client and attorney. Black saw matters differently. The client-attorney relationship did not apply in this case because Mac-Cracken was performing functions that did not fall within the generally recognized scope of legal duties. MacCracken, Black held, had been hired as a lobbyist to secure legislation favorable to his clients and to negotiate contracts with Federal agencies. These were not traditional legal services; these were services that could be performed by anyone who knew his way around Washington. MacCracken, though admitting his lobbyist's role, was unpersuaded. He would not yield the documents.

Black subpoenaed the files. This put MacCracken in a difficult position. He could either ignore the subpoena and put himself in contempt of the Senate or he could violate what he believed was a sacred trust. He chose to ignore the subpoena and appeared before the committee emptyhanded. A compromise was worked out. Black would not press the subpoena while MacCracken sought the permission of his clients to release the documents.[4]

The matter would have ended without further complications had MacCracken not gotten careless. All his clients except two readily gave him permission to release their correspondence. L. H. Brittin of Northwest Airways and H. M. Hanshue of TWA wanted to examine the files before releasing them. Hanshue dispatched his private secretary, one Gilbert Givvin, to pick up the material. MacCracken and Givvin went over the files together, selected a sheaf of documents, and mailed them to Hanshue. Meanwhile, Brittin appeared on his own. While MacCracken was tied up with other matters, the Northwest official secured permission from MacCracken's law partner, Fred Lee (the same Fred Lee who had helped draft the Air Commerce Act), to go through the files for material that he termed strictly personal. Brittin took what he wanted — perhaps no more than half a dozen letters — went directly to his own office in the National Press Building, tore the letters to shreds, and dumped them in his wastebasket. All the while, MacCracken's office files had been under the Senate subpoena.

When Black got wind of what had occurred, he hailed Brittin, Givvin, and MacCracken before the committee. Brittin explained that the papers he destroyed were of a personal nature, while Givvin could not say precisely what the packet sent to Hanshue contained. In his defense, MacCracken pleaded that Brittin went through his office files without his knowledge; as to turning over documents to Hanshue, he argued that he represented the TWA executive in two capacities — as a lobbyist and as a lawyer — and that the documents in question did not bear on lobbying activities.

The committee members were in no mood for explanations. "Those papers were in [MacCracken's] files, in his custody, in his control," Pat McCarran said, expressing the committee's outrage. "He had no right to permit them to be removed . . . while the subpoena was in full force and effect." Even White, who had previously defended MacCracken's claim to privilege, voted with the Democrats to impound MacCracken's files.[5]

On February 5, Black took the matter before the Senate. And while the committee itself declined to make a specific recommendation for contempt, Black, under questioning, offered his judgment that MacCracken, Givvin, Brittin, Hanshue, and Lee had engaged in "a deliberate effort to deprive the Senate of papers which were under subpoena and which were material in order to reach the facts." The Senate, sparing Lee, its former legislative counsel, directed the other four men to appear before it on Friday, February 9, "to show cause why they should not be punished for contempt."[6]

Meanwhile, Brittin's and MacCracken's contention that the documents in question did not pertain to airmail matters collapsed. Postal inspectors rummaged through trash sacks in the National Press Building basement and pieced together the documents shredded by Brittin; all concerned airmail business. And when Hanshue handed over to the committee what he claimed were the papers mailed by Givvin, one memorandum turned up that clearly dealt with matters under investigation. Though logic might dictate that the document would not have been returned if MacCracken and Hanshue were conspiring to withhold evidence from the committee, MacCracken had nevertheless committed a contemptuous action. Moreover, the recovery of the material did not guarantee that he had successfully purged himself of contempt, for the committee had no way of verifying that all the documents removed had been returned.[7]

On the day of the trial, the Senate's Sergeant at Arms, Chesley W. Jurney, sporting a morning coat, gray-striped trousers, 10-gallon hat, and silver-headed walking stick, set out to arrest MacCracken and bring him before the Senate. The accused was nowhere to be found. Jurney did locate MacCracken's defense attorney, Frank Hogan, who told him that he would produce the defendant in the chambers of a judge. Black saw through the plot. MacCracken and Hogan had been maintaining that the Senate could cite but not try; the contempt charge, they held, had to be brought before a court of law. Hogan obviously wanted Jurney to arrest his client in the presence of a judge, whereupon he could immediately apply for a writ of habeas corpus. Black called Jurney off. The trial proceeded with only Brittin, Givvin, and Hanshue in the dock.[8]

When the Senate adjourned for the weekend, MacCracken came out of hiding. Since he could not be hauled before the Senate until Monday, he now wanted to be arrested in order to institute habeas corpus proceedings. But no Jurney appeared to make the arrest. It was Mac-Cracken's and Hogan's turn to see through Black's plot. Obviously, the Senator wanted to time the arrest so that Hogan had no opportunity to secure a writ. Well, if the law would not go to the fugitive, the fugitive would go to the law. Saturday evening, MacCracken appeared at Jurney's apartment and told the somewhat befuddled Sergeant at Arms that he had come to surrender. Recovering his presence of mind, Jurney said that he could not possibly make an arrest because the warrant was locked in a Senate safe. "That's your problem," MacCracken shot back, and refused to leave. Jurney got Black on the telephone and was told that under no circumstances was MacCracken to be arrested during the weekend. Jurney's wife made up a bed for the unexpected overnight guest.

Come morning, Jurney plotted his escape. He had to go to the Senate Office Building on some business, he said, but MacCracken could remain behind at the apartment. No, said MacCracken; it was unwise to leave a prisoner unguarded. The two men went off together. At the Senate Office Building they were joined by a Jurney acquaintance. Leaving the building, the three men strolled down a street fronting the Capitol, with MacCracken keeping a few paces behind Jurney and his companion. Suddenly, the men in front bolted, jumped into a car, and roared off, leaving MacCracken dead in his tracks.

Jurney spent the rest of the weekend in hiding; but on Monday morning he emerged, armed himself with the warrant for MacCracken's arrest, and took after his quarry in earnest. He found him outside of the District of Columbia Court House, arrested him, and brought him before the Senate. The Senate, while acquitting Hanshue and Givvin, convicted MacCracken and Brittin and sentenced each to 10 days in the District of Columbia Jail. For MacCracken, this was the beginning of the end of his long association with aviation.[9]

IV

While MacCracken and Jurney played hide and seek, the administration was doing some sleuthing of its own. Walter Brown, as soon as it became public knowledge that he had carted off the Government's files, returned them personally to James A. Farley, his successor. Karl Crowley, the Post Office Department Solicitor, worked day and night, seven days a week, poring over the recovered documents and other materials. On January 26, Black lunched with Roosevelt and urged him to cancel all domestic airmail contracts. Roosevelt made a vague reference to the discussion later that day at a news conference — the first public admission that cancellation was being discussed within administration circles.[10]

Crowley wrapped up his investigation on February 7. He had satisfied himself that the carriers had colluded to prevent competitive bidding. He had also concluded that Brown had illegally granted six-month contract extensions in 1929 and that the route extensions made under the Watres Act were of doubtful legality. The next morning he confronted Farley with his findings, contained in a 100-page report supported by two volumes of documents and accompanied by a strong recommendation that the contracts be annulled. Farley picked up the phone and made an appointment with the President. At 4:30 that afternoon, Farley, Crowley, William W. Howes, the First Assistant Postmaster General, and Harllee Branch, the Second Assistant, filed into the Oval Office. Thus began a series of conferences between administration officials that would stretch over the next 48 hours.[11]

Crowley's report was compelling. "Unquestionably adequate grounds [for cancellation]," declared Attorney General Homer Cummings, who had been brought into the discussions by Roosevelt and had spent the night examining the evidence. The question was what to do about it. Everyone favored cancellation. Farley, however, urged that the date be postponed until new contracts could be bid on under new ground rules. That way there would be no disruption in service. Justice Department lawyers shot down the idea. Once convinced of fraud, they argued, the Postmaster General had to cancel the contracts immediately or else place himself in the position of condoning the crime. Roosevelt, too, came down on the side of immediate cancellation. He struck a moral chord: the beneficiaries of a corrupt system could not be allowed to continue to profit from it.

Now remaining to be settled was what to do with the airmail after cancellation. The service was not all that critical to the nation's postal system and could have been suspended until a permanent solution was worked out. But someone suggested that the Army Air Corps fly the mail on an interim basis. Roosevelt liked the idea. He wanted assurances, however, that the Army was equal to the task.[12]

Maj. Gen. Benjamin G. Foulois, the Chief of the Air Corps, had been following the airmail scandal in the newspapers. But when Harllee Branch called him on the morning of February 9, asking that he drop by his office that afternoon, Foulois did not connect the call with the unfolding crisis. He, Branch, and Eugene Vidal were members of the

Interdepartmental Committee on Civil Airways, and Foulois automatically assumed that Vidal had called a committee meeting to discuss airway matters. He was completely unprepared, therefore, when he arrived at Branch's office and was asked without any preliminaries whether the Air Corps could carry the mail if the President canceled all domestic contracts. The question should never have been put to the spunky Foulois, who had seen his beloved Air Corps struggle through 12 years of tightfisted Republican rule. The "sad shape" of the Corps immediately flashed through the general's mind. It had no cargo-carrying equipment to speak of and few of its flying officers had engaged in instrument or night operations. Flying the mail would be an invaluable experience for these men. More importantly, with the Air Corps becoming the focus of national attention, its chances of receiving adequate appropriations in the future would improve immeasurably. Foulois gave Branch an unqualified yes. How much time would the Air Corps require to get ready? Branch countered. A week to 10 days, Foulois said casually, thinking that Branch "certainly didn't mean how much time *from that moment on*." How Foulois could have misinterpreted the question remains a mystery. Since Branch had specified no date, he had to mean from *that* or any other moment, otherwise there was no point in asking the question.[13]

Foulois's word was all the administration was waiting for. Roosevelt promptly signed an Executive order assigning the task of flying the mail to the Air Corps. News of the President's action spread rapidly through administration circles, arriving at Army Headquarters ahead of Foulois, who was immediately accosted on his return by a redfaced Douglas MacArthur, the Army Chief of Staff, and told: "You're on your own now, Foulois. . . It's your ball game."[14]

At 4 p.m., Farley announced to the press that he had annulled 40 domestic route certificates held by nine carriers, effective midnight February 19. The carriers had violated an 1872 statute, which read in part: "No contract for carrying the mail shall be made with any person who has entered or proposed to enter into any combination to prevent the making of any bid for carrying the mail, or who has made any agreement, or given or performed or promised to give or perform, any consideration whatever to induce any other person not to bid for any such contract; and if any person so offending is a contractor for carrying the mail, his contract may be annulled . . . ." The administration had embarked upon an adventure that it would come to regret.[15]

The press and the Republican minority in the Congress were virtually as one in condemning the action. *U.S. Air Services* called it "the most ruthless, unprovoked, and unjust blow Government has ever inflicted upon a legitimate business . . . ." The *New York American* labeled the order "un-American," while the *New York Times* termed it an "impulsive action." To Hiram Bingham, canceling all the contracts was "incredibly stupid." Hamilton Fish, a conservative Republican Congressman who represented FDR's home district, described the cancellation as "arbitrary, high-handed, and dictatorial." Such an act, Fish said in an impassioned radio address, was "worthy of fascism, Hitlerism, or Sovietism in their most . . . arrogant moods."[16]

The sweeping nature of the order and the fact that it was issued without granting the affected lines a hearing troubled both friendly and unfriendly critics. "It's like finding a crooked railroad president, then stopping all the trains," Will Rogers cracked. "Even the ferocious . . . Pancho Villa . . . was accustomed to shoot only every tenth man," commented the *Los Angeles Times*. "It is not necessary," the *New York Sun* declared, "to lynch a whole industry to get the offenders in it." Warren Austin, who sat on the Black committee, believed that the nine contractors should have been given a hearing either before the President or the Postmaster General and an "opportunity for severance of [their] defenses;" instead, "all of them were condemned as crooks, *en bloc*." Even critics who conceded Farley's charge recoiled at the punishment and the way it was meted out. "That there has been fraud appears obvious," said the *Newark Sunday Ledger*. "But it is not in keeping with the established process of this government to take such a snap judgment . . . without an orderly and legal hearing . . . ."[17]

On February 12, Charles Lindbergh, now in the employ of TWA, shot off an angry telegram to Roosevelt: "Your present action does not discriminate between innocence and guilt . . . . [Cancellation] of all air mail contracts condemns the largest portion of our commercial aviation without just trial." Lindbergh released the telegram to the press, which prompted Steve Early, Roosevelt's press secretary, to ignore the issue raised in the telegram and accuse Lindbergh of not granting the President the courtesy of receiving his message in private. Billy Mitchell, emerging from the isolation of his Virginia farm, declared that "Lindbergh has disclosed himself as the 'front man' of the Air Trust . . . . He is a commercial flyer. His motive is principally profit." "Be not deceived," roared Senator Joseph P. O'Mahoney (D-Wyo.). "They are not disturbed about the liberties of the people. They are distraught because the license of the exploiters has been taken away. The voice is the voice of Jacob, but the hand is the hand of Esau — a hand that itches once again to gamble with the savings of the people." But the administration came off second best in this exchange of insults. "The notion that you must not answer a critic, but must discredit him," wrote Walter Lippmann, "is bad medicine anywhere at any time in any cause, however noble and however righteous."[18]

By no means, however, was the administration losing the larger debate. The American press, firmly in the grip of Republican publishers, had been railing against New Deal policies all along; it had never been expected to give the cancellation order a gleeful reception. Nor was the opposition party expected to sit by while a Republican administration was charged with collusion in the handing out of Federal contracts. Moreover, Roosevelt's policy did not lack for an able defense. Answering the charge that the mail operators should not have been condemned en masse, Congressman Donald C. Dobbins (D-Ill.) told the administration's critics what they already knew to be true: "Where a number of men participate in a collusive agreement by which a part of them derive benefit, all participating in the agreement are likewise guilty, although some of the participants may not have profited thereby." As to the charge that the operators received no hearing, Dobbins asked: "Where was all the interesting testimony given that we have been reading about in the newspapers for many weeks?"[19]

Hugo Black, the most vigorous defender of the administration, got closer to the point. No hearing was required under the law, he maintained, and cited example after example where none was held under similar circumstances.* Black further argued that the administration had no choice but to do what it did. "Where a party desires to rescind [a contract] upon the ground of mistake or fraud," Black said, reading from a Supreme Court decision (*Grymes* v. *Sanders*), "he must, upon the discovery of the facts, at once announce his purpose and adhere to it. If

---

*In 1834, Postmaster General Amos Kendall cut off the beneficiaries of a fraud without a hearing. In 1881, President James A. Garfield, acting solely on the strength of a postal inspector's report, peremptorily reduced the face value of fraudulent mail contracts. Theodore Roosevelt, in turn, canceled contracts tainted with fraud, and, as late as 1927, Postmaster General Harry S. New canceled a contract when he discovered that the contractor had colluded with others to prevent competitive bidding.

he be silent . . ., he will be held to have waived the objection and will be conclusively bound by the contract, as if the mistake or fraud had not occurred." The administration was clearly treating this case as a civil matter, and had acted according to recognized procedures for civil fraud. The opposition, Black charged, was deliberately trying to mislead the public by applying the rules of criminal prosecution to a civil case. Moreover, he argued, no one was depriving the operators of their day in court. They could all take their cases to the U.S. Court of Claims.[20]

Black was equally effective on the offensive, playing on a depression-ridden public's distrust of monied interests. "It was never intended by patriotic citizens that [Federal mail subsidies] should be diverted by collusive agreements into the pockets of favored bankers, brokers, or stock manipulators, politicians, and lobbyists," he said before a nation-wide radio audience.[21] On the floor of the Senate, he charged that the record of the Hoover administration in airmail matters revealed "a network of intrigue, chicanery, manipulation, and fraud . . . ." Billy Mitchell struck a similar theme before a House committee hearing. Aviation, he said, had fallen into the hands of "commercial interests" — interests that had contributed nothing to its development, interests that were solely concerned with raking in profits. "The Government . . . should . . . not let these gambling air-mail contractors run wild all over the country with [Federal mail subsidies]," he said. Liberal weeklies joined the chorus. "One can not help discerning a certain amount of poetic justice in all this," said the *Nation* with satisfaction. "And after all, gentlemen who made profits of millions on modest investments can perhaps afford to let somebody else take the profits for awhile." It seemed clear to the *New Republic* that "the contracts made in the Hoover administration were collusive" and Roosevelt had no alternative "except to cancel them." As the Air Corps was preparing to carry its first load of mail, the public appeared to agree with this assessment. In a poll conducted by the *New York Post*, a Roosevelt supporter, 8 out of 10 people questioned believed the President had acted correctly.[22]

V

Meanwhile, the Army was working feverishly to establish a nation-wide airmail transport system in 10 days' time. Foulois, Branch, and

Vidal met and determined that the Army could not possibly duplicate the service performed by the private carriers. The small open-cockpit aircraft used by the Corps could only carry a 150-pound load; to equal the normal load of one airliner, six or more Air Corps flights would be required. The Army had neither the airplanes nor the pilots to launch such an extensive operation. The three men decided, therefore, that the Army would fly only 12 routes, linking the 12 cities in which Federal Reserve banks were located.[23]

On February 16, three days before Army operations were scheduled to begin, an outwardly confident Foulois went before the House Post Office Committee. "We have assigned to this work the most experienced pilots . . . . We have had a great deal of experience in flying at night, and in flying in fogs and bad weather, in blind flying, and in flying under all other conditions," Foulois assured the committee. In actual fact, pilots with this kind of experience (such as Lt. Elwood R. Quesada, who would himself burst on the civil aviation scene some 20 years hence) were so few in number that they were assigned to "blackboard" duty, giving would-be mail pilots a concentrated course in instrument flying. Indeed, all the young men chosen for airmail flying duty had earned their wings within the past two years. Only hours after Foulois delivered his assurances, three Army airmen were killed in airmail training flights. The accidents were no different from those plaguing the Air Corps of that period during normal training operations, but this did not deter Eddie Rickenbacker, now an airline executive, from publicly labeling the deaths as "legalized murder." This was only a sample of the vituperation that would ultimately be heaped on the administration.[24]

On the very first day of Army operations, a major winter storm swept through the northern half of the country. By noon of the 19th, the northeast was engulfed in snow, rain, and fog, while the Rocky Mountain states were lashed by a severe snowstorm. Operations in the east were canceled. Winter's rage subsided only enough to permit the Corps to go airborne. Pilots riding in open cockpits struggled through below-zero temperatures, blinding storms, and squalls as they suffered frostbitten fingers, noses, and ears. The elements ultimately conspired with the Army's inexperience to bring forth calamity. On February 22, two more crashes took two more lives, one of an officer who was merely en route to supervise mail runs. The very next day, an aircraft ferrying a group of mail pilots crashed into the sea off Rockaway Point, N.Y.; one passenger drowned.[25]

The Roosevelt administration now came under the severest criticism since it took office. "The senseless butchery of young Army aviators . . . MUST STOP," declared the *New York Evening Journal.* "It isn't fair," said the *Pittsburgh Post-Gazette*, "to send these brave young men out in the weather conditions to be encountered at this season of the year without providing them with the BEST of everything." The cancellation order, declared Congresswoman Edith Nourse Rogers (R-Mass.), was "written in the blood of . . . young Army flyers . . . ." *New York Times* columnist Arthur Krock, noting the sudden change in the New Deal's fortunes, commented that "if no army pilots had crashed fatally on the frozen winter fields . . ., the probability is that the administration would have maintained throughout its first year the record of being able to 'get away with anything.'" As matters now stood, Krock concluded, "the administration feels the air mail is a bear it has by the tail."[26]

When March 9 dawned, the administration was on the defensive, but not yet retreating; by the end of that day, which saw four Army fliers perish in three mishaps, its defenses collapsed. One month (to the day) had elapsed since Farley's cancellation order; in that time, 10 men had died as a direct consequence of that order. It was not merely the loyal opposition that was now critical of the administration. "It's a shame to send some of these kids out in crates like that in the weather we've been flying," grumbled an Army officer. The public, stunned by the seeming incompetence of the nation's air arm, reacted with a mixture of grief and shock. "The country is sick at heart . . .," observed the *New York Herald Tribune* in an editorial entitled "Stop the Slaughter." But *Aviation* detected an element of confusion. "Public opinion is enveloped in a fog of unprecedented density," the journal noted. "The typical American has an agitated conviction that something ought to be done immediately, but he has no concrete idea what it should be." Senator Simon D. Fess (R-Ohio) typified the confusion, calling on the Congress to take an immediate but unspecified action. The Washington *Evening Star* advised the administration that it might as well face up to the fact that it had blundered: "Nothing is to be gained by keeping it up . . . . The Army should be relieved of a task it was not ready to assume, and the air mail should be grounded until the lawmakers decide what they want to do about it."[27]

Roosevelt was stung. The charge that he and Farley had moved hastily in a vain gesture to demonstrate their adherence to governmental purity now appeared to carry weight. Moreover, the fatalities were being played up so prominently that they were diverting attention from the real issue. As a matter of fact, the aviation imbroglio, by becoming the leading political issue of the day, was sidetracking the administration from the main business of the New Deal. The President moved to extricate himself from the wreckage of his aviation policy.

On March 10, FDR called MacArthur and Foulois on the carpet. Ushered into the Lincoln bedroom, the two generals found an irate President propped up in bed. "The man I saw wasn't the man whose picture was everywhere," Foulois noted. The familiar smile had been replaced by a deep scowl, and the voice that had consoled millions during the darkest days of the Great Depression now boomed with fury. "General," Roosevelt demanded without any preliminaries, "when are these air-mail killings going to stop?" After asking whether the crashes were the result of sabotage and being assured they were not, Roosevelt ripped into the two men. "For the next ten minutes MacArthur and I received a tongue-lashing which I put down in my book as the worst I ever received in all my military service," Foulois recalled years later. The lecture over, Roosevelt informed MacArthur and Foulois that he had just dictated a letter to Secretary of War George H. Dern instructing him to "issue immediate orders to the Army Air Corps stopping all carrying of air mail, except on such routes, under such weather conditions and under such equipment and personnel conditions as will insure . . . against constant recurrence of fatal accidents." A thoroughly dressed-down Foulois returned to Air Corps headquarters and ordered a 10-day halt to all airmail operations and a planned resumption on a reduced route structure. The 10-day layoff was a welcome respite for everyone.[28]

VI

Roosevelt also began working toward a permanent solution. On March 7, he had written a letter to Black, Kenneth McKellar (chairman of the Senate Post Office committee), and James M. Mead (chairman of the House Post Office Committee) outlining new airmail legislation. The President proposed that new contracts be let for a period not exceeding three years "on full, open and fair competitive bidding . . . ." He also proposed that airmail rate setting become, at the expiration of these contracts, the province of the Interstate Commerce Commission. Once let, moreover, contracts should not be sublet or sold by the holders to other companies. Roosevelt then proceeded to set down two conditions for qualifying as an airmail bidder. Companies having any corporate connection or affiliation with operators of competitive routes or aircraft or aircraft-part manufacurers should be prohibited from holding airmail contracts. Roosevelt, in short, would force the breakup of the large aviation holding companies. The other condition represented the punishment he would exact from carriers for their past misdeeds. "Obviously . . .," he wrote, "no contract should be made with any companies, old or new, any of whose officers were party to the obtaining of former contracts under circumstances which were clearly contrary to good faith and public policy." Spoils conference participants would be banished from the air transport scene. Within two days, a bill drafted by Karl Crowley and Harllee Branch was introduced by McKellar, for himself and Hugo Black.[29]

The operators greeted Roosevelt's proposal with mixed emotions. The provision for ICC rate-setting was welcome. And air transport companies could also welcome their prospective independence from their holding-company parents. The tie-in with manufacturing concerns, though it gave transport lines an added measure of financial security, tended to put them at a competitive disadvantage. United Air Lines, for example, had been confining its equipment purchases to aircraft manufactured by Boeing, a manufacturing affiliate of United Aircraft — this despite the fact that Douglas Aircraft, an independent manufacturer, had in the DC-2 an aircraft superior to anything Boeing could offer at that time. But being subjected to genuine competitive bidding — the first such bidding since the original routes were awarded in the 1920's — was a fearful prospect. And it was not merely the independents that engendered such fear; with Brown no longer around to rein in the appetities of the established mail carriers, there was no telling who might bid for a particular route. Of special concern was the recent emergence of E. L. Cord as a force in the aviation industry. This mercurial industrialist had gained control of Aviation Corporation — and thus of American Airways — after the spoils conference. He had clean hands, therefore, and would not be subject to any punitive measures that Congress might enact. He was reputed to be, moreover, an ardent Roosevelt supporter, a friend of Farley, and a big contributor to the Democratic Presidential campaign. Might not he, with Roosevelt's encouragement, bid on and acquire the most lucrative routes?[30]

But nothing in Roosevelt's proposal was initially so traumatic as the banishment of the spoils conference attendees. And no other provision drew quite the fire that this one attracted. "If they expect all the executives to resign who attended the so-called collusive meeting . . ., they would separate from the industry the only men who are qualified to run it," declared Eddie Rickenbacker, exhibiting once again a tendency for exaggeration. Chester W. Cuthell, the TWA general counsel, labeled the provision "a bill of attainder." Congressman Elmer E. Studley (D-N.Y.) saw in Roosevelt's proposal "an element of vengeance. . . that smacks of medieval law." Charles Lindbergh, testifying before a congressional committee, characterized it as "one of the most unjust acts I have ever seen in American legislation." But Kenneth McKellar saw things differently. "One of the first maxims of equity upheld in our courts is no one can come into court with unclean hands," said the crusty Tennessean, "and no one should come before the Government to contract with unclean hands." When the House Post Office Committee struck the provision from its version of the bill, Roosevelt served notice that he would bar the spoils conference participants, come what may, by reverting to powers he possessed in other mail statutes. "If they struck out the ban," he asked a reporter during a news conference, "did they repeal the old law?"[31]

While the ban was being debated, Secretary of War Dern launched an investigation of the Air Corps. He invited prominent civilians, Charles Lindbergh among them, to serve on a study group. Lindbergh, still in a pique, refused to serve on the grounds that the use of the Army to carry the mail "was unwarranted and contrary to American principles." The public was treated to another exchange of insults between Lindbergh supporters and detractors before a civilian board was finally constituted under the chairmanship of former Secretary of War Newton D. Baker.[32]

In the midst of all this, the Army suffered another fatality when, on March 17, two days before the Air Corps was to resume mail operations, a young lieutenant cracked up his plane during an airmail training flight.[33] Pressured by renewed rumblings of Air Corps incompetence, Roosevelt decided that he could not wait for congressional action before returning the mail to private contractors. Farley went to work on an interim plan for private carriage.

On March 30, the Post Office Department advertised for bids on temporary 90-day contracts. The advertisements specified that no company whose contracts had been canceled for fraud or collusion could bid. The operators scrambled to reorganize themselves. This process was relatively painless. A slight name change and a new corporate charter was enough to do the trick. Thus, American Airways became American Airlines; Eastern Air Transport, Eastern Air Lines; Northwest Airways, Northwest Airlines; United Air Lines, United Air Lines Inc. These and other lines had also begun the process of freeing themselves from holding-company control. Cutting loose blacklisted officials (*Black-listed*, according to pun-addicted sympathizers in the press) was a great deal more painful. But no line hesitated to perform the surgery. Airmail was the lifeblood of air transport. As it was, the short cancellation had already nearly crippled some lines financially. The choice came down to conforming or going bankrupt. The lines chose to conform.[34]

On the same day that bids were advertised the Air Corps suffered another fatality — mercifully, its last. The Corps had resumed operations much better prepared for its task than in February. New Martin B-10 bombers were beginning to arrive from the factory, and Foulois pressed these aircraft, which were well-suited for cross-country operations, into airmail service. Reduced schedules, better weather conditions, and growing experience also helped account for the Corps's improved safety record from March 19 forward.[35]

The bids on the temporary contracts, opened on April 20, surprised many observers. Competition centered on secondary routes, not on the more lucrative major routes. The established mail carriers limited their bids to routes they had previously operated. They were more interested in preserving their investments on their old lines than in expanding into someone else's territory. And, with the exception of E. L. Cord, they bid ridiculously low for these routes — in some cases 17.5 cents an aircraft mile as against the 45-cent limit established by the Post Office. The independents, on the other hand, were interested only in routes that they were equipped to handle. The transcontinental and other major routes would have strained their resources. The conflicting objectives of the bidders produced a wide spread between high and low bids. On routes that carriers had an investment to protect, they bid low; where they had no investment, they bid high. Few appeared interested in making capital expenditures on a new route unless the rate of return justified the outlay. The presumed temporary nature of the route awards undoubtedly operated as a restraining factor on everyone, including prospective investors outside the industry. It was senseless to make large investments on routes that would be opened for bids again when Congress decreed a permanent solution. Had operators known that Congress would freeze these awards, the bidding pattern would undoubtedly have been different.

The independents made some successful incursions into territory previously held by the original mail carriers. The single biggest grab was made by Braniff, which took the Chicago-Dallas route from United. National became a mail carrier by winning two New England routes, over which it had previously provided passenger service only. Central Airlines, newly organized to take part in the bidding, won a route between Washington and Detroit. Another new company, Chicago & Southern, captured the Chicago-New Orleans route. Wedell-Williams, started up again after a year's hiatus, successfully bid on the New Orleans-Houston route, penetrating deep into the territory of American Airlines. Delta took an even bigger prize from American, which sustained the heaviest losses among established operators, by making off with the Charleston (S.C.)-Dallas route, a major leg of the old southern transcontinental airway. Cord, to say the least, had failed to live up to his ogreish reputation. But there was a double irony here. Though Cord lost heavily in route mileage, his losses, in the long run, were a blessing. He emerged with a simpler and more efficient route system — a system that was destined to become the most profitable on the domestic scene.

Cord could also balance his losses in route mileage against the relatively high mail rate that he would earn. If there was a disturbing element in the bidding pattern it was that, with few exceptions, no bidder would earn fees that were truly remunerative. Principally interested in recouping the strategic positions they had lost in February, operators submitted bids that guaranteed their carrying the mail at a loss. On May 14, as the first mail pouches were loaded on commercial planes, operators looked to Congress for relief. And they needed this relief desperately, particularly United and TWA, both of which had made multi-million-dollar investments in new equipment.[36]

VII

Relief did not come immediately. The Black-McKellar Act, passed by the Congress in June, gave permanence to the three-month contracts by authorizing the Postmaster General to extend their life for an additional nine months, after which they could be "continued in effect for an indefinite period." New contracts could be let for one year and could also be extended indefinitely. The legislation set a maximum rate of 33.5 cents per airplane mile for a mail load not exceeding 300 pounds. The rate for contracts extended indefinitely, however, would be fixed by the ICC, though the maximum rate could not be exceeded. Thus, after a year was up, *Aviation* noted optimistically, the ICC would set fair and reasonable rates, and low bidders "could expect to be in clover." *Aviation*'s editor, like others, had failed to read the fine print in the Black-McKellar Act.

The rest of the act more or less followed Roosevelt's recommendations: interlocking interests between contractors and holding companies or concerns engaged in any phase of aviation were prohibited; spoils conference attendees were blacklisted; a ceiling was placed on the salaries of contracting company officials. All in all, it was not a measure that the airline industry was especially happy with. Neither, for that matter, were most thoughtful observers.[37]

The act, in point of fact, was a hodgepodge of conflicting ideologies. On the one hand, it embraced the concept of competitive bidding, which had become something of a New Deal battle cry; on the other, it adopted the idea of economic regulation — albeit on a limited scale. It was as if the framers of the act had no clear perception of the precise character of air transportation. The framers also appeared to suffer from tunnel vision. They limited public policy to but one aspect of civil air transportation — airmail carriage — and ignored the rest. If events of the previous five years had demonstrated anything, it was that airmail and air-passenger transport were intimately interwoven. It all came down to the fact that few people in Government were doing any hard, detached thinking about civil aviation. Of course, it was difficult to be detached in the highly charged political and emotional environment of the winter and spring of 1934; it was, in fact, difficult to do any thinking at all. Congress and the White House were merely engaging in some legislative patchwork.

No one recognized this more clearly than Franklin Roosevelt. As early as January 1934, when the Black hearings were beginning to heat up, Roosevelt had a short exchange with some reporters on the possibility of cancellation. The airmail, the President said on that occasion, was "a pretty big and complicated subject"; its disposition had implications not only for the whole of aviation, but for transportation in general. The

Government's objective, he continued, taking a page out of his Salt Lake City speech, should be "to coordinate all transportation, which means [placing] railroads, air, canals, waterways, and shipping under some directing body . . . ." But in March, when he made his legislative proposal to Congress, he gave no indication that he was interested in forging a comprehensive policy. He resorted, like his predecessors, to piecemeal measures. Edward P. Warner called him to account. "Some time in the very near future," he wrote in the April issue of *Aviation*, "it will become apparent that [aviation] policy must be considered not only in several parts, but also as a whole." Warner suggested that the President appoint a committee of prominent private citizens to study aviation in its entirety. Meanwhile, Pat McCarran introduced a measure in the Senate that did treat the subject in comprehensive fashion. Partly to head off McCarran and partly because he saw intrinsic merit in Warner's suggestion, Roosevelt called Black and McKellar to the White House and asked them to provide in the then-pending airmail legislation for the establishment of a commission "to make immediate study and recommend to the next Congress a broad policy covering all phases of aviation and the relationship of government thereto." Congress adopted the suggestion. In doing so, it admitted the Black-McKellar Act was a temporary piece of legislation.[38]

While Congress was deferring a permanent solution, Pat McCarran believed he had found one. In the short time that he had been in the Senate, the junior member of the Black committee had done a great deal of thinking about the essential nature of the air transport industry. The industry, he concluded, was as much a public utility as a gas or water company. That being the case, the public services it performed — the carriage of mail, express, and passengers — should come under Federal economic regulation. Establish an independent regulatory agency, he told his Senate colleagues, and endow it with the power to regulate economic activity and issue certificates of convenience and necessity. This was the way to deal with civil aviation — the same way the nation had dealt with the railroads. Yet Roosevelt, Black, and McKellar wished to continue the domination of air transport by the Post Office Department, which was not and was never meant to be a regulatory agency. "Commercial aviation should be out of the Post Office Department," he declared. "It has no place there." The Post Office had a commodity to ship. That fact was no reason why this Department should control the avenues of commerce.

McCarran's solution was essentially the same as that first proposed by Sam Bratton in 1929. And while McCarran's bill, like Bratton's, got short shrift from the Congress, it was received with a great deal more enthusiasm by the aviation community than the earlier measure. *Aviation*, sampling opinion within the industry, found McCarran's proposal being hailed as "the most constructive" of all the aviation measures before the Congress. "American aviation is solidly behind the McCarran bill," asserted the *Washington Herald*. United Air Line officials in particular were receptive to the idea of comprehensive economic regulation. The industry, said Paul Henderson, needed the protection and stability that certificates of convenience and necessity would afford; and if the Government granted such certificates, "then it will be only fair that the Government also regulate us as to make it impossible for us to make unusual profits." William A. Patterson expressed the same sentiment, but, at the same time, made it clear that the industry wanted its own regulatory body, not the rail-oriented ICC. The *Washington Herald* also found the proposal to its liking: "It simply provides a sane, businesslike foundation upon which American airlines can resume their operations — free from politics and politicians and with reasonable assurance against further change and disruption." With McCarran fighting virtually alone and working outside of the Senate's power structure, the measure never really had a chance. And while it did, surprisingly, attract the support of 26 Senators, most were Republicans whose principal objective was to deal the administration a political reversal. McCarran's proposal was slightly ahead of its time; but the tide of informed opinion was running, if ever so slowly, in the direction of comprehensive economic regulation. McCarran would ride with it.[39]

VIII

Herbert Hoover, in recalling the airmail cancellation in his memoirs, gave this short account of the event:

> After I left the White House, the New Deal, bent on making an appearance by any method, honest or dishonest, that corruption or malfeasance marked my administration, picked upon the negotiations of Postmaster Brown which had brought about order in the aviation companies. They canceled all contracts, killed a number of Army airmen trying to fly the mails, and in the end had to restore the contracts to the same operators, and,

in several cases, pay heavy damages. They were unable to find an atom of corruption.[40]

The former President's perception was faulty on many counts. The New Deal was not bent on showing that the Hoover administration was corrupt. Roosevelt did not have to play that variety of politics. There was no need to discredit the Hoover administration; it had long since been discredited in the public's eye by its inability to govern effectively during a woeful economic crisis. Yet the impression abounded among Hoover supporters that the New Deal's motives were blatantly political. "The whole affair was and will remain one of the most ruthless exhibitions of unscrupulous politics in our records," declared the *Chicago Tribune* in March 1934. The culprit in this scenario was James Farley, who, as the *Indianapolis Star* charged, "had been chiefly desirous of tossing a political bomb at his predecessor, Walter F. Brown . . . ." The fact of the matter was, however, that Farley, far from harboring such intentions, served merely as Roosevelt's instrument throughout the affair. The New Deal acted — whether wisely or unwisely — because action was required, because, considering the revelations on Capitol Hill, there was no turning its back on the matter.[41]

Assuredly, if corruption is narrowly defined, the New Deal did not uncover a single particle. Government officials had not been induced by the airlines, through bribery or other improper considerations, to render favors to private interests. This was no Teapot Dome, and the New Deal never charged that it was. What the New Deal did charge was that Government contractors had colluded with each other and the Postmaster General to prevent competitive bidding — an act contrary to law. But did Brown and the airlines violate the law? Much controversy centered around the spoils conference. Senator Austin, the Hoover administration's most able defender, had argued that holding the conference did not on its face constitute a conspiracy to eliminate competition. Brown, Austin correctly pointed out, had two types of authority — one gave him the power to award contracts through competitive bidding, the other through extensions to existing routes. The Postmaster General could proceed under either power. "The conferences were called under his extension authority," Austin said. "Since the extension authority was essentially non-competitive, the conference could not have been a conspiracy to eliminate competition." It was an effective argument, but it ignored certain crucial facts. While Brown did have these powers and others, each was granted for different purposes. Brown, at his discretion, could use noncompetitive means (extensions and route certificates) to deal with existing contractors. The Watres Act, however, gave him no discretion in dealing with carriers that did not possess mail contracts; he could grant contracts to independents through one method and one method only — competitive bidding. Not only was the law itself clear on this point, but the background to the Watres Act — dominated as it was by the denial of comprehensive negotiation powers to the Postmaster General — permitted no other interpretation. This denial was no mere whim on Congress's part. Though it believed, as did Brown, that throwing open existing routes to competitive bidding was a brand of economic mischief, it found, however, no compelling reason why new routes should not be awarded on a competitive basis. But Brown, instead of dealing with these various categories of carriers and routes separately and in a manner prescribed by law, dealt with them collectively in a manner that did not befit all. He called both contractors and independents to the conference — a conference held, according to Brown himself, for the purpose of accommodating passenger-carrying lines that possessed no mail routes — and declared at the outset that he intended to proceed without competitive bidding. This violated both the spirit and the letter of the Watres Act.[42]

Brown's defenders made much of the fact that the spoils conference failed to achieve its intended results and that the Postmaster General ultimately turned to competitive bidding. But the failure of the operators to agree on a division of the spoils did not necessarily mean that they did not collude to avoid competitive bidding. It was at this conference that Brown announced his selections for the southern and central transcontinentals. And the operators not selected — both out of fear and self-interest — abided by his wishes and did not bid on these routes. The bidding that followed was pure sham. The night-flying provision, the systematic elimination of interested independents, the deal with Halliburton, the deal with Letson — all of this was calculated to circumvent the law. So, too, was the device of granting extensions to established operators with the understanding that they would sublet them to favored independents.

The carriers did go to court, but were not, as Hoover maintained, awarded "heavy damages." A number of lines—Northwest, Western Air Express, TWA, American, and United — filed suits in the U.S. Court of Claims asking for payment of withheld mail fees accrued prior to February 19, 1934, the return of performance bonds, and damages. In

1936, Northwest, American, Western Air, and TWA proposed to dismiss their suits with prejudice if the Government would return their bonds and back pay. The Government agreed. United Air Lines, however, pressed its suit to its conclusion. The Court of Claims found in favor of the Government, though it did award the carrier $364,000 in withheld pay earned during January and February 1934. In handing down its judgment, the court said that United had entered into "agreements and combinations . . . for the purpose of preventing competitive bidding for air mail contracts and thereby excluding from the industry persons who desired to enter or continue in the industry . . . ."[43]

Hence, without question, Roosevelt had ample grounds on which to justify cancellation. Why, then, did the cancellation order lead to a political setback for the New Deal? Walter Lippmann put his finger on part of the answer. "A government," he said, "must not only do justice; it must also at all times appear to do justice." Though the Government was under no obligation to grant the carriers a hearing, doing so would have denied the New Deal's critics the opportunity to charge — and charge effectively — that the administration acted precipitously and without due process.[44]

But failure to grant a hearing was not nearly as consequential as the ill-starred decision to employ the Army in carrying the mail. Lippmann had noted in the midst of the crisis that "the air mail is perhaps a luxury which can be suspended for a time without serious consequences." Had the administration arrived at a similar conclusion early on, it would have spared the country a great deal of emotional distress. And there would have been no death toll, the daily recitation of which made it impossible for the public to concentrate on the real issues or for the administration to explain its position effectively.[45]

A substantial share of the responsibility for the Air Corps debacle belongs to Benjamin Foulois. He decided to gamble on a long shot and lost. Even worse, fully aware of the odds, he withheld them from the President. Nor was the press, which did not exactly cover itself with glory during the affair, blameless. Openly hostile to the administration, it conveyed the impression that the administration, acting out of political motives, had wronged innocent businessmen and callously sent young fliers to their deaths. No effort was made to put the Air Corps's performance in some kind of perspective. In point of fact, the Army's safety record in carrying the mail was not dramatically different from its record in conducting its usual peacetime operations. Short periods with high fatality rates were not uncommon. For example, during a 10-week period in 1933 (March 19-June 1), the Corps suffered 16 fatalities (as against 12 fatalities in a 15-week period while carrying the mail), yet neither the press nor the Congress took notice. During the five-year period 1929–1933, the Air Corps's fatal accident rate per 1,000 aircraft-hours flown was 0.109; during 1934, the rate was 0.091. During the same five-year period, the accident rate per 1,000 aircraft-hours flown was 1.25; during 1934, 1.09. Thus, the Air Corps's performance during 1934 compared quite favorably with its performance over the previous five years. The Corps, in fact, considering its past record, the unusually severe weather conditions, and its lack of experience in cross-country and instrument flying, performed creditably. It had carried nearly 777,400 pounds of mail in 78 days without losing a single pouch. And though it had lost 12 men, only 5 had been killed while actually carrying the mail.[46]

The Air Corps, then, had performed no better or no worse than it was accustomed to performing. Compared to commercial carriers, however, the Corps had an atrocious safety record. This fact and what it implied — that the nation's air arm was in an extreme state of unpreparedness—was as shocking to the national consciousness as the death of the young airmen. With the shock came a remedy. Flying the mail, recalled H. H. Arnold, an eventual successor to Foulois, "gave us wonderful experience for combat flying, bad weather flying, night flying; but best of all, it made it possible for us to get the latest navigational and night-flying equipment in our planes." As Foulois had calculated, taking on the assignment led the Congress and the administration to follow a more generous approach towards Air Corps needs. But Foulois himself was not around very long to enjoy the new equipment harvest. Under fire from the Congress and the press, he retired in 1935.[47]

Foulois's career was only one of many that ended in the wreckage of the New Deal's aviation policy. Paul Henderson and nearly a score of other airline executives were cast adrift to make their way in other fields. Some, like Henderson, who emerged a broken man, never found another niche for themselves. Others, like MacCracken, who saw his aviation clients evaporate, but managed to build a new law practice from scratch, were made of sterner stuff. Roosevelt, miraculously, emerged unscathed; Farley, acting as his lightning rod, had absorbed most of the heat.

There was no denying, however, as the *New York Times* noted, that cancellation and its aftermath had produced "the worst blow to the [New Deal's] prestige which has yet befallen it." The New Deal, hitherto seemingly politically invincible, had been proven mortal. In the long run, however, the affair produced localized, rather than general, consequences — consequences confined to the New Deal's relations with the aviation community. Scarcely a year before, the aviation community had welcomed the New Deal with open arms; now a large segment of this community had been disaffected. When Roosevelt proclaimed the week of October 14 as Air Navigation Week, *Aviation* judged that the administration was extending "the right hand of fellowship to the air transport industry of America"; the journal cautioned its readers, however, not to allow themselves to be lulled into a state of complacency: "[It] is well to bear in mind that the administration packs a wicked left . . . ." Many needed no reminder to be wary. "The aviation record of this administration can be written in one word . . . M-E-S-S," wrote Frank A. Tichenor, president of *Aero Digest.* "Mr. Roosevelt and his bright boys . . . kept their promise all right — they gave us a New Deal. But what a Deal! Every single card has been marked." The administration had a long way to go to repair the damage.[48]

As for the carriers, they took the consequences and hoped for the best. They could not afford the kind of open hostility to the administration indulged in by the likes of Tichenor. Besides, cancellation had not been devoid of good. The carriers had broken loose from holding-company control. With quick profits no longer on the horizon, carriers no longer had to worry about speculative raids on their securities, a factor making for management stability. The independents, given their long-sought opportunity to bid, were now of no concern. Finally, when carriers took the trouble to make a dispassionate appraisal of the administration's intentions, they could look to the future with lightened apprehension. The administration had done a curious thing. It had canceled the airmail contracts because they had been let without competitive bidding. One would have expected it, therefore, to restore competition to airmail carriage — a prospect that struck fear in the hardiest of carriers. Instead, in what must have brought a twinge of wry pleasure to Walter Folger Brown, the New Deal restricted competition. Might not this same administration, at some time in the near future, abandon competition altogether in favor of comprehensive economic regulation? The carriers clung to this hope as they looked with anticipation to the report of the Federal Aviation Commission — the group established by the Black-McKellar Act to review aviation policy. Roosevelt had appointed exceptional people to serve on this group; they were people who could be depended on to look after the industry's and the nation's interests. Thus, in assessing the recent tumult, *Aviation* concluded that the credits outweighed the debits. The year 1934, the journal's editor commented, was "the year in which the crack of doom proved to be only a starting gun." This assessment was correct except in its implied anticipation of quick results. The starting gun had sounded, but the runners broke ever so reluctantly off the block.[49]

11. Safety: A Crisis in Confidence

The aviation community, the Congress, and the public at large could be excused if, by 1935, they viewed the New Deal as fumbling and incompetent in aviation affairs. There was nothing in the record to suggest that Roosevelt had, or that he even intended to get, a firm grip on things. The airmail cancellation had been a political disaster. The austerity program at the Bureau of Air Commerce, thought to be a temporary aberration, was continued into fiscal 1935 and 1936. The report of the Federal Aviation Commission, hailed by many as a policy breakthrough, was filed away and seemingly forgotten. In only one civil aviation area — safety — did the administration appear to be immune from criticism. In the three-year period 1930-1932, scheduled domestic air carriers experienced one passenger fatality per 4.8 million passenger-miles flown; in the next three years, they suffered only one passenger fatality for every 18 million passenger-miles. These were truly amazing statistics. But statistics can be a poor line of defense in the aftermath of an airline crash; they were no defense at all in 1935, when even the New Deal's friends were questioning its competence in aviation matters, and an air disaster — headlined in newspapers across the land — took the life of a U.S. Senator.

II

Investigating and determining the probable cause of aircraft accidents was a burden that the Bureau of Air Commerce and its predecessor, the Aeronautics Branch, had difficulty bearing. Controversy had surrounded the function from the beginning. The Branch, uncomfortable in carrying out this responsibility, had shrouded its accident investigations in secrecy. Congress, mindful of the need for public disclosure, demanded a full airing of the facts. In the investigation of the Rockne crash, when Clarence Young finally recognized that secrecy was patently unacceptable, the Branch handled itself clumsily, issuing half-baked conclusions in its rush to still the public's clamor for an explanation. After this incident, it was clear to all that public disclosure would become a way of life. The problem now was to secure legislation that would put more teeth into the Department's investigative powers and, at the same time, protect the air carriers by prohibiting the use of accident reports in legal suits. Hiram Bingham tried to get such legislation through two successive Congresses, but failed. When Vidal took office, he pressed for passage and succeeded. In mid-1934, Congress passed an amendment to the Air Commerce Act that (1) compelled the Secretary of Commerce to make public a report on the probable cause of each fatal aircraft accident, (2) gave the Secretary the power to subpoena witnesses and evidence in probable-cause proceedings, and (3) prohibited the Government's accident report or other evidence gathered by Federal investigators from being admitted as evidence in court.[1]

But this legislation, while it resolved the issue of public disclosure, did nothing to correct the basic flaw of the probable cause provision. The responsibility of determining probable cause was misplaced in the Department of Commerce. The Bureau of Air Commerce issued and enforced safety rules, established routes, and maintained navigation aids. Hence, when it investigated an accident, it investigated not only the performance of a pilot, an air carrier, or an aircraft manufacturer, but its own performance as well. Clearly, there was a conflict of interest here. And though few people had as yet thought about the matter, given time and the appropriate circumstances, the Bureau's detractors would turn the question into a live issue.

The appropriate circumstances presented themselves on May 6, 1935, when a TWA airliner crashed outside of Kansas City, killing, along with four others, Senator Bronson M. Cutting (R-N.Mex.). Cutting, a political progressive of the Robert M. La Follette school, had supported Roosevelt during the 1932 election only to find himself at odds with the President over the reduction of veterans' pensions. This prompted FDR to throw his support to Cutting's opponent, Denis Chavez, when the New Mexican ran for reelection in 1934. Cutting eked out a narrow victory, which Chavez, with the President in his corner, promptly disputed. The contested election went to the Senate for resolution. Cutting was returning from New Mexico, where he had gone for the sole purpose of securing affidavits supporting his case, when he was killed.[2]

Progressives in the Congress had bristled when Roosevelt turned on Cutting. After all, they reasoned, though Cutting had opposed Roosevelt's austerity program, he had supported many other New Deal measures. And now that Cutting had been killed, their feelings turned to bitterness. Some progressives even blamed the President for Cutting's death. They reasoned that he would not have been on the ill-fated airliner if Roosevelt had not urged Chavez to contest the election. The outcome was that disgruntled progressives, anti-New Deal conservatives, and those with nagging doubts about the administration's slashing of the Bureau of Air Commerce budget joined forces to push a resolution through the Senate directing the Committee on Commerce, or a subcommittee thereof, to investigate the accident. The resolution, on its face, was a vote of no-confidence in the Bureau of Air Commerce. To exacerbate matters, Ewing Y. Mitchell, fired by Roosevelt shortly after the accident, used the occasion of his dismissal to criticize Vidal. "It may well be," Mitchell stated, "that the lives of Senator Cutting and those who died with him . . . might have been spared if one with knowledge, experience, and stability suited to the position had been in charge, for the past two years, of the Bureau of Air Commerce." This was but the first of a long series of accusations leveled at the Bureau and its personnel.[3]

Royal S. Copeland, chairman of the Committee on Commerce, organized a five-man subcommittee, which he would head, to carry out the Senate resolution. Copeland's choices to fill the subcommittee — Hiram Johnson (R-Calif.), Wallace H. White, Jr. (R-Maine), Bennett Champ Clark (D-Mo.), and A. V. ("Vic") Donahey (D-Ohio)—were not likely to make the administration feel at ease. Johnson, admittedly, was in sympathy with the New Deal's broad aims. It was also true, however, that he belonged to that small band of progressive Republicans of which Cutting had been a member and had deeply resented the treatment accorded his dead colleague. When Denis Chavez, appointed by New Mexico's governor to succeed Cutting, arrived to be sworn in, Johnson got up and walked out of the Senate Chamber. White was on the other end of the Republican Party's political spectrum. He had been a member of the Black Committee, and, for the most part, had resented the turn this probe had taken. White now had an opportunity to give the Roosevelt administration a taste of its own medicine. Clark and Donahey were both conservative Democrats who had given no more than luke-warm support to New Deal legislative goals. And Copeland, who had strong ties to William Randolph Hearst and Tammany Hall, was even less sympathetic to the New Deal. The Commerce Committee chairman, moreover, had a political ax to grind. Roosevelt had withheld his support from Copeland's bid for reelection in 1934. Thus, there was not one man on the subcommittee who, at this point in time, could be called a friend of the administration.[4]

The accident that killed Bronson Cutting and four of his fellow travelers had been weather related, though to say this is to skim the surface of a complex incident. The airliner (TWA flight No. 6), bound from Los Angeles to New York via Albuquerque, Kansas City, Colum-bus, and Pittsburgh, had encountered instrument flying conditions approximately 100 miles west of Kansas City. At 1:52 a.m., when the flight was 45 minutes out of Kansas City, it received a weather broadcast reporting that the ceiling at Kansas City's airport was 600 feet. The landing minimum from that airport was 700 feet. The pilot and the TWA dispatcher in Kansas City had a number of options. They could detour the flight to Wichita or Omaha, both of which were clear, thus enabling the aircraft to refuel, by-pass Kansas City and the weather, and proceed to its next stop, Columbus. They could overfly Kansas City and land at an intermediate field in Burlington, Iowa, or Kirksville, Mo., where they could refuel and then proceed to Columbus. Or they could plow ahead and attempt to land in Kansas City. Weather conditions alone demanded a reasonably conservative course. But the weather was not the only consideration demanding such a course. The aircraft, plagued by an erratic radio transmitter from the outset of its flight, was having difficulty maintaining two-way communication with the ground. Air commerce regulations required aircraft engaged in protracted instru-ment flying to maintain two-way radio contact. Thus, merely to abide by this rule, the pilot should have avoided the instrument flying weather around Kansas City by putting in either at Wichita or Omaha, where he could have had his transmitter repaired or replaced. These consider-ations notwithstanding, the pilot chose to bring his flight into Kansas City.

Meanwhile, another coast-to-coast flight (TWA flight No. 8), which had taken off from Los Angeles 30 minutes ahead of the aircraft carrying

Cutting, experienced extreme difficulty in landing in Kansas City. The pilot first attempted a visual landing, which he was forced to abort. His next attempt, an instrument landing, was aborted by a regularly scheduled weather report. The ground-based radio equipment of that day was incapable of giving both directional signals and weather reports simultaneously. The four-course directional range, therefore, was periodically interrupted for the transmission of regularly scheduled weather reports. Accordingly, the flight No. 8 pilot was forced to go through another complicated procedure to reorient himself with the range (he spent close to 30 minutes in all over Kansas City) before making a third and successful landing attempt. On landing, he told the TWA dispatcher that he had encountered a ceiling of no more than 450 feet — a fact promptly verified by the TWA meteorologist on duty. Even with this information before him, the TWA dispatcher did not move to redirect flight No. 6 to another airport until 3:00 a.m., some 36 minutes after flight No. 8 had landed. Having ascertained that Kirksville had a visibility of five miles and a ceiling of 1,200 feet, the dispatcher instructed flight No. 6 to fly toward Burlington and land at the first available field. By this time the flight was 30 minutes overdue. Whether it received the message is problematical. An hour earlier, the copilot had noted on the ship's log, "Radio transmitter out, two-way receiver very weak."

In any case, the pilot did try to land in Kansas City. After circling the airport for an indeterminate period — all the while wasting valuable fuel — he set out for Kirksville. Just minutes away from the intermediate field, the pilot, concerned about his dwindling fuel supply, lowered the aircraft below the overcast and flew visually. In places he was flying no higher than treetop level. He was only 16 miles from the Kirksville runway when he failed to pull the aircraft out of a fog-shrouded draw.[5]

In their accident report, released on June 4, 1935, Department of Commerce investigators laid the blame for the accident squarely on TWA and the pilot in command, who, along with the copilot, had been killed in the crash. TWA ground personnel at Alburquerque and Kansas City were guilty of errors in judgement, according to the report. TWA personnel in Alburquerque should not have cleared the flight when they knew its radio was malfunctioning. Ground personnel in Kansas City failed to reroute the aircraft expeditiously to a field with tolerable weather conditions after it became apparent that the Kansas City airport was below the authorized landing minimums and while the aircraft still possessed sufficient fuel to fly to an alternate landing field and still maintain the 45-minute fuel reserve required by Federal regulations. The pilot had also committed an error in judgment, according to the report, by pushing ahead after discovering that he was not communicating effectively with the ground.[6]

In a separate action, the Bureau of Air Commerce cited TWA and TWA personnel for a variety of violations. One of the more serious charges was that the pilot and copilot had not met the technical requirements for the flight to which they were assigned. The pilot and copilot had earlier flown the ill-fated airplane into Los Angeles as a charter flight; the return charter was canceled and the company pressed the airplane and its crew into service on a regularly scheduled flight. Federal regulations stated, however, that a pilot who had not flown a particular scheduled route in more than six months could not be reassigned to that route without prior Bureau of Air Commerce approval. Perhaps because this was a one-time flight for the pilot, TWA did not secure such approval. The pilot, it was further discovered, had missed his last regularly scheduled medical examination and thus was technically ineligible for assignment to any scheduled flight. Neither was the copilot eligible for his assignment. Regulations set a limit of eight consecutive flying hours between approved rest periods for pilots on scheduled routes. The normal flying time between Los Angeles and Kansas City was 8 hours 15 minutes. The Bureau, however, could waive the 8-hour rule for certain routes, which it had done for the Los Angeles-Kansas City route at the request of TWA. But whenever such a waiver was in force, the standards for the copilot were automatically raised; the company was required, in such a case, to assign to the flight a copilot with a scheduled air transport rating, the same rating required of the pilot in command. The copilot on flight No. 6 had not qualified for this rating.

In addition to these three violations, TWA was charged with (1) failing to carry reserve fuel sufficient for 45 minutes' flying (an aircraft was required to have this much reserve at its point of destination; the reserve had been depleted in the futile attempt to land in Kansas City); (2) engaging in instrument flying without effective two-way communication; (3) attempting a landing in Kansas City when the ceiling was below the landing minimum for that airport. In all, the airline incurred civil penalties totaling $3,500. The Bureau also fined the pilot of flight No. 8 a sum of $500 for landing in Kansas City when the ceiling was below the specified minimum.[7]

TWA was not about to take this verdict sitting down. Jack Frye, the TWA president, fired off an open letter to William Randolph Hearst disputing the findings of the accident board. The accident occurred, Frye charged, "because the favorable landing condition reported by the observer at the Kirksville field did not exist." Expecting to find a ceiling of 7,000 feet, the pilot "actually found . . . practically a zero-zero condition . . . ." The airline denied committing the violations it was charged with and refused to pay the penalties assessed against it.[8]

Frye's primary concern was protecting his company from legal damages. The Cutting crash was the first air disaster involving a TWA airliner in scheduled passenger operations since the passage of the public disclosure amendment. Never before had the events leading up to an accident been laid out in such detail before the public. And though the Government's findings could not be used as evidence in court, Frye had much to be concerned about. Any lawyer could use the Government's report as a road map to locate his own evidence. Some lawyers were no doubt doing just that before filing suit for Cutting crash survivors injured in the crash. TWA simply could not afford to do anything that left even the slightest impression that it was admitting negligence.

Frye's use of the Hearst newspapers as a forum suggests, though by no means conclusively, that Frye and Copeland were cooperating in establishing TWA's defense. Copeland had been a former Hearst employee; a medical doctor before entering politics, he had for many years written a health column for the Hearst chain. Hearst had supported Copeland, both personally and in his editorial pages, each time the New Yorker ran for election. Copeland had broken with Roosevelt, and Hearst was himself on the verge of an open break. The three men could thus find common ground in seeking to discredit the Bureau's accident report, though their motives may not have precisely coincided. Hearst's motives were perhaps the simplest — one more opportunity to attack Roosevelt. Copeland's were more complex. Beside his New Deal animus and his dislike of Roosevelt were his sympathy for TWA and his genuine interest in promoting aviation safety.[9]

The Copeland Committee staff, headed by Harold E. Hartney — the same Harold E. Hartney that had interested MacCracken many years before in the founding of the National Aeronautic Association — now launched a concerted effort to prove the contention set forth in Frye's letter. They soon came up with a theory that the airways keeper on duty at Kirksville on the night of the crash had left his post and had persuaded a friend to fill in for him by sending out canned weather reports over the Bureau's teletype network. The committee staff also gathered a batch of affidavits from local residents holding that the weather in Kirksville at the time of the accident was zero-zero. With this evidence before him, Copeland called E. Y. Mitchell's successor, J. Monroe Johnson, and reportedly said, "We have found the man who murdered Senator Cutting" — meaning the Kirksville airways keeper. Johnson promptly dispatched a team of postal inspectors to the scene, who found Copeland's evidence less than convincing. Indeed, they shot the entire theory full of holes.[10]

The committee staff was forced to pursue another tack. They found a disgruntled former Bureau of Air Commerce employee — one Jay A. Mount, who had been fired as Superintendent of Maintenance for falsifying travel vouchers and for other misdeeds—and persuaded him to concoct his own version of the probable cause of the accident. Even before Mount had gotten into his project, he wrote a friend, "I believe I'm going to work up a darned good case placing the blame of the crash on the radio range at Kansas City being out of alinement." To assure that he did so, Jack Frye talked to him personally over the telephone and ultimately dispatched TWA's Kansas City superintendent to help Mount "get some matters clear in my mind" — thus providing further evidence that TWA and the Senate committee were working hand in glove. Relying entirely on secondary sources (and his own considerable imagination), Mount constructed a theory that placed the blame for the accident on faulty maintenance of navigation aids. He had enough knowledge of the Bureau's maintenance procedures to give his theory a ring of plausibility. Copeland and Hartney paraded Mount before the committee, where he read his account in open session.[11]

Meanwhile, Jack Frye came forth with yet another version of events, and put the Bureau on the defensive on other fronts. In his testimony before the committee, the TWA president maintained that the critical point in the flight occurred when the Bureau turned off the Kansas City range for a weather broadcast, thus forcing the pilot of flight No. 8 to abort his instrument landing. Frye pointed out, correctly, that TWA had asked for a continuous beam for flight No. 8 — a request that was normally granted as a matter of course, but which the Bureau, inexplicably, failed to honor on this occasion. Had the request been honored, flight No. 8 would have landed three minutes after its initial approach;

instead, the flight required 25 minutes to land. In the interim, Frye explained, TWA ordered flight No. 6 to stand by until flight No. 8 landed. If flight No. 6 had not been ordered to stand by, it would have arrived in Kansas City before the ceiling had fallen below the landing minimum. None of this squared with the available record, but no matter — Frye had pointed to a serious weakness in the radio range then in use, a weakness that the Bureau would have been overcoming if it had had sufficient research and development funds available.[12]

Frye also attempted, with a great deal more attention to factual accuracy, to demonstrate that the Department's regulations on scheduled air transport operations had been improperly promulgated and were, therefore, not in force at the time the accident occurred. TWA, therefore, could not be charged with violating regulations that had no legal standing. (He made it plain, however, that both flight No. 6 and No. 8 followed these regulations to the letter during the morning of May 6.) Frye appeared to be introducing a technicality into the proceedings. All air carriers, including TWA, had considered the regulations valid when they were promulgated; to have done otherwise would have invited anarchy in the skies. But Frye had put his finger on a decided weakness in the Bureau's regulatory process: regulations were issued in such a haphazard manner that even Bureau personnel themselves sometimes had difficulty determining what was in force. Frye capped his assault by attacking the air commerce regulations on other grounds — sloppy draftmanship. Again, because the facts were on his side, he made telling points.[13]

III

The facts relating to the probable cause of the Cutting crash were clearly on the Bureau's side — and Denis Mulligan and Shorty Schroeder had made a brilliant recitation of them before the Copeland Committee. The trouble was that no amount of brilliance could make the Bureau's position altogether convincing. The Bureau of Air Commerce, just as much as TWA, was a party in interest. This was the crucial fact on everyone's mind; this was the fact from which the Bureau had no escape. The controversy between the Department of Commerce and TWA, Frank Tichenor wrote, "goes right to the heart of the Government's system of regulating the aviation industry." TWA's contentions, if correct, exposed a hidden disease gnawing at the vitals of America's air transport system — the disease of "face saving." "Can a Government agency," Tichenor asked, "sit in judgment upon an activity in which it itself participates?"[14]

A Copeland Committee staff member, Carl Dolan, conducted a review of Department of Commerce accident reports between 1927 and 1935 and found that out of a total of 101 fatal accidents 30 had been attributed to human error, 27 to a combination of weather and human error, 26 to weather, and 18 to other or undetermined causes. In no case had the Department attributed the cause of an accident to itself. Dolan concluded that Bureau personnel had "whitewashed themselves for 10 years." Yet he offered no proof to back up his charge except the probability suggested by his statistics. David L. Behncke, president of the Air Line Pilots Association, did not go quite so far in impugning the Bureau's motives, but he did detect a tendency on the part of accident investigators to "conveniently blame" the pilot whenever "immediate concrete evidence" for an accident had not turned up in the investigation.

Vidal, put on the defensive, tried to transfer the onus of face-saving from the Bureau to the airlines. It was to be expected, he said before the Copeland Committee, "that an air-line operator might attempt to shift the blame for an accident to the Bureau if possible, because the air line, after all, has more at stake." Bennett Champ Clark pounced on Vidal's statement. Vidal, Clark said, had touched "the very crux of the whole problem." Conceding that it was in the operator's interest to shift blame, he asked whether it was not "equally of interest to the Department, in order that its heads may save their own scalps, to shift the blame to the operator, and particularly to the pilot who may have died?" Vidal's statement, Clark held, amounted to an indictment of a system that employed a party in interest to conduct a disinterested investigation. There was no combating Clark's reasoning. This was a case where the facts could not speak for themselves. It did not matter, as Fred Fagg put it, that "there wasn't one investigation that wasn't conducted . . . properly"; the fact was that "the public didn't believe that that was the case."[15]

Vidal readily admitted that the accident investigation function was misplaced. The uproar over the Cutting accident, he told the Copeland

Committee, had made it "inadvisable in the future for Bureau personnel to investigate probable causes of accidents." Having Bureau personnel judge their own inspection and airway services was proving embarrassing. But he stopped short of offering a concrete alternative. Joseph B. Eastman, Federal Coordinator of Transportation, set down a rule for Copeland to follow. Where a Federal function involves dealing with parties with conflicting interests, the hearing of these parties, and the making of decisions based on the record, he said, that function "should be carried on by what we have come to call an independent agency . . . ." Edward P. Warner agreed. It was folly, he said, to entrust everything aeronautical to a single agency. Where the paramount objective was administration, an executive agency was called for; "where the natural thought is . . . of even-handed justice as between contending claimants," a commission or board was called for. Administrative and quasi-judicial functions should not be mixed. David Behncke made a concrete proposal. All except the promotional activities of the Bureau of Air Commerce should be transferred to, and made a separate branch of, the ICC; at the same time, a safety board concerned with accident prevention and investigation should be established — a board that would be separate and distinct and would have "nothing to do with any other functioning or regulating body." Few things would have pleased Vidal more than the establishment of such an independent board; in its absence, he was forced to live with the specter of public distrust.[16]

The Copeland Committee had not been established long before it became evident that it was interested in more than just the specific cause of a single accident or who should or should not be charged with determining probable cause. "It is apparent," *U.S. Air Services* declared in October 1935, "that the Cutting tragedy will be only a peg on which to hang a penetrating investigation of air transportation and associated organizations."[17] Chief among the "associated organizations" was the Bureau of Air Commerce. The accident had afforded an opportunity to those who believed that all was not well with this Federal agency to give their opinions free expression. Some men seized the opportunity with a vengeance.

A favorite subject of the Bureau's detractors was the workings of the spoils system and its debilitating effects on the organization's efficiency.

Even Edgar Gorrell, the president of the Air Transport Association, who was not on unfriendly terms with Johnson and Vidal, asserted that the Bureau's basic problems could be traced to politics. Aviation, he told Senator Harry S. Truman (D-Mo.), should be placed "behind an insulated wall, where politics cannot get at it . . . ." E. Y. Mitchell's political machinations while he was Assistant Secretary received prominent billing during the hearings. The former Assistant Secretary's tampering with the rolls of aviation medical examiners was spotlighted, as was his blatant attempt to turn a hearing board meeting, convened to determine the fate of three district managers charged with incompetence, into a political confessional. According to a board member, Assistant Secretary John Dickinson, Mitchell asked each of the accused "Whether they did not think that the approval of the New Deal by the people of the United States as expressed in the election of President Roosevelt required a clean sweep of Government employees connected with the old deal and whether they did not think that having held their jobs for a number of years it was time for them to get out and let others have a chance at these attractive and lucrative jobs." The board voted to dismiss the three employees, who, as it turned out, had been unfairly charged by a cantankerous superior who was himself guilty of misdeeds.[18]

Precious little else was uncovered to suggest that the Department was playing fast and loose with the civil service system (though, admittedly, employees not covered by the system were often replaced for no other reason than to make room for Democratic Party faithful). The fact that Mitchell's actions were disapproved of by his peers and near-peers in the Department, and that Mitchell himself was unceremoniously dismissed, had no impact on the Committee or on the public's conception of the Bureau. Vidal could counter that 90 percent of the Bureau's employees were blanketed under civil service and that the minimum qualification for certain job categories had been raised — but such rebuttals were to little or no effect. The exaggerated picture of the Bureau as a spoils system stronghold, first painted in 1933 by disenchanted aviation editors and copied by Copeland-hearing witnesses, could not be easily altered.[19]

Thus, Franklin K. Lane, Jr., who had served on the Federal Aviation Commission, talked of the necessity of making tenure in the Bureau of Air Commerce "more or less permanent." The Bureau, he lectured, was a "technical and scientific" agency — an organization of professionals whose appointment and advancement procedures should be governed by individual merit. David Behncke in turn stressed the need for continuity and professionalism. Under the present system, which he believed was controlled by political considerations, there was too much uncertainty and too little continuity. A job at the Bureau of Air Commerce should be looked upon as a career. "I do not think we are going to get what we want in aviation until we take the Department of Commerce out of politics," said another critic, Charles H. Payne. "You have got to have the most competent men that this country can produce. They should not be changed at the end of 4 years." *U.S. Air Services* had a suggestion. Remove Vidal, replace him with a qualified man, and allow the new man to choose, under the civil service system, the professionals best fitted to perform "the technical duties in the noble profession of protecting and saving human lives." Only then, the journal observed, would the public be assured that "the aids to safety" were being operated at "an EFFICIENCY OF 100 PERCENT . . . ."[20]

Critics were on more solid ground when they pointed to the strained and decidedly unhealthy relationship between the members of the Bureau's triumvirate. "There is a wide-spread suspicion that many of the higher officials of the Bureau of Air Commerce are more intent on building themselves up politically than building up aviation," Frank Tichenor asserted. "You might suggest to the three musketeers in the Bureau of Air Commerce," Cy Caldwell wrote to a Copeland Committee aide, "that it would help matters if they all stopped playing politics and attended to their knitting — and that goes for all three of them, my dear friend Carroll Cone as well as the other two."[21]

It was not without reason that Caldwell put special emphasis on Cone, who, from the day Vidal was named Director, devoted a large measure of his energies to establishing himself as pretender to the throne. "For four long years J. Carroll Cone . . . has basked in the spotlight at the entrance to his side-show in the Commerce building, cultivating the impression among his followers that he is the real ringmaster and not Vidal," *U.S. Air Services* charged. As if all this was not bad enough, Cone's supporters openly campaigned to install him in Vidal's post. "I think it is a common belief . . . that the Bureau, as it is administered, does not have the confidence and respect of those who are engaged in aviation," wrote Charles F. Horner, president of the National Aeronautics Association, to J. Monroe Johnson. "That situation is so nearly intolerable that any attempt to defend it until there is an indication of necessary changes would be futile and would probably make a bad situation worse." Horner's solution was to fire Vidal and put Cone in charge of the Bureau. Even Clark Howell, who had headed the Federal Aviation Commission and should have known better, offered precisely the same advice to Johnson. The tendency, though by no means universal, was to blame Vidal for most of the ills plaguing the Bureau. Few bothered to discern that Vidal was in an impossible position and that the confusion and uncertainty caused by the clash of personalities and ambitions could have been ended just as easily—and more appropriately —by firing Vidal's disputatious deputies. But any change — even that sought by Cone's supporters — was preferable to the status quo. Roosevelt and Roper, though they knew this to be true, continued for the time being a state of affairs that everyone recognized as intolerable.²²

Implicit in the charges of face-saving, political cronyism, and dissension at the top was the larger charge that the Bureau of Air Commerce was not doing its job, which implied, in turn, that the airways were unsafe. Critics bore in on specific matters that appeared to support this larger contention. The nature of flight No. 6—the length of time it spent in the air, its use of both visual and instrument flight rules, its dependence on ground organization, its rerouting to an intermediate field — lent itself to a critical examination of Federal rules and practices.

Jack Frye had already questioned the validity of the rules governing scheduled air carrier operations, thus focusing attention on Department of Commerce rulemaking procedures. Others questioned the wisdom of the rules themselves. The accident drew particular attention to the regulation that permitted the waiving of the 8-hour rule governing a pilot's flight time.

The Air Line Pilots Association (ALPA) had been conducting a running battle with the Commerce Department over the number of flight hours pilots could safely log in scheduled air transport operations. The question emerged in the early 1930's when ALPA, then a fledgling organization, discovered that some operators were working their first pilots as many as 170 hours per month. In the fall of 1931, the Department of Commerce acted by limiting the first pilot to a maximum of 110 flight hours per month. The Department also limited the number of flight hours for any 7-day period to 30, and for any 24-hour period to

8, with a rest period of 24 consecutive hours during each 7-day period. Largely to accommodate operators, however, a waiver of the 8-hour rule could be secured over certain routes. Copilots, moreover, were not covered by any of these limitations.[23]

ALPA was less than happy with the new rule. When the Roosevelt administration took office, Behncke undertook an aggressive campaign to get the limitation reduced to 90 hours per month. He was supported in this campaign by the Aero Medical Association, which, in September 1933, recommended that a flying limitation of 85 hours per month be established for first pilots on scheduled transport operations. When the Department of Commerce held fast to its 110-hour limitation, and negotiations with individual operators failed, the pilots association turned to the National Labor Board, which had been established by Roosevelt in August 1934 to handle disputes arising under NRA. The Labor Board, relying heavily on information supplied it by the Aero Medical Association, laid down an 85-hour monthly limitation, or 1,020 hours per year. The NLB, however, had no power, other than moral suasion, to back up its decision. The result was that the Bureau of Air Commerce and most of the operators ignored it. "The operators seem determined to break down the 85 hour limit set by the Labor Board," Behncke complained to Shorty Schroeder. "These chiselers never seem to be satisfied. Eighty-five hours is plenty . . . ."[24]

Meanwhile, the pilots association was receiving a more sympathetic hearing in Congress. Thus, the Black-McKellar Act included a provision that empowered the Secretary of Commerce "to prescribe the maximum flying hours of pilots on air-mail routes" — a power he already possessed under the Air Commerce Act; Black-McKellar also required all airmail contractors to conform to the decisions of the NLB on rates of compensation and working conditions for pilots, mechanics, and laborers. The latter provision had no binding effect on Department of Commerce regulations; nevertheless, the legislation increased the pressure on the Bureau of Air Commerce to bring its rules into closer conformity with the Labor Board decision. In October 1934, the Bureau adopted a new rule limiting the first pilot to 100 flight hours a month and not more 1,000 hours in any 12-month period. The 8-hour rule was retained, as was the provision permitting its waiver on certain routes. The copilot's flight hours were limited for the first time, to 100 per month or a maximum of 1,200 per year.[25]

ALPA was still not satisfied. Though the yearly maximum of 1,000 hours for the first pilot was lower than the number of hours under the NLB formula, Behncke still held out for the 85-hour monthly limitation. He also questioned the wisdom of granting waivers of the 8-hour rule. When the Cutting crash occurred, Behncke pounced on the waiver rule. "A tired pilot is an unsafe pilot," he declared. And, in truth, the pilot of flight No. 6 had been on duty for 9 hours 30 minutes before he cracked up his aircraft. The last two or three hours, which required flying in instrument weather, had been particularly stressful. When he made the fatal error of dropping into the draw, he must have been something less than the pilot he had been a few hours earlier. Though one could only speculate whether a fresher pilot could have avoided disaster, Behncke had made his point that Federal regulations were not as rigorous as they might be.[26]

The Department, through its actions, as much as admitted Behncke's point. To its credit, it suspended the waiver rule a few weeks after the accident and ultimately rescinded it in a January 1936 revision of the air commerce regulations, thus closing the matter permanently. But the impression left on many people was that the Bureau would not act unless a tragedy forced it to act. In this case, at least, this impression did not wholly square with the facts. No one had made a scientific determination of the critical points of pilot fatigue. All the contending positions in the matter — even that of the Aero Medical Association — had been arrived at empirically. Under the circumstances, the Bureau of Air Commerce was at sea with no rigorously arrived-at data to guide it.[27]

The character of the Air Commerce Regulations, while a concern, was not a major worry. More troubling was the state of the Federal airways — the state they had been reduced to by the administration's austerity program. The expectation that the Bureau of Air Commerce budget would rebound after the deep cuts suffered in 1933 failed to materialize. By fiscal 1936, the Bureau's budget had dwindled to 57 percent of its fiscal 1932 allotment. Aggravating matters, air carrier activity tripled during the period, while general aviation activity increased by 20 percent. All Bureau divisions were hit hard and had to scramble just to stay in place; none, however, were hit as hard as the Airways Division. Airway appropriations were scarcely sufficient to keep facilities in working order. What funds were expended on new airway construction and the installation of improved aids came from the

Public Works Administration; but even with the infusion of PWA money, New Deal expenditures for airway development in the four fiscal years 1933-36 amounted to only a third of the funds allotted by the Republicans over the previous four fiscal years. A Vidal boast that his administration had cut the cost of maintaining and operating a mile of airway from $350 to $330 per year had a false ring. Skeptics wondered whether these savings were truly the result of increased efficiency; they wondered even more whether these savings had not compromised the airway system's safety. As *Fortune* exclaimed, "The watchword of the Department of Commerce has been 'economy' — economy so short-sighted that the citizen whose life it jeopardizes is utterly unable to comprehend it . . . ."[28]

"As matters now stand," declared Fred Smith, an Ohio aviation official, "except in a few isolated instances, our airways are not developed adequately even for scheduled air transport . . . ." Some people who agreed with Smith did not hesitate to link the Cutting crash with the state of the airways. "I am satisfied," Senator Copeland declared, "that the Cutting disaster could have been prevented if we had had all of the equipment and the use of the equipment that we should have had." Others were not ready to go so far. Airline operators, fearful of frightening their customers away, approached the subject gingerly. C. R. Smith, president of American Airlines, after enumerating for the Copeland Committee a list of well-traveled airways that were without navaids, was careful to point out that he had no complaints about the functioning of existing aids; he merely wanted more. "We have never had an accident that could be charged to the failures of an airway aid or facility," declared W. A. Patterson, president of United Air Lines. Edgar S. Gorrell, president of the newly created Air Transport Association, told a Senate appropriations committee that "whoever laid out these air-ways aids . . . did a marvelous job . . . . [It] was a monument to somebody's brains and intelligence . . . ." But, he continued, the time had come to expand and modernize these aids. Only TWA seemed to be somewhat out of step with the industry. The carrier had aided and abetted Jay Mount, who delivered a scorching, if unwarranted, indictment of the airway system before the Copeland Committee. Subsequently, in April 1936, when a TWA airliner crashed into a mountain near Uniontown, Pa., TWA blamed the accident on a malfunctioning radio range. But the company (as well as other carriers, no doubt) must have had second thoughts about the wisdom of such tactics; it quickly retracted its statement and left the determination of probable cause to Federal investigators.[29]

For their part, Federal officials tried to explain that navigational aids were not safety devices; they were needed, Vidal said, "only for completing schedules in unfavorable weather." "The matter of safety is merely a matter of balancing regulations against aids," J. Monroe Johnson pointed out. "You can make any airway safe without any aids, if you restrict them to perfect weather." Airlines often got into trouble, Vidal suggested, when, in their desire to meet schedules, they pushed existing aids beyond their known capabilities.[30]

Johnson and Vidal were indulging in an oversimplification. Navaids did exist for navigation; but a malfunctioning aid was a safety hazard. The loop antennas employed on most four-course ranges were subject to a so-called "night effect" — a severe swinging of courses through a wide arc during hours of darkness. An unsuspecting pilot following such a course could easily plow into the side of a mountain. The Bureau of Air Commerce knew the cure for this condition — the replacement of loop antennas with T-L antennas, which were not subject to the night effect. But it lacked the funds to prosecute this replacement program vigorously. The same thing held true for the introduction of a visual-type radio range (which permitted the simultaneous transmission of course and weather information), Z-markers, and fan markers, all of which would not only increase efficiency but also add a measure of safety. None of these critical programs could be financed out of the Bureau's no-growth budget. Time had overtaken the airways. "It must be remembered that most of the [aids] were engineered around 1930," declared Paul Goldsborough, president of Aeronautical Radio, Inc. The Bureau readily admitted that the airways had not kept pace with technology. "I consider . . . that every radio range that we possess of the loop type antenna is an obsolete range," said Rex Martin. Eugene Vidal added: "You might compare certain of our radio equipment with a home radio set built about 10 years ago."[31]

The Department of Commerce was not insensitive to the implications of Vidal's statement. J. Monroe Johnson had worked overtime trying to pry airway funds loose from all available sources. Responding to pressures from the Copeland Committee, the National Aeronautic Association, the Air Transport Association, the Business Advisory

Council, and the National Accident Prevention Conference, he put a $9 million airway modernization package together and presented it to Harold Ickes, the PWA head. Ickes turned it down, as did Harry Hopkins, the administrator of the Works Progress Administration. Johnson pared the program down to $5 million and took it to the Bureau of Budget. He got another rebuff for his trouble.[32]

Every bit as disturbing was the extent to which austerity had handicapped the Bureau's safety function. "I am ashamed to admit that at the present time only three inspectors are engaged in aircraft factory inspections," Cone told the Copeland Committee in May 1936. "Any lack of inspection on the part of the Bureau," Cone said, "is due wholly to the lack of sufficient personnel, or to facilities and funds for travel." The Bureau's total inspection force numbered only 60 men, who had to pass upon 14,000 licensed fliers, 24,000 student pilots, 8,000 aircraft, and 2,500 mechanics. Edgar Gorrell calculated that each member of the force had to conduct 800 inspections per year. "It is more than a man can do," he said, "especially when you come to realize how far-flung [the airway system] is." Aircraft for flight-inspection use were in short supply. "Strange to say," Assistant Secretary Johnson asserted, "we regulate and inspect all of these modern airplanes, and yet we in the Bureau have only small fabric-covered planes, only four of which are equipped to [flight-test navigation aids]." At the rate that Congress was appropriating funds for new aircraft, Vidal told a House subcommittee, "it will take over 50 years . . . to replace [the Bureau's obsolescent fleet]." The general decline in the level of safety services rendered came down to a simple matter of arithmetic. In fiscal 1932, the appropriation for the regulating and inspection service was $1.4 million; in fiscal 1936, it was $0.644 million. And there was no relief in sight. For fiscal 1937, the Bureau of the Budget granted the function a token increase of $90,000.[33]

Aviation safety, whether by coincidence or as a result of the administration's tightfisted policies, began to deteriorate badly. Air carriers had a disastrous safety record in 1936. The passenger fatality rate per 100 million passenger-miles flown, which had stood at 4.78 in 1935, jumped to 10.1 — the highest rate since 1932. David Behncke, pointing to the hazards faced by professional airmen, calculated that over the last five years one air carrier pilot was killed, on the average, every 28 days. "The vice president of the Pilots' Association was killed in an airplane crash," he said, inserting a personal note, "and I was myself a

little over a year ago severly injured . . . ." A vague sense of ill-feeling
gripped the aviation community and the flying public. "There is great
disquiet in the public mind about safety of life in the air," J. Monroe
Johnson asserted. Cy Caldwell, an aviation journalist and pilot, assayed
the industry's safety record and dashed off a letter to Harold Hartney.
"We're nowhere near the safety record of railroads or even steamships or
buses or private automobiles, and we probably won't be for some time,"
Caldwell wrote. "But we are engaged in a noble experiment, and the
public is in the position of the uncomprehending guinea pig in the
medical labratory, who contentedly munches his lettuce until a medical
student gives him a jab with a needle and proceeds to dissect him."
Caldwell exaggerated, but it was the kind of exaggeration that was being
fed by the feeling of malaise — a malaise that could be traced directly to a
public loss of confidence in the ability of the Bureau of Air Commerce to
carry out its responsibilities in aviation safety.[34]

IV

It was in this atmosphere of general uneasiness that Copeland, on
June 30, 1936, issued a preliminary report of his committee's findings. In
many ways — in its unrepressed bias, its disdain for facts, and its gross
distortions — the report probably had no parallel in the annals of the
Congress. The report was also extraordinary in its free wheeling criticism
of public officials.

The Cutting crash, according to the report, had been caused by three
malfunctioning Bureau of Air Commerce navaids — the Kansas City
four-course range, the Kirksville radio marker, and the Kirksville
rotating light beacon. The committee, of course, was entitled to its
opinion; but in reaching this conclusion, it systematically disregarded
any and all facts that did not support it. Reams of disinterested testimony
that would have led the committee to a different conclusion was ignored.
Indeed, the report did not give the slightest hint that such testimony even
existed. But while taking no notice of crucial facts that were within its
reach — indeed, its knowledge — the committee attempted to report
events that were beyond its ken. It even went so far as to attempt to
reconstruct what was going on in the dead pilot's mind as he flew the ill-
fated airplane from Kansas City to Kirksville, and neatly arranged these
reconstructed thoughts between quotation marks.[35]

John H. Wigmore, retired Dean of the Northwestern University Law School, who had worked as a legal adviser to the Copeland Committee, delivered what was perhaps the most accurate contemporary description of the committee's handiwork. Wigmore found the report "deeply disappointing" as a document "purporting to be the result of an impartial study, setting forth sufficient evidence from which the public may fairly draw conclusion . . . ." Wigmore continued:

> It is incomplete and incoherent in its statement of the crucial issues of fact. It gives the impression of bias against the Bureau of Air Commerce; as a partisan brief it would read well. It omits a number of principal data that would lead to a different finding; and these omissions are so consistent that they indicate deliberate choice. The result is that the readers can only be misled as to the balance of probabilities in respect to the precise causes of the accident and the allotment or responsibility for them.[36]

Wigmore had discerned the truth of the matter. The Copeland Committee had deliberately painted a distorted picture of events. Copeland's motives were mixed; it seems clear, however, that one of his objectives was to protect TWA by constructing a counterweight to the Bureau of Air Commerce findings. No other purpose can fully explain the lengths to which he went to distort the record.

Having blamed the accident on the Bureau of Air Commerce, the report unleashed a one-sided assault on Vidal and Martin. Martin, according to the report, engaged in office politics, was disloyal to Vidal, and lacked the necessary "professional equipment" to head the Airway Navigation Division. The report concluded that "a larger man" than Martin was needed to fill this "place of great responsibility." It also recommended that Vidal be replaced, though it threw a few compliments his way. Vidal possessed all the necessary technical qualifications and experience for his job, the committee granted; what he did not possess was the temperament of an administrator. He was too amiable; he was lacking "in iron, positiveness, and the determination to keep the employees under his direction functioning according to schedule." The Director of Air Commerce must possess "greater firmness, greater experience with men."

The committee gave Cone a clean bill of health. "Concerning Colonel Cone, we have no recommendation to make," the committee stated in its report. "He came through the ordeal without criticism." But to many it seemed like a strange business to criticize Martin for playing office politics, while letting Cone, a master practitioner of the art, off the hook. It seemed strange, too, that Martin was attacked as incompetent, while Cone, who, at the time of the Cutting crash, had the responsibility for flight-checking the very navaids the committee contended had caused the disaster, escaped unscathed. Once again the committee had selected only those "facts" that suited its purpose.[37]

But that purpose was more than what immediately came to the surface. True, Copeland was indulging in an unseemly business: distorting the truth to protect an air carrier; unfairly attacking a Federal agency which, on balance, was doing a passable job under difficult circumstances; turning a tragedy into a political football; taking sides in a bureaucratic controversy that had no higher purpose than self-aggrandizement. Copeland did this and thereby intensified the malaise gripping the aviation community. But the New Yorker had a higher purpose, too. Even Vidal and Johnson freely admitted that all was not well at the Bureau of Air Commerce. The Federal airways suffered from neglect. The regulatory and inspection functions of the Bureau were desperately shorthanded. Political ambition divided the Bureau's leadership. It was Copeland's higher purpose to deal with these matters, for he had, in the final analysis, a genuine interest in aviation safety. And his report, in spite of its glaring faults, had the merit of driving a vital point home to Roosevelt and the Congress. That point was that the time had come to attend to the civil aviation affairs of the nation.

12. Cutting Up the Sky

"Hot on the trail of Senator Copeland's condemnation of the Bureau of Air Commerce comes the news that the government is taking over active control of air traffic," reported *Business Week* in July 1936.[1] The Bureau of Air Commerce, under siege by the Congress, the aviation press, and assorted segments of the aviation community, was manifesting a surprising resiliency and an unexpected capacity to respond to a new challenge. All may not have been well at the Bureau, but things were not so bad as the Copeland report suggested. Indeed, while Copeland's staff was still assembling its report, the Bureau was preparing to undertake the staggering responsibility of controlling air traffic. In consequence, 1936, an otherwise wretched year for the air agency, finished on an upbeat. The beleaguered Bureau of Air Commerce was finally rebounding from the sharp policy and political reversals it had sustained during Franklin Roosevelt's first term.

II

It was in and around terminal areas that air traffic control first became necessary. "Terminals," said Harry H. Blee, an Aeronautics Branch official, in May 1932, "always have been, and probably always will be the 'bottle-necks' of transportation, whether of ground, water, or air systems."[2] En route traffic could operate on a see-and-be-seen basis; but because all operations began and ended within the limited confines of an airport, there was an early need to regulate the flow of takeoffs and landings.

The earliest control methods were crude by any standard. A controller, equipped with a set of flags, stationed himself at a prominent spot on the field. A wave of a green or checkered flag signaled the pilot to proceed; a red flag, to hold. This signaling system was more effective in controlling takeoffs than landings, and was useless at night. In the early 1930's it was displaced at such major airports as Cleveland Municipal, Newark, Hoover Field in Washington, D.C., and Lambert Municipal in St. Louis by a system of light guns. Mounted on standards and equipped with sights, the guns were aimed at incoming or outgoing aircraft, which could detect their red or green beams at a distance of a mile or more in clear weather. Some airports made use of hand-carried light guns, which were employed principally to control takeoffs.[3]

Both flags and lights had a common shortcoming: neither could control the approach or departure of aircraft beyond visual range. As early as the late 1920's a number of airport operators began experimenting with a low-power radio transmitter. Limited to 15-watts by the Federal Radio Commission, the transmitter could reach appropriately equipped aircraft within 15 miles of an airport. In 1930, the City of Cleveland made a quantum jump in airport traffic control techniques. It constructed a radio-equipped control tower — the first of its kind — at its municipal airport. The tower was so located as to offer an unobstructed view of the airport and all of its approaches. The radio equipment possessed a simple single-wire antenna that stretched between the top of the tower and a support on the roof of the building. The tower controller contacted approaching aircraft, informed them of weather and landing conditions and of the presence of other aircraft airborne in the vicinity or taxiing on the runway, and ultimately gave them permission to land. The controller could follow the progress of approaching aircraft on a position map, which was updated by periodic position reports transmitted by the pilot to the company dispatcher and relayed to the tower. Aircraft preparing for takeoff were similarly controlled.[4]

This kind of system was considered adequate enough, provided traffic was light, air speed relatively low and relatively uniform, and the weather good. But traffic began to burgeon after the passage of the Watres Act, and the newly introduced DC-2's and B-247D's, which cruised at speeds in excess of 180 m.p.h., began sharing the airspace with much slower aircraft, making for a dangerous traffic mix.

Newark and Chicago, the nation's busiest terminals in the mid-1930's, were handling between 50 and 60 landings and departures per hour during peak traffic periods. This traffic was not beyond the ability of airport control to handle safely, if it arrived in orderly fashion. But with no airway control to regulate its flow, traffic came in randomly,

The Cleveland Municipal Airport control tower, the first radio-equipped ATC tower in the United States

often arriving at the same time to compete for a portion of the congested airspace around the terminal and ultimately for a piece of concrete on the ground. "Often airplanes were compelled to waste time circling in the air waiting for a safe chance to land, or alternately, to risk the danger of landing while others were taking off or landing," Jerome Lederer reported. "Rivalry, sometimes dangerous, developed between the pilots of competing companies to land their passengers first." Air traffic congestion, noted *Aviation* in August 1935, was causing consternation at the busier terminals. "There are many excellent pilots who would rather do anything than land a private airplane at Newark, Cleveland or Chicago," the magazine observed.[5]

The introduction of instrument flying brought more woes. "We have planes coming [into Chicago and Newark] from different directions at about the same time," related D. W. Tomlinson, a TWA test pilot. "They are coming in on the radio beams with no visibility . . . ." Gill Robb Wilson, a New Jersey aviation official, reported that Newark Airport often had "as many as fifteen planes circling [it], all of them blind flying and trying to keep at a different altitude, and some of them low on gas." Hair-raising experiences were common. One incident, perhaps apocryphal, is worth relating. An airmail flight from Albany arrived over the Newark radio range in a blinding snow storm. The pilot radioed the Newark tower and asked about the visibility below, pointing out that he was at 3,000 feet and could not see his wing tips. Before the tower could answer, the pilot of another incoming aircraft radioed the pilot of the first plane that he too was over the radio range at 3,000 feet. A long pause followed before the second pilot radioed back that there was no cause for alarm because he had just climbed to 3,500 feet. "We both better worry," shot back the first pilot. "I climbed to 3,500 too. Now you stay there and I'll start down." Congressman James M. Mead, chairman of the House Post Office Committee, recounting reports of similar incidents over congested airports, told the House: "Something must be done about uniformly controlling the ever-increasing air traffic around our major airports, and practically all of our airways, if public safety is to be served." In the judgment of the airline operations committee of the Aeronautical Chamber of Commerce, airway traffic control was "one of the most serious problems facing air lines at present . . ."; the early adoption of a standard method of controlling traffic was "vitally necessary." Obviously, pilots could no longer be allowed to fend for themselves.[6]

New Jersey officials were having grave concerns. Worried state legislators introduced bills providing for the establishment of air traffic control along the airways feeding into Newark. The idea of state control was patently unworkable. "There was a great question legally as to whether we could pick up a ship and tell it to stay in a certain place . . .," explained Gill Robb Wilson, "or whether we could tell a ship over one state to stay there." Reacting to New Jersey's legislative proposals, Congressman Mead placed the blame on the failure of the Federal Government to grapple with a problem that was "purely interstate." "This is definite proof that it is high time action is taken by the Federal Government, or we shall be faced with as many different kinds of air traffic control laws as there are States, which will strangle and hamper the industry to a point where progress will be impossible." TWA's vice president in charge of operations told Harold Hartney in October 1935 that it was absolutely essential that all airway traffic "be brought under the control of the Department of Commerce."[7]

By this time, the Bureau of Air Commerce had already decided to take a hand in order to head off disaster, though it was scarcely prepared to contribute more than advice and encouragement. In April 1935, Vidal had called a conference of airline operators to consider their air traffic control problems. The operators recommended that the Bureau study the airway situation and come up with a method of controlling it. Vidal accepted the recommendation. A week later, he called on the military services, including the Coast Guard, to appoint representatives to join with Department of Commerce officials and draw up regulations to deal with the hazards fast being created by the increase in instrument flying. The situation demanded, Vidal told Rear Admiral Ernest J. King, "one central authority . . . to regulate all [instrument] flying by means of clearances . . . and designating courses and altitudes at which such flying should be done." In September, the military services agreed that they would look to the Department of Commerce for the regulation of all en route traffic on designated civil airways. From this point on, events moved rapidly. Working groups, involving Federal, civilian, military, and airline personnel, were organized. Airlines began drawing up inter-line agreements governing traffic along mutually used routes. And a Washington meeting was scheduled, for November 12-14, to hammer out a final solution.[8]

As things turned out, the Bureau could not wait for the November meeting before taking action. As early as August 21, Schroeder warned Cone that traffic conditions at Chicago and Newark were becoming so menacing that immediate regulatory initiatives were necessary. As a preliminary step, Vidal decided to move against private fliers. On November 1, he signed a notice ordering all airway users except airline operators to refrain temporarily from making instrument flights within 25 miles of the center line of a radio beam or within 25 miles of an air carrier airport. The order, according to the New York Times, was met "with a squawk that echoed from Mines Field, Los Angeles, to Roosevelt Field, L. I." "With their increasing schedules, destined to much further increase, [airlines] are the air highway users par excellence," observed one critic. "But they neither are nor should be the only beneficiaries."

Louis R. Inwood, a representative of the Aeronautical Chamber of Commerce, pointed out that "not only do miscellaneous fliers sometimes get in the way of the scheduled air transport, but sometimes, very decidedly, the air transports get in the way of the miscellaneous flier." Vidal really had little choice but to be arbitrary. The Air Transport Association had been conducting an active campaign against uncontrolled flights around air carrier airports. "Private flying," Edgar Gorrell told a congressional committee, "is today a menace when the private flier is allowed to land, uncontrolled, at these congested terminals . . . ." Vidal was forced to establish priorities, and in doing so he had to give preferential treatment to air carriers. Aircraft carrying one or two people could not be allowed to interfere with public carriers loaded with mail and passengers. "We perhaps may have unnecessarily antagonized the itinerant flyers when we issued our original bulletin," Cone explained later, but "several near-collisions" involving air carriers and military and private aircraft forced the Bureau to act as rapidly as possible, without prior consultation with all affected parties.[9]

On November 12, and on the following two days, representatives of all segments of the aviation community (except manufacturers) met at the Commerce Building in Washington with Bureau of Air Commerce officials and heard the reports of the various study groups established by Vidal. Though the conference was confronted with a host of important questions, the chief question was whether to accept a recommendation by the study group on airway traffic control — viz., "that a uniform and centralized system of air traffic control be set up by [the Bureau of] Air Commerce, such system to be handled by a group of government employees . . . ." If any of the conferees opposed this recommendation, they remained silent. The problem was, however, that the Bureau was in no position to assume such a large responsibility. The Bureau's budget had no slack, and the quest for additional funds would take months. Meanwhile, winter weather was bound to increase the level of instrument flying and thereby compound the hazards on the airways.

The conference had few options. All intentional instrument flying could be prohibited until such time as the Bureau was financially able to establish an air route traffic control system; or someone other than the Bureau could undertake to control traffic. The first option would have dealt a severe blow to the airlines' blossoming scheduled passenger operations; the second, though it would require a considerable outlay in private funds, seemed preferable. Vidal confronted the operators with a proposition. If they undertook to establish airway traffic control immediately, he promised that the Bureau of Air Commerce would take over the operation within 90 to 120 days. Realizing that they were already in a race against time, the operators accepted.[10]

No one was deluding himself that the airlines could operate the system as well as the Bureau, which could back up its operations with rules that had the effect of law. But any control, however inadequate, was freely conceded to be better than none at all. Moreover, the airlines could save the Bureau valuable time by working out ATC procedures, training ATC personnel, and generally accumulating experience in the control of airway traffic.[11]

On November 15, Vidal approved an interairline air traffic agreement between carriers flying the Chicago-Cleveland-Newark airway. At the same time, he relaxed the general ban on instrument flying by private fliers; these pilots could now fly by instruments if they filed a flight plan with the Bureau of Air Commerce and with at least one airline flying over the route they planned to use. On December 1, four air carriers — United, American, TWA, and Eastern — established a small experimental airway traffic control unit at Newark. Each of the lines assigned at least one man to the unit, which was eventually incorporated.[12]

Encouraged by the success of the Newark unit in establishing some order along the airways leading into the New Jersey terminal, the operators laid plans for opening additional units. At an operators meeting on March 10, 1936, they decided to establish airway stations at Chicago, Cleveland, Pittsburgh, and Oakland. Chicago's unit began operations in April, Cleveland's in June. Personnel who had gained experience at Newark were put in charge of the new operations. Each of these three units cost the airlines approximately $6,000 a month to run.[13]

Immediately after the March 10 meeting, ATA president Edgar Gorrell began pressuring Vidal and Assistant Secretary Johnson to live up to the gentleman's agreement of the previous November. Not that the airlines were concerned about continuing to bear the expense of running the units; rather, their principal care was that they could not do the job nearly so well as the Bureau of Air Commerce. "Any amount of money provided by the operators cannot solve the problem . . .," Gorrell informed J. Monroe Johnson. In a letter to Johnson on March 11, Gorrell argued that the effective scope of the ATC units was restricted because they had "but questionable authority over air transport flight and [none over] military and miscellaneous flight operations." Carroll

Cone, who was eager for the Bureau to take over the operation, explained to a congressional committee that "a competing airline cannot regulate another; . . . and they certainly cannot regulate private . . . flyers. The Army and Navy will not submit to orders from private or commercial operators . . . ." Nor, Cone could have added, were pilots of airlines not belonging to the ATC consortium a very submissive breed.[14] Earl F. Ward, a former American Airlines employee who had put together the Newark station, issued a warning to Shorty Schroeder on March 14:

> The fact that there have been no major disasters caused by collision in the air has so far been a matter of luck rather than forethought, and I cannot urge too strongly, basing my statement on first-hand knowledge, that the Bureau of Air Commerce move in on this problem with the utmost speed, as the consequences of such a collision would provoke . . . a storm of comment and criticism such as has never been seen before.
>
> To summarize, funds should be made available at once to enable the formative work to go forth under the auspices of the Bureau of Air Commerce rather than the air lines and coincidentally regulations should be promulgated and plans formed looking toward the ultimate set-up.[15]

It had been 90 days since the Bureau struck its bargain with the operators. About all the Bureau had done in this time to carry out its end of the agreement was to hire Earl Ward, on March 6, and give him authority to act for the Bureau in ATC matters and assist the airlines in the establishment of the Chicago and Cleveland units. In fact, while Gorrell was urging Johnson and Vidal to act, the Department of Commerce was mired in an internal legal debate.[16]

During the November 1935 conference Vidal had asked the Department's Solicitor to determine whether the Secretary of Commerce possessed the legal authority to control air traffic. "There does not appear to be any doubt . . . that the necessity for such control [arises] from the duty to protect and to advance interstate air commerce," James J. O'Hara, the Acting Solicitor, ruled in early December. Moreover, O'Hara argued, the Air Commerce Act specifically charged the Secretary with the responsibility for establishing air traffic rules, "including rules as to the safe altitudes of flight and rules for the prevention of collisions . . . ." This authority, O'Hara said, was so broad that it encompassed all flight, intrastate as well as interstate. It appeared to O'Hara, however, that before the Secretary established ATC facilities he should first formally designate as "civil airways" those routes over which he intended to exercise control. This would effectively remove state jurisdiction over these airways and avoid any possible conflict between state and Federal authority.

O'Hara's opinion should have settled the matter, but didn't. Denis Mulligan, in helping to frame a reply to Gorrell's March 11 letter, told Vidal that he doubted that the Air Commerce Act gave the Bureau the power to do the things sought by Gorrell. The Secretary could establish and operate air navigation facilities over designated airways; "but whether he can take part in the operation of aircraft over such airways . . . seems . . . to be a distinct question in itself," Mulligan argued. "That the Congress . . . intended to thrust the Government this intimately into the aviation business is not at all clear." Johnson sought another opinion from the Solicitor, all of which infuriated Cone no end. "What we need . . . more than anything else is a lawyer to help us find a way to do things rather than to find out reasons why we cannot," he told Vidal.

Vidal did not really take the legal issue seriously; he believed that the only impediment before the Bureau was money, which he intended to raise little by little by making judicious savings in on-going Bureau activities. Cone probably didn't take it seriously either, though this did not stop him from pointing to the issue as evidence of footdragging, hoping, perhaps, that the ensuing denials would inspire a greater sense of commitment. In fact, Gorrell's March 11 letter, in which he spoke of the Bureau's "duty" to assume the responsibility for ATC, appears to have been partially inspired by reports from Cone and his staff that the Bureau was having second thoughts about the November gentleman's agreement. Vidal, irritated by these tactics, told Cone flat-out that "someone in your division has misrepresented the facts" to Gorrell. It is doubtful that Cone accomplished much more than to widen the gap between himself and his chief.[17]

Cone and Vidal were still at loggerheads when, on March 24, they went before a subcommittee of the House Appropriations Committee to ask for supplemental funds. The divergent positions that these men took must have left more than one Congressman slightly incredulous. The request, as it came from the Bureau of the Budget, was for $500,000 for some badly needed airway facilities. Vidal proposed to amend the request by allotting $100,000 of the total for the hiring of more inspectors to bolster the Bureau's undermanned regulatory force. Thomas S. McMillan (D-S.C.), the subcommittee chairman, suggested that since the problem of air traffic control was so pressing the $100,000 might better be spent for that purpose. Vidal had just painstakingly pointed out to McMillan that he desperately needed more inspectors; thus Robert L. Bacon (R-N.Y.) sought a way out by suggesting that $100,000 earmarked for radio aids be used for air traffic. Vidal explained that the entire $400,000 for airway facilities would support the projected ATC system by providing key radio aids along critical approaches. As for ATC startup costs, Vidal told of his intention to secure these funds by cutting back on airway beacon lights. "It is a question of making a saving in what is becoming less important and putting that amount of money on what is now more serious," he said. Vidal obviously wished to preserve his flexibility by not being tied to a specific budetary line item for air traffic control. Cone would have none of it. "I do not know just how he proposes to save the money," he told McMillan and Bacon, seizing the opportunity to contradict his chief. Vidal rose to the occasion. If the subcommittee left his request intact, he countered, he would promise not to commit any money for airway markers until he had worked out something for air traffic control. The subcommittee let Vidal have his way.[18]

In the next few weeks Vidal scraped up $175,000 for the takeover of the ATC units early in fiscal 1937. On June 3, in an anticlimatic eleventh hour decision, Solicitor O'Hara reaffirmed his earlier ruling that air traffic control was "absolutely necessary to foster air commerce, prevent disasters and protect lives and property." On June 6, the Bureau of Air Commerce assumed control of the Newark, Chicago, and Cleveland ATC units, designating them airway traffic control stations.* At the same time, the Secretary of Commerce formally designated 73 air routes as civil airways of the United States. The Federal Government had undertaken a responsibility that would ultimately become, in terms of manpower and facilities employed, its most demanding civil aviation function.[19]

III

Taking over the three ATC stations was, in the first instance, largely a matter of paperwork; the facilities themselves became Federal property

---

*The modern name for these facilities is air route traffic control centers.

and controllers and station managers were made Federal employees and eventually blanketed under civil service.*

The rest of it, for the moment, became a matter of adopting the ATC procedures that had been worked out at the three stations, primarily by Earl Ward and Glen Gilbert. These two men, more than any others, were responsible for creating a new enterprise, and a new profession, from scratch — Ward contributing his substantial managerial skills, Gilbert his conceptual powers. Ward, incidentally, whose title was Supervisor, Airway Traffic Control, served in this capacity until the spring of 1937, when he was placed at the head of a new Airways Operation Division, created during a wholesale reorganization of the Bureau of Air Commerce. At the same time, an Airway Traffic Control Section was also created within the Operation Division; Gilbert moved from his job as manager of the Chicago station to become chief of the new section.[20]

Each station was manned by a crew of five — a manager, assistant manager, and three controllers. The stations operated 16 hours a day, from 8 a.m. to midnight; but the availability of air traffic control services itself created more traffic and the stations eventually went on a 24-hour schedule. The crews worked overlapping shifts. The largest on-duty contingent, present during periods of heaviest traffic, numbered three; the smallest, one.[21]

Each station was equipped with a blackboard, a large table map, a teletype machine, and a telephone.†

---

*In addition to Earl Ward, who had been hired earlier, the Bureau brought on board 15 controllers: from Newark, John Huber, R. A. Eccles, Hugh McFarlane, E. A. Westlake, and William H. Cramer; from Chicago, Glen A. Gilbert, Lee E. Warren, Emerson R. Mehrling, J. V. Tighe, and R. E. Sturtevant; from Cleveland, L. Ponton de Arce, Homer Cole, C. J. Stock, Harry D. Copland, and Clarence T. Tolpo. W. H. Cramer to N. A. Komons, April 3, 1975.

†At this early juncture, the Bureau of Air Commerce was unable to provide the stations with logistical and engineering support. This forced each station to rely on its staff and local suppliers for equipment design and fabrication. Hence, though equipment was similar in type, models differed from station to station.

The Bureau relied on the ingenuity of working controllers to introduce equipment improvements. John L. Huber, a Newark controller, was instrumental in helping design the first telephone recording equipment; Huber also designed the first "flight progress board," which eventually supplanted the blackboard. J. V. Tighe, a Chicago controller, designed the first satisfactory shrimp boat. Not all controller-inspired equipment changes were equally successful. As a replacement for the cumbersome blackboard, Lee E. Warren, the Washington station manager, designed a "sequencing board" of 20 interchangeable slate panels, or slats. When all the slats were in place, the affair resembled a blackboard with 20

Earl F. Ward poses with the original group of Bureau of Air Commerce airway controllers. Left to right (front row): *Hugh McFarlane, C. T. Tolpo, Ward, Harry D. Copland, & R. E. Sturtevant;* (middle row): *J. V. Tighe, Glen A. Gilbert, E. A. Westlake, C. J. Stock, R. S. Roose, & R. A. Eccles;* (back row): *Lee E. Warren, Emerson R. Mehrling, L. Ponton de Arce, Homer F. Cole, & John L. Huber. Of the 15 controllers entering the Federal service on June 6, 1936, only William H. Cramer is missing from this photograph. Roose was not a member of the original 15*

---

horizontal lines running across it. The controller kept flights in vertical sequence by interchanging the slats, which fitted into a metal frame and were locked into place by rods; in interchanging, the controller unlocked and pulled out a slate panel from its metal frame and lifted the rest of the panel into their new positions with a foot treadle connected by cables and pulleys. "Anyone who could work a full shift without getting a bruised finger or a skinned shin bone got a free drink after hours," cracked Lee Warren. This cumbersome device soon gave way to the flight progress board.

Standardization did not emerge until 1938, after the creation of the Civil Aeronautics Authority, when Warren and C. E. Wise, a CAA engineer, took ideas from all locations and assembled a standard ATC station configuration in a prefabricated building at Washington Hoover Airport. From this prototype, CAA made engineering drawings and began converting stations (now called centers) to this configuration. Enclosure to ltr., Lee E. Warren to Nick A. Komons, April 2, 1977, FAA Historical Files.

Flights were posted on the blackboard, which detailed their progress and their estimated time of arrival and altitude over designated geographical fixes. The information on the board was transferred to the map, on which all airways were plainly marked. Small brass markers shaped like shrimp boats, one for each flight in the control area, dotted the map. Each marker was equipped with a clip, to which could be attached a slip of paper. The controller noted on the paper the name of the airline, the flight number, the flight's time of departure, and cruising altitude. Placed in positions on the map table corresponding to the actual flight progress of aircraft, these markers showed by their pointed ends the direction of flight and gave a clear, concise picture of what would probably take place as incoming aircraft converged around the terminal area. Each marker was moved every 15 minutes to conform to the estimated or actual progress made by aircraft.[22]

When three controllers were on duty, each performed a distinct function. The so-called "A" controller issued all necessary instructions to aircraft, including clearances, and maintained the dispatch board and the inbound flight log. The "B" controller (or coordinator) handled the weather sequences, maintained two other logs, and positioned the shrimp boats on the map. The "C" controller (or calculator) calculated the speed of incoming ships, estimated the time they would arrive over designated fixes, and entered these estimates on the blackboard. During periods of low traffic activity, one man performed all three functions. When two men were on duty, the functions of the coordinator were split.[23]

Only passive control was exercised over aircraft flying in controlled areas during periods of good weather. Nevertheless, their progress was followed as if they were under active control, and pilots were informed of other aircraft within 15 minutes or less of their line of flight and of the estimated time and altitude these aircraft would pass over designated points.[24]

Aircraft came under active control only during instrument flight. When ATC was under airline jurisdiction, its function was to keep en route airline traffic separated and flowing in such a manner that it arrived at terminal areas in an orderly sequence. The Bureau recognized that under its jurisdiction airway control had to be expanded to include all aircraft flying the civil airways on instruments. "We have been prone, perhaps subconsciously, to think of airline transports when air traffic control is mentioned," Earl Ward cautioned. "However, the safety of

The Newark airways control station, 1936

passengers in and operations of other than scheduled air transports must be given consideration; . . . an air transport . . . can be jeopardized by lack of supervised control of an operator of any other aircraft . . . ." Safety required that all instrument flights "proceed from origin to destination in a prescribed manner."[25]

Accordingly, following the formal designation of the nation's civil airways, the Bureau issued a set of regulations, effective August 15, 1936, governing instrument flight. Under the new rules, all civil pilots desiring to fly intentionally by instruments over a civil airway were required to have a federally licensed aircraft equipped with a two-way radio and federally prescribed instrument-flying equipment. The pilot himself had to possess an instrument rating. Agreements were worked out with the Armed Services, which issued directives requiring military aircraft to have equivalent equipment, and military pilots equivalent qualifications. Pilots were also required to file a flight plan if they intended to fly by instruments or along a civil airway when visibility was

Airway controllers plot aircraft movements

less than one mile. Flight plans were subject to the approval of airway traffic control. These rules had the effect of keeping general aviation aircraft, few of which were equipped for instrument flying, and general aviation pilots, few of whom had an instrument rating, off the airways frequented by air carriers during instrument weather conditions. Aircraft not equipped with instrument-flying equipment could, however, fly between the bottom layer of the overcast and the ground.[26]

Active control was exercised by separating aircraft horizontally and, if the need arose, vertically. All aircraft on civil airways, whether flying by instruments or visually, during good or bad weather, were separated horizontally. Eastbound aircraft (i.e., those on a heading of 360° to, but not including, 180°) were required to fly at odd thousand-foot altitudes (1,000, 3,000, 5,000, etc.); westbound aircraft (i.e., those on a heading of 180° to, but not including, 360°), at even thousand-foot altitudes (2,000, 4,000, 6,000, etc.). Pilots could deviate from these altitudes only in an emergency, at the express request or authorization of ATC, or when crossing an intersecting airway; in the last case, they were required to cross an intersecting airway at 500 feet above their normal altitude.*[27]

Controllers did not have direct radio contact with aircraft under their control. Pilots and airway controllers communicated with airline dispatchers, Department of Commerce radio operators, and airport traffic controllers, who acted as middlemen, relaying messages between pilots and airway control. The chief means of communication between ground personnel was a private telephone circuit. The telephone unit at ATC stations was like the headset used by a telephone operator. Worn by the controller, it made him immediately available to anyone on the interphone system. The practice was soon adopted of recording every word spoken to or by controllers over the system; the wax cylinders were filed for future reference in the event of controversy or shaved and reused.[28] The interphone system could not begin to handle all the information required by ATC. Weather reports came over the Bureau's teletype network. This system was also used by airways communications stations to transmit position reports and other information on itinerant pilots. In no time, this system, which possessed only a single circuit, was overburdened. Because weather information took precedence, periods of as long as three hours when no time was available for the transmission of aircraft movements were not uncommon. Accordingly, in 1937, the Bureau established another teletype circuit, the so-called white net, for the exclusive use of air traffic control. As procedures evolved, the interphone system was reserved primarily for controlling airline operations, and the white net for private and military aircraft; procedures, however, were flexible enough to accommodate necessary deviations. The original teletype circuit, now dubbed the black net, was used exclusively for weather reporting.[29]

An airway station's involvement with traffic began as soon as a pilot filed a flight plan. The airline dispatching office immediately relayed the plan to the controller on duty and asked for clearance to take off. Depending on traffic conditions, the controller would either approve the

---

*In November 1937, as a way of increasing orderly flow, the airways were color-coded. The main east-west routes were coded green; secondary east-west, red; main north-south, amber; secondary north-south, blue. Under this system, green had the right of way over all traffic; amber, over red and blue; red, over blue. Glen A. Gilbert, *Air Traffic Control* (New York, 1945), 15.

plan as filed or assign the flight a different takeoff time or cruising altitude or both. Once in the air, the pilot was required to report to his dispatcher the time he passed over a designated radio fix and the estimated time he expected to pass over the next fix.* This information was also relayed to air traffic control, which entered it on the blackboard and adjusted the position on the map of the brass marker representing the flight.

A radio fix was a geographical point at which the pilot could obtain a definite check on his position along the airway without visual reference to the ground. Radio markers, which sent out characteristic signals, were most extensively used for this purpose. The point at which two radio range beams intersected also served the purpose, as did a radio range's "cone of silence." †

The last fix over which a pilot passed was the so-called inner marker. It was at this point that traffic control became most intense, since several airways often converged at this fix. Even as few as three aircraft arriving over this marker at approximately the same time required the controller to exercise extreme care. At Newark, for example, aircraft coming in from both Cleveland and Buffalo were required to pass over the same inner marker. An airway controller might have an aircraft arriving from Buffalo at 7,000 feet and two from Cleveland, one at 5,000 and the other at 7,000 — all three approaching the marker at approximately the same time. A glance at the blackboard or the table map would tell the controller that two aircraft were on a collision course. But long before an emergency could eventuate, the controller could anticipate the situation and take corrective action. He might order the first Cleveland aircraft to pass over the marker at 3,000 feet, the second Cleveland plane at 5,000 feet. At the same time, he would direct the Buffalo plane to "hold" at 7,000 — that is, circle around the marker at that altitude and await further orders. In this way, by separating traffic horizontally and vertically, the controller could hand off aircraft to the airport's tower in an orderly sequence. Of course, if the terminal area was congested, the

---

*Earlier procedures only required pilots to report their geographic positions at hourly intervals.

†A four-course range transmitter sent no signals directly overhead; the silent, or area spread skyward like a cone, hence the term "cone of silence." A pilot knew when he passed directly over a range because he momentarily lost radio contact.

controller might find it necessary to keep all three aircraft in a holding pattern.[30]

Where the jurisdiction of airway traffic control ended and where that of airport traffic control began varied with conditions. Usually, the airport tower took control within a radius of three miles from the center of the landing area. But as conditions of visibility decreased the jurisdiction of airway control expanded. Earl Ward explained: "The differentiation between the two Control functions might be illustrated by saying that, in effect, the Tower Controls an aircraft only as far as the Tower operator can see the aircraft and the pilot of the aircraft can see the airport, all of the remainder of the flight being controlled by Airways."[31]

IV

Even before the Bureau assumed responsibility for air traffic control, it had become apparent that the three ATC stations in operation were only the beginning. Detroit, Pittsburgh, and Washington, D.C., were beset with the same traffic problems that had plagued Newark, Chicago, and Cleveland prior to December 1935. The same held true for the nation's major west coast metropolitan centers, Los Angeles and the San Francisco-Oakland area. The Department had promised the Senate and House Appropriations Committee and the Copeland Committee to establish ATC stations at each of these five locations before the winter of 1936-37 set in. The Bureau missed its objective.

As early as August 1936, Cone was warning that "at the rate we have been moving . . . there is doubt in my mind as to whether or not we will have the set-ups all completed [on schedule]." On October 19, 1936, the Detroit station went operational, followed by the Pittsburgh station on November 16. Plans to open the Washington station in December went awry, as did the scheduled early winter opening of the two west coast stations.[32]

Funds, now ample, were no problem this time. "I believe that practically all concerned fully realize that setting up a reasonable air traffic system is the most complicated . . . problem which we have yet had to deal with . . .," Vidal concluded in August 1936. Improving the procedures handed down by the airlines, working out complex new procedures for new control areas, and finding appropriate locations for the new stations took more time and effort than originally expected.[33]

The greatest cause of delay was a lack of skilled personnel. "We have had much difficulty in training men . . .," Vidal told a congressional committee in explaining the Bureau's failure to open stations on schedule. "We put these men through an exacting training course," he went on. "We not only had that delay, but we must continually search the country for qualified men." Qualified men were few and far between. All the airway traffic controllers in the United States were already in the Bureau's employ; moreover, few professions adequately prepared a man for the job of air route controller. Tower controllers — few in number to begin with— performed analogous duties that were not, at this period in time, nearly so demanding as the duties of airway controllers. Airline dispatchers were greater in number, and it was from this group that the Bureau hoped to acquire the largest percentage of its early trainees. The entrance requirements for trainees were stiff — a high school degree plus one of the following: 1,000 hours flying time; one year's experience in an airline operations office; or experience in controlling traffic. Later, when controllers were blanketed under civil service, the education requirement was dropped (though the four-hour examination was rigorous) and the experience factors were expanded somewhat. Salary, moreover, was not what many might have expected. "I had Weir Cook come to Chicago yesterday and it appears that he is not greatly interested [in the Chicago manager's job]," Earl Ward related. "He had an idea that salaries ran from six to eight thousand and that a private airplane went with the job. So his interest waned considerably when he got the facts." The facts were that an airway traffic control station manager earned $3,500 per annum, an assistant manager $2,900, and a controller $2,000. Even the original airline controllers balked at the low pay. They had been paid $200 a month by the ATC corporation. Nearly all had been airline employees, and in transferring to this corporation they had been promised that they could return to their old airline jobs if they did not like the new work. When the Bureau announced its pay scale, which was $400 a year lower than the private scale, former airline personnel threatened to return to their old jobs. Only the persuasive powers of Earl Ward and Glen Gilbert, who spent many anxious hours on the telephone, and a promise that the old pay rate would soon be restored prevented a wholesale turndown of Federal employment.[34]

The attraction of being at the creation of something new and exciting was there, and many a talented young man opted for the low pay and the long, sometimes nerve-racking hours. The publicity surrounding the

Federal takeover no doubt generated interest in the profession. The news was carried over the wire services and in wide-circulation magazines. Newspapers serving the areas at which the stations were located gave the story prominent coverage. The National Broadcasting Company, not to be outdone, presented a special half-hour program on "aerial traffic cops." The program, broadcast from the Newark station amidst the whirl of engines and the shouting of ATC instructions, included a three-minute talk by Cone from Washington and interviews with personnel at the Cleveland and Chicago stations. The fact that some cities — Dallas and Fort Worth were prime examples — vied with each other for the privilege of having an ATC station within their borders (". . . HELP US GET IT FOR DALLAS," a Dallas booster wired Cone) also served to excite interest. Public curiosity about ATC, while clearly not of spectacular proportions, was nevertheless there. More than 18,000 people visited ATC stations during their first 33 months of operation.[35]

It was February 9, 1937, before the Los Angeles station, in Burbank, Calif., could be opened, and then only on a part-time basis; the station was not staffed for 24-hour operations until the end of that year. Meanwhile, the Washington station had opened on April 1, and the Oakland station on May 15. Though new stations would be commissioned at an accelerated pace beginning in 1939, Oakland was the last station to open during the existence of the Bureau of Air Commerce.[36]

V

Controlling traffic on the airways was a vast, complex undertaking and, initially at least, not without its moments of confusion. "When these new [air traffic] regulations were first started they were generally misunderstood and very greatly criticized . . .," Cone wrote in October 1936. Even as he was writing these words the system was still ragged along the edges. Flying in controlled airspace demanded a discipline and self-control that the pilot of the mid-1930's was unaccustomed to. Some carefree spirits simply refused to follow procedures and take orders from Federal ground personnel. Frequently, pilots refused or neglected to report their time over check points; dispatchers failed to relay instructions from ATC to pilots in the air; pilots took off before receiving clearances. Eastern Air Lines pilots based in the South, where they enjoyed relative freedom until they first encountered air traffic control at Washington, were perhaps the most stubborn breed. Some of them even refused to file a flight plan. Matters eventually got so out of hand that the airline was temporarily restricted to visual flight rule operations until it fell in line with ATC procedures.

What irritated pilots most was being forced into a holding pattern. The tendency was to blame the ensuing delay in landing on air traffic control rather than on the traffic itself. Indeed, dispatchers even went so far as to enter a late departure or arrival in their logs by writing, "Delayed account of air traffic control." (Some airlines displayed a sign behind their ticket counter informing customers, "All Flights Delayed by Air Traffic Control.") This practice was so general that Earl Ward felt it necessary to write the Air Transport Association in protest. "It is our thought that delays should be charged to 'traffic' rather than 'Airway Traffic Control', this distinction being made for the reason that, although Airway Traffic Control may actually issue an order causing a delay, if no Airway Traffic Control station were controlling the point in question, exactly the same precautions should be taken by the companies or pilots involved." The manager of Cleveland Municipal Airport, irritated by frequent takeoff and landing delays, apparently did not see this distinction. "I have told Earl Ward that something must be done about Airway Traffic Control in Cleveland," he raged, "and if he dosen't do something pretty soon, I will — and through Washington, too." In one case at Newark, a United Air Lines pilot who had been holding over a fix for 45 minutes informed his dispatcher: "To Hell with Control, I'm going to land" — and he did. Only time, bringing with it a greater appreciation of the air traffic function, would instill the necessary discipline in airway users.[37]

If some airline pilots took a cavalier attitude toward air traffic control, many private pilots were virtually up in arms over it. Though the restrictions placed on general aviation flights in November 1935 were eventually eased, these pilots still believed that their freedom to use the nation's airways was being unduly restricted. "We find ourselves more or less on the spot between itinerant flyers and the air line operators," Cone noted. "A great many of itinerant flyers insist that the new regulations are much too rigid and place unnecessary hardships and inconvenience on [them]." The truth was that private aircraft without instrument flying equipment — and they were the overwhelming majority — had virtually been banished from designated civil airways during instrument weather. But with a two-way radio and instrument equipment, the private pilot had the same rights and privileges on the airways as the airline pilot. The problem, according to Cone, was that some private pilots did not know this: "Due to a careless reading of the regulations they have the idea that the regulations restrict their operations even when they are operating away from civil airways and under good weather conditions."[38]

Though private pilots recoiled at the new airway restrictions, others believed that the government had not gone far enough in keeping itinerants under control. The presence of private aircraft at air carrier airports, whether in good weather or foul, produced a measure of interference with airline movements. "I think that at a large terminal like Newark or Chicago or Kansas City, where there are many transport planes coming in every 15 minutes, that the private plane without the two-way radio should go to some other field," suggested Congressman Robert L. Bacon. Vidal was willing to grant that point and go a step further. "I think," he said, "we will ultimately prohibit privately owned planes landing at these congested terminals under any conditions." Cone was in absolute agreement, for once, contending that airports other than those used by air carriers should "have to take care of itinerant flyers." The temptation to promulgate such a rule was real, but so was the growing influence of the private flier and his determination to preserve his place in the sky. Reacting to talk of additional restrictions on private flying, William Barclay Harding wrote the Bureau that "if there is any truth in this ominous report, kindly consider this letter as a protest. As one who has indulged in private flying for nearly ten years, I wish to request that you give us 'our day in Court' before issuing the death sentence." Manufacturers of general aviation aircraft were no less disturbed. "Such drastic regulations menace the business of ALL Aircraft Manufacturers, except those building Airline and Military Planes . . .," declared the president of the Stinson Aircraft Corporation. The regulation would "turn the air over to the Airlines." Thus, though Vidal declared, late in 1936, that "within a year . . . we will prohibit privately owned aircraft from going into certain terminal airports," he never made good on his threat.[39]

Bureau personnel, like private pilots, also had difficulty interpreting the hastily drawn air traffic rules. "There appears to be considerable misunderstanding, on all sides, regarding the authority invested in an

Airway Traffic Control Station to issue or refuse clearance to aircraft," L. Pontón de Arce, manager of the Oakland station, wrote to Glen Gilbert in December 1937. Specifically, de Arce wanted to know whether controllers should "grant all requests for clearances regardless of weather conditions." Emerson Mehrling, the Pittsburgh station manager, did not share de Arce's confusion. In August of the same year he had told a Pittsburgh newspaper reporter, "If weather conditions here and en route are adverse to flying, our men will not approve the flight and the pilot will be grounded . . . until the poor conditions are cleared." As it turned out, Mehrling was laboring under a misconception. "Air Traffic Control will base clearances on traffic conditions only," Earl Ward informed de Arce, "and will not base clearances on weather conditions." Only private aircraft without instrument flying equipment could be denied a clearance because of weather. There was a reluctance, and there would be for a long time to come, on the part of the Federal Government to make all dispatching decisions for the airlines. As to the confusion over rules, time, once again (and revised, unambiguous regulations), was needed to erase the gray areas and promote a surer understanding of procedures.[40]

There were those who believed that all dispatching functions should be handled by disinterested Federal employees. Robert Bacon, for one, argued that Federal dispatchers should have the "final say as to whether a flight shall start and . . . final determination of whether that flight shall be prohibited on account of bad weather." The Bureau's position, as expressed by Cone, was that the weather minimums established by the Department offered sufficient protection to the public. Bacon's point, however, was that airline dispatchers, in their concern to complete as many flights as possible, forced pilots to fly under less than safe weather conditions. R. W. Schroeder admitted that a Federal employee would be "free from the money award . . . and free from the malice of the operators . . .," thus implying that airline employees did not enjoy the same freedom. But the Bureau would not take the step suggested by Bacon. Rather, it established more rigorous certification requirements for airline dispatchers.[41]

Other problems arose from the fact that a number of stations were housed in physical plants that were strictly makeshift affairs, though, here again, the problem was of a transitory nature. The Washington station, for example, was located on Hoover Field in a room measuring approximately 125 square feet. Jammed into this space were two teletype machines, a large map table, two radio receivers, a filing cabinet, a desk, and control boards, not to mention chairs and other odd pieces of furniture. For eight hours of the station's 24-hour work day, five men labored in this space. "It can be readily realized that the most efficient operations of the Washington Airway Traffic Control Station cannot be accomplished in such restricted quarters," complained Lee E. Warren, the station manager. "Our station equipment is cut to a bare minimum because of space requirements and actually we are operating without some items considered necessary." The station needed three and a half times its existing space to function at top efficiency. To relieve the situation while permanent quarters were being constructed, the station was moved into roomier temporary facilities, only to be plagued by other problems. The roof leaked, the floor was covered with ridges, making walking difficult, and the doors, warped by the elements, could be open or shut only after a struggle. "Around both doors are cracks large enough to permit rain and dust to enter," Warren related.[42]

This problem was solved when the Washington station moved into a new building toward the end of 1938. But other problems, only vaguely understood at this early date, were by no means transitory; they would remain a permanent part of the ATC function. Air traffic control was a high-pressure occupation even in 1937. Matters were exacerbated by the fact that stations were so shorthanded they could not grant controllers their regular allotment of annual leave. "Three of the men at Burbank have nearly two months due them and the other three have at least one month," R. E. Sturtevant wrote to Glen Gilbert in April 1938. "Of course, it will be impossible to give everyone his allotted time, but in order to divide what vacation time is available equally, it will be necessary for me to know just when to expect an additional man at Burbank." The 44-hour week, though standard, was seldom observed; controllers often worked 10 to 12 hours a day, six to seven days a week, as needed, and, in the recollection of one former controller, "there was no such thing as overtime [pay] or complaining." The Burbank station opened for operations woefully undermanned, with a total force of three controllers. The Detroit station, in order to have an adequate work force during its busiest hours (between 7 and 11 a.m., and 4 and 8 p.m.), went on a split shift, forcing those men who lived a considerable distance from Wayne County Airport to spend 13 hours a day at the station.[43]

Controllers began showing the effects of overwork and stress. They had periods of irritability in which they displayed a low threshold for noise and other annoyances. The pounding of the teletype machines was a common complaint. Irritability was often accompained by fatigue. "In the proportion that physical work is at the same time mentally fatiguing," wrote C. W. Schott, the assistant manager of the Detroit station, in citing an independent study on fatigue, "the greater the alertness required, so much sooner does fatigue appear. This is the case with all occupations where an extreme and unremitting attentiveness is required." Such was undoubtedly the case with ATC work. Schott went on:

> It appears logical to assume that those of us engaged in the work are subject to fatigue at certain times. Since fatigue is defined as that state when an individual is capable of less general activity (physical and mental) than would be expected from his general mental and physical equipment . . ., and since the symptoms are lack of interest, inattentiveness, irritability, and a general tired feeling, it is logical to assume that every possible step should be taken to limit the fatigue stimuli in an ATC office. . . ."[44]

Schott was primarily interested in improving the working environment of the controller — cutting down noise and constructing more pleasant surroundings. These were things that would be improved in time. But the most powerful fatigue stimuli proved intractable, for they were inherent in the job. Their effects became more pronounced as aviation grew and air traffic control became a more complex and demanding occupation. Decades passed before the Federal Government seriously turned its attention to this problem.

Of more immediate concern to Federal officials were the controllers in the towers. "Due to the very close interlocking of control between airway traffic control and airport traffic control, it is necessary, and has been strongly urged by interests as widely varied as Army, Navy, municipalities, air lines, and organizations of private and sportsman pilots, that the Bureau of Air Commerce take over the airport functions," Earl Ward said in October 1937. Leaving airport traffic control to the devices of individual municipalities was proving less than satisfactory. "The Wayne County Airport Control Tower is not operating in an efficient manner," complained Harry D. Copland, the Detroit airway station manager. "This, we believe, is due chiefly to the fact that the tower operators are required, while on duty in the tower, to act as telephone switchboard operators handling all airport incoming and outgoing telephone calls." This was the kind of thing that the Bureau could not regulate. Control towers, funded by hardpressed local governments, had to live within their means, and it was usually fruitless for the Bureau to ask them to hire telephone operators or other tower personnel. It was equally difficult to get dozens of municipalities to agree on standard airport control procedures. There was, too, the matter of personnel qualifications. Nearly as many standards existed as towers, with the result that many towers, in the Bureau's opinion, were manned by incompetents.

Taking over the towers, which would have been a more expensive proposition than the airway control takeover, was out of the question in 1937. Neither the Budget Bureau nor the Congress was psychologically prepared for such a broad extension of Federal authority, and the Department did not even broach the subject with them. About the only device left to the Bureau was to require Federal certification of tower personnel. This would at least guarantee that all controllers met minimum qualification standards. In August 1936, R. W. Schroeder began urging his superiors to "move in on the . . . problem of licensing Control Tower operators." The need for such an action was acute, Schroeder argued, "particularly so, in that it will provide an avenue whereby the safety factor around congested airports can be greatly increased . . . ." Some members of the aviation community counseled a go-slow approach. "I do feel that a great many of the major factors in the industry are resentful of too much Departmental control of their activities," advised John Berry, an Ohio aviation official. "Control operators should be licensed by the Department. Let's take time to do it right and not rush it."

Considering the level of personnel at some towers, time was a luxury the Bureau believed it did not have. Neither, it developed, did it have the power to set employment standards for city employees. It could not, as in the case of airmen flying interstate, compel every tower controller to possess a Federal certificate. The Bureau got around the problem by turning to its air traffic control powers. A May 1938 amendment to the air traffic rules prohibited aircraft operations at airports designated by the Secretary of Commerce as "control airports" (i.e., those serving air carriers and other interstate and foreign commerce) when the ceiling dropped below 500 feet or visibility was less than one mile unless "a certificated airport control tower operator on duty at a radio equipped airport control tower" authorized such operations. At the same time, the Department issued standards for an airport control tower operator rating. The effect of the rule change was to force major airports either to shut down operations during severe instrument conditions or require some, if not all, of their tower personnel to secure a Federal tower rating.

The new rule, though it improved matters substantially, was no more than a stopgap until the Department could take control of airport towers. As late as 1939, only three of eight controllers in the Boston tower were rated. Buffalo had no certificated controller. At Akron, control tower operators were obliged to divide their time between controlling traffic, selling tickets, answering the telephone, and handling baggage. The Atlanta tower was undermanned and had inferior radio equipment, and Ward had to admit that conditions would have been worse "if the airport manager had not been able to prevail upon the city to furnish funds for additional operators." With 53 control airports, each under the jurisdiction of nearly as many municipalities, it was impossible to achieve a uniform airport traffic control system operating under common standards. And though as early as 1937 one congressional committee discerned that "the present system of airway-traffic control has in it a missing link, caused by the fact that the control of the Federal Government does not reach within the boundaries of the air terminals," and recommended an immediate Federal takeover of towers, Congress would not come to grips with this problem until forced to do so by the exigencies of war.[45]

But if the system had its limitations, the Bureau of Air Commerce had probably assumed all the responsibilities that it could reasonably handle. At the same time, it had undertaken an enterprise that had vast implications for aviation. "The sky isn't the limit any more," observed the *Washington Herald* in October 1936. "They've started limiting the sky. Not only limiting it but cutting it up into lanes and channels, and channels with designated intersections and traffic rules and watchful policemen and fines for reckless drivers."[46] In 10 short years, aviation in the United States had come a long way from "the chaos of laissez faire in the air."

13. The Bureau Revitalized

The Bureau of Air Commerce had to scrimp, scrape, and juggle to raise the necessary funds for airway traffic control. Had the ATC takeover been delayed by a year, the Bureau could have assumed its new responsibilities in style, for, with fiscal 1938, the long financial drought had finally come to an end. The Cutting crash, a frightening series of air disasters in the winter of 1936–37, and the vigorous efforts of Royal S. Copeland and J. Monroe Johnson persuaded the Budget Bureau and the Congress to come to the air agency's rescue and fund a long-overdue airway modernization program. At the same time, in a move that many had been eagerly awaiting, the administration swept away the old guard and installed new leadership at the Bureau's helm.

II

Eugene Vidal, luckless from the start, was denied the opportunity to enjoy the sudden change in the Bureau's financial fortunes. Beginning on December 15, 1936, when a Western Air Express flight disappeared between Los Angeles and Salt Lake City, an appalling succession of scheduled air carrier aircraft began falling out of the sky. By January 12, 1937, when a second Western Air Express flight met with disaster, there had been five fatal airline crashes and 32 people killed in the short space of 28 days. It was one of those inexplicable periods when the gods of chance rain ill-luck on air transports; the weather had been extremely bad, and the aircraft of this prejet age were forced to fly in the thick of it, if they flew at all. Nonetheless, people looked for more concrete explanations. "Every cause from failure of the Department of Commerce radio facilities to interline jealousy among pilots to complete schedules has been put forward," *Aviation* observed. They also looked for scapegoats. Eugene Vidal was an easy target.[1]

On February 28, Vidal, described by *Time* as "tired and exasperated" after seeing the Bureau through the most tumultuous years in U.S. civil aviation history, called a press conference to announce his resignation, effective immediately. "You can quote me as saying I feel very chipper now," he told assembled newsmen. "And stress the *now*!" The resignation, largely anticipated, was welcome news to most segments of the aviation community. "His objectives were the wrong objectives during the past four years . . .," *U.S. Air Services* declared. Senator Copeland was more generous. "I am sorry to see him go," he said. "Of course I scolded him . . . but he wasn't to blame. . . . It was the system that was wrong not Mr. Vidal."[2]

The next day Secretary Roper called a press conference of his own. He announced that a Northwestern University law professor, Fred D. Fagg, Jr., would succeed Vidal. He also announced that J. Carroll Cone and Rex Martin had been given new assignments abroad; Cone would study and report on European aviation developments, Martin on Latin American. *Time* correctly discerned that Martin and Cone were being "sent to Siberia." And no doubt the two former assistant directors discerned the same thing. On his return from Europe, Cone left the Bureau for a post with an air carrier. Martin would doubtless have taken a similar course had not the aircraft on which he was returning home been lost in a tropical storm over the Caribbean. The triumvirate had finally been disbanded. It now remained for the new director to exercise the leadership that had been so sorely missing over the last four years.[3]

Fred Fagg had been coming to Washington on various short assignments since 1934, when he was barely 38 years of age. He was part of what George Peck, the veteran farm leader, termed the "plague of young lawyers" who settled on the Federal City in droves during the early days of the New Deal. Bright, imaginative, superbly educated young men still in their late thirties and early forties, they set about changing things, bringing with them a zest for work, a dedication to public service, and a multiplicity of talents perhaps unmatched in American annals. In the process, according to a contemporary news correspondent, they transformed Washington from a sleepy Southern town to "a gay, breezy, sophisticated and metropolitan center." They also worked a profound and lasting change in the responsibilities of government and in governmental policy. Before he was through, Fred Fagg would help work such a change in Federal civil aviation policy.[4]

Fagg first came into intimate contact with aviation during the First World War, when, as a 21-year-old flying officer, he served as a bomber pilot with the 92d Aero Squadron in England. The war over, he completed his interrupted undergraduate studies at the University of Redlands (1920), went on to Harvard for an M.A. in business economics (1921), and to Northwestern University Law School, where he earned a J.D. degree in 1927. Between 1921 and 1928, he taught transportation economics at Harvard, Northwestern, and the University of Southern California.

In 1928, Fagg went to Germany for a year as an exchange professor in law at the Institute fur Luftrecht, at Konigsberg. At the time, Konigsberg was the only organized air institute in the world and possessed the greatest air law library anywhere. A year at Konigsberg not only afforded the tall, lantern-jawed law professor a rare opportunity for further study in his specialty; it also gave him ideas. On his return to the United States, having been invited by Dean John H. Wigmore to accept a position on the Northwestern Law School faculty, he immediately set about putting those ideas into effect. In 1929, he and Wigmore established at Northwestern the Air Law Institute—the first school of its kind in the United States; Fagg became the Institute's managing director. The following year he founded and became the editor of the *Journal of Air Law*—the first publication of its kind in the United States. There followed four productive years of legal scholarship that established Fagg as a leading expert in aviation law and forecasted, to a degree, the kind of ideas he would put into practice once given the opportunity.

The opportunity arrived in 1934 when, as a representative of the National Association of State Aviation Officials, Fagg came to Washington to testify before the Federal Aviation Commission. He so impressed FAC Chairman Clark Howell that he was invited to stay on as the commission's legal adviser. In the end, the commission adopted Fagg's position that air carrier economics should be regulated by a Federal aviation agency, just as railroad economics were regulated by the Interstate Commerce Commission — a recommendation that Roosevelt was still sitting on in 1937. A few months after the work of the Federal Aviation Commission was over, Fagg was called on once again to interrupt his teaching to become legal adviser to the Copeland Committee, which, unfortunately, took very little of his counsel. But having now stepped into the pressure cooker that was the Bureau of Air Commerce, he could no longer be easily ignored. Fagg proved in a short time that he was a rarity among public men; a brilliant scholar and teacher, he was also a brilliant administrator and doer.[5]

Fagg was no stranger to the Bureau of Air Commerce. Indeed, he had already performed yeoman's work in its behalf. In 1936, he and Wigmore were invited by J. Monroe Johnson to undertake a monumental task — the rewriting and codification of the air commerce regulations.[6] This attempt to bring order to the Bureau's great body of rules and regulations was in response to two unrelated attacks on Federal rulemaking procedures — one initiated by Jack Frye, who maintained that a portion of the air commerce regulations had been improperly promulgated and were therefore invalid, the other stemming from the U.S. Supreme Court in the hot oil cases (*Panama Refining Co.* v. *Ryan*).

Frye had embarrassed the Bureau during the Copeland hearings by pointing to the sloppy rulemaking procedures at the Department of Commerce. In brief, the Department had undertaken in mid-1934 to revise and reissue its rules governing scheduled operations of interstate air carriers. The airlines participated in the early stages of the revision and were thus fully aware of what was going on; moreover, in November, the Bureau mailed to each airline a full set of the new rules, bearing an effective date of October 1, 1934. Finally, the rules were printed in the December 15, 1934, issue of the *Air Commerce Bulletin*, an official publication of the Bureau of Air Commerce. But as Frye observed, neither the mimeographed version mailed to the operators nor the printed version bore the signature of the Secretary of Commerce, the only official within the Department who could promulgate air regulations. It turned out that Roper had never signed the regulations in their final form, though he had seen earlier versions and had approved of them in principle.[7]

It may have appeared to some people that Frye had raised a mere technicality, but he had actually touched on a serious problem. The Bureau followed no standard method in drawing up and publishing its regulations. No central clearing office existed to review new rules or revisions. Often, individuals of varying rank wrote and issued rules governing activities within their jurisdiction with little or no consultation with an Assistant Director, the Director, or the Secretary. The Bureau failed to make a distinction between regulations and information in its publication practices. The organization issued a boundless volume of valuable printed information of all kinds, which largely took the form of notices or bulletins. These issuances were either mimeographed or printed. Revisions of individual rules often appeared as notices, which had the same format as a news release. Massive revisions were printed in individually numbered bulletins. But the same bulletin format was also employed in issuing material of a purely informational character — aviation statistics, a description of the airways, or advances in radio technology. At the same time, the Bureau published a bimonthly magazine, the *Air Commerce Bulletin*, which also intermingled informational and regulatory materials. No one could look between the same two covers and find a complete and up-to-date version of the air commerce regulations. The regulations were scattered everywhere. "Neither the flying public, not the State officials, nor perhaps even the Bureau officials, were enabled to find just what each needed without a wasteful search through an accumulated mass of material, some of it stale and out-of-date," Dean Wigmore observed.[8]

The Bureau was not alone in practicing these slipshod methods; indeed, in this respect, the Bureau was a microcosm of the entire executive branch. The New Deal, a maelstrom of administrative activity, had inundated the country with a tidal wave of rules and regulations. Roosevelt alone had issued 674 Executive orders in his first 15 months in office; this was more than Hoover had issued in four years and nearly six times more than 10 Presidents had issued in the 39 years between 1862 and 1900. Some of these orders were published, some not, though they possessed a general applicability and legal effect. But the President's personal rulemaking production, though voluminous by previous standards, was dwarfed by the activities of the various Federal departments and agencies. No agency was more active in rulemaking than the National Recovery Administration. In the course of its 18-month existence, this agency promulgated a set of industrial codes that filled 13,000 pages and issued orders clarifying these codes that filled an additional 11,000 pages — a body of regulations that exceeded the cumulative bulk of the *United States Code* after 146 years of congressional legislation. The *United States Code*, however, was a rationally organized body of work that could be found in any law library. The NRA codes and the rules of other Federal agencies were like the Bureau of Air Commerce regulations — here, there, and everywhere — scattered, jumbled, amorphous.[9]

Confusion was inevitable. In October 1933, Federal officials brought suit against the Panama Refining Company for violating a section of the petroleum code prohibiting oil production in excess of assigned state quotas. When the indictment was handed down, neither the accused, the prosecutor, nor the courts knew that, at the time of the alleged violation, this section of the petroleum code had been rescinded; through a clerical error it had been amended out of existence. True, unofficial copies of the code, which had been distributed throughout the industry and used by the prosecutor, contained the rescinded provision; moreover, the President had rectified the error, once it was discovered, by issuing a new Executive order, thus making true the state of facts that all parties had assumed to exist. The U.S. Supreme Court was unimpressed. Since the code in question had been rescinded before the alleged violation took place, a majority of the Justices refused to treat the code as being properly before the Court.[10]

The decision sent a minor shock wave through the Bureau of Air Commerce. A search was immediately instituted to locate a complete, current set of regulations bearing the Secretary's signature. "Will you . . . kindly make search and provide all of the originals of said regulations," Denis Mulligan requested the Aeronautics Information Division on March 4, 1935. The search failed to turn up the original copy of the October 1934 amendment regulating scheduled air carrier operations; it was at this point that the Bureau discovered that Roper had never signed these regulations into effect. But instead of having Roper approve the regulations at this late date, E. Y. Mitchell, believing the matter came within the scope of his delegated powers, put his initials on a mimeographed copy of the regulations, believing this sufficient validation.[11]

Frye obviously thought differently, and, given the reasoning in the *Panama* case, the chances were good that the Supreme Court would have agreed with him. As it was, the matter was never adjudicated, for TWA and the Department of Commerce settled their differences stemming from the Cutting crash out of court. But the affair was a clear signal to the Department that is must get a firm grip on its rulemaking process. The *Panama* case, moreover, sent a signal to the Congress, which, in July 1935, passed the Federal Register Act, requiring the President and the various Executive agencies to publish in the *Federal Register* all Executive orders and rules having general applicability and legal effect.[12]

When Fagg and Wigmore settled into their task, they concluded that the air regulations should form "a single set of source material," uniform in size, style, and general plan, "which would give to each participant in aeronautics a complete picture of the Federal Government's position in the control of aviation." Specifically, the two men decided that the regulations should form a single "book," but looseleaf in form so that changes could be made by inserting new pages for superseded ones. They also determined that this "book" would be structured according to classifications — aircraft, airmen, facilities, air carriers — and that these classifications, though inclusive, must allow for future developments by including such categories as "unassigned" or "miscellaneous." The various categories and subcategories (i.e., parts and sections) would be numbered by an expansible decimal system; in other words, the work would be codified. This method, first adopted by Wisconsin for its statutes, was "the only method that makes feasible a permanent citing figure and yet allows changes to be absorbed into the system without confusion," Wigmore asserted. For an art as rapidly changing as aeronautics, such a system was "indispensable." In 1937, two years after passing the Federal Register Act, Congress enacted legislation requiring, by July 1938, the codification of all Federal regulations into a *Code of Federal Regulations*. The Bureau of Air Commerce, thanks to Fagg and Wigmore, had anticipated this congressional action by at least a year.[13]

Fagg spent a solid eight months on the project, working day and night. "If I carry away one memory of Washington," he said years later, "it is of how many lights were burnt past 11 o'clock at night when John Q. Public used to think that the boys went home at 4:30 in the afternoon and . . . the girls dropped the inkwells the minute the bell rang." When he was named Director of Air Commerce, the rule codification project had been only half completed. Another attorney, Howard C. Knotts, was retained to finish up the work, but Fagg's connection with the project remained intimate throughout. The final product, according to John H. Geisse, was "a masterpiece worthy of the efforts of Mr. Fagg." But it was a cold, complex, and heavily legalistic piece of work, sacrificing the simplicity and directness of the old rules in favor of thoroughness and precision. Still, Fagg's style was a model of simplicity compared to present-day standards of draftsmanship.[14]

Fred Fagg had no illusions about the job before him. "I was invited to take on a headache and do something with it," he admitted years later. When Gene Vidal stepped down, Royal S. Copeland had been heard to

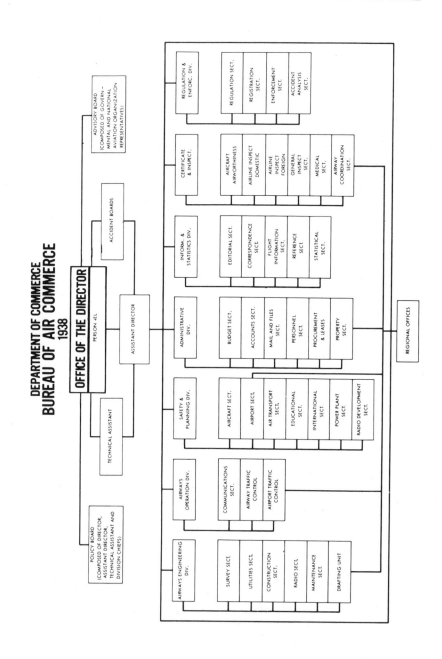

DEPARTMENT OF COMMERCE
BUREAU OF AIR COMMERCE
1938

exclaim, "It won't change things a bit to put in a new director. God couldn't run the bureau as it is now organized." No one knew this better than Fagg.[15]

Within two months, Fagg had junked the old headquarters organization, which had diffused both responsibility and authority and adopted a scheme that placed final authority where it belonged, in the hands of the Director of Air Commerce. The posts of Assistant Director for Airway Development and Assistant Director for Regulation — the positions held by Martin and Cone — were abolished. A new position of Assistant Director was created, but the incumbent—first R. W. Schroeder, until he left for private industry in May 1937, and then Howard Rough — did not have line authority over a functional area, as did Cone and Martin. Rather, he served simply as Fagg's deputy, or second in command.

Fagg sharpened the lines between the Bureau's various functional responsibilities by recasting the two large, dominant divisions — Air Navigation and Air Regulations — and the two sections — Administrative and Information — into seven coequal divisions — Airways Engineering, Airways Operation, Safety & Planning, Administrative, Information & Statistics, Certification & Inspection, and Regulation & Enforcement — each headed by a division chief reporting to the Director. In creating both an Airways Engineering and an Airways Operation Division, Fagg was the first man to draw a sharp distinction between the installation and the operation of airway facilities. The distinction would be preserved by the Bureau's successor agencies.

Establishment of the Safety & Planning Division also represented a new departure. As its name implied, the new division became the Bureau's planning arm, with safety as its central concern. Hitherto, the operational divisions were responsible for long-term planning within their functional areas. "It was difficult, if not impossible, to effect coordination and stability within the Bureau with reference to working toward planned objectives," observed Richard C. Gazely, the chief of the new division. "Furthermore, the various Divisions were so pressed with a large volume of imperative routine work that it was impossible for them to give full consideration to anything else." Not surprisingly, the press of day-to-day business had made operational people prisoners of the present. The solution was to put planning in the hands of planners and give them a bailiwick of their own.

Fagg made one more innovation at the Washington headquarters. He created a Policy Board composed of himself, the Assistant Director, and the seven division chiefs. Broad policy matters were dealt with by this cabinet-like group.[16]

Fagg also laid plans for reorganizing the Bureau's field structure. The plan adopted, and put into effect in May 1938, called for abolishing the nine general inspection districts and the six airway districts and consolidating their functions at seven regional offices headquartered at Kansas City (Mo.), Los Angeles, Newark, Atlanta, Chicago, Fort Worth, and Seattle. Each region was placed under the general direction of a regional manager, who was responsible for a host of matters that had previously been the province of Washington. The new scheme made possible a closer coordination of field activities. Moreover, with the decentralization of responsibility, the Bureau's field units could respond more quickly to local needs.*[17]

Finally, Fagg moved to restore public confidence in the Bureau as an impartial investigator of aircraft accidents. He knew that the loss of public trust had been at the root of most of Vidal's problems and had eventually proved his undoing. Fagg's solution was simple. He adopted the practice of inviting one or more aviation experts domiciled in the state in which an accident occurred to sit on the Bureau's accident board as fully participating members. Inviting such outsiders, whose impartiality and integrity could not be challenged, went a long way in restoring public trust and dampening the fires of controversy.[18]

Before 1937 was out, Fagg could sit back and listen to the singing of his praises. "I have faith, I have confidence in the gentlemen [Fagg and Johnson] in this new set-up within the Department of Commerce," Edgar Gorrell told a congressional committee. "Out of the chaos of conflicting ambitions and petty jealousies that had been the rule rather than the exception when he inherited the job," *Aviation* said of Fagg, "he has succeeded in building up an *esprit de corps* that was entirely lacking before." *Time* Magazine, in referring to Fagg as one of Washington's "most brilliant young men," observed that in seven months he had transformed the Bureau of Air Commerce from "an Administration headache to a smile." Part of that smile was doubtless engendered by the sight of new-found riches flowing into the Bureau's previously empty

---

*The Civil Aeronautics Authority, created in mid-1938, retained the Bureau's basic regional organization.

coffers — riches that would be used to revitalize a Federal airway system badly in need of repair.[19]

III

In the midst of the accident-plagued winter of 1936–37, the Bureau of Air Commerce called airline officials, airline pilots, and other members of the aviation community to a three-day safety conference, beginning February 4. The conference, though marred by a dispute between David Behncke and the operators, agreed on a program to improve safety on the airways; the capstone of the program was the deployment of additional and more reliable radio navigation aids. The following month, the Copeland Committee issued a second report. Radically different in tone and substance from the first, the report recommended the immediate appropriation by the Congress of $12,414,000 — $10,000,000 for ground-based radio aids, the rest for improved weather reporting. The pressure on the Congress and on the Bureau of the Budget to modernize the airways was mounting.[20]

Copeland, Edgar Gorrell, J. Monroe Johnson, and Fagg made certain the pressure did not let up. Johnson, rebuffed by the Budget Bureau in 1936, told the Senate Appropriations Committee, "We propose to go back to the Budget Bureau" for the money — and he did. Meanwhile, Fagg began conducting a more personalized campaign and doing things "that hadn't been done before" by Bureau Directors. He took to inviting key Congressmen and Senators, "particularly those associated with the appropriations," to visit airports and airway installations and talk to pilots and airway personnel in order "to see the problems of aviation right in the grass roots." Gorrell, too, began touching important bases on Capitol Hill. "In order to make ourselves right with the country and with God, as I see it, we have to spend a lot of money," he told the Senate Appropriations Committee. He later told the same committee: "In my judgment, the Budget's idea of 'efficient orderly procedure' is responsible for the death of American citizens . . . ." Going before a House subcommittee looking into new aviation legislation, he told Congressman Clarence F. Lea (D-Calif.), "The serious trouble is that the airways are full of gaps." And these gaps could be closed only by congressional appropriations for airway facilities. "I would suggest that any administrative body needs not only a proper law," he said before a Senate subcommittee chaired by Harry S. Truman, "but also needs ample funds." If Congress wished to stop the recent rash of accidents, he continued, it could do so by adopting "the high spots" of the second Copeland report.[21]

Copeland himself expanded his activities. A plodding, tenacious legislator, he had the ability to direct all his energies toward the limited number of public causes that interested him. Once he dug in for the long haul, he became a formidable, if ponderous, advocate, who usually got results. Thus, he suddenly began making appearances at congressional hearings dealing with aviation matters and inevitably ended up taking the witness stand to urge the adoption of this or that reform, to hold out for an increase in the air commerce budget, or to strike out at what he termed "false economy." During the fiscal 1937 appropriation hearings, Copeland had predicted disaster if Congress did not appropriate large sums for airway modernization; Congress failed to do his bidding and disaster struck. The following year, now wrapped in the mantle of a prophet, he again made dire predictions: "And if we do not get the money we will continue to kill the people."[22]

This time, the administration and the Congress yielded. The fiscal 1938 appropriation made available to the Department of Commerce $7 million for a two-year airway modernization program. The appropriation, even by the standards of that day, was not great; but to the money-starved Bureau of Air Commerce, it represented a princely sum. "We were grateful for peanuts," Fagg said in retrospect.[23]

The airway modernization program thrust out in two directions — the expansion of facilities, to fill gaps in the airways, and the improvement of existing aids or their replacement by more capable facilities. The bulk of this effort, both in terms of the number of facilities involved and the amount of money spent, went into radio ranges and markers.

Two new types of markers, the "Z" and fan, both employing very high frequencies, were introduced. The Z-marker, deployed in large numbers beginning in 1938, was developed to supplement the cone of silence as an aid in helping pilots positively identify their position over a range station. The cone of silence was an intrinsic byproduct, not a deliberately designed characteristic, of the four-course range. When first discovered, this silent zone, which fanned out skyward from the top of a beacon station like an inverted cone, was considered of no consequence.

It was soon realized, however, that it might serve a useful purpose —
either as a convenient checkpoint or as a definite fix from which to start a
letdown. For these purposes, it was believed, pilots could distinguish a
true cone of silence from a momentary fadeout (or a false cone) by the
rapid surge of signals at the edges of the cone. The cone of silence
assumed increased importance with the advent of airway traffic control
by serving at many locations as an inner marker. Unfortunately, it was
less than adequate for this purpose. Even experienced pilots occasionally
confused it with a momentary fading of range signals, caused by a faulty
airborne receiver, a drop in the aircraft's battery voltage, a malfunctioning transmitter, or interference induced by the surrounding terrain.
Moreover, at low altitudes, the cone was so small that it was often
difficult to locate; many a pilot passing on one side or the other of a cone
of silence missed it entirely. Conversely, at high altitudes, the cone was
spread out over such a wide area that it was virtually valueless as a
precise position check. Finally, the cone was a "negative" indicator
employed to meet a need that could better be met by a "positive"
indicator.[24]

The shortcomings of the cone of silence were apparent to the Bureau
from the first. These shortcomings were magnified by poorly sited
ranges. Pilots complained of the cone of silence over the Washington
range station, which was difficult to locate, and over the Pittsburgh
station, which was plagued by the surrounding terrain. "Over the river
gap about 5 miles southeast of Connellsville, difficult and complete false
cones of silence were observed . . .," reported a group of TWA pilots
regularly flying the Pittsburgh range. Starting in 1934, the Bureau
installed experimental Z-markers at seven selected sites, including Washington and Pittsburgh. The aids operated on a frequency of 75 megacycles — the first devices on the airways to use the very-high-frequency
spectrum — and transmitted a signal that flashed a light on the instrument panel of aircraft passing directly over a radio range's cone of
silence.* The signal could also be picked up aurally, superimposed on the
range signals. By 1936, the device had been perfected to a point that it
was ready for regular installation on the airways. But it was not until two
years later that widescale deployment, made possible by the $7 million

---

*The earliest models operated on a frequency of 93 megacycles.

modernization program, could begin. Nearly 200 units were commissioned before the program ran its course.[25]

The fan marker, an outgrowth of the Z-marker development program, was devised as a replacement for the class "M" marker, which was located at strategic points along the airways to enable pilots to check their distance from a radio range station. The "M" marker had never performed satisfactorily as a device for fixing the pilot's position along his chosen course. Most of its shortcomings stemmed from the fact that it operated on the same low-frequency band as the four-course range. Its power had to be kept low in order not to interfere unduly with range signals; in consequence, its signals were weak and rarely reached a range of 10 miles. Moreover, they were plagued by static and possessed all the vagaries of the low-frequency range, which were not insubstantial.[26]

Development of a very-high-frequency course marker had been high on the Bureau's priority list for as long as the Z-marker, but no serious work was done on the device until 1936. In the summer of that year, R. G. Nichols, a radio expert, was assigned the task of surveying and reporting on the condition of the Bureau's radio facilities. "It is my opinion," Nichols told J. Carroll Cone, that [the development of a fan marker] must go forward with more zeal than has been displayed in the past . . . or let's quit talking about it." Vidal ordered the development program to proceed. Rather than begin from scratch, personnel from the Bureau's Radio Development Section decided to convert a Z-marker into a very-high-frequency replacement for the "M" marker. The converted device was designed to emit its signals in a vertical fanlike pattern instead of the circular pattern of the Z-marker. The first experimental fan-marker was installed at Hunter's Point, Va., the site of the Washington, D.C., radio range station, and later moved to Bowie, Md., where it was perfected and keyed to emit a continuous identifying signal (two dashes, the Morse Code symbol for the letter "m").[27]

The first fan marker to go into regular service on the airways was commissioned in March 1938. An additional 20 markers were ordered and deployed during the two-year modernization program. The late start in development made impossible a more rapid deployment rate. This rate did pick up dramatically, however, during the early 1940's.[28]

Though the introduction of very-high-frequency markers filled an almost desperate need on the airways, it could not, in 1937–38, match in importance the necessity for improving the performance of the four-course range. In consequence, the Bureau put most of its modernization dollars into this device.

The shortcomings of the four-course range were legion. Equipped with a loop antenna, it was an eccentric, unpredictable device highly sensitive to changing weather conditions, the rise and fall of the sun, the contour of the earth's surface, and the presence of conductive elements. As a result, phantom beams, shifting, bending, and multiple courses, signal reversals, static, and false cones of silence were an all-too-common part of the experience of flying by instruments in the 1930's. Coping with all the vagaries of this facility was hopeless. The facility could be refined and re-refined and still have serious shortcomings; they were intrinsic in the device. The low-frequency radio waves employed by the four-course range did not propagate uniformly over nonuniform terrain. Unlike light waves, which travel in a straight line, they tended to cling to the curvature of the earth. Moreover, they were refracted and reflected by conductive matter. Because a low-frequency radio beam underwent a gradual rate of attenuation, errors introduced by conductive obstacles had a long-range effect.[29]

Given the nature of low-frequency radio waves, the surest solution for the Bureau would have been to abandon this spectrum for the emerging very-high-frequency technology, which it had done in its marker program. The shorter waves populating the VHF spectrum, besides being relatively static-free, do not follow the curvature of the earth; they travel within a line-of-sight path straight out into space, all the while relatively unaffected by changing weather conditions and the influence of conductive materials. VHF technology had been sitting on the shelf for years waiting to be pulled off. Unfortunately, it was not a solution open to the Bureau in 1937–38. None of the Bureau's activities had been hit harder by the austerity of Roosevelt's first term than long-range research and development. Not until 1937 did the Bureau finally launch a program to develop a VHF range. With this device still years away from being perfected, the Bureau was reduced to making as many fixes on an obsolescent piece of equipment as its nature would allow. The Bureau's predicament raised a natural question. "Since [very]-high-frequency beacons must eventually replace the present low-frequency installation, an awkward question presents itself: What about the $7,000,000 now being spent on modernizing equipment admittedly obsolescent in principle?" asked a radio engineer. "The answer is that, since the world began, laws and appropriations have yet to catch up with scientific advancement."[30]

The immediate consequence of this shortsightedness was that the flying public was forced to put up with the vagaries of the four-course range for a much longer period than would otherwise have been necessary. The problems associated with refracted waves would remain. Mountains, large deposits of coal, iron or other ore, railroad tracks, and rivers, when lying obliquely to the path of a low-frequency wave, bent it and sent it on a new path. Little attention had been paid to the potential for wave refraction when the ranges were sited in the early 1930's. The Washington range station had been located on the banks of the Potomac River. Its beams, reported the operations manager of Pennsylvania Airlines, "are bent so badly that they will not stay on course, which is a decided hazard considering all of the obstructions surrounding Washington-Hoover Airport." The Knoxville, Tenn., range was in an even poorer location. It was sited right in the middle of rough terrain traversed by a network of railroad tracks and power lines — all of which played havoc with its signals. Nothing could be done with such poorly located stations as Knoxville except, as one radio expert advised in 1938, to move them to more suitable sites — a step the Bureau was not prepared to undertake on a wide scale. Fortunately, although the amount of bend varied somewhat with weather conditions, refracted courses were fairly stable and pilots flying them regularly knew what to expect.[31]

Reflection, like refraction, was also an intractable problem. "The most prolific source of difficulties in radio navigation — and one most prone to lead to an accident — is the phenomenon of multiple courses," wrote a radio expert in 1937. Though the phenomenon was not well understood in 1937, it was believed that a beam ricocheting off a hill or other reflecting objects broke up into a number of beams. "I once counted fourteen [beams] in the west 'A' quadrant of the Elmira, N.Y., range within a twenty-mile radius from the station," recounted an American Airlines instrument flying instructor. Multiples had one saving factor — they could be easily recognized by their narrowness and by the fact that they emitted the same signal on both their sides. Moreover, they could not be flown for a great distance before they disappeared. Nevertheless, they were a distinct hazard because they occurred over mountainous terrain and presented a substantial orientation problem to any pilot encountering them. To reorient himself, a pilot was forced to take a 90° turn and fly a considerable distance before picking out his true course from the many encountered. This was a dangerous maneuver over treacherous mountain terrain during instrument weather. As early as 1933, a Department of Commerce official was saying, "Sooner or later something has to be done about [multiple beams], because we have had some pretty close calls." Nothing was done because, given the doddering technology of the four-course range, nothing could be done.[32]

There were fixes that the Bureau could and did make to improve the performance of the radio beacon. The problems associated with false cones of silence had been overcome by the Z-marker. And the swinging beam phenomenon (commonly known as "night effect" because it was most noticeable between sunset and sunrise) was brought under control with the widespread use of TL antennas. In common with other nonpolarized radiation, low-frequency radio emissions possess two wave systems — a "ground wave," which travels in a plane approximately parallel to the ground, and a "sky wave," which travels to the ionized region of the stratosphere—the so-called Kennelly-Heaviside layer—and is reflected back to earth. A four-course range equipped with an antenna system of two crossed loops intersecting at their centers threw a disproportionate amount of its energy at the Heaviside layer, which sent it bouncing back to earth. The rebounding sky waves distorted the ground pattern — the wave system on which aircraft depended for navigation — causing it to swing. "I have flown down beams on perfectly clear nights when I could see six or eight beacons ahead and where the ship was kept absolutely lined up with these beacons and the gyro heading never budged and where I should have been receiving a clean on-course signal," related one pilot. "Instead, I would receive everything from a clean off-course 'A' to a clean off-course 'N'. The beam would swing from 'A' to an 'A' bi-signal, to an on-course, to an 'N', and then back again, the whole cycle requiring probably one to two minutes." Eddie Rickenbacker appropriately dubbed these loop-type stations "revolving ranges."[33]

Department of Commerce radio engineers had discovered the solution to this problem as early as 1932. A TL, or modified Adcock, antenna system, consisting of four vertical steel-tower radiators connected to a transmitter by underground cables, threw an insignificant portion of its signals at the Heaviside layer. Yet, except for an initial effort launched in fiscal 1932 to replace 50 loop antennas with the TL variety, the conversion program moved at a snail's pace. "It is my urgent recommendation that all present loop stations be converted to TL stations," wrote a Bureau of Air Commerce radio expert in September 1936. "Swinging of these beams at night constitutes a distinct hazard." The Bureau put the matter permanently to rest by investing approximately $1.6 million of its modernization funds in TL antennas.[34]

The Bureau of Air Commerce was also successful in eliminating the need to shut down a radio range in order to broadcast weather reports. When the Aeronautics Branch installed the first radio range stations, in the late 1920's, it adopted the practice of providing range service on one radio frequency and radiotelephone communications on another. Under this arrangement, a directional beam was available to the pilot continuously. If a pilot wanted a weather report, he merely switched to the weather broadcast frequency. This was fine for receiving regularly scheduled broadcasts; the pilot, however, was deprived of special spot reports on changing weather conditions — reports that may have contained vital information. In time, another difficulty arose with this arrangement. As more range stations were established, the Department found that it did not have enough channels available to assign each station two distinct frequencies. In 1929, therefore, it assigned each station one frequency for both range and weather broadcasts, and adopted the practice of alternate transmission.[35]

Alternate transmission on the same frequency relieved the pilot of the necessity for retuning his receiver and assured his receiving critical spot reports. But it also created, in the words of one veteran pilot, "a terrific conflict of interests." A pilot heading into unexpected instrument flying conditions wanted a weather report, even if it meant doing without range signals momentarily; a pilot in the middle of an instrument approach wanted a continuous beam. Many a pilot was deprived of directional signals just when he needed them most. "This is one of the worst things that we have to put up with . . . and one that should be eliminated if it is at all humanly possible . . .," David Behncke told a congressional committee. In 1935, the Bureau resorted to an expedient at six stations serving important terminal areas. It set aside one frequency — 236 kilocycles — as a weather-broadcast channel. This was essentially the same system practiced in the late 1920's and, therefore, because of crowded frequencies, it could not be further extended. Moreover, unless his aircraft possessed two receivers, a pilot was again faced with the dilemma of choosing between range signals and weather reports. What was really needed was a system permitting the simultaneous broadcasting of range signals and weather over the same frequency.[36]

Department of Commerce radio engineers had been working on the problem of simultaneous transmission virtually from the moment the first four-course range went into operation. They attacked the problem by developing a visual-type range. A reed-like instrument on the aircraft's panel visually indicated the pilot's course; voice broadcasts were sent on the same frequency. To accomplish this, a voice transmitter was added to the range transmitter and a fifth tower was located in the middle of the block of four radio-beacon antenna towers. The voice broadcast was superimposed on the range signal. The aircraft receiver filtered the signals and directed the range signals into a converter for visual interpretation, the voice signals to the pilot's headphones. This system had an added advantage in that it relieved the pilot of the tiresome, monotonous chore of continuously listening to range signals. The new range was field tested in 1932; unfortunately, the visual indicator was never completely debugged. But the basic concept, without visual indicator, could still be used. Both voice and range signals could be directed to the headphones; when transmitted simultaneously, both could be picked up by the pilot in the same way that one can listen to a voice broadcast with music in the background.[37]

In 1934, a simultaneous transmission range was deployed at Pittsburgh for extensive testing. By October 1936, the facility had been refined sufficiently for the Bureau to begin installing simultaneous ranges at eight more locations. This was one case where development dovetailed very nicely with appropriations. Simultaneous transmission had reached the practical stage just as the Bureau was coming out of its funding drought. Full conversion to simultaneous transmission was now just a matter of spending money.[38]

The establishment of airway traffic control, the coming of Fred Fagg, and the modernization program all served to revitalize the Bureau of Air Commerce and went a long way toward repairing the damage inflicted by the austerity program, the airmail imbroglio, and the Cutting crash. Thanks in large part to Fred Fagg, the Bureau had indeed been transformed from a "headache to a smile." Yet the newly invigorated Bureau was an organization whose days were numbered. The march of time and the forces released during Roosevelt's first four years in office — forces that could not be contained either by generous appropriations or by deft administration — moved relentlessly toward a new and significant departure in Federal civil aviation policy — a policy that left no room for the Bureau of Air Commerce as an entity. Ironically, Fred Fagg had a big hand in the Bureau's eventual demise.

14. The Civil Aeronautics Act

In October 1936, a correspondent of James A. Farley's introduced Edgar S. Gorrell as "a man who represents a considerable bunch of people, and what he wants—help on air safety—is certainly a good thing." Gorrell did represent an important constituency—19 U.S. airlines that had banded together to form the Air Transport Association of America, "sort of a 'chamber of commerce' for air line activities." And he was interested in improving aviation safety; he and the association he headed had worked unstintingly for airway modernization. But this forceful, muscular, slightly balding former Army aviator, who had flown everything from crates held together with baling wire to modern transports and had made a small fortune building fancy motor cars, was interested in other matters, too, not all of which would have been judged a good thing by the Postmaster General. Gorrell sought to free the airline industry from the clutches of the Post Office Department and the stultifying effects of the airmail contract system. He sought, indeed, to secure a national legislative charter for the industry—a charter that would recognize the interests of existing carriers and, through Federal regulation, promote their orderly growth with a minimum of competition.[1]

The Bureau of Air Commerce got caught up in this legislative drive. Three Federal agencies were involved in commercial aviation affairs— the Post Office Department, which, besides being the airlines' biggest customer, exercised control over airmail carrier routes and schedules; the Interstate Commerce Commission, which set airmail carriage rates; and the Department of Commerce. In the minds of some people, scattering these responsibilities throughout the Government needlessly impaired the formulation of a coherent policy and the execution of the Federal civil aviation role. As the drive for comprehensive economic regulation gathered momentum, the idea of placing all Federal civil aviation

concerns in one new aviation agency began to gain increased popularity—a popularity that ultimately could not be denied.

II

The case for comprehensive economic regulation of airline affairs
had been given perhaps its clearest, though not earliest, expression by the
Federal Aviation Commission, which Roosevelt had appointed in the
aftermath of the 1934 airmail scandal to formulate a Federal civil
aviation policy. The Commission, headed by newspaper publisher Clark
Howell and counting among its other members such well-known aviation
experts as Edward P. Warner and Jerome C. Hunsaker, came down
foursquare for the idea of Federal economic regulation. The Post Office
Department, the Commission asserted in its report, should "take towards the air lines exactly the same attitude that it takes towards
railroads. We recommend that all air lines that are maintaining regular
service should be considered as common carriers available for the
transport of mail, and we assume that the Post Office Department would
desire to follow the uniform rule of putting the mail upon those aircraft
which would forward it most expeditiously to its destination." Once
freed from Post Office domination, however, the industry should not be
left to its own devices. "There should be a check on development of any
irresponsible, unfair, or excessive competition such as has sometimes
hampered the progress of other forms of transport," the Commission
asserted. It was "plainly destructive of the general welfare" to permit a
new operator, offering an inferior service, to wean traffic away from an
established operator by cutting rates. Air transport, in the opinion of the
Commission, had "grown up to the point where at least one administrative device common in other forms of transportation should be introduced"; this device was the certificate of convenience and necessity. Such
a certificate should be issued by the Federal Government to those
carriers "who make a proper showing of their ability to render a service
which will meet an unsatisfied public need or, by the inauguration of a
new route or otherwise, materially improve upon the service previously
available." No interstate airline would be allowed to operate without
such a certificate. Carriers already actively engaged in air transport

would be automatically certificated. At the same time, the Federal Government would set the conditions of service and establish all rates — passenger, mail, and freight.

To carry out these functions, the Commission recommended the establishment of a new independent aviation board, or commission. This commission must be independent from the executive branch because the functions of rate control and the issuance of certificates were quasi-judicial in character. And it must be a new commission because "it is inappropriate that the control of civil aeronautics simply be relegated to the Interstate Commerce Commission as now constituted." Placing an additional burden on an agency that was already "heavily loaded" was fraught with danger at the formative stage of a new regulatory undertaking; there would be a tendency to draw "analogies with other forms of transportation where such analogies may be superficially attractive but valid only in a very limited degree and actually misleading beyond that point." But once airline economic regulation was established on a secure footing, it could well be integrated with the regulation of other transportation modes in an all-inclusive transportation agency.[2]

The industry, still smarting from the airmail cancellation, the disastrous bidding of May 1934, and the failure of the Black-McKellar Act to provide immediate relief, had looked forward to the Federal Aviation Commission report. "Everyone was exceedingly optimistic, and there was every indication of a New Deal in aviation," declared Fred L. Smith, a state aviation official sympathetic to the carriers. The Commission did not disappoint the industry. In fact, as *Aviation* observed, industry spokesmen had, without exception, recommended to the Commission the creation of a new regulatory board. The industry also had reason to be optimistic from the public reception given the Commission report. "The document is the most important utterance in aeronautical circles to appear in this country since the report of the Morrow board . . .," *U.S. Air Services* declared. In the opinion of *Business Week*, the Commission arrived at "so sound a conclusion" in recommending the creation of an independent board "that such action by Congress is made clearly logical."[3]

Franklin Roosevelt did not find the recommendation so compelling. If the President had clearly enunciated one point in his pronouncements on transportation, it was that transportation policy should be coordinated and integrated. Establishing an independent aviation board, far from serving this end, would further splinter an already badly splintered policymaking apparatus. Roosevelt did not like the idea on another count. The President believed that the Federal bureaucracy was running out of control, primarily because of the proliferating number of independent regulatory agencies functioning outside of Presidential authority.

Up to this point, Roosevelt had made only a few halfhearted attempts to bring these agencies under his control. He had fired a member of the Federal Trade Commission merely because he was a Republican—an action the U.S. Supreme Court would reverse (in *Humphrey's Executor* v. *United States*), holding that the FCC, since it included quasi-legislative functions among its responsibilities, was an agent of Congress, not of the executive; the President, therefore, could not remove its members without assigning a statutory cause. Earlier, FDR had suggested to ICC Commissioner Joseph B. Eastman that heads of independent agencies report to the President. Roosevelt was again rebuffed when Eastman replied that the ICC, like other quasi-judicial agencies, "is by law a creature of Congress, and it is our duty to report direct to it." But the President had no intention of backing down. In 1936, he would launch an exhaustive study on executive reorganization and, early in his second term, would submit a bill to Congress asking for broad reorganization powers. And while all this was still in the future, creating another independent agency did not fit into the President's plans, even in 1935. Thus, he informed the Congress that he did not concur in the recommendation of the FAC for a new regulatory board, even as a temporary measure. "As I have suggested on many occasions," he told the Congress, "it becomes more and more apparent that the Government . . . should bring about a consolidation of its methods of supervision over all forms of transportation." He would, at a later date, propose to Congress legislation "centralizing the supervision of air and water and highway transportation." Meanwhile, the multiplication of regulatory agencies should be avoided. He went on: "Therefore in the interim before a permanent consolidated agency is created or designated over transportation as a whole, a division of the Interstate Commerce Commission can well serve the needs of air transportation." It should be noted that beyond discussing this organizational question Roosevelt said nothing. One could only surmise, therefore, that the President, by broaching this question, was signaling the Congress to act.[4]

Pat McCarran had been following developments closely. In the midst of the airmail crisis of 1934 he had introduced an ill-fated bill that had largely anticipated the recommendations of the Federal Aviation Commission. His judgment seemingly reinforced by the Commission, McCarran decided to try again. On January 22, 1935, the same day the Commission released its report, he introduced a measure similar to his 1934 bill that contemplated the establishment of an independent aviation commission. A few days later, Representative Clarence F. Lea introduced a bill drawn up by the Federal Aviation Commission staff that closely reflected the FAC recommendations. On June 7, Roosevelt again told Congress that "a separate commission need not be established." Realizing the hopelessness of opposing Roosevelt, McCarran introduced another bill, which, in his words, was "in keeping with the message of the President." "Never for a moment did I abandon my thought that . . . an independent commission [should be created]," McCarran later explained; but he had laid his preference aside and provided that economic regulation of the air "should go over under the Interstate Commerce Commission thinking that, perchance, we might thereby get legislation that would be for the best interests of the industry . . . ."[5]

The airlines, too, would have preferred an independent commission, but they, like McCarran, bent to accommodate the President. Airline executives, representing both old-line carriers and those recently chartered, got solidly behind McCarran's new measure. But McCarran and the carriers suddenly found themselves virtually alone in advocating the bill's passage. Not that Roosevelt shifted gears and decided to disavow all the work of the Federal Aviation Commission; he simply did nothing to further the Commission's objectives, as encompassed in McCarran's bill. Worse yet for the bill's prospects, the President allowed members of his administration to conduct an open campaign against it. The McCarran bill threatened the vested interests of powerful executive departments, particularly the Post Office. This department was not going to hand over its interests to the ICC or any other agency without a struggle. Hence, James Farley informed Burton K. Wheeler, chairman of the Senate Committee on Interstate Commerce, that the airline industry had not yet sufficiently matured to be regulated in the same manner as railroads. Farley further stated that Post Office control over routes and schedules "should not be taken away from it so long as the planes are used for the transport of mail."[6]

Nor did the bill gain favor among powerful groups within the Senate. Black and McKellar were proud of their work in shaping and shepherding through Congress the airmail act that bore their name. They were not eager to see this work discarded. Roosevelt, of course, could have ordered Farley to fall in line with the Federal Aviation Commission recommendations; he likewise could have influenced the position of recalcitrant or uncommitted legislators. He chose to do neither; instead, he kept a discreet silence, as one above the battle. The 74th Congress adjourned on June 30, 1936, without taking action on either the McCarran or Lea bill.

III

By the time the 75th Congress assembled, on January 3, 1937, the majority of domestic operators were in desperate economic straits. Operating under the Black-McKellar Act, they claimed with but slight exaggeration, had brought them to the edge of ruin.

As passed in 1934, Black-McKellar stretched out the life of the 90-day mail contracts awarded in May 1934 to one year, after which they could be extended by the Postmaster General for an indefinite period. The rates on contracts so extended would be fixed by the ICC; however, the act prohibited the ICC from revising mail rates upward—that is, the original contract, or bid, rate could not be exceeded, even if it was below what the Commission believed was a fair or reasonable rate or below the maximum 33 1/3 cents per airplane mile fixed by the statute. The airlines, in the scramble for routes in 1934, had entered bids that did not begin to represent the true cost of transporting the mail. They did this, however, in the expectation that remedial legislation would be forthcoming; what followed was the Black-McKellar Act, which locked the operators into these absurdly low rates.

As if Congress had not created enough difficulties for them, the lines proceeded to create difficulties for themselves. With mail carriage no longer profitable, the lines looked to passenger traffic to pay the fare. The search for customers brought carriers into head-on competition, with some lines encroaching on the territory of others. TWA, for example, moved into Chicago and established passenger routes between that city and Kansas City and Pittsburgh; this drained traffic from United Air Lines, which operated a mail route between New York and San Francisco via Chicago. Carriers could ill-afford to indulge in such practices. "This competition," a Senate committee headed by Harry S. Truman declared in 1935, "has been carried to an extreme which tends to undermine the financial stability of the carriers and jeopardize the maintenance of transportation facilities and services appropriate to the needs of commerce . . . ."[7]

"We very badly need some relief legislation," C. R. Smith of American Airlines told a congressional committee in 1935; indeed, Smith said, an amendment to the Black-McKellar Act, enabling the ICC to increase, as well as decrease, airmail rates and prohibiting off-line competition, was more pressing than passage of the McCarran bill. Even the Post Office Department, which was doing quite well under the 1934 arrangement, requested Congress to grant the carriers relief. Congress responded favorably; in August 1935, it authorized the ICC to revise rates upward and prohibited mail-carriers from establishing passenger or express service "which in any way competes with passenger or express service available upon another air-mail route . . . ." Off-line competitive service established prior to July 1, 1935, could be continued, however.[8]

The Black-McKellar Act was still an unsatisfactory piece of legislation. Its greatest shortcoming, perhaps, was in splitting rate-setting responsibility between two agencies. Serious difficulties arose immediately after the ICC began revising rates upward, leading, according to Kenneth McKellar, to "a state of war . . . between the Interstate Commerce Commission and the Post Office Department." "The Commission has interpreted the air-mail law differently from the way we have interpreted it," Karl Crowley, the Post Office Department Solicitor, told the Congress. The ICC, Crowley complained, had not consulted the Department on critical facts concerning airline operations; it had treated postal officials "more as litigants than as part of the Government"; it had paid no attention to postal appropriations. "I feel that if the Commission will give due regard to the amount of money allotted by Congress for us to spend on air-mail subsidies . . .," he asserted, "a proper rate could be fixed." The Department did have its budgetary problems from time to time; on the other hand, the ICC was charged with setting fair and reasonable rates, and postal appropriations were only one of many factors it had to consider. With their interests and responsibilities clashing, the two agencies were bound to come into conflict; given the tactics employed by the Post Office and the leverage it enjoyed under the

Black-McKellar Act, it was a conflict that the ICC—and ultimately the air carriers—could not win.[9]

The Post Office Department, long supreme in the field, simply refused to allow the ICC to have the final say on rates of airmail compensation. "Air mail rate adjustments upward by order of the ICC are countered by threatened curtailment of. . . schedules by Post Office officials," *U.S. Air Services* reported. Such threats, Pat McCarran told a congressional committee, served to restrain the ICC from setting what it believed were fair and reasonable rates. How much influence these tactics had on the ICC is difficult to say; what is certain is that the Post Office did make such threats. Making matters worse was a provision in the Air Mail Act permitting the Postmaster General to negotiate rates on certain routes. Consequently, in case after case, airlines carried the mail at a rate below the base fixed by the ICC. As the Commission itself noted in November 1936, "It is apparent that rates prescribed by us could not insure fair and reasonable compensation to the carriers when applied in conjunction with a system of free service and negotiated rates exclusively under the control and authorization of another agency of the Government burdened with the cost of the service."[10]

Not all air carrier problems were of the Post Office's making. The carriers continued to hurt themselves by bidding low on new mail routes. In their desire to expand into new territory, the lines, according to a congressional committee, had "virtually evinced a willingness to pay for the privilege of carrying the mail over a particular route." The height of absurdity was reached in July 1937 when one carrier made off with a postal route with a bid of eight ten-thousandths of a mill. With the 1935 amendment to the Black-McKellar Act allowing the life of new contracts to run for three years, winning bidders appeared to be inviting disaster.[11]

Not surprisingly, airlines recorded heavy losses on their books. Over the three-year period of 1934–36, only 6 of 19 carriers showed a net profit. Total losses for the period were in excess of $3.5 million, while the profitable lines netted for the entire three years a combined profit of only $134,000. These were the kind of figures that the lines regularly paraded before the ICC and the Post Office in their quest for higher rates. Postal officials were unmoved. They pointed, with some justification, to the fact that carriers were buying new equipment at a record pace and writing it off in three or four years—an unusually rapid depreciation rate, which, according to the Post Office, helped magnify losses. They also pointed out that the ICC, in setting rates, did not sufficiently discriminate between losses sustained in mail operations and those in off-line passenger operations. Some observers saw an element of vindictiveness and distrust in the Post Office's attitude. "'Father' Post Office, remembering the airmail scandal, treats the airlines like boys in a reform school," *Time* remarked. But whatever the precise truth about airline balance sheets, or of Post Office motives, it was clear that the operators faced a very uncertain profit picture, largely because of the chaotic and unstable airmail rate system. Meanwhile, as the carriers continued to show heavy losses, the Post Office Department airmail operations began to show a profit for the first time in history.[12]

With the airmail no longer a bonanza, the carriers turned to passenger traffic to sustain them. The operators' business strategy underwent a dramatic change after the airmail scandal—a traumatic and sobering experience that had signaled an end to large mail subsidies. Operators that had not done so before now recognized that commercial aviation's prospects lay with passenger service. The lines' continued willingness to carry mail below cost was part of this new strategy; winning an airmail route also meant winning a nearly exclusive passenger route, since, under the Air Mail Act of 1935, mail carriers were forbidden to conduct new off-line operations on the routes of other mail carriers.

Beginning in 1936, with the introduction of the Douglas DC-3 into scheduled passenger service, the lines could pursue this policy with a reasonable prospect of success. Scheduled air transportation could charge rates in excess of surface transportation because of the time it saved its customers. The premium charged, however, could not exceed the value placed on the time saved by the traveler or shipper. Prior to 1936, even with the Federal Government paying for the cost of developing and operating airways and local and state governments shouldering the burden of building and maintaining airports, the rates that air carriers could charge and still remain competitive with railroads and buses were not high enough to cover the cost of transporting passengers; the aircraft of that period, even when fully loaded with passengers, could not turn a profit unless they also carried mail. The DC-3 changed all this. Larger, faster, and possessing a greater range than older aircraft, this airliner could carry 21 passengers between New York and Los Angeles in 16 flying hours and return them in 14; the B-247D could carry only 10 passengers and make the same trip west in 20 hours. More importantly, the DC-3's direct operating costs were nearly 50 percent lower than the B-247's. "The DC-3 freed the air lines from complete dependency on government mail pay," noted C. R. Smith, the first airline executive to order the new machines. "It was the first airplane that could make money just by hauling passengers." By 1937, passenger traffic was easily producing more revenues than mail carriage, a development that cried out for scrapping a system whereby routes and schedules were fixed to meet the parochial needs of the Post Office, not the traveling public.[13]

The coming of the DC-3 had its self-contradictory aspects. It was a liberating influence, to be sure, freeing the carriers from their near-total dependence on mail revenues; on the other hand, more than any other single event since the airmail cancellation, the introduction of this aircraft made Federal economic regulation imperative to the carriers' well-being. The Air Mail Act of 1935, though it prohibited mail carriers from poaching on each other's passenger traffic, did not prevent a nonmail carrier from establishing a passenger route wherever he chose. As long as seat-mile costs were too high to yield a profit, interlopers presented no serious threat to existing lines; but, as *U.S. Air Services* pointed out, in 1937, "This year and hereafter this competitive menace is very real because airplane manufacturers are producing transports capable of economical operations without air mail revenues." Briefs railing against competition began coming from unexpected sources. "It is believed to be sound public policy," asserted the U.S. Chamber of Commerce, making common cause with the air transport industry, "that an air-line operator who makes the necessary investment to establish and maintain service on a given route should be entitled to protection against unlimited competition so long as he renders adequate and efficient service at reasonable rates." Edgar Gorrell could not have agreed more. "We cannot ask people to put money into this industry . . . when their investment can be taken away from them by some unregulated and irresponsible competing company," he told Congressman Clarence Lea. Speaking before a Senate committee, he presented Harry Truman with a peculiar slant on U.S. economic development. The airlines' problems, he said, should be solved in the "traditional American way, a way which invited the confidence of the investing public by providing a basic charter that promises the hope of stability and security, and orderly and intelligent growth under watchful governmental supervision." The DC-3 was clearly a mixed blessing.[14]

The Douglas DC-3

IV

"A paper storm of aviation bills fell on the Capitol this session," noted *Aviation* in reviewing the furious legislative activity of 1937. "Many of them are trivial. . . . But a half dozen of them are heavy-duty documents written by able Congressmen. . . ." Among the heavy-duty documents were two bills providing for the economic regulation of air transportation by the ICC. One had been introduced by Clarence Lea, the other, inevitably, by Pat McCarran, who was now admitting that the practice had become "more or less a hobby with me." The two bills were virtually identical, reflecting the fact that this time around the people looking to economic regulation had joined forces in a coordinated legislative effort. Lea, McCarran, Joseph Eastman of the ICC, and representatives of the Air Transport Association had met periodically to put together an acceptable bill. The ATA went so far as to retain a prestigious law firm — Covington, Burling, Rublee, Acheson & Shorb —

to assist in the drafting. The proponents of economic regulation were now decidedly more organized. Opponents of the legislation, however, were as formidable as ever.[15]

"[The McCarran] bill would freeze the present air service," Karl Crowley charged before a Senate committee. "It would create a monopoly . . . . No little fellow with a new idea, with plenty of capital, could go out and establish a line . . . ." Crowley struck the same theme before a House committee: "I do not think that [aviation] ought to be stifled and controlled and held down by any governmental agency. I think that it ought to be just as free as it can be . . . . Let it alone. Let it develop. Let competition develop." But when it became a question of the Post Office relinquishing its control over the carriers, Crowley's tune changed. "We have to, the Post Office Department must, regulate the schedules for this service to be effective," he told Clarence Lea. Lea chafed. "The Post Office Department has taken a rather destructive attitude against constructive legislation . . .," he complained to Roosevelt.[16]

No less obdurate in their opposition were the chairmen of the House and Senate Post Office Committees, James M. Mead and Kenneth McKellar. These men were as jealous of their jurisdiction as officials of executive agencies. McKellar, in addition, saw sinister forces at work and made much of a weekend drafting sessions held at Gorrell's suite in the Carlton Hotel in Washington between ATA and ICC officials. Both McCarran and McKellar testified before the Senate subcommittee holding hearings on McCarran's bill. The two men snapped at each other, and when Harry Truman, the subcommittee chairman, tried to intervene, either in McCarran's defense or in an effort to hold down McKellar's rambling discourses, tension filled the committee room. After one particularly acrimonious exchange with Truman, McKellar stalked out of the hearings in a huff, saying: "It is your committee; yes, sir. I will take the privilege of withdrawing and will discuss this on the floor of the Senate." Truman and McCarran had aroused the ire of the wrong man. When the bill was brought before the Senate, McKellar, all the more convinced of a dark, nefarious purpose behind the ICC and ATA collaboration, announced that he was prepared to filibuster. McCarran fell ill, and while Truman tried to carry on, he could not overcome the opposition of the crusty Tennessean. The bill was never put to a vote. "This means . . .," *U.S. Air Services* observed, "that officials of the Post Office Department, with Senator McKellar, . . . are resolved to hold onto their control over the air mail until the cows come home — the cows to be delayed by every obstacle these men can throw in their way."[17]

Clarence Lea had no more success with his bill. Mead made it clear that he did not like the measure and that he would oppose it on the House floor. Lea appealed to Roosevelt. "I believe legislation can yet be promptly passed this session if, within the next few days, you find it possible to advise us of your desires," he wrote the President on July 23. A week later, with Roosevelt still maintaining his silence, Lea appealed to him again: "We need only your approval, I think, to get the measure through during this session. I hope you can conclude to give us that help." On August 5, Roosevelt wrote Lea that "it would be desirable to postpone the matter" until the executive branch had a better opportunity to work out a solution. Lea knew he was beaten; he did not bother to call his bill up.[18]

Other legislative activity concerning aviation had also occupied the 1st session of the 75th Congress. And though this activity did not attract the attention received by the economic proposals, it would, in the long run, have a profound effect on the final legislative outcome. The sponsors of this legislation, though generally sympathetic to the airlines' plea for economic regulation, were primarily interested in aviation safety.

The Cutting crash, the Copeland hearings, and the lag in airway development had shaken many people's confidence in the Bureau of Air Commerce. But scarcely anyone, Royal S. Copeland included, had proposed very radical solutions. People tended to think that a turnover in key personnel and an infusion of funds would set things right. David L. Behncke was an exception. "I think the main trouble is that the air transportation industry has outgrown the present Government regulatory vehicle, which is the Air Commerce Act . . .," he testified before the Copeland Committee. In April 1936, the central executive council of Behncke's airline pilots union passed a resolution recommending that those functions of the Bureau of Air Commerce dealing with regulation, safety, and navigation of scheduled air transportation be placed in a separate branch of the ICC. "This would take [aviation safety] out of politics and other harmful influences and give it the benefit of the Interstate Commerce Commission's long and extensive experience in the field of transportation," Behncke explained. ALPA also proposed the creation of a separate and independent five-man air safety board, which would also be lodged in the ICC, to investigate the probable cause of aviation accidents and make safety recommendations. The Department of Commerce would still have jurisdiction over general aviation and retain its promotional functions.[19]

Few people took Behncke's proposal very seriously until the winter of 1936–37, with its spate of air carrier accidents. These mishaps moved Pat McCarran to attach a new section to his economic regulatory bill embodying ALPA's proposals. Congressman Robert Crosser (D-Ohio) quickly followed suit by introducing a similar air safety measure in the House. McCarran ultimately split his bill in half and reintroduced two separate measures, one pertaining to economic regulation, the other to safety.

Both the McCarran and Crosser safety bills received a favorable hearing in committee. The recent accidents, said New York Mayor Fiorello La Guardia, were "sufficient to justify the belief that this function ought to be transferred from the Department of Commerce to the Interstate Commerce Commission." After all, La Guardia argued, the Department of Commerce had the responsibility for promoting commercial aviation — a function that did not mix well with regulatory responsibilities. On the other hand, the ICC was a disinterested agency. "It has no leanings one way or the other," he said. "It does not get 'chummy' with railroads or people that it has under its supervision." A writer in *Forum* picked up the theme. Bureau of Air Commerce officials had consistently yielded to airline pressures and had thereby compromised safety in the air. But, he said, "when the Interstate Commerce Commission issues an order to railroads, they don't begin a barrage of telephone calls to congressmen. They do as they are told."[20]

David Behncke had more to say on the same point. "Career men, not political appointees who change with each administration, are necessary to increase public safety," he said. These men should have employment security, or else they would be "looking for another job while they are working for the Bureau." And where would they go for employment when they are removed from their jobs during a change in administrations? "The only place they can go is back to the aircraft industry, where most of them originated," Behncke held, answering his own question. "Therefore it is only natural that they lean toward the people whose industry they are regulating, because, in reality, they are regarded as their future employers." To prove his point, Behncke cited the examples of MacCracken, Young, and Vidal, all of whom formed one connection or another with the air transport industry after leaving the Department of Commerce.[21]

Joseph Eastman, not wishing to get mired even deeper in controversy, refused to take a clear-cut stand. He admitted, however, that there was grave dissatisfaction in many quarters with the way the Department of Commerce handled its safety reponsibilities and predicted "a strong movement in favor of giving the Commission jurisdiction [over aviation safety], such as in the case of railroads and motor carriers." Edgar Gorrell was equally cautious. He was getting along well with Johnson and Fagg. The modernization program was underway. So why plunge unnecessarily into the unknown? Why take a step that might open up a hornet's nest? But the idea must have had its attractive aspects, particularly the safety board proposal, for Gorrell was careful not to reject it. "The air lines do not care what governmental body administers safety," he declared. The Truman subcommittee, which also held hearings on this proposal, was not so equivocal. "We do not feel that safety of air transportation should be left under the jurisdiction of the Secretary of Commerce . . .," it stated in its report.[22]

Just as the Post Office Department fought the economic regulatory bills, the Department of Commerce attacked the safety bills, and with equal success. But the significance of these bills far transcended their failure to attain passage. These measures injected a potent new theme — safety — into the overall drive for comprehensive aviation legislation. It was a theme that those seeking Federal economic regulation could use to their advantage.[23]

V

Franklin Roosevelt must have been a puzzle to many an observer of the aviation scene. He had persuaded Congress to authorize the establishment of a commission to study and recommend new approaches to Federal civil aviation policy. He had seemingly accepted the approach recommended by this commission, except for one particular: he wanted no part of a new independent agency. Advocates of economic regulation willingly altered their views to accommodate the President. Yet the President lifted not one finger in behalf of their legislative program — the very program that had been recommended by his commission. He talked of a coordinated transportation policy, but when it came to act he appeared content to let matters stand — to continue a crazy-quilt aviation policy, with a limited amendment here and there to existing aviation statutes.

Why Roosevelt did not act is still something of a mystery, though it was certainly not uncharacteristic of the man. He often detached himself from issues that appeared to others of great moment. The aviation issue probably did not have the urgency for the President that it had for others. Moreover, it was a sticky issue in many ways; Roosevelt must have taken into account that there was substantial support for the status quo within the executive branch and the Congress. "There is one point that is bothering me here," Congressman Alfred L. Bulwinkle (D-N.C.) said. "The President comes along and recommends that air transportation be put under the Interstate Commerce Commission, and the Post Office Department says that it should not be done."[24] This kind of behavior was puzzling and bothersome, but it was also characteristic of the man. Far from stamping out dissenting views within his administration, Roosevelt often went out of his way to foster them. He did not demand that his subordinates close ranks until he was prepared to act, and it is certain that he was not prepared to act between January 1935 and July 1937. It should be remembered that the Federal Aviation Commission had been forced on him by events; he had adopted the idea as a way of blocking McCarran's 1934 bill dealing with economic regulation. Roosevelt may have agreed with the findings and recommendations of the Commission, but he may also have believed that immediate implementation was premature. In any event, other matters occupied the President during the period: the continuing economic crisis, the election of 1936, governmental reorganization, and his court-packing scheme.

Roosevelt's inconsistencies bedeviled those trying to read his mind. In 1935, he had signed into law the Motor Carrier Act, which entrusted to the ICC the economic regulation of buses and trucks engaged in interstate commerce. This action was in line with his recommendation on aviation legislation. The following year, however, he approved the Merchant Marine Act, which created an independent regulatory agency. Had the President changed his mind on stopping the proliferation of independent agencies? Not at all. Early in 1937, he submitted to the Congress for its consideration the fruits of many months of study on reorganizing the executive branch, the so-called Brownlow Report. This report, the product of Louis Brownlow, a public administration expert,

Charles E. Merriam, a University of Chicago political scientist, and Luther Gulick, another public administration expert, looked askance at the sprawl of Federal commissions and agencies independent of the President's executive powers. These entities, according to Brownlow, were minature independent governments. "They constitute a headless 'fourth branch' of the Government, a haphazard deposit of irresponsible agencies and uncoordinated powers," the report said. "They do violence to the basic theory of the American Constitution that there should be three major branches of the Government and only three." Congress had found no effective way of supervising them; the Executive could not control them; the judiciary touched them only during litigation. What bothered the report's authors and the President was not that these agencies exercised quasi-judicial and quasi-legislative powers independently; they believed this was both necessary and proper. What bothered them was that these agencies also exercised "non-judicial" powers, which, they believed, properly belonged to the President. Thus, these agencies constituted "areas of unaccountability."

Brownlow proposed a radical solution. The 100 or so independent agencies, administrations, boards, and commissions would be placed within 12 executive departments (the 10 existing departments and two new ones, Social Welfare and Public Works, which Congress was asked to create). Once in these departments, the commissions would be divided into two sections, one administrative and one judicial. The administrative section would be a regular division or bureau of the department in which it was housed and would be headed by a chief directly responsible to the Secretary and through him to the President. The judicial section, however, would be completely independent of the Secretary's control and would be in the department purely for administrative support. The President's inconsistencies aside, it appeared a fair assumption that if subsequent aviation legislation were to meet with Roosevelt's approval it would have to take the Brownlow Report into account.[25]

While Clarence Lea was pleading with the President to speak out in favor of his ill-fated bill, Roosevelt was thinking ahead to the next congressional session. On July 31, 1937, when both the Lea and McCarran bills were still pending, he dashed off a short memorandum to Harllee Branch, the Second Assistant Postmaster General:

It looks now as if there will be no aviation legislation at this session. I suggest that as soon as the session closes, the Interde-

Royal S. Copeland

J. Monroe Johnson

Fred D. Fagg, Jr.

partmental Committee on Civil International Aviation be expanded to cover the whole aviation field, taking in the Interstate Commerce Commission . . ., and that this Committee charge itself with the preparation of a Bill for the next session in January, covering the whole subject of aviation, including mail . . . .[26]

This was the first visible evidence that Roosevelt had finally decided to engage the civil aviation issue. What prompted him to act at this time can only be speculated. He knew, of course, that the forces spearheaded by Gorrell, Lea, and McCarran would be back with their legislative proposals in the next congressional session; he could sense that these forces were building momentum, and that their chances of success were improving. He would therefore join them, but on his own terms — with a bill of his own making. It is probable, too, that he realized that the Black-McKellar Act was not working and that the need for comprehensive economic regulation was pressing.

Meanwhile, Fred Fagg was thinking along analogous if not precisely parallel lines as the President. Fagg had been convinced since 1934 that airlines should be treated as common carriers. Indeed, he and Dean Wigmore had drafted Clarence Lea's 1935 bill. Fagg was thinking in terms of assembling an ad hoc executive branch committee to draft a bill for the next session. The committee, he believed, should be composed of representatives from the various executive departments having an aviation interest; these men should come together and achieve an executive branch consensus. Fagg did not wish to invite the ICC into the proceedings, and for good reason. He wanted to return to the idea originally proposed by the Federal Aviation Commission — the establishment of a new Federal aviation agency.

Fagg won J. Monroe Johnson over to the proposition. Johnson, in turn, won Secretary Roper over. Soon after McCarran's and Lea's legislative drive had stalled, Roper and Johnson took the idea to the President. Roosevelt concurred, though grumpily. He dropped his thought of including the ICC in the proceedings and agreed to Roper's appointing representatives from six Departments — War, Navy, Commerce, Post Office, State, and Treasury — to prepare a legislative proposal. The President set down no guidelines. He merely directed Roper, as Roosevelt himself later explained to the press, to issue orders to the committee members "to go into a room and not come out until they had reached an agreement." "Of course you know that for the past two years every proposal that has been made on the Hill . . . has met opposition from one branch of the Government or another," the President elaborated. "This summer I told them to go into a room and bring me a unanimous report."[27]

On September 15, Roper announced the creation of the Interdepartmental Committee on Civil Aviation Legislation. The Committee's six members were all assistant secretaries or the equivalent. J. Monroe Johnson represented Commerce. Each Department also designated an alternate member; the alternate for Commerce was Fred Fagg. The regular members attended hearings and other meetings irregularly. The real work was done by the alternates, particularly by a subcommittee of three, composed of Fagg, Major St. Clair Streett of the War Department, and Clinton M. Hester, a Treasury Department attorney, who also served as the subcommittee chairman. Hester had found his way to the Committee through no mere accident. He was the author of the administration's reorganization bill — a piece of draftsmanship that had pleased the President. It was therefore a fair assumption that Hester was there to see that the Interdepartmental Committee did not do too much violence to the principles expressed in the Brownlow Report.[28]

Fagg did not have to be told any of this. He knew that the Committee's job entailed more than reaching a consensus among interested Departments by, as *Aviation* put it, untangling and rewriting "the maze of conflicting air transport legislation left in a heap by the last session of Congress"; he knew that the Committee had to construct a piece of legislation that was satisfactory to Franklin Roosevelt and appealing enough to the Congress and the various aviation interests to assure its passage. Early on, therefore, Fagg offered two suggestions, which the Committee members acceded to. One was that the Committee take account of the Brownlow Report; the other, that they frame a bill creating a single independent agency that would be responsible for all Federal civil aviation affairs.[29]

Both of these matters had to be approached gingerly. The Brownlow-inspired reorganization legislation was running into very rough weather on Capitol Hill, and would in fact meet with defeat in April 1938.[30] Hence, it was likely that an aviation bill with strong strains of unadulterated Brownlow would encounter heavy congressional resistance. Moreover, the two suggestions appeared incompatible. An independent agency charged with executive functions, as those exercised by the Bureau of Air Commerce, and quasi-judicial functions, as those exercised by the ICC, ran counter to Brownlow's basic thrust. Somehow, the Committee would have to reconcile these two divergent conceptions.

Accordingly, Fagg and Hester did not take the Brownlow Report neat; they diluted it with their own commonsense ideas. The result was a finely balanced bill that reflected the interplay of these two divergent conceptions. The draft ultimately approved by the Interdepartmental Committee established a Civil Aeronautics Board composed of three members appointed by the President to serve a term of six years. To this Board were transferred the powers and responsibilities exercised by the Secretary of Commerce under the Air Commerce Act. In addition, the Board was given the power to issue certificates of convenience and necessity and regulate all rates. The Board was an independent agency — that is, it would not be housed within an existing Department — which ran counter to the Brownlow Report; nor was the agency split into an "administrative" and "judicial" section, which also ran counter to Brownlow. On the other hand, the Interdepartmental Committee had Brownlow in mind when it —

- Provided that "the President shall designate annually one of the members of the Board as chairman, who shall be the executive officer of the Board . . . ." This provision surely gave the President leverage in influencing affairs.

- Remained silent on the President's powers to remove Board members. By failing to specify grounds for removal, the bill was saying, in effect, that Board members would serve at the President's pleasure, just as any Presidential appointee in the executive branch. Clearly, Fagg and Hester had not forgotten the *Humphrey* case.

- Provided that certificates issued to American-flag and foreign-flag carriers were subject to the approval of the President. This provision recognized the President's hegemony over foreign affairs.

- Provided, in a section entitled "Administrative Review," that any power or duty conferred on the Board "not subject to review by courts of law shall be subject to the general direction of the President . . . ." With no attempt made to specify what was and what was not subject to the review of the courts, this provision represented a sweeping grant of Presidential powers.[31]

The Committee finished its work in less than four months. Roosevelt approved the bill readily, at which point Hester, who was now made the administration's official spokesman on aviation legislation, called in Clarence Lea, whom the administration had decided to work with instead of Pat McCarran. The Congressman agreed to use the Interdepartmental bill as a foundation from which to draft his own measure. He circulated the Interdepartmental bill as a confidential committee print and elicited comment from his own staff and the ATA. Once the comments were in, Lea's, Hester's, and Gorrell's staffs drafted a new bill. This work was completed within 60 days, and on March 4, 1938, Lea introduced H.R. 9738 — a bill different from the Interdepartmental bill in many details but similar in its treatment of Presidential powers. Four days later, though stopping short of an out-and-out endorsement, Roosevelt remarked during a press conference that "Lea's bill is in line with the desires of the large majority of the industry and is in line, substantially, with the recommendations of the Interdepartmental Committee." Thus, Fagg's and Hester's careful balancing act had worked, and Roosevelt, after insisting that airline economic regulation go to the ICC, had now reverted to the original idea of the Federal Aviation Commission. "There's one nice thing about a merry-go-round — even the Washington kind," *Aviation* noted in commenting on the President's aboutface. "If you give it a little time, it will always bring your pet horse back to where you are waiting for it."[32]

Meanwhile, largely ignored by the administration, Pat McCarran appeared somewhat befuddled by the swift pace of events. In November 1937, when J. Monroe Johnson called an airport operators conference in connection with the work of the Interdepartmental Committee, McCarran publicly labeled the conference "pure camouflage." After four frustrating years, he had come to distrust the administration and believed the recent surge in activity was chiefly designed to throw obstacles in his path. "I am fed up with the obstructions Washington bureaucracy tries to put in the way of honest legislative endeavor for aviation," he told a *New York Times* reporter. Early in January, Roosevelt called the disgruntled McCarran to the White House. He told him, according to the Senator, that "I should proceed to draft legislation carrying out the idea of an independent authority to have full and absolute control over all matters pertaining to aviation." But the President, perhaps, did not sufficiently impress upon the Senator some of the finer points desired by the administration. McCarran's bill, largely the result of fusing his safety and economic measures of the previous session, scarcely took account of the Brownlow Report.[33]

    Shortly after convening his aviation subcommittee for another round of hearings, Harry Truman detected "a change in the attitude toward aviation legislation" — a distinct change for the better. No doubt, the knowledge that Clarence Lea's bill was largely the work of the administration had something to do with this shift. But so did the character of the bill. Fred Fagg's suggestion that all aviation affairs be lumped into one agency had proved a brilliant stroke. As a piece of tactics, it was near flawless. Edgar Gorrell, though actually content to leave safety regulation and airway development to the Bureau of Air Commerce, quickly perceived the appeal of combining safety, airway development, and economic regulation in a single bill. Fagg's conception "offered distinct possibilities for sloganeering that would enhance the chance of success in securing the critically needed legislation," noted Howard C. Westwood, a Covington & Burling attorney who had worked on ATA's legislative drafts. "An argument stressing the diffusion among existing government agencies of various powers over civil aviation and the virtue of bringing all into a coherent unity under a new body would sound good in Congress."[34]

    Fagg's conception also served to bring together all the factions looking to aviation reform — those wishing to strengthen air safety and those seeking economic regulation. This had the effect of greatly expanding the issue. It was no longer merely a question of regulating airline economics; it was now also a question of promoting air safety — and saving lives. Airline economic regulation possessed an extremely narrow political base. The kind of circumstances that had led to the establishment of the ICC and to railroad economic regulation did not prevail in the case of the airlines. The ICC had been created not to save the railroads from economic ruin but, simply put, to save the country from the railroads and their questionable business practices. The movement for air carrier regulation had as its overriding objective the stabilizing of airline economics by reducing competition and setting fair and reasonable rates, without which, the operators contended, the lines faced disaster. The problem was that very few people cared how air carrier operators fared financially. But people did care about air safety.

    None of this, of course, would have had much appeal had the Bureau of Air Commerce not been under virtual siege since the Cutting crash. Indeed, in the opinion of one highly placed Department of Commerce official, this incident was the pivotal event in the background to the Civil Aeronautics Act. "Those who aspired to see your Uncle really plunge into [the field of airline economic regulation] got their opportunity when it was charged that not TWA but the old Bureau of Air Commerce killed . . . Bronson Cutting . . .," Denis Mulligan said some years after the event. "That was the starting point which enabled Senator Copeland . . . to really launch what evolved into the 1938 statute . . . ." And so it was that the Bureau of Air Commerce became a sacrificial pawn in a game played by the airlines to insure their own survival.[35]

VI

Clarence Lea's measure differed from the Interdepartmental bill in a number of specifics. Five key differences should be noted. Lea's proposal (1) created a five-member Civil Aeronautics "Authority," instead of a three-member Civil Aeronautics "Board"; (2) established, in accordance with ALPA's recommendations, a Safety Board (later changed in committee to a Safety Division) to investigate and determine the probable cause of aircraft accidents; (3) gave the Authority jurisdiction over intrastate flying; (4) provided that certificates of convenience and necessity could remain in effect indefinitely (instead of the 10-year limit set by the Interdepartmental Committee) on the condition that the possessor render satisfactory service; (5) strengthened the wording of the "grandfather clause," making the issuance of certificates to existing carriers automatic.[36] It was a measure of how times had changed in the 12 years since the Air Commerce Act had been debated that the state rights issue was not raised. Legislators had come to recognize that aviation safety transcended state lines. As a matter of fact, attitudes had changed since the last congressional session. Scarcely anyone disputed the necessity for the legislation. Most of the debate, both at the hearings and on the floors of the House and Senate, centered on matters related to the Brownlow Report.

A number of legislators, particularly Republicans, displayed an acute frustration over the administration's sudden shift in attitude. Congressman Charles A. Wolverton (R-N.J.) posed a series of sharply

worded questions in a vain effort to get administration spokesmen to
explain why Roosevelt liked this year's bill but not last's. Congressmen
James W. Wadsworth (R-N.Y.) and B. Carroll Reece (R-Tenn.) jumped
on the obvious inconsistencies in Roosevelt's evolving position. "I am
wondering," Reece said, throwing Roosevelt's oft-stated position back at
him, "if we continue to set up separate commissions to deal with each of
these agencies of transportation if it is going to be possible under such a
policy to bring about the development of interrelated planning of our
national transportation system." If the administration continued to
support this kind of legislation, Wadsworth pointed out, the prospect of
ever getting rid of the profusion of independent boards and commissions
would become hopeless. "Congress has yielded to [administration and
special interest] suggestions and importunities time after time," Wadsworth told Fagg. And Congress had "gone on, and on" piling up one
commission after another. "Now you make a strong plea for . . . a
separate body on civil aeronautics . . . ." Inconsistencies aside, administration spokesmen and their supporters in the Congress successfully
countered these arguments. "There comes a time when you have a very
important industry which needs special attention," James M. Mead said,
"and when that time comes . . . you create a new body." When this
exchange took place, Roosevelt's reorganization plan was three weeks
away from being rejected by Congress. With congressional sentiment
thus aligned, deviations from the Brownlow plan gave the Lea bill's
supporters few problems; administration spokesmen ran into their biggest difficulties defending those sections of the bill that conformed, or
seemed to conform, with Brownlow.[37]

The most contested provision of the bill was easily that section
giving the President jurisdiction over all matters "not subject to the
review of the courts." Carl E. Mapes, the ranking Republican on the
House Interstate and Foreign Commerce Committee, objected to the
vagueness of the provision and, by implication, to the fact that it
appeared to be Brownlowian in character. Hester denied that the
provision was in harmony with Brownlow. (Moments earlier Hester had
delivered to the committee a Brownlow-inspired discourse on the Constitution, in which he deplored the lack of executive control over independent commissions. Consistency was not a strong suit in the administration's arguments.) Mapes then posed what was perhaps the most crucial
question of the House hearings. "Have you any language in mind which

might be incorporated in the bill that would set out what powers and duties in the judgment of the Congress should be subject to review of the courts and what would come under the general direction of the President?" he asked. Hester gave a patently unsatisfactory answer: "No . . . . We feel that the matter should be left to the courts to eventually determine exactly what the line of demarcation is." No amount of questioning could bring Hester to enumerate the President's powers under this section.[38]

Republicans and some Democrats continued to wrangle with Lea and the administration over this provision. Congressman Alfred L. Bulwinkle offered a suggestion that resolved the issue. He proposed dropping the offending provision and adopting in its place a new section creating an "Administrator," appointed by the President with the advice and consent of the Senate, who would be "in" the Authority and would exercise specified executive powers — essentially the same powers exercised by the Secretary of Commerce under the Air Commerce Act, except safety rulemaking and accident investigation. Thus, the Administrator, possessing only executive powers, would be the creature of the President, while the five-man Authority, possessing quasi-legislative powers, would be the creature of the Congress. The suggestion, its Brownlowian overtones notwithstanding, was adopted by a majority of the Committee. In addition, since the five-man Authority had now been stripped of its executive functions, the Committee adopted a provision that limited the power of the President to remove these five members to cases of inefficiency, neglect of duty, or malfeasance. No limitation was placed on the President's power to remove the Administrator. The bill was favorably reported out of committee on April 28; interestingly enough, the Republicans filed a minority report recommending that the new organization be placed in the Interstate Commerce Commission.[39]

The House Interstate and Foreign Commerce Committee made another change to Lea's original bill — a change that would have a profound, if delayed, effect on the nation's airport system. The Committee removed the words "except airports" from that portion of the bill that dealt with the proposed new agency's authority to establish and maintain air navigation facilities. Lea had borrowed the deleted language from the Air Commerce Act.

The airport question had been a major concern of the Interdepartmental Committee. This committee had not been in existence for many days before it realized that the question required special treatment. Indeed, it found the subject too sizable to handle by itself. Thus, early in December, after the Committee had held hearings on airport policy, the Department of Commerce called a two-day conference on airports. Representatives of 14 national organizations interested in airport development attended.[40]

The conference took dead aim at Herbert Hoover's "dock" theory, which held that airports were analogous to docks and, therefore, the responsibility of municipalities. Not that the conference believed that the entire airport should become a Federal responsibility. In calling for a national public airport system, the responsibility for which would be shared by Federal, state, and local governments, the conference limited Federal reponsibility "to the actual landing area and the necessary air navigation facilities." The conference made two key recommendations to the Interdepartmental Committee. It proposed that Congress (1) provide the Bureau of Air Commerce with $150,000 for an immediate survey of the nation's airport needs, and (2) enact legislation establishing a Federal-aid airport program with an initial appropriation of $12 million for the two-year period 1938–39. Before adjourning, the conference established an Airport Advisory Committee to give the Department of Commerce a standing source of expert opinion on airport matters.

The Interdepartmental Committee unanimously approved the first recommendation and sent it on to the White House. It tabled the second, without prejudice, while awaiting the administration's position on the survey. The Budget Bureau turned down the request for $150,000. Fagg and Hester went to Budget Director Daniel Bell and asked him to reconsider. Bell now agreed to the survey, but stated his firm opposition to a Federal-aid airport program.[41]

Lea steered clear of the question in his bill, but soon found, as witness after witness testified before his committee, that he could not long ignore it. What these witnesses said in effect was that the nation's airport system was in a chaotic state, largely because of a lack of overall planning and an inadequacy of local development funds. This chaos could be brought under control only by a Federal planning and aid program. Witnesses could point with logic to the fact that the Federal Government, through its relief and recovery programs, was already financing the lion's share of airport development. During Roosevelt's first six years in office, Federal funds accounted for 76.7 percent of all funds spent in the United States on airport development. Almost without exception, modern airports capable of handling the DC-3 and other aircraft of its generation had been built with Federal money. "Had it not been for Works Progress Administration airport work, air traffic in the United States would have been brought to a practical stop by the advent of the big ships," Gill Robb Wilson, president of the National Association of Aviation Officials, told the Lea Committee. There was, then, a kind of subterranean Federal-aid airport program. But the program was conducted without a national airport plan; as a matter of fact, its principal thrust was not airport development but economic recovery. It seemed logical, therefore, that this subterranean program should give way to a more systematic program with specific aviation goals.[42]

Aside from trying to establish need, witnesses attacked the "dock" theory of airports as a way of establishing a clear Federal reponsibility in the matter. "A runway is an aid and just as necessary as a radio range station," said Richard Aldworth, chairman of the New Jersey State Aviation Commission and a member of the Airport Advisory Committee established by the Department of Commerce in December. To Aldworth, an airport was akin to a waterway or harbor. "In the city of New York, the New York harbor is used by the French Line, the Cunard Line, and other lines, and they are not required to dig the harbors, so that the *Normandie* or the *Queen Mary* can dock," he said. Federal funds paid for the digging of these waterways.[43]

Administration witnesses were hard put to defend the position of the Bureau of the Budget. They argued that the words "except airports" should be retained in the bill; otherwise Congress would be committing the Federal Government "to the building of Federal airports throughout the United States that might involve hundreds of millions of dollars." James Wadsworth believed that retaining this language was a needless complication. The airport survey, he contended, would more than likely indicate the necessity for some measure of Federal assistance. "In that event you would have to come back to Congress and get a bill passed to take out that language." "Why would it not be better," he asked Hester, "to take it out now . . . ?" Hester could only convey the Budget Bureau's fear of a raid on the Federal treasury.[44]

In the end, the Lea Committee, as well as its counterpart in the Senate, was persuaded by the superior arguments of the airport-aid proponents. Both the Senate and House bills dropped the airport prohibition contained in the Air Commerce Act and authorized an airport survey.[45]

Meanwhile, Harry Truman, chairman of the Interstate Commerce subcommittee to which McCarran's bill had been referred, was having difficulties. Like the administration, he was committed to the approach taken by Clarence Lea. McCarran's bill was clearly not in the image of the House measure. This, therefore, would have to be remedied. Moreover, in order to facilitate compromise in a House-Senate conference, Truman wanted the Senate bill to be as nearly identical to the Lea bill as possible. The problem was McCarran. Truman was uncertain how ready the Nevada Senator was to compromise differences. Truman concluded that working entirely within his subcommittee and trying to trade off one provision for another was entirely too risky. He and Royal S. Copeland got together and decided to outflank McCarran.

On March 30, Truman and Copeland, working in tandem, each introduced kindred bills that were virtually identical to the unamended version of H.R. 9738. Truman's bill, offered as a substitute for McCarran's measure, went to the Committee on Interstate Commerce; Copeland's went to the Committee on Commerce. In this way, if Truman was unsuccessful in resolving his differences with McCarran and bringing out a satisfactory bill, Copeland would stand ready to report his own bill out. Moreover, the ploy might work to persuade McCarran to convert to the Lea position.[46]

The maneuver succeeded. "There seem to be some who think there is only one ambition I have and that is to have my name on a bill," McCarran said, trying to hide his chagrin as Truman began hearings on his substitute measure. "Just forget that. Take my name off the bill if you want to. We need this legislation more than I need my name on the bill." Of course, Truman knew better, and was depending on McCarran's ambition to assert itself. As for McCarran, he realized he had been outflanked and that he was in danger of being frozen out of the legislative process. He also knew, as he listened to administration and industry witnesses express their preference for Truman's substitute, that he had introduced the wrong measure. On April 14, eight days after Truman had recessed his hearings, McCarran introduced a new bill, which was referred to Copeland's Commerce Committee; five days later, McCarran introduced a nearly identical measure, which was referred to the Committee on Interstate Commerce. The bills, McCarran explained, followed the general outlines of the Truman and Copeland proposals, without unduly sacrificing "the principles and provisions" of his earlier bill. McCarran had converted to Lea's overall approach, though, unfortunately, important differences still remained between his bill and Lea's. Nevertheless, Truman and Copeland could now proceed without fear that a disgruntled McCarran, sensing that he had been pushed out of the way, would revolt and precipitate an impasse in the Senate. Indeed, in a move desigend to placate the Nevadan, Copeland reported McCarran's bill, not his own, out of committee.[47]

The strategy now called for Truman, Copeland, and their allies to offer amendments on the floor in order to bring McCarran's bill as close as possible to the House version. If this failed, Truman let it be known just prior to the Senate debate, he was prepared to offer his substitute bill. A series of amendments were adopted without difficulty. Then Truman moved to strike out a provision in the bill limiting the President's power of removal to cases of inefficiency, neglect of duty, or malfeasance. McCarran rumbled and raged like a wounded warhorse. He had worked for constructive aviation legislation since 1934; he had fought a long uphill battle. But if this amendment passed he would remove his name from the bill and "stand on the floor of the Senate as long as I have the strength to stand to defeat the bill, because the amendment destroys everything worthwhile in the bill." On May 13, a Friday, the Senate passed the amendment and then waited over the weekend to learn whether McCarran would carry out his threat. "I have had more than a score of telephone calls this weekend from air lines and others interested in this legislation," McCarran explained on Monday. "They said the industry was so in need of some legislation, they asked me to do the best I could." The Senate passed the bill the same day and sent it to the House.[48]

Two days later, on May 18, the House took up and passed the Lea bill. Immediately thereafter, Lea moved that the House strike out all but the enacting clause from the Senate bill and "insert in lieu thereof the provisions of the bill just passed . . . ." The House agreed and sent its bill to the Senate in the form of an amendment to the McCarran measure.[49]

Substantial differences still existed between the House and Senate versions as passed, though nothing that could not be resolved in conference. The Senate had not adopted the device of an "Administrator," which helped draw reasonably clear lines between executive and quasi-legislative and quasi-judicial powers. Moreover, the Senate bill placed no restriction on the President's power to remove members of the Authority. The House bill did. Finally, the Senate bill established an independent Air Safety Board "within" the Authority to investigate accidents; the House version established a Safety Division that was somewhat less independent. As between the two versions, the administration still preferred the Lea bill. So did Harry Truman, who particularly favored the idea of an Administrator responsible to the President. Thus, when the House bill arrived in the Senate, Truman asked that body to concur in the House's action. In so moving, Truman did not know that McCarran was absent from the Senate because of a death in his family. A question was immediately raised about the propriety of taking up this matter in the absence of the Senate bill's sponsor. "I think it would be perfectly agreeable to the Senator from Nevada when the explanation is made," Truman answered. But his explanation failed to sway the Senate.[50]

Truman had been wrong, moreover, in thinking that McCarran would readily agree to the House amendment. The Nevadan returned to Washington two days later and made an impassioned speech before the Senate. He related how he had traveled 3,000 miles from his home to the Capital within a single day. "Every inch of the way there sat at the controls of that great plane a young man who had in his hands my life . . . . Yea, more! Everyone of those boys . . . is a potential soldier, because were this country to be called into war tomorrow there is not a man who sits today at the controls of a commercial plane who would not be a soldier . . .," he said in his best Fourth of July style. Thus, the Senate was dealing with a "big subject" — a subject that "should take the regular course and go to a conference committee, so that out of it all America . . . may take her place in the forefront of this great science and this great industry." McCarran's rhetoric carried the day.[51]

Now it was Truman's turn to be squeezed. He was not picked to serve on the conference committee. No one had deliberately blocked his appointment; the Missourian had been victimized by his own early maneuvering, which had resulted in a bill first being reported out of Copeland's Commerce Committee, of which he was not a member. Truman believed his presence in the conference necessary to insure against McCarran's blocking the adoption of the Administrator concept.

Bennett Champ Clark, a fellow Missourian who had been picked to serve on the conference committee, came to Truman's rescue. Going to Vice President John Nance Garner and in the course of registering a strongly worded complaint, Clark asked that he be replaced on the committee by Truman. "This put me on the conference committee," Truman later recalled, "where I was able to keep McCarran from deleting the provision for setting up an . . . administrator. . . ."[52]

As for the other two major differences, one was settled in favor of the House, the other in favor of the Senate. An independent three-member Air Safety Board was adopted, as was the provision limiting the President's power to remove members of the Authority. The House agreed to the conference report on June 11, the Senate two days later. Roosevelt signed the Civil Aeronautics Act into law on June 23. The act became operative on August 22, at which time the Bureau of Air Commerce went out of existence — its functions, personnel, and facilities transferred to the new Civil Aeronautics Authority.[53]

Thus, the air carriers finally got their economic charter. They had broken loose from Post Office Department control, secured permanent rights to their routes, and rid themselves of the specter of competition. In the process, they had brought down the Bureau of Air Commerce — an act dictated more by political than substantive considerations. Not that the Air Commerce Act was wholly adequate for the times. Its proscription of Federal airport development would not do; but that shortcoming could have been remedied by the deletion of two words. The old act's state rights philosophy could also have been excised with little trouble. And its other major failing — conferring on the Secretary of Commerce the responsibility for accident investigation and the determination of probable cause — was scarcely anything that another amendment could not have cured. The 1926 charter required no more than a fix here and there. But the sad series of events that had begun with Eugene Vidal's appointment and reached their climax with the Cutting crash, coupled with the allure of placing all civil aviation concerns in a single agency, had worked to sweep aside a politically weak, but nevertheless viable, organization operating under a statute that, with few exceptions, was equal to the task ahead.

This is not to say that the Civil Aeronautics Act was wholly unnecessary. The airmail contract system under the Black-McKellar Act was hopelessly out of joint. The airlines needed a new economic charter that recognized and treated them as common carriers. This was the crying need in 1938, not a thorough revamping of the safety and airway development functions. But Congress was in a particularly creative mood and fashioned a delicately balanced tripartite organization with executive, quasi-legislative, and quasi-judicial powers — an Administrator responsible for fostering air commerce, controlling air traffic, and establishing airways; an Authority that promulgated both safety and economic rules; an independent Air Safety Board that determined the probable cause of accidents. It was a unique organization, and certainly the most complex ever created by the Congress. But uniqueness and complexity would not necessarily bring better things; indeed, they brought with them their own special set of problems. This, however, is another story.

What one cannot fail to note in passing is how far U.S. civil aviation had come in the 12 years since the enactment of the Air Commerce Act. In 1926, U.S. airlines flew 4.3 million revenue miles and carried 5,782 passengers; in 1938, they flew 69.7 million revenue miles and carried 1.3 million passengers. Revenue passenger-miles flown in 1926 were virtually nil; revenue passenger-miles flown in 1938 came to 476 million. It was this dramatic growth in traffic, exponential in character and impossible of achievement without the fostering hand of Federal air regulation and airway development, that ultimately spawned the Civil Aeronautics Act. U.S. airlines had assumed the aspects of common carriers, and they demanded to be treated accordingly. And therein lies the chief significance of the Civil Aeronautics Act—it recognized that U.S. commercial aviation had come of age.[54] But this was no ordinary coming of age. Attaining its majority brought the industry no new measure of independence. Indeed, the Civil Aeronautics Act assured a growing airline dependence on Federal policy.

Bibliographical Comment and Notes

The National Archives, in Washington, D.C., houses the largest collection of primary sources used in this study. The Civil Aeronautics Administration Central Files (Record Group 237), which contain the records of the Aeronautics Branch and the Bureau of Air Commerce, were disappointing; I suspect that records were either mindlessly destroyed or carted off by departing officials. Nevertheless, what remains is indispensable to the study of Federal civil aviation policy. The U.S. Department of Commerce General Records, Office of the Secretary (Record Group 40), contain a small but important collection of documents on civil aviation affairs. I also made selective use of the U.S. Post Office Department Files, Bureau of the Second Assistant Postmaster General, Division of the Air Mail Service (Record Group 28). On the background to the Air Commerce Act, the most important collection of documents outside of Washington are in the Herbert Hoover Papers, at the Herbert Hoover Presidential Library, West Branch, Iowa. The Franklin D. Roosevelt Library, Hyde Park, New York, has surprisingly little on domestic civil aviation affairs. The National Aeronautic Association, Washington, D.C., granted me access to its files; without this rich source, I could not have understood the aviation community's position on Federal regulation in the pre-1926 period or grasped the importance of the role played by the private sector in securing passage of the Air Commerce Act. Finally, the FAA Historical Files, in the FAA Headquarters Building, Washington, D.C., contain some materials not found elsewhere.

Printed public documents abound. The annual hearings of the House and Senate Appropriation Committees are a mine of information. So are congressional hearings conducted on specific aviation questions. Among the more important Senate hearings are the following: *Investigation of Air Mail and Ocean Mail Contracts, Hearings* before a special committee, 73d Cong., 2d sess., 1933-34 (Black Committee); *Revision of Air-Mail Laws, Hearings* before the Committee on Post Offices and Post Roads, 73d Cong., 2d sess., 1934; *To Amend the Air Mail Act of 1934, Hearings* before a subcommittee of the Committee on Post Offices and Post Roads, 74th Cong., 1st sess., 1935; *Safety in Air, Hearings* before a subcommittee of the Committee on Commerce, 74th Cong., 2d sess., & 75th Cong., 1st sess., 1936-37 (Copeland Committee); *Regulation of Transportation of Passengers and Property by Aircraft, Hearings* before a subcommittee of the Committee on Interstate Commerce, 74th Cong., 1st sess., 1935; *Regulation of Transportation of Passengers and Property by Aircraft, Hearings* before a subcommittee of the Committee on Interstate Commerce, 75th Cong., 1st sess., 1937 (Truman Committee); *Civil Aviation and Air Transport, Hearings* before a subcommittee of the Committee on Interstate Commerce, 75th Cong., 3d sess., 1938 (Truman Committee); *Civil Aeronautics Authority, Hearings* before the

Committee on Commerce, 75th Cong., 3d sess., 1938. Notable hearings on the House side include *Bureau of Civil Air Navigation in the Department of Commerce, Hearings* before the Committee on Interstate and Foreign Commerce, 68th Cong., 2d sess., 1924; *Inquiry into Operations of the United States Air Services, Hearings,* 68th Cong., 2d sess., 1925 (Lampert Committee): *Air Mail, Hearings* before the Committee on Post Office and Post Roads, 73d Cong., 2d sess., 1934; *Aviation, Hearings* before the Committee on Interstate and Foreign Commerce, 75th Cong., 1st sess., 1937 (Lea Committee); *To Create a Civil Aeronautics Authority, Hearings* before the Committee on Interstate and Foreign Commerce, 75th Cong., 3d sess., 1938. Hearings conducted by the Executive Branch should not be overlooked, particularly U.S. President's Aircraft Board, *Hearings* (4 vols.; Washington, 1925) (Morrow Board).

About a dozen congressional reports and documents are worth noting: *Bureau of Aeronautics in Department of Commerce,* S. Rept. 460, 67th Cong., 2d sess., 1922; *The Promotion of Commercial Aviation,* S. Rept. 2, 69th Cong., 1st sess., 1925; *Report of the Federal Aviation Commission,* S. Doc. 15, 74th Cong., 1st sess., 1935; *Air Transport Act, 1935,* S. Rept. 1329, 74th Cong., 1st sess., 1935; *Safety in the Air,* S. Rept. 2455, 74th Cong., 2d sess., 1936; *Reorganization of the Executive Departments,* S. Doc. 8, 75th Cong., 1st sess., 1937 (Brownlow Report); *Inquiry into Operations of the United States Air Services,* H. Rept. 153, 68th Cong., 2d sess., 1925 (Lampert Report); *Air Commerce Act of 1926,* H. Rept. 1162, 69th Cong., 1st sess., 1926; *Amend the Air Mail Act of February 2, 1925,* H. Rept. 966, 71st Cong., 2d sess., 1930; *Amend the Air Mail Act,* H. Rept. 1209, 71st Cong., 2d sess., 1930; *Investigation of the United States Postal Air Mail Service,* H. Rept. 2087, 72d Cong., 2d sess., 1933; *Civil Aeronautics Bill,* H. Rept. 2254, 75th Cong., 3d sess., 1938. A pivotal Executive Branch report is U.S. President's Aircraft Board, *Report of the President's Aircraft Board* (Washington, 1925) (Morrow Report).

The annual reports of the Secretary of Commerce provide a running account of Aeronautics Branch and Bureau of Air Commerce activities. They are, however, uneven; earlier reports tend to be more informative than those of the late 1930's. For the pre-1926 period, I relied heavily on the annual reports of the Postmaster General and of the National Advisory Committee on Aeronautics. The Aeronautics Branch and the Bureau of Air Commerce published a wealth of information. Aeronautics Bulletins (numbered 1 through 27), covering a wide range of topics, were issued and periodically updated. The most important of these are Bulletin 7 ("Air Commerce Regulations") and Bulletin 24 ("The Federal Airways System"). Bulletins 7A through 7H deal with special regulations. *Domestic Air News* (1926-1929) and its successor, the *Air Commerce Bulletin* (1929-1938), are bimonthly periodicals containing both aeronautical news and regulatory information. Both the Aeronautics Bulletins and the *Air Commerce Bulletin* were particularly useful for tracing the evolution of the airways; but I also relied on the Civil Aeronautics Authority Development Reports, for developments in the late 1930's, and on the *Bureau of Standards Journal of Research* and the *Scientific Papers of the Bureau of Standards,* for earlier developments. The *CAA Statistical Handbook* (issued annually beginning in 1945) was my principal source for aviation statistics; for the pre-1926 era, however, I was forced to rely on the *Aircraft Year Book,* which should be used with care. For nonaviation statistics, I used, among other sources, U.S. Bureau of the Census, *Historical Statistics of the United States: Colonial Times to 1970* (2 vols.; Washington, D.C., 1975).

Plowing through the trade journals of the period was both a rewarding and a frustrating experience. *Aviation,* I believe, best reflected the views of the aviation community and was the most thorough in covering aviation developments. *U.S. Air Services* was not far behind. *Aero Digest,* though it contained many excellent technical articles, was strident and biased. I found the *Journal of Air Law* a superb source, both for legal questions and other topics. *Time* and other national news magazines played up prominent aviation events. Among newspapers, I relied most heavily on the *New York Times,* which had no peer among dailies in covering aviation news. I used other newspapers selectively. Incidentally, the *Congressional Record* is, among other things, an excellent clipping service.

Regrettably, very few of the principal participants wrote memoirs. Michael Osborn and Joseph Riggs (eds.), *"Mr. Mac": William P. MacCracken, Jr., on Aviation, Law, Optometry* (Memphis, 1970) is essentially oral history rather than formal autobiography; MacCracken unwinds in a long, somewhat rambling, but interesting and informative, series of interviews. Herbert Hoover exaggerates his role in helping secure passage of the Air Commerce Act in his *Memoirs* (3 vols.; New York, 1951-52). Benjamin D. Foulois with C. V. Glines, *From the Wright Brothers to the Astronauts: The Memoirs of Major General Benjamin D. Foulois* (New York, 1968) contains a first-hand, if one-sided, account of the airmail cancellation incident. Ewing Young Mitchell wrote a tract in defense of himself, *Kicked In and Kicked Out of the President's Little Cabinet* (Washington, D.C., 1936), that does not succeed in salvaging his reputation. In 1962, Charles E. Planck, a former FAA public affairs officer, conducted a series of interviews with former Federal civil aviation officials; I used with profit the MacCracken, Young, Vidal, Fagg, and Mulligan transcripts. The tapes are held by the FAA Library.

Professional historians have written little on the history of the Federal role in regulating and fostering civil aviation. In consequence, the secondary literature is patchy and uneven. Arnold E. Briddon, Ellmore A. Champie, and Peter A. Marraine, *FAA Historical Fact Book: A Chronology, 1926-1971* (Washington, 1974) is a handy, reliable reference work that needs updating. Donald R. Whitnah, *Safer Skyways: Federal Control of Aviation, 1926-1966* (Ames, Iowa, 1966) is marred and should be used with care. Two works written in the early 1930's, Laurence F. Schmeckebier, *The Aeronautics Branch, Department of Commerce: Its History, Activities and Organization* (Washington, 1930) and Charles C. Rohlfing, *National Regulation of Aeronautics* (Philadelphia, 1931) are still useful. Among works of a more general character, Henry Ladd Smith, *Airways: The History of Commercial Aviation in the United States* (New York, 1942) is by far the most satisfying. Edward Pearson Warner, *The Early History of Air Transportation* (Northfield, Vt., 1937) is an insightful older work. John H. Frederick, *Commercial Air Transportation* (5th edition; Homewood, Ill., 1961) is stiff but informative. Lloyd Morris and Kendall Smith, *Ceiling Unlimited* (New York, 1953), Charles J. Kelly, Jr., *The Sky's the Limit: The History of the Airlines* (New York, 1963), and Elsbeth E. Freudenthal, *The Aviation Business* (New York, 1940) all touch on aspects of Federal involvement in civil aviation affairs. For airline history, nothing approaches the scholarship of R. E. G. Davis's *A History of the World's Airlines* (London, 1964). Among works of a more specialized nature, I borrowed heavily from Thomas Worth Walterman, "Airpower and Private Enterprise: Federal-Industrial Relations in the Aeronautics Field, 1918-1926," unpublished Ph.D. dissertation, Washington University,

1970, in reconstructing the background to the Air Commerce Act, and from Ellmore A. Champie, *The Federal Turnaround on Aid to Airports, 1926-38* (Washington, 1973), in discussing the early development of Federal airport policy. No student of the Civil Aeronautics Act can afford to ignore Howard C. Westwood and Alexander E. Bennett, "A Footnote to the Legislative History of the Civil Aeronautics Act of 1938 and Afterword," *Notre Dame Lawyer*, February 1967. I cribbed from Nick A. Komons, *The Cutting Air Crash: A Case Study in Early Federal Aviation Policy* (Washington, 1973). The standard work on the development of the airplane is Charles Harvard Gibbs-Smith, *Aviation: An Historical Survey from Its Origins to the End of World War II* (London, 1970), which can profitably be supplemented by Peter W. Brooks, *The Modern Airliner: Its Origins and Development* (London, 1961), a classic in its own right. A highly technical source on airway development is William E. Jackson (ed.), *The Federal Airways System* (Washington, 1970). Finally, the casual reader can do worse than turn to Editors of American Heritage, *The American Heritage History of Flight* (New York, 1962), a popular, highly illustrated history that captures the romance of flight. Students wishing more bibliographical information on specific topics can turn to the notes that follow.

In order to conserve space, an abbreviated form of citation has been used throughout for the following sources:

- Civil Aeronautics Administration Central Files, Record Group 237, National Archives, cited as RG 237 (followed by file or box number).
- Herbert C. Hoover Papers, Herbert Hoover Presidential Library, National Archives and Records Service, West Branch, Iowa, cited as Hoover Papers.
- National Aeronautics Association Files, Headquarters, National Aeronautics Association, Washington, cited as NAA Files.
- U.S. Department of Commerce General Records, Office of the Secretary, Record Group 40, National Archives, cited as RG 40 (followed by file number).
- U.S. Post Office Department Files, Bureau of the Second Assistant Postmaster General, Division of the Air Mail Service, Record Group 28, National Archives, cited as RG 28, AMS.

Prologue

1. Robert L. Heilbroner, *The Worldly Philosophers* (Revised paperback edition; New York, 1961), 214, 215; Frederick Lewis Allen, *Only Yesterday: An Informal History of the Nineteen Twenties* (New York, 1931), 182.

2. Arthur M. Schlesinger, Jr., *The Crisis of the Old Order* (New York, 1957), 57; U.S. Bureau of the Census, *Historical Statistics of the United States: Colonial Times to 1957* (Washington, 1960), 166, 167; John D. Hicks, *Republican Ascendancy, 1921-1933* (New York, 1960), xi-xii.

Chapter 1

1. [Washington] *Evening Star*, July 18, 1921.

2. *Aviation*, March 8, 16, & 22, 1926, 340, 376, 416–17.

3. See, for example, U.S. Congress, Senate, *The Promotion of Commercial Aviation*, S. Rpt. 2, 69th Cong., 1st sess., 1925, 4.

4. Quoted in *Aero Digest*, January 1924, 42.

5. John B. Rae, *The American Automobile, A Brief History* (Chicago, 1965), 87.

6. U.S. Bureau of the Census, *Historical Statistics of the United States: Colonial Times to 1957* (Washington, 1960), 431.

7. Rae, *Automobile*, 91.

8. *Ibid.*, 87–88.

9. *Historical Statistics*, 72, 73, 91, 116, 126, 128.

10. Rae, *Automobile*, 87–88.

11. *Historical Statistics*, 462–63.

12. Michael Osborn and Joseph Riggs (eds.), *"Mr. Mac": William P. Mac-Cracken, Jr., on Aviation, Law, Optometry* (Memphis, 1970), 35–36.

13. Lester J. Maitland, "Lincoln Beachey: Forgotten Eagle," in James F. Sunderman (ed.), *Early Air Pioneers, 1862–1935* (New York, 1961), 58–62; Henry Ladd Smith, *Airways: The History of Commercial Aviation in the United States* (New York, 1942), 25–30; Lloyd Morris and Kendall Smith, *Ceiling Unlimited* (New York, 1953), 101–109.

14. Smith, *Airways*, 47–49; Morris and Smith, *Ceiling Unlimited*, 227–28.

15. Smith, *Airways*, 47–49; U.S. Congress, House, *Inquiry into Operations of the United States Air Services, Hearings* before a select committee, 68th Cong., 2d sess., 1925, 1046, hereinafter cited as *Lampert Hearings*.

16. Editors of American Heritage, *The American Heritage History of Flight* (New York, 1962), 198.

17. *Ibid.*, 196–97; Cecil B. De Mille, "The Plane in Motion Pictures," *Aero Digest*, September 1924, 134–46.

18. Joint Committee on Civil Aviation of the U.S. Department of Commerce and the American Engineering Council, *Civil Aviation: A Report* (New

York, 1926), 93; *Aircraft Year Book,* 1921, 10 & 1924, 15; Allan J. Cameron, "Skywriting Pilots Have Covered United States," *Aero Digest,* December 1923, 406–407.

19. *Aircraft Year Book,* 1922, 11–12 & 1925, 45–47, 50, 51–52; Joint Committee, *Civil Aviation,* 86; Sherman M. Fairchild, "Photographing New York From the Airplane," *Aero Digest,* December 1923, 434–35.

20. W. V. King and G. M. Bradley, "Airplane Dusting Controls Malaria Mosquitoes," *Aero Digest,* December 1925, 652–53; Joint Committee, *Civil Aviation,* 79; U.S. President's Aircraft Board, *Hearings* (Washington, 1925), 350–57, 1444–46, hereinafter cited as *Morrow Board Hearings.*

21. *Aircraft Year Book,* 1921, 8, 9.

22. *American Heritage History of Flight,* 234; Harve E. Partridge, "Aerial Liquor Runners Teaching Public the Use of the Airplane," *Aero Digest,* September 1924, 155.

23. *Aircraft Year Book,* 1923, 22–23 & 1925, 55; Smith, *Airways,,* 85–86.

24. *Aircraft Year Book,* 1921, 7 & 1925, 54.

25. R. E. G. Davies, *A History of the World's Airlines* (London, 1964), 42; Smith, *Airways,* 84.

26. *U.S. Air Services,* November 1920, 22; C. F. Redden to Herbert C. Hoover, April 22, 1924, Hoover Papers; Davies, *Airlines,* 42–44; Edward Pearson Warner, *The Early History of Air Transportation* (A James Jackson Cabot Professorship Lecture; Northfield, Vt., 1937), 30–32; Smith, *Airways,* 86–88; Joint Committee, *Civil Aviation,* 58–59; *American Heritage History of Flight,* 199.

27. *Aircraft Year Book,* 1923, 16–17 & 1925, 54; Joint Committee, *Civil Aviation,* 48; William Knight, "An Appeal to Congress on the Matter of Aeronautical Appropriations," *Aero Digest,* November 1922, 194–95; Will H. Hays, "Aerial Navigation—Its Development and Possibilities," *U.S. Air Services,* March 1925, 19–22; Elsbeth Freudenthal, *The Aviation Business* (New York, 1940), 62–63.

28. *Morrow Board Hearings,* 1471; Paul Henderson, "The Air Mail—Its Future," *Aero Digest,* March 1925, 128–29; Joint Committee, *Civil Aviation,* 50.

29. Warner, *Air Transportation,* 3; Laurence F. Schmeckebier, *The Aeronautics Branch, Department of Commerce: Its History, Activities and Organization* (Washington, 1930), 3–4.

30. Smith, *Airways,* 55; Harold F. Ambrose, "Post Office Department Observes Air Mail Growth," *Air Commerce Bulletin,* May 15, 1938, 267–68.

31. Schmeckebier, *Aeronautics Branch*, 4; Ambrose, "Post Office," 268.

32. *Aerial Age Weekly*, April 15, 1918, 248.

33. Warner, *Air Transportation*, 12–15; *Morrow Board Hearings*, 266.

34. *Morrow Board Hearings*, 266.

35. U.S. Post Office Department, *Annual Report of the Postmaster General for the Fiscal Year Ended June 30, 1920* (Washington, 1920), 57–59; Ambrose, "Post Office," 269.

36. U.S. Post Office Department, *Annual Report of the Postmaster General for the Fiscal Year Ended June 30, 1925* (Washington, 1925), 29; Joint Committee, *Civil Aviation*, 52.

37. E. H. Shaughnessy, "The Aerial Mail Service," *Aerial Age Weekly*, February 13, 1922, 538; U.S. Post Office Department, Second Assistant Postmaster General, "A Brief History of the Air Mail Service" (mimeographed pamphlet), 9–10.

38. A. J. Jackson, *De Havilland Aircraft Since 1915* (London, 1962), 22–25.

39. *Ibid.*, 41; Warner, *Air Transportation*, 16. In the beginning, modifications were done under contract by aircraft manufacturers. This turned out to be an expensive proposition, and the Post Office itself established a factory at Maywood Field, Chicago, where it rebuilt and serviced its aircraft and engines. Doc., C. H. Clarahan, *et al.*, to the Postmaster General, October 28, 1925, RG 28, AMS.

40. *Morrow Board Hearings*, 281, 286, 287, 288; Joint Committee, *Civil Aviation*, 52–53, 64.

41. Henderson, "Air Mail," 127; *Morrow Board Hearings*, 265–66; enclosure to ltr., Charles D. Walcott to Herbert Hoover, March 23, 1921, Hoover Papers. See also Knight, "Appeal to Congress," 194; *Lampert Hearings*, 1212–13.

42. Herbert Hoover to Frederick C. Hicks, December 30, 1921, Hoover Papers; U.S. Congress, Senate, *Bureau of Aeronautics in the Department of Commerce*, S. Rpt. 460, 67th Cong., 2d sess., 1922, 2.

43. Unsigned memo to Herbert Hoover, Subj: "Notes for Meeting of the Air Craft Men Monday," July 16, 1921, Hoover Papers.

44. S. C. Mead to Herbert Hoover, December 29, 1922, Julius H. Barnes to Hoover, May 29, 1924, and H. P. Stellwagen to Hoover, January 28, 1924, Hoover Papers; Warner, *Air Transportation*, 48; *Aviation*, October 26, 1929, 831.

45. Robert H. Wiebe, *Businessmen and Reform: A Study of the Progressive Movement* (Cambridge, Mass., 1962), 13, 14, 52, 55, 136, 212, 215, 217.

46. See Thomas Worth Walterman, "Airpower and Private Enterprise: Federal-Industrial Relations in the Aeronautics Field, 1918–1926," unpublished Ph.D. dissertation, Washington University (St. Louis), 1970, 241–42.

47. *Aircraft Year Book*, 1926, 114; Minutes of Business Session of the Second National Aero Congress, Detroit, Mich., October 12, 13, & 14, 1922, NAA Files. The remark about mules is attributed to William P. MacCracken, Jr.

48. *Aero Digest*, September 1922, 66; *Morrow Board Hearings*, 1446; Charles J. Glidden to Calvin Coolidge, August 21, 1923, Hoover Papers; Charles M. Schwab, "Safe and Sane Flying," *Aero Digest*, February 1923, 67.

49. Joint Committee, *Civil Aviation*, 108; *Aircraft Year Book*, 1926, 114; *Morrow Board Hearings*, 1098.

50. *Lampert Hearings*, 1660, 1665.

51. S. S. Bradley to Herbert Hoover, August 24, 1922, Hoover Papers. See also Floyd Miller to Herbert Hoover, April 5, 1922, Hoover Papers.

52. [Washington] *Evening Star*, May 31, 1922.

53. Bradley to Hoover, August 24, 1922, Hoover Papers; *Promotion of Commercial Aviation*, 2.

54. *Morrow Board Hearings*, 1482–83; George Gleason Bogert, "Problems in Aviation Law," *Cornell Law Quarterly*, March 1921, 280–87; Joint Committee, *Civil Aviation*, 99–100, 102.

55. Bogert, "Aviation Law," 290–91; Schmeckebier, *Aeronautics Branch*, 6.

56. Bogert, "Aviation Law," 290; *Lampert Hearings*, 834.

57. Bogert, "Aviation Law," 287–89; U.S. Congress, Office of the Legislative Counsel, *Civil Aeronautics: Legislative History of the Air Commerce Act of 1926* (Washington, 1928), 54.

58. *Civil Aeronautics*, 67.

59. *Ibid.*, 97–98, 100; Joint Committee, *Civil Aviation*, 110, 121; *Morrow Board Hearings*, 1097, 1482–83.

60. *Civil Aeronautics*, 132–33; *Aero Digest*, November 1922, 189.

61. *Bureau of Aeronautics*, 18; *Morrow Board Hearings*, 1483; *Aero Digest*, September 1925, 481; *Aircraft Year Book*, 1926, 116; *Lampert Hearings*, 816.

62. E. N. Gott, "Flying and Its Relation to the General Public," *U.S. Air Services*, October 1922, 19–23; *Aero Digest*, September 1922, 67; Charles F. Redden, "The Outlook for Commercial Aviation in America," *Aero Digest*, February 1923, 100; *Lampert Hearings*, 1877; *Aircraft Year Book*, 1922, 3, 7; Joint Committee, *Civil Aviation*, 106, 108.

63. *Lampert Hearings*, 283; *Aircraft Year Book*, 1922, 7; Annual Report of the British Air Attache, Washington, for 1922, March 31, 1923, Records of the Air Ministry, AIR 2/246, Public Record Office, London.

64. *Aircraft Year Book*, 1923, 21; *Aero Digest*, April 1923, 274.

65. *Aero Digest*, November 1922, 188; Stellwagen to Hoover, January 28, 1924, Hoover Papers; Walterman, "Airpower," 246.

66. *Lampert Hearings*, 2748; John F. Stover, *American Railroads* (Chicago, 1961), 88–89; *Historical Statistics*, 455, 458.

67. Joint Committee, *Civil Aviation*, 35, 37; *Aero Digest*, February 1923, 113; Clarence W. Barron, "Aviation Development," *Aero Digest*, December 1923, 392. For McLeod's proposal, see *Aero Digest*, January 1925, 28.

68. *Morrow Board Hearings*, 1471.

69. *Ibid.*; Vincent Burnelli, "Commercial Aviation," *Aero Digest*, March 1925, 151; *Morrow Board Hearings*, 307; Schwab, "Safe and Sane," 144. See also *Lampert Hearings*, 1074, 1213.

70. *Morrow Board Hearings*, 318–19.

71. *Ibid.*, 319.

72. *Ibid.* See also *Aircraft Year Book*, 1923, 16, & 1924, 9.

73. *Lampert Hearings*, 2157; enclosure to ltr., Walcott to Hoover, March 23, 1921, Hoover Papers.

74. *Morrow Board Hearings*, 306–307, 323, 1097, 1471; *Lampert Hearings*, 29–30.

Chapter 2

1. R. Earl McClendon, "The Question of Autonomy for the United States Air Arm, 1907-1945," Air University Documentary Research Study (Maxwell Air Force Base, Ala., 1950), 47-48.

2. *Flying*, April 1916, 109-11, July 1916, 248, December 1916, 464; *New York Times*, September 13, 1918.

3. National Advisory Committee for Aeronautics, *Fifth Annual Report* (Washington, 1919), 17.

4. National Advisory Committee for Aeronautics, *Sixth Annual Report* (Washington, 1920), 10-11; Thomas Worth Walterman, "Airpower and Private Enterprise: Federal-Industrial Relations in the Aeronautics Field, 1918-1926" (unpublished Ph.D. dissertation, Washington University, 1970), 384-89.

5. Laurence La Tourette Driggs, "Necessity for a Separate Department of Aeronautics," *U.S. Air Service* (November 1919), 29.

6. I. B. Holley, Jr., *Ideas and Weapons* (New Haven, 1958), 119-21; Lloyd Morris and Kendall Smith, *Ceiling Unlimited* (New York, 1953), 188-90.

7. Holley, *Ideas and Weapons*, 118; Elsbeth E. Freudenthal, *The Aviation Business* (New York, 1940), 59-61.

8. Henry Ladd Smith, *Airways: The History of Commercial Aviation in the United States* (New York, 1942), 45–46.

9. *Ibid.*, 46.

10. Holley, *Ideas and Weapons*, 68-69; McClendon, "Autonomy," 63-67.

11. McClendon, "Autonomy," 70-71; Alfred F. Hurley, *Billy Mitchell: Crusader for Air Power* (New York, 1964), 39ff.

12. *Aircraft Year Book* (1920), 101ff; Walterman, "Airpower," 204-05.

13. Walterman, "Airpower," 205-08.

14. McClendon, "Autonomy," 74-75; for extracts from the Dickman report see U.S. Congress, House, *Inquiry into Operations of the United States Air Services, Hearings* before a select committee, 68th Cong., 2d sess. (1925), 1723-24, hereinafter cited as *Lampert Hearings*.

15. See U.S. Congress, House, *War Expenditures, Hearings* before Subcommittee No. 1 (Aviation) of the Select Committee on Expenditures in the War Department, 66th Cong., 1st sess., 1919, *passim.*

16. *U.S. Air Service*, November 1919, 27; Driggs, "Necessity," 29.

17. *Lampert Hearings*, 1724-25; Walterman, "Airpower," 212.

18. *Congressional Record*, 66th Cong., 2d sess., 2185-98, 2243-44, 2301-02.

19. *U.S. Air Service*, November 1919, 28; *Congressional Record*, 66th Cong., 2d sess., 2244.

20. Walterman, "Airpower," 287.

21. National Advisory Committee for Aeronautics, *Seventh Annual Report* (Washington, 1921), 13; enclosure to ltr., Charles D. Walcott to Herbert Hoover, March 23, 1921, Maj. Gen. Charles T. Menoher to John W. Weeks, April 1, 1921, Hoover Papers.

22. NACA, *Seventh Annual Report*, 12-15.

23. *U.S. Air Service* (May 1921), 37; U.S. Congress, Office of the Legislative Counsel, *Civil Aeronautics: Legislative History of the Air Commerce Act of 1926* (Washington, 1928), 146; E. Y. Chamberlain to Herbert Hoover, July 5, 1921, Hoover Papers.

24. James W. Prothro, *The Dollar Decade: Business Ideas in the 1920's* (Baton Rouge, 1954), 239; S. S. Bradley to Herbert Hoover, August 24, 1922, Hoover to Samuel E. Winslow, August 30, 1922, Hoover Papers.

25. S. S. Bradley to Herbert Hoover, July 1,1921, Hoover Papers; Benedict Crowell to W. P. MacCracken, January 11, 1922, NAA Files; L. D. Gardner to Hoover, June 20, 1921, unsigned memo to Hoover, Subj: "Notes for Meeting of the Air Craft Men Monday," July 16, 1921, S. W. Stratton to Hoover, June 30, 1921, Hoover Papers; *New York Times*, June 21, 1921; Luther K. Bell to Richard S. Emmet, July 11, 1921, Hoover Papers.

26. Benedict Crowell to W. P. MacCracken, January 11, 1922, NAA Files; H. E. Coffin to Herbert Hoover, April 18, 1922, Hoover Papers.

27. Walterman, "Airpower," 393-94.

28. U.S. Congress, Senate, *Bureau of Aeronautics in Department of Commerce*, S. Rpt. 460, 67th Cong., 2d sess. (1922), 2, 23-29.

29. Aero Club of America Resolution, January 21, 1922, Hoover Papers; Walterman, "Airpower," 395-96.

30. Walterman, "Airpower," 395-99.

31. Michael Osborn and Joseph Riggs (eds.), *"Mr. Mac": William P. Mac-Cracken, Jr., on Aviation, Law, Optometry* (Memphis, 1970), 3, 4-5, 8, 10-11, 33, 50, 55, 180; *Aviation* (July 13, 1929), 142; Minutes of Second Annual Convention of the NAA, Dayton, Ohio, October 2, 3 & 4, 1922, W. P. MacCracken to Ralph W. Cram, July 21, 1924, NAA Files.

32. Osborn and Riggs, *Mr. Mac*, 33-34.

33. *Ibid.*

34. Report of the Special Committee on the Law of Aviation to the Executive Committee of the American Bar Association, 1921, NAA Files.

NOTES FOR PAGES 35-64

35. Osborn and Riggs, *Mr. Mac*, 38-39.

36. William P. MacCracken, "Fact Sheet on Civil Aeronautics Bill," January 25, 1924, NAA Files; *Legislative History*, 53.

37. *Legislative History*, 85-89, 98-99, 101-04, 146-47.

38. Benedict Crowell to W. P. MacCracken, January 11, 1922, NAA Files. For MacCracken's views see U.S. Congress, House, *Bureau of Civil Air Navigation in the Department of Commerce, Hearings* before the Committee on Interstate and Foreign Commerce, 68th Cong., 2d sess. (1924), 54ff.

39. W. P. MacCracken to Hugh W. Roberts, December 4, 1922, S. S. Bradley to MacCracken, February 10, 1922, Benedict Crowell to MacCracken, January 11, 1922, NAA Files.

40. W. P. MacCracken to B. H. Mulvihill, April 13, 1923, MacCracken to Philip Carroll, February 27, 1922, NAA Files; Joint Committee on Civil Aviation of the U.S. Department of Commerce and the American Engineering Council, *Civil Aviation: A Report* (New York, 1926), 109-10.

41. Osborn and Riggs, *Mr. Mac*, 40-41.

42. *Legislative History*, 62-63. The case in question was *Railroad Commission of Wisconsin* v. *The Chicago, Burlington & Quincy Railroad Co.*

43. George G. Bogert to W. P. MacCracken, February 3, 1922, Bogert to MacCracken, March 15, 1922, S. S. Bradley to MacCracken, February 28, 1922, Bradley to MacCracken, March 7, 1922, NAA Files.

44. W. P. MacCracken to Philip Carroll, September 16, 1922, NAA Files.

45. *Aircraft Year Book* (1922), 2.

46. H. E. Coffin to B. H. Mulvihill, May 23, 1923, Harold Hartney to W. P. MacCracken, May 31, 1923, Godfrey Cabot to Lester D. Gardner, May 11, 1923, NAA Files; Walterman, "Airpower," 262, 274.

47. Philip A. Carroll to W. P. MacCracken, November 9, 1922, Charles A. Boston to MacCracken, September 20, 1922, Godfrey Cabot to MacCracken, November 10, 1925, NAA Files.

48. Coffin to Mulvihill, May 23, 1923, NAA Files; *Lampert Hearings*, 1281; Herbert Hoover to Maurice G. Cleary, June 25, 1921, Hoover Papers; *Aviation*, April 27, 1925, 473; Harold E. Hartney to All Members of the Original Organization Committee of Five Hundred, September 13, 1922, & September 22, 1922, NAA Files.

49. *Lampert Hearings*, 1281; Harold E. Hartney to L. D. Gardner, August 31, 1922, NAA Files.

50. W. P. MacCracken to B. F. Castle, July 26, 1923, MacCracken to W.
     Jefferson Davis, October 28, 1922, Davis to MacCracken, January 6, 1922,
     MacCracken to Davis, January 19, 1922, George G. Bogert to Mac-
     Cracken, March 15, 1922, Minutes of the Business Sessions of the Second
     National Aero Conference, October 12-14, 1922, B. H. Mulvihill to Mac-
     Cracken, January 27, 1923, Howard E. Coffin to MacCracken,
     September 30, 1923, Mulvihill to MacCracken, December 16, 1922, Coffin
     to MacCracken, September 2, 1922, Porter Adams to MacCracken,
     November 1, 1922, NAA Files.

51. S. S. Bradley to W. P. MacCracken, November 9, 1922, MacCracken to H.
     E. Coffin, December 5, 1922, NAA Files.

52. S. S. Bradley to William E. Lamb, August 3, 1922, Hoover Papers; Bradley
     to W. P. MacCracken, April 10, 1922, NAA Files.

53. William E. Lamb to Richard S. Emmet, April 15, 1922, Lamb to Herbert
     Hoover, May 26, 1922, Hoover to Samuel E. Winslow, June 12, 1922,
     Hoover to Winslow, June 13, 1922, Hoover to Winslow, June 19, 1922,
     Hoover Papers.

54. James J. O'Hara to Richard S. Emmet, August 7, 1922, Hoover Papers;
     Frederic P. Lee to W. P. MacCracken, September 12, 1922, H. E. Coffin to
     B. H. Mulvihill, July 31, 1922, S. S. Bradley to MacCracken, August 16,
     1922, NAA Files; S. E. Winslow to Herbert Hoover, September 15, 1922,
     Hoover Papers; MacCracken to Coffin, November 22, 1922, Winslow to
     MacCracken, December 8, 1922, NAA Files.

55. George G. Bogert to S. E. Winslow, December 23, 1922, W. Jefferson
     Davis to Solicitor, Department of Commerce, December 21, 1922, NAA
     Files; Herbert Hoover to Winslow, January 12, 1923, Hoover Papers;
     Walterman, "Airpower," 405.

56. W. P. MacCracken to Harold Hartney, January 10, 1923, NAA Files; *Aero
     Digest*, February 1923, 113; S. S. Bradley to MacCracken, January 22,
     1923, Bradley to MacCracken, January 23, 1923, NAA Files.

57. H. W. Karr to W. P. MacCracken, January 12, 1924, MacCracken to Fred
     Smith, January 25, 1924, NAA Files; Walterman, "Airpower," 408.

58. James W. Wadsworth to Herbert Hoover, November 28, 1924, Hoover
     Papers. See text of bill in *Bureau of Air Navigation Hearings*; see also
     Walterman, "Airpower," 400-401.

59. Philip A. Carroll to W. P. MacCracken, December 20, 1922, NAA Files;
     Lampert Hearings, 1200; Clarence M. Young to Herbert Hoover,
     December 7, 1925, Hoover Papers; W. Jefferson Davis to Soliciter, Depart-
     ment of Commerce, December 21, 1922, NAA Files.

60. John Ahlers to W. P. MacCracken, May 13, 1924, Minutes of Meeting of
     the Legislative Committee of the NAA, September 2, 1924, F. C. Wallace
     to Lester D. Gardner, May 13, 1924, NAA Files.

61. W. P. MacCracken to E. B. Heath, March 6, 1924, F. B. Patterson to MacCracken, June 12, 1924, NAA Files.

62. Godfrey Cabot to E. W. Porter, May 28, 1926, Cabot to Lester E. Gardner, September 3, 1924, Gardner to F. C. Wallace, April 29, 1924, NAA Files.

63. W. F. Fullam to W. P. MacCracken, July 3, 1924, Godfrey Cabot to L. E. Gardner, September 3, 1924, Fullam to MacCracken, September 26, 1924, Terence Vincent to the National Aeronautic Association, November 28, 1924, NAA Files.

64. W. F. Fullam to F. H. Russell, June 7, 1924, NAA Files; U.S. President's Aircraft Board, *Hearings* (Washington, 1925), 1448-49, 1450, 1483 (hereinafter cited as *Morrow Board Hearings*); L. E. Gardner to F. C. Wallace, April 29, 1924, NAA Files. See also for the efforts of the NAA to remain free of manufacturing interests and other special groups, Minutes of the Second Aero Conference, 1922, & H. E. Hartney to All Members of the Original Organization Committee of Five Hundred, September 13, 1922, NAA Files.

65. Godfrey Cabot to Terence Vincent, December 1, 1924, NAA Files; *Lampert Hearings*, 829-30; F. B. Patterson to W. P. MacCracken, May 21, 1924, Patterson to MacCracken, June 12, 1924, NAA Files.

66. W. P. MacCracken to F. B. Patterson, May 24, 1924, MacCracken to W. F. Fullam, July 22, 1924, Minutes of Meeting of the Legislative Committee of the NAA, September 2, 1924, NAA Files.

67. W. P. MacCracken to S. S. Bradley, September 2, 1922, Minutes of Meeting of the Legislative Committee of the NAA, September 2, 1924, MacCracken to Bradley, March 7, 1923, MacCracken to George G. Bogert, April 11, 1923, MacCracken to Bogert, December 13, 1923, Bradley to MacCracken, March 5, 1923, Bradley to MacCracken, March 9, 1923, NAA Files.

68. Hugh W. Robertson to W. P. MacCracken, December 1, 1922, George G. Bogert to MacCracken, April 9, 1923, NAA Files.

69. S. S. Bradley to B. H. Mulvihill, March 7, 1923, Mulvihill to W. P. MacCracken, April 11, 1923, MacCracken to Mulvihill, April 13, 1923, MacCracken to Mulvihill, July 21, 1923, Godfrey Cabot to MacCracken, June 23, 1925, MacCracken to Cabot, June 25, 1925, NAA Files.

70. S. E. Winslow to W. P. MacCracken, April 7, 1924, Winslow to MacCracken, May 3, 1924, MacCracken to John Ahlers, April 18, 1924, H. W. Karr to MacCracken, February 6, 1924, Karr to MacCracken, January 12, 1924, NAA Files.

71. Elton J. Layton to W. P. MacCracken, June 9, 1924, NAA Files; *Bureau of Civil Air Navigation Hearings*, 54ff; F. P. Lee to MacCracken, January 16, 1925, MacCracken to S. E. Winslow, December 3, 1923, NAA Files.

72. "The Winslow bill has practically no significance as a party measure and is, therefore, apt to be overlooked by the present Congress," MacCracken wrote to F. B. Hubacheck in December 1923. See also MacCracken to W. Frank Carter, November 8, 1923. Others placed more emphasis on the belief that the Winslow bill was a piece of special-interest legislation. "One of the rocks on which the Winslow Bill was wrecked was the allegation on the part of various interested parties that particular provisions of that bill were specifically designed to favor certain individual manufacturers," Cabot wrote to Lester Gardner in September 1924. All in NAA Files.

Chapter 3

1. Harold Nicolson, *Dwight Morrow* (New York, 1935), 280–81.

2. *Ibid.*, 34, 281.

3. *Ibid.*, 291; Herbert Hoover, *The Memoirs of Herbert Hoover: The Cabinet and the Presidency, 1920-1933* (New York, 1952), 55-56; William Allen White, *A Puritan in Babylon* (New York, 1938), 74, 433.

4. C. G. Grey, "Civil Aviation in the United States," *Aviation* (January 5, 1925), 17.

5. Eugene M. Emme, *Aeronautics and Astronautics: An American Chronology of Science and Technology in the Exploration of Space, 1915-1960* (Washington, 1961), 19; Thomas Worth Walterman, "Airpower and Private Enterprise: Federal-Industrial Relations in the Aeronautics Field, 1918-1926" (unpublished Ph.D. dissertation, Washington University), 415-16. "As I've always viewed it, the Air Mail Act of 1925 was the key to the whole thing. Once arrangements were made for turning over the Post Office's airmail operations to commercial carriers, there simply *had* to be an air commerce act." Dr. Richard K. Smith to author, September 11, 1975.

6. Howard J. Hamstra, "Two Decades—Federal Aero-Regulation in Perspective," *The Journal of Air Law and Commerce* (April 1941), 109; Henry Ladd Smith, *Airways: The History of Commercial Aviation in the United States* (New York, 1942), 84; S. S. Bradley to W. P. MacCracken, July 23, 1942, NAA Files.

7. *Aero Digest,* May 1925, 265; *U.S. Air Service,* May 1925, 18; Lloyd Morris and Kendall Smith, *Ceiling Unlimited* (New York, 1953), 276; Edward Pearson Warner, *The Early History of Air Transportation* (A James Jackson Cabot Professorship Lecture; Northfield, Vt., 1937), 49-50; *U.S. Air Services,* September 1925, 23-24; *Aero Digest,* January 1926, 18; *Aviation,* April 27, 1925, 473; Herbert Hoover to Henry Ford, August 22, 1925, Hoover Papers; *Aero Digest,* November 1926, 360.

8. *Aircraft Year Book* (1925), 58; *New York Times*, December 15, 1925; Smith, *Airways*, 107-08.

9. W. Irving Glover, "Air Mail Service," *Aviation*, April 5, 1926, 488-89.

10. For material on Mitchell see Alfred F. Hurley, *Billy Mitchell* (New York, 1964) & Burke Davis, *The Billy Mitchell Affair* (New York, 1967).

11. U.S. Congress, House, *Air Service Unification, Hearings* before Committee on Military Affairs, 68th Cong., 2d sess. (1925), 10-11; Wesley Frank Craven and James Lea Cate (eds.), *The Army Air Forces in World War II*, Vol. I: *Plans and Early Operations* (Chicago, 1948), 25-26.

12. Hurley, *Mitchell*, 84-86; Craven and Cate (eds.), *Plans and Operations*, 26.

13. Walterman, "Airpower," 24-25; *Air Service Unification Hearings*, 39, 54; Craven and Cate (eds.), *Plans and Operations*, 19.

14. Minutes of Second Annual Convention of the NAA, Dayton, Ohio, October 2-4, 1924, NAA Files; U.S. Congress, House, *Inquiry into Operations of the United States Air Services, Hearings* before Select Committee of Inquiry, 68th Cong., 2d sess. (1925), 292-93, hereinafter cited as *Lampert Hearings*.

15. W. P. MacCracken to Harold Hartney, January 22, 1925, Godfrey Cabot to MacCracken, March 6, 1925, NAA Files; U.S. President's Aircraft Board, *Hearings* (Washington, 1925), 1488, hereinafter cited as *Morrow Board Hearings*.

16. *Air Service Unification Hearings*, 352; *Lampert Hearings*, 1829; Mason M. Patrick, "Recommendations for Improving the Air Service," *U.S. Air Services*, February 1923, 15-16; *U.S. Air Services*, September 1921, 7 & December 1921, 21; Edwin Denby to Herbert Hoover, April 18, 1922, John W. Weeks to Herbert Hoover, April 11, 1922, Hoover Papers.

17. Emme, *Aeronautics and Astronautics*, 18.

18. Walterman, "Airpower," 412-13, 415.

19. *Aircraft Year Book* (1926), 5-6.

20. See Walterman, "Airpower," 391-92.

21. Hurley, *Mitchell*, 95-98; Craven and Cate (ed.), *Plans and Operations*, 27.

22. Charles H. Coleman, "Given Up As Lost, Navy Hawaiian Flight Plane Found After Nine Days," *U.S. Air Services*, October 1925, 15-18; *Aviation* September 14, 1925, 309, 311-14, 315 & September 21, 1925, 345, 350.

23. *Aircraft Year Book* (1926), 133. Mitchell's statement is printed in full in *Aviation*, September 14, 1925, 318-20.

24. U.S. President's Aircraft Board, *Report of the President's Aircraft Board* (Washington, 1925), 1 (hereinafter cited as *Morrow Report*); H. F. Ranney, "President Coolidge Names Board of Nine to Decide Aviation's Needs," *U.S. Air Services*, October 1925, 23-25.

25. Walterman, "Airpower," 463-64.

26. *Morrow Board Hearings*, 495ff; Nicolson, *Morrow*, 283-84; Davis, *Mitchell*, 228-30.

27. *Morrow Report*, 6-10.

28. *Ibid.*, 14-15, 19, 24-25.

29. U.S. Congress, House, *Inquiry into Operations of the United States Air Services*, H. Rpt. 1653, 68th Cong., 2d sess. (1925), 1-2, 7, 8, hereinafter cited as *Lampert Report*.

30. *Ibid.*, 5-6, 7, 8-9.

31. J. Walter Drake to Howard Coffin, May 26, 1925, Drake to Coffin, June 6, 1925, Kenneth MacPherson to C. M. Keys, July 25, 1925, RG 40, FN 83272; Joint Committee on Civil Aviation of the Department of Commerce and the American Engineering Council, *Civil Aviation: A Report* (New York, 1926), *passim.*; *Morrow Board Hearings*, 320.

32. *Aviation*, December 28, 1925, 905; *Aero Digest*, February 1926, 66; S. S. Bradley to W. P. MacCracken, December 5, 1925, NAA Files; *New Republic*, December 15, 1925, 98; *Nation*, December 16, 1925, 695; Henry W. Bunn, "The Most Statesmanlike Act of the Present Administration," *U.S. Air Services*, March 1927, 33. *Philadelphia Record* quoted in *Aero Digest*, February 1926, 105. See also Nicolson, *Morrow*, 286.

33. Walterman, "Airpower," 497.

34. Hiram Bingham to Herbert Hoover, October 13, 1925, Hoover Papers; *Cong. Rec.*, 69th Cong., 1st sess., 474.

35. *Cong. Rec.*, 69th Cong., 1st sess., 829-31; *Morrow Board Hearings*, 329; Herbert Hoover to W. L. Jones, December 9, 1925, Hoover Papers.

36. U.S. Congress, Senate, *The Promotion of Civil Aviation*, S. Rpt. 2, 69th Cong., 1st sess. (1925), 8; see also Herbert Hoover to W. L. Jones, December 9, 1925, Hoover Papers.

37. *Cong. Rec.*, 69th Cong., 1st sess., 926.

38. Frederic P. Lee to W. P. MacCracken, December 29, 1925, Godfrey Cabot to MacCracken, September 24, 1925, in NAA Files.

39. W. P. MacCracken to Godfrey Cabot, November 22, 1925, Cabot to

MacCracken, January 2, 1926, MacCracken to Cabot, January 16, 1926, NAA Files.

40. Godfrey Cabot to Howard Coffin, February 10, 1926, Cabot to William P. MacCracken, February 10, 1926, NAA Files; Michael Osborn and Joseph Riggs (eds.), *"Mr. Mac": William P. MacCracken, Jr., on Aviation, Law, Optometry* (Memphis, 1970), 52-53. For a comparison of the Senate and House bills see *Promotion of Civil Aviation,* 10-14.

41. *Cong. Rec.,* 69th Cong., 1st sess., 7312-30. Merritt had introduced this amended version of S. 41 on March 17. *Ibid.,* 5818.

42. For analysis of vote see Walterman, "Airpower," 521.

43. *Promotion of Civil Aviation,* 10-14.

44. *Ibid.,* 13.

45. National Advisory Committee for Aeronautics, *Twelfth Annual Report* (Washington, 1926), 10; *Lampert Hearings,* 284; *Morrow Board Hearings,* 307; Ellmore A. Champie, *The Federal Turnaround on Aid to Airports, 1926-1938* (Washington, 1973), 2-4.

46. NACA, *Twelfth Annual Report,* 11.

47. *Ibid.*

48. *Promotion of Civil Aviation,* 10-14; J. Walter Drake to Hiram Bingham, April 16, 1926; Drake to Everett Sanders, April 19, 1926, RG 40, Series 1, F.N. 83272.

49. MacCracken to A. H. Amick, Jr., June 19, 1926, NAA Files.

50. *Cong. Rec.,* 69th Cong., 1st sess, 9356, 9391, 9811.

51. Craven and Cate (eds.), *Plans and Programs,* 29.

52. Osborn and Riggs (eds.), *Mr. Mac,* 56; Martin Madden to Calvin Coolidge, July 31, 1926, Hoover Papers; *Philadelphia Public Ledger,* June 17, 1926; Herbert Hoover to George Wharton Pepper, June 23, 1926, Hoover Papers.

53. Frank MacIntyre to Herbert Hoover, July 29, 1926, Hoover to Hiram Bingham, July 30, 1926, Howard Coffin to Hoover, August 13, 1926, Godfrey Cabot to Hoover, August 10, 1926, Madden to Coolidge, July 31, 1926; Charles S. Deneen to Hoover, July 31, 1926, Hoover to Coolidge, August 3, 1926, Hoover Papers; *New York Times,* August 10, 1926.

54. George S. Carll, Jr., "Congress Provides for Commercial Aeronautics," *U.S. Air Services,* July 1926, 22-24; *New York Times,* December 11, 1926.

55. Hewitt H. Howland, *Dwight Whitney Morrow, A Sketch in Admiration*
     (New York, 1930), x; Nicolson, *Morrow,* 286.

Chapter 4

1. William P. MacCracken, Jr., to E. B. Heath, March 6, 1924, NAA Files;
    Cong. Rec., 69th Cong., 1st sess., 830; National Advisory Committee for
    Aeronautics, *Twelfth Annual Report* (Washington, 1926), 11.

2. J. S. Marriott, "Regulating Air Commerce, Article I--Inspection," *Avia-
    tion*, January 18, 1930, 96. On the built-in conflict, see for example,
    Aviation, January 1938, 55.

3. Aeronautics Branch, *Annual Report of the Director of Aeronautics to the
    Secretary of Commerce for the Fiscal Year Ended June 30, 1927* (Wash-
    ington, 1927), 1-2; Nick A. Komons, *The Cutting Air Crash: A Case Study
    in Early Federal Aviation Policy* (Washington, 1973), 5.

4. Department of Commerce Order, July 18, 1927, RG 40, FN 83272;
    Arnold E. Briddon *et al.*, *FAA Historical Fact Book: A Chronology,
    1926-1971* (Washington, 1974), 12; *Aviation*, July 13, 1929, 142.

5. J. Walter Drake to Director, Bureau of Standards, July 24, 1925, Drake to
    Commissioner of Lighthouses, July 24, 1926, DOC Order, July 18, 1927,
    RG 40, FN 83272; Komons, *Cutting*, 5.

6. Michael Osborn and Joseph Riggs (eds), *"Mr. Mac": William P. Mac-
    Cracken, Jr., on Aviation, Law, Optometry* (Memphis, 1970), 63; *Aviation*,
    January 22, 1926, 249; U.S. Department of Commerce, Transcript of
    Aeronautical Conference, December 5-9, 1927, Washington, D.C., 25;
    William P. MacCracken to Russell Owen, November 23, 1927, RG 237,
    FN 845; Charles L. Lawrance, "The Opportunity of the States," *Aviation*,
    October 1931, 579.

7. Osborn and Riggs (eds), *Mr. Mac*, 63; U.S. Congress, Senate, *Departments
    of State, Justice, Commerce and Labor Appropriation Bill, 1928, Hearings*
    before a subcommittee of the Committee on Appropriations, 69th Cong., 2d
    sess., 1927, 23-24; *Aero Digest*, November 1926, 408; *Aviation*, January 3,
    1927, 13; *Domestic Air News*, January 31, 1927, 1 & February 28, 1927, 1.

8. Aeronautics Branch, *Annual Report of the Director of Aeronautics to the
    Secretary of Commerce for the Fiscal Year Ended June 30, 1928* (Wash-
    ington: 1928), 2-3; Charles C. Rohlfing, *National Regulation of Aeronau-
    tics* (Philadelphia, 1931), 84-85; Marriott, "Inspection," 96.

9. Osborn and Riggs (eds.), *Mr. Mac*, 105-106; *Domestic Air News*, July 15,
    1927, 4-5.

10. *Air Commerce Regulations*, 1927, *passim*, FAA Library.

11. *Ibid.*, 29-31; *Domestic Air News*, December 1926, 8; *Aviation*, July 13, 1929, 143-44; Osborn and Riggs (eds.), *Mr. Mac*, 66.

12. L. H. Bauer, "The Hazards of Aviation," unpublished paper, CAA Central Files, RG 237, FN 802; *Air Commerce Regs*, 34-35; Osborn and Riggs (eds.), *Mr. Mac*, 66-67; *Domestic Air News*, January 31, 1927, 2; Briddon *et al.*, *FAA Fact Book*, 11; *Aviation*, August 1, 1927, 252; Aeronautics Branch, *FY 1927 Annual Report*, 8; Aeronautics Branch, *Annual Report of the Assistant Secretary of Commerce for Aeronautics to the Secretary of Commerce for the Fiscal Year Ended June 30, 1930* (Washington, 1930), 5.

13. Osborn and Riggs (eds.), *Mr. Mac*, 64-65; U.S. Congress, House, *Department of Commerce Appropriation Bill, 1934, Hearings* before a subcommittee of the Committee on Appropriations, 72d Cong., 2d sess., 1932, 87.

14. Aeronautics Branch, *FY 1928 Annual Report*, 7; Kenneth M. Lane, "Regulating Air Commerce, Article II--Engineering," *Aviation*, January 25, 1930, 154; U.S. Congress, House, *Department of Commerce Appropriation Bill for 1930, Hearings* before a subcommittee of the Committee on Appropriations, 70th Cong., 2d sess., 1928, 23.

15. Rohlfing, *Regulation*, 78-79.

16. William P. MacCracken to Harry A. Babcock, August 30,1926, RG 40, FN 83272.

17. U.S. President's Aircraft Board, *Hearings* (Washington, 1925), 322-23; House Doc. No. 395, 69th Cong., 1st sess., May 22, 1926.

18. Osborn and Riggs (eds.), *Mr. Mac*, 69-70.

19. *Ibid.*, 67; Aeronautics Branch, *FY 1928 Annual Report*, 3; *Domestic Air News*, November 15,1928, 7; U.S. House of Representatives, *Commerce Appropriation Hearings for FY 1928*, 26.

20. Briddon *et al.*, *FAA Fact Book*, 278; Aeronautics Branch, *FY 1928 Annual Report*, 3, 7.

21. Aeronautics Branch, *FY 1928 Annual Report*, 4-5; Fred L. Israel (ed.), *The State of the Union Messages of the Presidents, 1790-1966*, Vol. III: *1905-1966* (New York, 1966), 2735. Young quote from Aeronautics Branch, *FY 1928 Annual Report*, 5.

22. Rohlfing, *Regulation*, 82, 84-85.

23. Aeronautics Branch, *FY 1928 Annual Report*, 4-5.

24. *Aviation*, October 20, 1928, 1253; Rohlfing, *Regulation*, 73-74; U.S. House of Representatives, *Commerce Appropriation Hearings for FY 1930*, 22, 65.

25. Rohlfing, *Regulation*, 63, 71; U.S. House of Representatives, *Commerce Appropriation Hearings for FY 1930*, 22; Aeronautics Branch, *Annual Report of the Director of Aeronautics for the Fiscal Year Ended June 30,1929*(Washington, 1929), 11; Marriott, "Inspection," 94.

26. Aeronautics Branch, *FY 1929 Annual Report*, 3, 5.

27. Osborn and Riggs (eds.), *Mr. Mac*, 64, 119.

28. Lawrance, "The States," 580.

29. E. McD. Kintz, "Regulating Air Commerce, Article IV--Enforcement," *Aviation*, February 22, 1930, 376; Aeronautics Branch, *FY 1928 Annual Report*, 9.

30. Osborn and Riggs (eds.), *Mr. Mac*, 79-80.

31. *Ibid.*, 82-83, 87-88, 90-91.

32. Aeronautics Branch, *FY 1928 Annual Report*, 9; Aeronautics Branch, *FY 1929 Annual Report*, 15; Rohlfing, *Regulation*, 90-91.

33. U.S. House of Representatives, *Commerce Appropriation Hearings for 1930*, 19-20; *Domestic Air News*, October 15, 1927, 3; Bauer, "Hazards of Aviation," RG 237, FN 802.

34. Aeronautics Branch, *FY 1930 Annual Report*, 9; Aeronautics Branch, *Annual Report of the Assistant Secretary of Commerce for Aeronautics to the Secretary of Commerce for the Fiscal Year Ended June 30,1931* (Washington, 1931), 7.

35. Transcript of December 1927 Aero Conference, 144, 178, 360.

36. *Ibid.*, 152-53, 155; William B. Robertson to William P. MacCracken, October 22, 1927, telegram, Robertson to MacCracken, October 24, 1927, Clarence Young to Robertson, October 26, 1927, MacCracken to Robertson, October 27, 1927, RG 237, FN 671.

37. Transcript of December 1927 Aero Conference, 145, 162-63, 165, 180, 187-89, 190-91, 198-99.

38. *Aeronautics Bulletin No. 7* (Air Commerce Regulations), September 1, 1929, 5.

39. U.S. House of Representatives, *Commerce Appropriation Hearings* for *FY 1930*, 21.

40. Russell Owen to William P. MacCracken, November 20, 1927, MacCracken to Owen, November 23, 1927, RG 40, FN 845.

41. Reed G. Landis to Clarence Young, February 6, 1931, Gilbert G. Budwig to Landis, February 10, 1931, RG 40, FN 612.002.

42. *U.S. Air Services,* October 1927, 58; *New York Times,* September 6 & 11, 1927; *Aircraft Year Book,* 1928, 120; *Literary Digest,* September 24, 1927.

43. *New York Times,* September 4, 6, 11 & October 30, 1927; *Outlook,* September 21, 1927, 78; *Nation,* September 21, 1927, 276; *U.S. Air Services,* October 1927, 1, 54.

44. *New York Times,* September 14 & 16, 1927.

45. *Aeronautics Bulletin No. 7* (Air Commerce Regulations), September 1, 1929, 14.

46. Transcript of December 1927 Aero Conference, 32; Roy D. Chapin to William M. Chadbourne, February 14, 1933, RG 40, FN 83272.

47. Curtiss Flying Service to William P. MacCracken, January 14, 1927, Don Cardiff to Walter Parkins, October 5, 1930, Gilbert G. Budwig to Cardiff, December 13, 1930, RG 237, FN 671 & 611.11.

48. Roy D. Chapin to William M. Chadbourne, February 14, 1933, Gilbert G. Budwig to Malcolm Kerlin, April 8, 1933, RG 40, FN 83272.

49. Kenneth Brown Collings, "How to Make Flying Safe," *American Mercury,* February 1937, 157; Warren E. Eaton to J.S. Marriott, April 2, 1931, RG 237, FN 611.01.

50. Eaton to Marriott, April 2, 1931, Marriott to Eaton, April 8, 1931, RG 237, FN 611.01; *New York Times,* April 13, 1931, & February 4 & 5, 1932.

51. Eaton to Marriott, April 2, 1931, Marriott to Eaton, April 8, 1931, RG 237, FN 611.01.

52. U.S. Congress, House, *Department of Commerce Appropriation Bill for 1931, Hearings* before a subcommittee of the Committee on Appropriations, 71st Cong., 2d sess., 1930, 37; U.S. Congress, House, *Department of Commerce Appropriation Bill, 1932, Hearings* before a subcommittee of the Committee on Appropriations, 71st Cong., 3d sess., 1930, 47-48.

53. John F. O'Ryan to Clarence Young, April 11, 1930, L. G. Fritz to G. G. Budwig, April 19, 1929, RG 237, FN 611.41 & 671.

54. O'Ryan to Young, April 11, 1930, G. G. Budwig to L. G. Fritz, April 25, 1929, RG 237, FN 611.41 & 671; memo, Clarence M. Young to Airline Operators, January 24, 1931, FAA Library.

55. Department of Commerce News Releases April 29 & May 7, 1932, RG 237, FN 611.41; *Aviation,* June 1932, 276.

56. *Aviation,* May 17 & 31, 1930, 1009, 1075; U.S. House of Representatives, *Commerce Appropriation Hearings for FY 1932,* 43; Fred D. Fagg, Jr.,

and Abraham Fishman, "Certificates of Convenience for Air Transport," *Journal of Air Law*, April 1932, 231, 232; Clarence M. Young to Delta Air Service, August 11, 1930, George E. Gardner to Fred Fagg, November 16, 1931, RG 237, FN 671 & 846.

57. Clarence M. Young to Wade H. Miller, September 24, 1927, R. D. Bedinger to Chief, Inspection Service, Aeronautics Branch, May 6, 1930, RG 40, FN 845 & 611.01; *Aviation*, August 1, 1927, 285, October 6 & December 15, 1928, 1089, 1988, September 7 & October 19, 1929, 523, 777; Donald E. Keyhoe, "Is Air Travel Safe?" *Saturday Evening Post*, October 5, 1929, 10-11; Rohlfing, *Regulation*, 115; T. Lee, Jr., "Flying Schools and State Legislation," *Journal of Air Law*, October 1930, 529-32. For a full airing of this issue see Transcript of December 1927 Aero Conference, 459-584.

58. Young to O'Hara, January 16, 1929, RG 40, FN 83272; Rohlfing, *Regulation*, 111, 112.

59. *Aeronautics Bulletin No. 7-B* (Air Commerce Regulations--School Supplement), May 1, 1929; "Proceedings of the First National Legislative Air Conference, August 18-20, 1930," *Journal of Air Law*, October 1930, 534.

60. Herbert Hoover to Senator Samuel M. Shortridge, May 7, 1928, RG 40, FN 83272.

61. Bauer, "The Hazards of Aviation," RG 237, FN 802.

62. *Aviation*, December 26, 1927, 1516–17.

63. Department of Commerce Information Bulletin No. 41 (Abstract of State Laws on Aeronautics), March 15, 1928, FAA Library; *New York Times*, September 27, 1929.

64. *Aviation*, July 13, 1929, 152; *New York Times*, September 24, 1930; House of Representatives, *Commerce Appropriation Hearings for FY 1931*, 37.

65. House of Representatives, *Commerce Appropriation Hearings for FY 1929*, 27; *Aviation*, January 11, 1930, 73; *New York Times*, March 1 & December 8, 1930.

66. Clarence M. Young to Oscar H. Morris, November 22, 1930, RG 237, FN 845; U.S. House of Representatives, *Commerce Appropriation Hearings for FY 1932, 45*; *U.S. Air Services*, January 1931, 11, 32, 34; U.S. House of Representatives, *Commerce Appropriation Hearings for FY 1933*, 119-20; memo, Colglazier to Young, February 9, 1932, RG 237, FN 615.

67. J. Walter Drake to H. E. Hartney, February 9, 1926, RG 40, FN 83272; Earl D. Osborn to Herbert Hoover, January 9, 1925, Harold Phelps Stokes

to Osborn, January 16, 1925, Hoover Papers; *Aviation,* June 7, 1926, 867, August 31 & October 12, 1929, 455, 733.

68. *Aviation,* July 1932, 318; *CAA Statistical Handbook of Civil Aviation,* December 1945, 93.

69. *CAA Statistical Handbook of Civil Aviation,* December 1945, 55.

70. *Commonweal,* October 23, 1929, 632; *Scientific American,* July 1929, 36-38; *Forum,* September 1930, 173; *Nation,* October 22, 1930, 438-39; memo, Colglazier to Young, February 9, 1932, RG 40, FN 615. See also *Saturday Evening Post,* October 5, 1929, 10; *Harper's Magazine,* March 1930, 424-35; *Collier's,* September 3, 1927, 7-8; *Forum,* July 1929, 17-22.

Chapter 5

1. Durant quoted in *U.S. Air Services,* December 1926, 33.

2. P. R. Bassett, "The Night Airway," *Aero Digest,* March 1925, 140; Henderson quoted in C. G. Grey, "Civil Aviation in the United States," *Aviation,* January 5, 1925, 16.

3. Page Shamburger, *Tracks Across the Sky: The Story of the Pioneers of the U.S. Air Mail* (New York, 1964), 23-24; Carroll V. Glines, *The Saga of the Air Mail* (Princeton, N. J., 1968), 65-66; Edward Pearson Warner, *The Early History of Air Transportation* (A James Jackson Cabot Professorship Lecture; Northfield, Vt., 1937), 7-8.

4. Ken McGregor, "Beam Dream," in *Saga of the U.S. Air Mail Service* (?, 1962), 16; Shamburger, *Tracks,* 62-66; Carlton Kemper to Superintendent, Aerial Mail Service, December 21, 1919, RG 28, AMS.

5. Jerome Lederer, *Safety in the Operation of Air Transportation* (A James Jackson Cabot Professorship Lecture; Northfield, Vt., 1939), 17-18; Warner, *Early History,* 11-12.

6. Doc., C. H. Clarahan, *et al.,* to the Postmaster General, Subj: "Investigation of the Air Mail Service," October 28, 1925, RG 28, AMS; U.S. Post Office Department, Second Assistant Postmaster General, "A Brief History of the Air Mail Service," (mimeographed pamphlet), 8-9; U.S. Post Office Department, *Annual Report of the Postmaster General for the Fiscal Year Ended June 30, 1921* (Washington, 1921), 47; Don Downie, "First Fifty Years of FSS," *APOA Pilot,* August 1970, 48.

7. Federal Aviation Administration, Air Traffic Service, "History of Air Traffic Control" (unpublished manuscript, 1971), 1; POD, "Brief History," 9; *FY 1921 POD Annual Report,* 47; U.S. Post Office Department News Release, April 22, 1921, RG 28, AMS.

NOTES FOR PAGES 125-145

8. Shamburger, *Tracks,* 90; E. H. Shaughnessy, "The Aerial Mail Service," *Aerial Age Weekly,* February 13, 1922, 539; Warner, *Early History,* 25-26.

9. U.S. President's Aircraft Board, *Hearings* (Washington, 1925), 304.

10. *FY 1921 POD Annual Report,* 46-47; Warner, *Early History,* 18-19, 26; "The Night the Mail Went Through," *FAA Aviation News,* August 1970, 12-13; *Aircraft Board Hearings,* 304, 308-309; D. L. Bruner and H. R. Harris, "The First Night Airways," *U.S. Air Services,* June 1924, 7, 10-11; Donald Duke, *Airports and Airways: Cost, Operation and Maintenance* (New York, 1927), 121; Benjamin B. Lipsner, *The Airmail: Jennies to Jets* (New York, 1951), 201.

11. U.S. Post Office Department, *Annual Report of the Postmaster General for the Fiscal Year Ended June 30, 1927* (Washington, 1927), 24, 26; POD, "Brief History," 11-12.

12. Paul Henderson to William P. MacCracken, April 26, 1924, NAA Files; *FY 1927 POD Annual Report,* 24-25; A. K. Lobeck, *Airways of America: The United Air Lines* (Kennikat Press Scholarly Reprints; Port Washington, N.Y., 1970), 1975.

13. Lobeck, *Airways,* 175; Shamburger, *Tracks,* 106-107; POD, "Brief History," 15-16.

14. C. G. Grey, "Civil Aviation in the United States," *Aviation,* January 5, 1925, 16-17; Warner, *Early History,* 49.

15. *Air Commerce Act of 1926, Statutes at Large,* 44 (1926), 568.

16. *Ibid.*

17. Aeronautics Branch, *FY 1928 Annual Report,* 10-11.

18. Michael Osborn and Joseph Riggs (eds.) *"Mr. Mac": William P. Mac-Cracken, Jr., on Aviation, Law, Optometry* (Memphis), 1970, 67; *Aviation,* July 13, 1929, 145; *Domestic Air News,* January 31, 1927, 3; Herbert Hoover to Dwight F. Davis, May 7, 1928, RG 40, FN 83272.

19. Aeronautics Branch, *FY 1927 Annual Report,* 4-5.

20. Warner, *Early History,* 26.

21. U.S. Department of Commerce, Aeronautics Branch, *The Federal Airways System,* Aeronautics Bulletin No. 24 (Washington, 1930), 18-19; D. C. Young, "Airways Lighting" (Reprint of a paper presented before the Silver Anniversary Convention of the Illuminating Engineering Society, Pittsburgh, Pa., October 12-16, 1931), 2, 5-6; F. C. Hingsburg, "Field Lighting, Radio and Interfield Communications," *Aero Digest,* June 1929, 59-62.

22. J. C. Breckenridge, "Airway Beacons," *Aero Digest,* June 1929, 76, 230, 232.

23. *Morrow Board Report,* 308-309; Bruner and Harris, "First Night Airways," 10-11; C. Moran, "The Gay White Way of the Air Mail," *U.S. Air Services,* February 1924, 36-37; *The Federal Airway System,* 18.

24. Aeronautics Branch, *FY 1927 Annual Report,* 7; Young, "Airways Lighting," 5-6.

25. Aeronautics Branch, *FY 1930 Annual Report,* 25; Young, "Airways Lighting," 8; *The Federal Airways System* (1936 edition), 6.

26. POD, *FY 1927 Annual Report,* 25; Young "Airways Lighting," 7; *Federal Airways System* (1930 edition), 20-21.

27. Lobeck, *Airways,* 175.

28. *Federal Airways System* (1930 edition), 10-18; Young, "Airways Lighting," 11-16.

29. U.S. Congress, Senate, *Departments of State, Justice, Commerce and Labor Appropriation Bill, 1928, Hearings* before a subcommittee of the Committee on Appropriations, 69th Cong., 2d sess., 1927, 12; U.S. Congress, House, *Appropriations, Department of Commerce, 1929, Hearings* before a subcommittee of the Committee on Appropriations, 70th Cong., 1st sess., 1928, 43, 47-48.

30. U.S. Department of Commerce News Release, February 16, 1931.

31. *Federal Airways System* (1936 edition), 12-13.

32. *Ibid.*

33. *Domestic Air News,* March 31, 1929, 20-21.

34. Osborn and Riggs (eds.), *Mr. Mac,* 68; Briddon, *et al., FAA Fact Book,* 15.

35. J. Walter Drake to W. Irvin Glover, June 19, 1926, memo, William P. MacCracken to J. E. Yonge, September 16, 1927, RG 40, FN 83272; U.S. Senate, *Fiscal Year 1928 Appropriation Hearings,* 12.

36. William P. MacCracken to Vern C. Gorst, Pacific Air Transport, September 3, 1926, memo, MacCracken to Captain Hingsburg, October 31, 1926, MacCracken to the Comptroller General of the United States, March 10, 1928, RG 40, FN 83272; U.S. Department of Commerce, *Annual Report of the Secretary of Commerce for the Fiscal Year Ended June 30, 1933* (Washington, 1933), 11; U.S. Congress, House, *Department of Commerce Appropriations Bill, 1934, Hearings* before a subcommittee on the Committee on Appropriations, 72d Cong., 2d sess., 1933, 113-14.

37. U.S. Congress, Senate, *Safety in Air, Hearings* before a subcommittee of the Committee on Commerce, 74th Cong., 2d sess. & 75th Cong., 1st sess., 1936-37, 21.

38. Young to the Secretary of Commerce, March 31, 1930, RG 40, FN 83272; Young to Herbert Hoover, May 8, 1931, FAA Historical Files; U.S. Congress, House, *Department of Commerce Appropriation Bill for 1931, Hearings* before a subcommittee of the Committee on Appropriations, 71st Cong., 2d sess., 1930, 53.

39. *Domestic Air News,* December 18, 1926, 1; Aeronautics Branch, *FY 1927 Annual Report,* 4-5; Laurence F. Schmeckebier, *The Aeronautics Branch, Department of Commerce: Its History, Activities and Organization* (Washington, 1930), 13-14; Aeronautics Branch, *FY 1928 Annual Report,* 12.

40. Aeronautics Branch, *FY 1929 Annual Report,* 22-25.

41. *Domestic Air News,* March 31, 1929, 20; Schmeckebier, *Aeronautics Branch,* 5; *Air Commerce Bulletin,* September 2, 1930, 115 & February 1, 1933, 365.

42. *Air Commerce Bulletin,* February 1, 1933, 365; Herbert Hoover, *The Memoirs of Herbert Hoover: The Cabinet and the Presidency, 1920-1933* (New York, 1952), 134; Clarence Young to Captain H. Weir Cook, January 11, 1933, RG 237, FN 615.

43. Warner, *Early History,* 26-27.

Chapter 6

1. See, for example, Clarence M. Young, "Civil Aeronautics in America," *Aero Digest,* December 1927, 646; F. C. Hingsburg, "Field Lighting, Radio and Inter-Field Communications," *Aero Digest,* June 1929, 59–62; Herbert Hoover, Jr., "Blind Flying and Radio (Part 1)," *Aero Digest,* July 1930, 59; G. G. Kruesi, "A New Homing Device for Blind Flying," *Aero Digest,* March 1931, 39.

2. Doc., "Air Mail Radio," presentation by Art Johnson at a meeting of the IAS in Los Angeles, June 29, 1962, FAA Historical Files.

3. J. H. Dellinger and Haraden Pratt, "Development of Radio Aids to Air Navigation," *Proceedings of the Institute of Radio Engineers,* July 1928, 894; U.S. Department of Commerce, Aeronautics Branch, *Annual Report of the Director of Aeronautics to the Secretary of Commerce for the Fiscal Year Ended June 30, 1927* (Washington, 1927), 13–14.

4. Herbert Hoover, Jr., "Two-way Radio Communication in Air Transport Service, Part II," *Aero Digest,* May 1930, 57, 260.

5. Dellinger and Pratt, "Development of Radio Aids," 891; Herbert Hoover, Jr., "Two-Way Radio Communication in Air Transport Service," *Aero Digest,* April 1930, 62.

6. Hoover, "Two-Way Radio," 62.

7. Aeronautics Branch, *Annual Report for Fiscal 1927,* 6, 13.

8. *Domestic Air News*: December 18, 1926, 6; April 30, 1927, 8, 9; July 15, 1927, 2–3; August 15, 1927, 7; March 31, 1928, 24.

9. U.S. Department of Commerce, Aeronautics Branch, *The Federal Airways System,* Aeronautics Bulletin No. 24 (Washington, 1930), 29–31.

10. Haraden Pratt and Harry Diamond, "Receiving Sets for Aircraft Beacon and Telephony," *Bureau of Standards Journal of Research,* October 1928, 543–63.

11. *Ibid.; Air Commerce Bulletin,* June 2, 1930, 10; George K. Burgess, "Aircraft Radio Beacon Development," *Aviation,* June 18, 1928, 1765; E. T. Allen to William P. MacCracken, December 8, 1928, RG 40, FN 671.

12. U.S. Department of Commerce, *Federal Airways,* 31–32; *Air Commerce Bulletin,* June 2, 1930, 4, 10.

13. Hingsburg, "Field Lighting," 62; U.S. Congress, House, *Department of Commerce Appropriation Bill, 1930, Hearings* before a subcommittee of the Committee on Appropriations, 70th Cong., 2d sess., 1928, 83; U.S. Congress, House, *Department of Commerce Appropriation Bill for 1931, Hearings* before a subcommittee of the Committee on Appropriations, 71st Cong., 2d sess., 1930, 50; U.S. Congress, House, *Department of Commerce Appropriation Bill 1934, Hearings* before a subcommittee of the Committee on Appropriations, 72d Cong., 2d sess., 1933, 81.

14. U.S. House of Representatives, *Fiscal Year 1931 Appropriation Hearings,* 48–50; *Air Commerce Bulletin,* July 15, 1929, 27; K. T. Road, "Eyes for Blind Flying," *Aero Digest,* July 1929, 61, 290; *Domestic Air News,* July 15, 1928, 30 and September 15, 1928, 15.

15. *Air Commerce Act of 1926, Statutes at Large,* 44 (1926), 568.

16. William E. Jackson (ed.), *The Federal Airways System* (Washington, 1970), 164–66; Aeronautics Branch, *Annual Report for Fiscal 1927,* 5–6; Department of Commerce, *Federal Airways,* 37–38.

17. U.S. Department of Commerce, Aeronautics Branch, *Annual Report of the Assistant Secretary of Commerce for Aeronautics to the Secretary of Commerce for the Fiscal Year Ended June 30, 1932* (Washington, 1932), 10; *Air Commerce Bulletin,* August 15, 1932, 83; U.S. Department of Commerce, Bureau of Air Commerce, *The Federal Airways System,* Aeronautics Bulletin No. 24 (1936 edition; Washington, 1936), 14–15.

18. Department of Commerce, *Federal Airways* (1936 edition), 14.

19. U.S. Department of Commerce, Bureau of Air Commerce, *Aeronautic Radio*, Aeronautics Bulletin No. 27 (Washington, 1937), 5; Jackson (ed.) *Federal Airways*, 172.

20. Department of Commerce, *Federal Airways* (1936 edition), 1–6.

21. U.S. Department of Commerce, *Annual Report of the Secretary of Commerce for the Fiscal Year Ended June 30, 1933* (Washington, 1933), 11; *Air Commerce Bulletin*, December 15, 1934, 151.

22. Doc., "Air Mail Radio," presentation by Art Johnson at a meeting of the IAS in Los Angeles, June 29, 1962; Don Downie, "First Fifty Years of FSS," *The AOPA Pilot*, August 1970, 49; U.S. Post Office Department News Release, November 8, 1919, Wesley L. Smith to Second Assistant Postmaster General, May 22, 1920, RG 28, AMS.

23. Henry W. Roberts, "Practical Aspects of Radio Navigation by Aircraft," *Aero Digest*, February 1937, 56; Dellinger and Pratt, "Development of Radio Aids," 893.

24. Dellinger and Pratt, "Development of Radio Aids," 891–93.

25. *Ibid.*, 893; F. H. Engel and F. W. Dunmore, "A Directive Type of Radio Beacon and Its Application to Navigation," *Scientific Papers of the Bureau of Standards*, January 1924, 281; Jackson (ed.), *Federal Airways*, 219.

26. Jackson (ed.), *Federal Airways*, 219; Engel and Dunmore, "A Directive Type Radio Beacon," 281–95; Rexmond C. Cochrane, *Measures for Progress: A History of the National Bureau of Standards* (Washington, 1966), 295.

27. Dellinger and Pratt, "Development of Radio Aids," 893–94.

28. *Ibid.*, 894; Jackson (ed.), *Federal Airways*, 219; see also, E. Z. Stowell, "Unidirectional Radiobeacon for Aircraft," *Bureau of Standards Journal of Research*, December 1928, 1011–22; *Domestic Air News*, June 30, 1928, 4; Burgess, "Aircraft Radio Beacon Development," 1764.

29. Department of Commerce, *Federal Airways* (1930 edition), 25.

30. Henry W. Roberts, "Flying the Radio Ranges," *Aero Digest*, July 1937, 52; F. C. Hingsburg, "Field Lighting," 61; Karl S. Day, *Instrument and Radio Flying* (Garden City, N.Y., 1938), 52–54; Herbert W. Anderson, "Instrument--Not Blind Flying," *Journal of Air Law*, April 1937, 199–200; William H. Murphy, "The Interlocking Equisignal Radio Beacon," *Aero Digest*, August 1927, 172–75.

31. D. M. Stuart, *Circuit Design for Low-Frequency Radio Ranges*, Civil Aeronautics Authority Technical Development Report No. 23, November

1939 (Washington, 1941), 1; Malcolm P. Hanson, "Radio Equipment for Airways," *Civil Airports and Airways*, ed. by Archibald Black (New York, 1929), 167.

32. Department of Commerce, *Aeronautic Radio*, 6–7.

33. *Air Commerce Bulletin*, June 2, 1930, 2.

34. Jerome Lederer, *Safety in the Operation of Air Transportation* (A James Jackson Cabot Professorship Lecture; Northfield, Vt., 1939), 19; Clarence M. Young, "The Federal Airways System," *Aero Digest*, March 1933, 20; Hanson, "Radio Equipment," 167–69; Department of Commerce, *Aeronautic Radio*, 12.

35. J. H. Dellinger, Harry Diamond, and F. W. Dunmore, "Development of the Visual Type Airway Radiobeacon System," *Bureau of Standards Journal of Research*, March 1930, 425–59; U.S. Department of Commerce, Aeronautics Branch, *Annual Report of the Director of Aeronautics to the Secretary of Commerce for the Fiscal Year Ended June 30, 1928* (Washington, 1928), 29; *Domestic Air News*, April 30, 1927, 8 and March 31, 1928, 24; memo, F. C. Hingsburg to W. P. MacCracken, November 1, 1927, R.G. 40, FN 83272.

36. U.S. Congress, House, *Appropriations, Department of Commerce, 1929, Hearings* before a subcommittee of the Committee on Appropriations, 70th Cong., 1st sess., 1928, 54, 61–62; U.S. Department of Commerce, Aeronautics Branch, *Air Commerce Regulations*, Aeronautics Bulletin No. 7 (Washington, 1933), 23.

37. Laurence F. Schmeckebier, *The Aeronautics Branch, Department of Commerce: Its History, Activities and Organization* (Washington, 1930), 47; U.S. Department of Commerce, Aeronautics Branch, *Annual Report of the Director of Aeronautics to the Secretary of Commerce for the Fiscal Year Ended June 30, 1929* (Washington, 1929), 32–33; U.S. Department of Commerce, Aeronautics Branch, *Annual Report of the Assistant Secretary of Commerce for Aeronautics to the Secretary of Commerce for the Fiscal Year Ended June 30, 1930* (Washington, 1930), 23.

38. See Department of Commerce Annual Reports for the appropriate years.

39. Rex Martin, "Improvements on the Federal Airways," *Aero Digest*, August 1934, 15–16; U.S. Department of Commerce, *Federal Airways* (1936 edition), 18; *Air Commerce Bulletin*, August 15, 1933, 31.

40. *Air Commerce Bulletin*, March 2, 1931, 437–38; see also Department of Commerce Annual Reports for the appropriate years.

41. U.S. House of Representatives, *Fiscal 1930 Appropriation Hearings*, 59–60; U.S. House of Representatives, *Fiscal 1931 Appropriation Hearings*, 48.

42. U.S. House of Representatives, *Fiscal 1930 Appropriation Hearings*, 59–60; F. C. Hingsburg to E. P. Lott, February 10, 1930, RG 237, FN 671; R. P.

Lamont to R. E. L. Pryor, September 29, 1931, W. P. MacCracken to M. V. Politeo, January 9, 1928, RG 40, FN 83272.

43. U.S. House of Representatives, *Fiscal 1933 Appropriation Hearings*, 108–11; H. D. Heister, "Developing the Airways and Their Radio Communications Stations, 1918–1975," unpublished manuscript, 75–76; doc., C. H. Clarahan, *et al.*, to the Postmaster General, Subj: "Investigation of the Air Mail Service, October 28, 1925," RG 28; H. D. King to the Secretary of Commerce, October 28, 1932, E. F. Morgan to the Attorney General, May 27, 1929, F. C. Hingsburg to the Secretary of Commerce, January 10, 1931, RG 40, FN 83272.

44. A. K. Lobeck, *Airways of America: The United Air Lines* (Kennikat Press Scholarly Reprints; Port Washington, N. Y., 1970), 186; "FSS: Pioneers of Flight Safety," *FAA Aviation News*, August 1970, 10; Downie, "First Fifty Years," 49; *San Francisco Chronicle*, August 17, 1970; Heister, "Communications Stations," 71.

45. Downie, "First Fifty Years," 48.

46. J. H. Dellinger, "Directional Radio as Transport Safety Factor," *Aeronautical World*, February 1929, 20.

Chapter 7

1. Frederick Lewis Allen, *Only Yesterday: An Informal History of the Nineteen-Twenties* (New York, 1931), 186, 190.

2. Michael Osborn and Joseph Riggs (eds.), *"Mr. Mac": William P. MacCracken, Jr., on Aviation, Law, Optometry* (Memphis, 1970), 72, 74; U.S. Congress, House, *Department of Commerce Appropriation Bill, 1933, Hearings* before a subcommittee of the Committee on Appropriations, 72d Cong., 1st sess., 1932, 43-44; *Domestic Air News*, March 31, 1927, 11; William P. MacCracken, Jr., to William P. MacCracken, Sr., November 24, 1928, FAA Historical Files; Craig Greiner to MacCracken, February 14, 1929, RG 237, FN 805.0.

3. *Aviation*, July 6, 1929, 25; *Domestic Air News*, January 31, 1928, 21-22.

4. E. McD. Kintz, "Regulating Air Commerce, Article IV--Enforcement," *Aviation*, February 22, 1930, 377; *Aviation*, October 19, 1929, 777, August 1930, 107, December 1932, 465; U.S. Congress, House, *Department of Commerce Appropriation Bill, 1934, Hearings* before a subcommittee of the Committee on Appropriations, 72d Cong., 2d sess., 1933, 89, 101-102, 120.

5. Gerrish Gassaway to Clarence Young, January 7, 1931, Gilbert Budwig to Gassaway, January 17, 1931, RG 237, FN 611.01.

6. *New York World* editorial quoted in *Aviation*, March 8, 1930, 507-508.

7. Amelia Earhart to Clarence Young, March 4, 1929, RG 237, FN 080.1.

8. Walter S. Ross, *The Last Hero: Charles A. Lindbergh* (New York, 1968), 146; Allen, *Only Yesterday*, 220-21; Lloyd Morris and Kendall Smith, *Ceiling Unlimited* (New York, 1953), 262, 263. But see also *Aviation*, June 13, 1927, 1330, June 20, 1927, 1349.

9. *Aviation*, June 20, 1927, 1398; Allen, *Only Yesterday*, 218.

10. Ross, *Last Hero*, 139; Donald E. Keyhoe, *Flying with Lindbergh* (New York, 1928), 3, 6, 7; Osborn and Riggs (eds.), *Mr. Mac*, 95-96.

11. Osborn and Riggs (eds.), *Mr. Mac*, 95; *Aviation*, January 2, 1928, 25.

12. Osborn and Riggs (eds.), *Mr. Mac*, 97-100; Watson B. Miller to Mac-Cracken, March 26, 1928, Hugo L. Black to MacCracken, March 23, 1928, Mrs. Henry [?] to MacCracken, March 29, 1928, RG 237, FN 805.0.

13. Osborn and Riggs (eds.), *Mr. Mac*, 100; J. Zach Spearing to MacCracken, March 26, 1928, RG 237, 805.1.

14. MacCracken to Charles A. Lindbergh, October 28, 1927, telegram, Paul Henderson to MacCracken, October 19, 1927, Greiner to MacCracken, February 14, 1929, John W. Summers to MacCracken, March 29, 1928, E. M. Hale to MacCracken, December 26, 1928, MacCracken to Miss Betty Gillies, January 11, 1929, [Secretary to MacCracken] to E. N. Hale, February 23, 1929, Leo E. Stevens to Clarence Young, October 11, 1930, telegram, J. C. Murphy to MacCracken, December 5, 1927, RG 237, FN 805.0.

15. Eugene M. Emme, *Aeronautics and Astronautics: An American Chronology of Science and Technology in the Exploration of Space, 1915-1960* (Washington, 1961), 10, 22; *Aviation*, May 21, 1928, 1449; Editors of American Heritage, *The American Heritage History of Flight* (New York, 1962), 243; Henry Ladd Smith, *Airways: The History of Commercial Aviation in the United States* (New York, 1942), 122, 123.

16. *New York Times*, September 8, 1926, & June 26, 1927; *Domestic Air News*, September 15, 1928, 3. See also *Aviation*, October 19, 1929, 776.

17. U.S. Congress, House, *Appropriations, Department of Commerce, 1929, Hearings* before a subcommittee of the Committee on Appropriations, 70th Cong., 1st sess., 1928, 29-30.

18. MacCracken to Peter J. Brady, May 23, 1928, RG 237, FN 671.

19. *American City*, January 1928, 117-19, October 1928, 116-18, & December 1928, 110.

20. "Proceedings of the First National Legislative Air Conference, August 18-20, 1930," *Journal of Air Law,* October 1930, 494, 500.

21. *New York Times,* June 26, 1927, & July 27, 1927; *Journal of Air Law,* October 1930, 535.

22. Ellmore A. Champie, *The Federal Turnaround on Aid to Airports, 1926-38* (Washington, 1973), 5, 12-13.

23. W. C. Broadman to MacCracken, July 2, 1928, doc., Walter L. Crocker, president, John Hancock Mutual Life Ins. Co., ca. 1927, R. H. Nichols to Wyoming Airways Corporation, June 6, 1927, RG 237, FN 671.81 & 802.

24. Doc., Walter L. Crocker, president, John Hancock Mutual Life Ins. Co., ca. 1927, A. W. Defenderfer to Chief of Aviation Section [MacCracken], July 18, 1927, R. W. Johnson to MacCracken, May 27, 1927, RG 237, FN 802.

25. Copy of ltr., President, National Aeronautics Association to "Gentlemen," undated, ca., 1927, J. P. Van Zandt to Admiral H. I. Cone, ca. May 1927, J. P. Van Zandt to MacCracken, May 27, 1927, MacCracken to J. P. Van Zandt, July 1, 1927, RG 237, FN 802.

26. H. Barber to MacCracken, April 21, 1927, memo, R. G. Lockwood to MacCracken, April 28, 1927, MacCracken to Barber, May 6, 1927, Barber to MacCracken, May 9, 1927. DOC News Release, May 19, 1930, H. R. Bassford to E. R. Strong, May 8, 1930, Bassford to Strong, May 22, 1930, Strong to Bassford, May 26, 1930, K. T. Redick to Strong, June 26, 1931, Strong to Floyd S. Prothero, July 21, 1931, RG 237, FN 802.

27. *Domestic Air News,* January 15, 1929, 23. See also Eugene Vidal [?] to J. R. Armstrong, February 28, 1936, RG 237, FN 802.

28. Harris M. Hanshue to MacCracken, February 14, 1927, W. M. Bishop to Robert P. Lamont, January 10, 1930, John B. Kohler to Gilbert G. Budwig, October 4, 1930, Budwig to Kohler, October 16, 1930, RG 237, FN 671; Ewing Y. Mitchell, *Kicked In and Kicked Out of the President's Little Cabinet* (Washington, 1936), 140-46; memos, John S. Collins to Chief Clerk, May 5, 1931, E. W. Libbey to Administrative Assistant, Aeronautics Branch, May 6, 1931, RG 237, FN 846.

29. *Washington Daily News,* October 9, 1929; *Aviation,* February 8, 1930, 258-59.

30. *Cong. Rec.,* 71st Cong., 1st sess., 3669-70.

31. *Ibid.,* 3670-71, 4612, 4989-90; *Aviation,* December 7, 1929, 1097.

32. *Cong. Rec.,* 71st Cong., 2d sess., 2995, 9044; *New York Times,* February 15, 1930.

33. *Literary Digest,* March 1, 1930, 104; *New York Times,* January 21, 1930; Charles C. Rohlfing, *National Regulation of Aeronautics* (Philadelphia, 1931), 95; *Aviation,* December 7, 1929, 1097; *New York Herald Tribune* editorial reprinted in *Aviation,* March 8, 1930, 508.

34. *New York Times,* February 14, 1930; *Journal of Air Law,* October 1930, 504; Pendleton Edgar, "Regulating Air Commerce, Article VI--Accidents," *Aviation,* March 29, 1930, 644; *New York Times,* February 13, 1930; *Aviation,* March 8, 1930, 489.

35. *Aviation,* February 8, 1930, 258-59; *New York Times,* February 13, 1930.

36. *Cong. Rec.,* 71st Cong., 2d sess., 2813, 6267; U.S. Congress, House, *Department of Commerce Appropriation Bill for 1931, Hearings* before a subcommittee of the Committee on Appropriations, 71st Cong., 2d sess., 1930, 38; *Aviation,* July 1934, 223.

37. See Peter W. Brooks, *The Modern Airliner* (London, 1961), 57-58, for Fokker form of construction. The 1930 edition of *Jane's All the World's Aircraft* gives additional details.

38. *New York Times,* April 1 & 3, 1931.

39. *Ibid.,* April 8, 1931; *Aviation,* May 1931, 266.

40. Dillard Hamilton to Gilbert G. Budwig, December 16, 1930, RG 237, FN 671.

41. Budwig to Hamilton, December 30, 1930, RG 237, FN 671.

42. *New York Times,* May 5, 1931; transcript of personal interview, Clarence Young by Raymond Heule, July 19, 1971, Hoover Papers.

43. *New York Times,* May 5, 1931; *Aviation,* June 1931, 329.

44. Henri Hegener, *Fokker--The Man and the Aircraft* (Letchworth, Herts, 1961), 75; *New York Times,* May 5 & 6, 1931.

45. *New York Times,* May 9, 1931; *Aviation,* June 1931, 329; J. S. Marriott to Gorst Air Transport, Inc., January 11, 1933, RG 237, FN 671.

46. *New York Times,* June 25, 1931; *Aviation,* August 1931, 459; Marriott to Gorst, January 11, 1933; Hegener, *Fokker,* 76; Morris and Smith, *Ceiling Unlimited,* 299. See also 1931 edition of *Jane's All the World's Aircraft,* 307c.

47. *New York Times,* May 9, 1931.

Chapter 8

1. C. T. Ludington to Peter J. Brady, June 5, 1928, NAT Release, "Passenger Service Information," July 19, 1928, Peter J. Brady to William P. Mac-Cracken, Jr., April 18, 1928, RG 237, FN 671; Boeing Air Transport Ticket Envelope, ca. 1928, FAA Historical Files; Howard J. Hamstra, "Two Decades—Federal Aero-Regulations in Perspective," *Journal of Air Law,* April 1941, 112.

2. *Statutes at Large,* Vol. 43, 805; Fred D. Fagg, Jr., "National Transportation Policy and Aviation," *Journal of Air Law,* April 1936, 165–66.

3. *Aviation,* February 21, 1927, 361.

4. Edward P. Warner, *The Early History of Air Transportation* (A James Jackson Cabot Professorship Lecture; Northfield, Vt., 1937), 54–55; Michael Osborn and Joseph Riggs (eds.), *"Mr. Mac": William P. Mac-Cracken, Jr., on Aviation, Law, Optometry* (Memphis, 1970), 44; Thomas Worth Walterman, "Airpower and Private Enterprise: Federal Industrial Relations in the Aeronautics Field, 1918–1926" (unpublished Ph.D. dissertation, Washington University, 1970), 529–30.

5. Henry Ladd Smith, *Airways: The History of Commercial Aviation in the United States* (New York, 1942), 112; *Aircraft Year Book* (1929), 22.

6. *Statutes at Large,* Vol. 44, 692; U.S. Congress, House, *Amend the Air Mail Act of February 2, 1925,* H. Rpt. 966, 71st Cong., 2d sess., 1930, 3.

7. U.S. Congress, Senate, *Regulation of Transportation of Passengers and Property by Aircraft, Hearings* before a subcommittee of the Committee on Interstate Commerce, 74th Cong., 1st sess., 1935, 124; U.S. Congress, House, Committee on the Post Office and Post Roads, *Investigation of the United States Postal Air Mail Service,* H. Rpt. 2087, 72d cong., 2d sess., 1933, 7, 35.

8. U.S. Bureau of the Census, *Historical Statistics of the United States, 1789–1945* (Washington, 1949), 224; U.S. Congress, Senate, *Investigation of Air Mail and Ocean Mail Contracts, Hearings,* before a special committee, 73d Cong., 2d sess., 1933–34, 1699 (hereinafter cited as *Black Hearings*); Elsbeth E. Freudenthal, *The Aviation Business* (New York, 1940), 88; *Aviation,* February 16, 1929, 467.

9. Freudenthal, *Aviation Business,* 88; *Aviation,* August 1932, 360.

10. *Aviation,* October 1930; Smith, *Airways,* 113–14.

11. Earl D. Osborn, "The Industry's Progress During 1928," *Aviation,* January 5, 1929, 24; H. Rpt. 2087, 11–12; Smith, *Airways,* 133–45, 147–55; Freudenthal, *Aviation Business,* 93–96, 100–107.

12. *Aviation*, March 1, 1930, 460; *New York Times*, January 27, 1961; Smith, *Airways*, 156–57; Arthur M. Schlesinger, Jr., *The Coming of the New Deal* (New York, 1958), 449.

13. Gilbert Goodman, *Government Policy Toward Commercial Aviation* (New York, 1944), 25–26; Herbert Hoover, *The Memoirs of Herbert Hoover: The Cabinet and the Presidency, 1920–1933* (New York, 1952), 244.

14. *Black Hearings*, 2580.

15. Osborn and Riggs (eds.), *Mr. Mac*, 147.

16. H. Rpt. 966, 4.

17. *Black Hearings*, 1470–72; Goodman, *Government Policy*, 15–16.

18. *Black Hearings*, 1472, 2777.

19. Hamstra, "Two Decades," 114; H. Rpt. 966, 6; Fagg, "National Transportation," 167.

20. Osborn and Riggs (eds.), *Mr. Mac*, 145–47; U.S. Congress, House, *Amended the Air Mail Act*, H. Rpt. 1209, 71st Cong., 2d sess., 1930, 2–4; *Cong. Rec.*, 71st Cong., 2d sess., 7372–73; Smith, *Airways* 161; Charles J. Kelly, Jr., *The Sky's the Limit: The History of the Airlines* (New York, 1963), 73–74.

21. *Statutes at Large*, Vol. 46, 259.

22. C. E. Woolman to Clarence Young, March 17, 1930, RG 237, FN 671; Erle P. Halliburton to Young, January 26, 1930, RG 237, FN 611.01.

23. Memo, W. Irving Glover to Earl B. Wadsworth, May 15, 1930, in *Black Hearings*, 2323; Brown quoted in *ibid.*, 2350.

24. *Black Hearings*, 1655, 2325–26, 2449, 2643, 3102; U.S. Congress, Senate, *Investigation of Air Mail and Ocean Mail Contracts*, S. Rpt. 245, pt. 2, 73d Cong., 2d sess., 1934, 27–28; Kelly, *Sky's the Limit*, 74.

25. *Black Hearings*, 1476, 3003–3005, 3007.

26. *Ibid.*, 2643, 3109.

27. Osborn and Riggs (eds.), *Mr. Mac*, 148; *Black Hearings*, 2551.

28. *Black Hearings*, 1549, 2045–46, 2326, 2555.

29. U.S. Congress, House, *Air Mail, Hearings* before the Committee on the Post Office and Post Roads, 73d Cong., 2d sess, 1934, 375; *Cong. Rec.*, 71st Cong., 2d sess., 7377; *Black Hearings*, 2392–93.

30. Smith, *Airways*, 171; Freudenthal, *Aviation Business*, 114; *Black Hearings*, 1658–59, 1671, 2379, 3096.

31. U.S. Congress, Senate, *Revision of Air-Mail Laws, Hearings* before the Committee on Post Offices and Post Roads, 73d Cong., 2d sess., 1934, 227–40.

32. *Cong. Rec.*, 73d Cong., 2d sess., 3123; *House Airmail Hearings*, 92; *Black Hearings*, 2714–15, 2801–802.

33. *Black Hearings*, 2714.

34. *House Airmail Hearings*, 95, 233; *Black Hearings*, 1624, 1642–47, 2737, 2808; *Revision of Air-Mail Laws*, 237.

35. *Black Hearings*, 1451–54, 1517, 1583, 1585–87, 1594, 1609–10.

36. *Ibid.*, 1488, 1499-1500, 2796, 3010.

37. *Ibid.*, 1489, 1492–93, 1495, 1517, 2734–35; Smith, *Airways*, 188–93, 195.

38. *Black Hearings*, 1478; *Cong. Rec.*, 73d Cong., 2d sess., 7000.

39. Smith, *Airways*, 197; H. Rpt. 2087, 3.

40. U.S. Department of Commerce, Civil Aeronautics Administration, *Statistical Handbook of Civil Aviation* (Washington, 1945), 33, 36.

41. Peter W. Brooks, *The Modern Airliner* (London, 1961), 67–90.

42. H. Rpt. 2087, 7; Hamstra, "Two Decades," 131.

43. Hoover, *Memoirs*, 244.

44. *Cong. Rec.*, 72d Cong., 2d sess., 2872; H. Rpt. 2087, 4, 6, 7, 15.

45. *Cong. Rec.*, 71st Cong., 1st sess., 4051, 4480; [Washington] *Evening Star*, September 17, 1929.

46. Thomas H. Kennedy, "The Certificate of Convenience and Necessity Applied to Air Transportation," *Journal of Air Law*, January 1930, 78, 82–83; [Washington] *Evening Star*, September 17, 1929.

47. Fred D. Fagg, Jr., and Abraham Fishman, "Certificates of Convenience for Air Transport," *Journal of Air Law*, April 1932, 240–41.

48. Kennedy, "Convenience and Necessity," 83 (note 19); *New York Times*, September 27, 1931, and March 3, 1932.

49. David L. Behncke to Clarence Young, June 8, 1932, RG 237, FN 846.

50. Behncke to Young, May 19, 1932, RG 237, FN 611.41; Kennedy, "Convenience and Necessity," 89; Fagg and Fishman, "Certificates," 226.

51. *Aviation*, December 1931, 665; H. Rpt. 2087, 3.

52. Alfred Anderson to Robert P. Lamont, February 28, 1931, RG 237, FN 671; *Black Hearings*, 2812; *Aviation*, January 1931, 54, November 1931, 619, & December 1931, 674.

53. *Aviation*, September 1931, 508; H. Rpt. 2087, 11.

54. *Aviation*, March 1933, 90; *Black Hearings*, 2551, 3062–63. For the decline of the independents, compare tables in *Aircraft Year Book*, 1931 issue (opposite 38) and 1934 issue (opposite 54).

Chapter 9

1. The secondary literature on the Great Depression and the Hundred Days is vast. I have relied on Dixon Wecter, *The Age of the Great Depression, 1929-1941* (New York, 1948), 1; John Kenneth Galbraith, *The Great Crash, 1929* (Boston, 1954), 134, 173; Arthur M. Schlesinger, Jr., *The Crisis of the Old Order, 1919-1933* (Boston, 1957), 243, 246, and *The Coming of the New Deal* (Boston, 1958), 3, 20-21; William E. Leuchtenburg, *Franklin D. Roosevelt and the New Deal, 1932-1940* (Paperback edition; New York, 1963), 1, 2, 13, 18, 19, 23, 24-25, 39, 41, 47; Frederick Lewis Allen, *The Big Change, 1900-1950* (Paperback edition; New York, 1952), 130-31, 134; William Manchester, *The Glory and the Dream: A Narrative History of America, 1932-1972* (2 vols.; Boston, 1974), I, 38; John Morton Blum, *Roosevelt and Morgenthau* (Boston, 1970), 26-27. I have also used U.S. Bureau of the Census, *Historical Statistics of the United States: Colonial Times to 1970* (Washington, 1975), 135, 164, 199, 224, 225, 226, 265, 912, and *Statistical Abstract of the United States: 1933* (Washington, 1933), 257, 279, 282, 560.

2. *CAA Statistical Handbook of Civil Aviation* (1948), 25, 38, 43.

3. U.S. Congress, House, *Department of Commerce Appropriation Bill, 1932, Hearings* before a subcommittee of the Committee on Appropriations, 71st Cong., 3d sess., 1930, 44; *Aviation*, December 1933, 369; *CAA Statistical Handbook*, 63, 66-70, 80, 83; *Aviation*, March 1931, 65-66 and August 1932, 360.

4. *New York World-Telegram*, March 7, 1934.

5. *Ibid.*; W. B. Courtney, "Wings of the New Deal," *Collier's*, February 17, 1934, 13; Frank A. Tichenor, "A Message to President Franklin D. Roosevelt," *Aero Digest*, March 1933, 22.

6. Courtney, "Wings," 13.

7. *Ibid.*; Tichenor, "Message," 22; *Aviation,* March 1933, 65-67; *Aero Digest,* April 1933, 16; *New York World-Telegram,* March 7, 1934.

8. *Aviation,* April 1933, 116; Samuel I. Rosenman (ed.), *The Public Papers and Addresses of Franklin D. Roosevelt* (5 vols.; New York, 1938-50), I, 716-17, 720, 723 & II, 153-54; Fred D. Fagg, Jr., "National Transportation Policy and Aviation," *Journal of Air Law,* April 1936, 155-56.

9. James MacGregor Burns, *Roosevelt: The Lion and the Fox* (New York, 1956), 149; Schlesinger, *Crisis,* 304; Michael Osborn and Joseph Riggs (eds.), *"Mr. Mac": William P. MacCracken, Jr., on Aviation, Law, Optometry* (Memphis, 1970), 154.

10. Aeronautics Branch News Release, July 6, 1933, FAA History Files; Malcolm Kerlin to Chief of Appointment Division, June 30, 1934, Daniel C. Roper to Hamilton Fish, Jr., April 21, 1934, RG 40, FN 83272; *U.S. Air Services,* August 1933, 23.

11. Osborn and Riggs (eds.), *Mr. Mac,* 155; Ewing Young Mitchell, *Kicked In and Kicked Out of the President's Little Cabinet* (Washington, 1936), 31-32.

12. Daniel C. Roper, "Memorandum Regarding Director of Air Transportation," May 26, 1933, RG 40, FN 83272.

13. Osborn and Riggs (eds.), *Mr. Mac,* 154.

14. Roper, "Memo Regarding Director," May 26, 1933.

15. *Aviation,* July 1933, 220.

16. Anonymous memorandum, July 9, 1935, RG 40, FN 83272; Eugene L. Vidal, transcript of personal interview with Charles E. Planck, 1962, FAA History Files; Osborn and Riggs (eds.), *Mr. Mac,* 155.

17. *Aviation,* October 1933, 329; Courtney, "Wings," 13-14; *Business Week,* April 18, 1936, 10.

18. Vidal, transcript of interview with Planck; *New York Times,* February 21, 1969; *Washington Post,* February 22, 1969; *Aviation,* January 1931, 54 and November 1931, 619; *Aero Digest,* September 1935, 16; Courtney, "Wings," 48; Henry Ladd Smith, *Airways: The History of Commercial Aviation in the United States* (New York, 1942), 216-20, 223, 226-27, 283.

19. *Aviation,* May 1936, 30; anonymous memorandum, July 9, 1935, RG 40 FN 83272; Nick A. Komons, *The Cutting Air Crash: A Case Study in Early Federal Aviation Policy* (Washington, 1973), 71; Mitchell, *Kicked In and Out,* 352; *U.S. Air Services,* November 1936, 8. "[It] is general knowledge that the director and the two assistant directors have been fighting each

other ever since they received their appointments . . .," a Department of Commerce official told a congressional committee in 1936. U.S. Congress, Senate, *Safety in Air, Hearings* before a subcommittee of the Committee on Commerce pursuant to S. Res. 146, 74th Cong., 2d sess., & 75th Cong., 1st sess., 1936-37, 1203, hereinafter cited as *Copeland Hearings.*

20. Mitchell, *Kicked In and Out,* 69ff, 90-91, 136, 340-41, 353-54; *Copeland Hearings,* 412-13; Fred D. Fagg, transcript of personal interview with Charles E. Planck, 1962, FAA History Files. See also Smith, *Airways,* 283, for the weakness of Vidal's position.

21. Mitchell, *Kicked In and Out,* 342; *Official Register of the United States* (1932), 100, (1933), 97 & (1934), 101; *Copeland Hearings,* 1228.

22. *U.S. Air Services,* September 1933, 7; *Aero Digest,* September 1933, 14; Komons, *Cutting,* 69-70; Daniel C. Roper to Frank W. Bireley, October 3, 1933, RG 40, FN 83272.

23. Schlesinger, *New Deal,* 13.

24. *Ibid.,* 8-10; *Statutes at Large,* Vol. 48 (1933), 8.

25. Arnold E. Briddon *et al., FAA Historical Fact Book: A Chronology, 1926-1971* (Washington, 1974), 278; U.S. Congress, House, *Department of Commerce Appropriation Bill, 1933, Hearings* before a subcommittee of the Committee on Appropriations, 72d Cong., 1st sess., 1932, 116-17.

26. U.S. House of Representatives, *Commerce Appropriation Hearings for FY 1933,* 94; U.S. Department of Commerce, Civil Aeronautics Administration, *A Digest of the Programs and Appropriations for Air Navigation Facilities, 1927-1947* (pamphlet, ca. 1947), 37; U.S. Department of Commerce, *Annual Report of the Secretary of Commerce for Fiscal Year 1933* (Washington, 1933), 10.

27. Briddon *et al., FAA Fact Book,* 278; Malcolm Kerlin to Heads of Bureaus, March 24, 1933, S. W. Crosthwait to Mr. Behn, July 21, 1933, Kerlin to Heads of Bureaus, July 15, 1933, RG 237, Box 68.

28. F. C. Hingsburg to Mr. Edgerton, June 17, 1933, in *Copeland Hearings,* 494.

29. Rex Martin, "Improvements on the Federal Airways," *Aero Digest,* August 1934, 15; E. Y. Mitchell to Benson R. Frost, October 10, 1933, RG 237, Box 8; Daniel C. Roper to G. Bromley Onam, January 11, 1936, RG 40, FN 83272.

30. U.S. Congress, House, *Department of Commerce Appropriation Bill for 1935, Hearings* before a subcommittee of the Committee on Appropriations, 73d Cong., 2d sess., 1934, 221.

31. *Air Commerce Bulletin,* September 14, 1933, 80, 81 & October 15, 1933, 117; Aeronautics Branch News Release, August 19, 1933; Martin, "Im-

provements," 15-16; *Copeland Hearings,* 98, 599-600, 679; Komons, *Cutting,* 63.

32. Briddon *et al., FAA Fact Book,* 276; U.S. House of Representatives, *Commerce Appropriation Hearings for FY 1935,* 213-20, 223; E. Y. Mitchell to Morris D. Canter, August 19, 1933, RG 237, Box 8.

33. *Western Flying,* September 1933, 20 & November 1933, 7.

34. E. Y. Mitchell to James M. Fitzpatrick, June 24, 1933, anonymous memo, "Reorganization of the Airways Division," July 8, 1935, E. W. Libby to General Accounting Office, July 21, 1934, RG 40, FN 83272; U.S. Department of Commerce, *Annual Report of the Secretary of Commerce for Fiscal Year 1934* (Washington, 1934), 9.

35. FDR quoted in Leutchenburg, *Roosevelt,* 48; Schlesinger, *New Deal,* 87-102.

36. Ellmore A. Champie, *The Federal Turnaround on Aid to Airports, 1926-38* (Washington, 1973), 4-5; *DOC Annual Report for FY 1934,* 10-11; *Air Commerce Bulletin,* February 15, 1934, 189, 190; *Aviation,* December 1933, 382; U.S. House of Representatives, *Commerce Appropriation Hearings for FY 1935,* 229-33; CAA, *Digest of Programs,* 41; doc., "Report of Proceedings of Airline Safety Conference," Washington, D.C., February 4, 1937, 318.

37. U.S. House of Representatives, *Commerce Appropriation Hearings for FY 1935,* 220.

38. *Aviation,* December 1933, 369; Howard J. Hamstra, "Two Decades—Federal Aero-Regulation in Perspective," *Journal of Air Law,* April 1941, 132.

39. *Aviation,* October 1933, 311-13, December 1933, 269, January 1934, 24 & February 1934, 39; *Western Flying,* October 1933, 8-10.

40. Eugene L. Vidal, "Low-Priced Airplane," *Aviation,* February 1934, 41; Tom D. Crouch, "An Airplane for Everyman: The Department of Commerce and the Light Airplane Industry, 1933-1937," unpublished paper, 1976, 1, 3.

41. Quoted in Crouch, "Airplane for Everyman," 3.

42. Quoted in Courtney, "Wings," 48.

43. Crouch, "Airplane for Everyman," 6; Aeronautics Branch News Release, November 8, 1933; Eugene L. Vidal, "The Poor Man's Airplane," *Western Flying,* February 1934, 9; Vidal, "Low-Priced Airplane," 41.

44. *U.S. Air Services,* August 1924, 15; Vidal, "Low-Priced Airplane," 40.

45. Vidal, transcript of personal interview with Planck; Vidal, "Poor Man's Airplane," 9, 10.

46. Vidal, transcript of personal interview with Planck; Courtney, "Wings," 48; Vidal, "Low-Priced Airplane," 41.

47. Aeronautics Branch News Release, November 22, 1933; Vidal, "Low-Priced Airplane," 41. See also U.S. House of Representatives, *Commerce Appropriation Hearings for FY 1935,* 222.

48. Resolution, Village of Bellwood (Cook County) Illinois, January 16, 1934, Vidal to Maj. Gen. B. D. Foulois, January 19, 1934, RG 237, Box 413.

49. *Aviation,* December 1933, 379; Crouch, "Airplane for Everyman," 9; William B. Stout, "A Few Fallacies Concerning the 'Cheap Airplane' Idea," *Aero Digest,* September 1935, 14; *National Aeronautic Magazine,* September 1935, 7; Robert J. Pritchard, "Ten Thousand Airplanes at $700?" *Western Flying,* December 1933, 8.

50. Pritchard, "Ten Thousand," 8.

51. *Aviation,* December 1935, 25 & February 1934, 50.

52. *Western Flying,* March 1934, 19; Vidal, transcript of personal interview with Planck. See also Crouch, "Airplane for Everyman," 11.

Chapter 10

1. *Cong. Rec.,* 72d Cong., 2d sess., 5008–5009; Michael Osborn and Joseph Riggs (eds.), *"Mr. Mac": William P. MacCracken, Jr., on Aviation, Law, Optometry* (Memphis, 1970), 180; Henry Ladd Smith, *Airways: The History of Commercial Aviation in the United States* (New York, 1942), 226–27.

2. Osborn and Riggs (eds.), *Mr. Mac,* 180; *Aviation,* June 1933, 177–78.

3. U.S. Congress, Senate, *Investigation of Air Mail and Ocean Mail Contracts, Hearings* before a special committee, 73d Cong., 2d sess., 1933–34, 1437ff (hereinafter cited as *Black Hearings*); Osborn and Riggs (eds.), *Mr. Mac,* 149–52; Richard W. Robbins to James A. Farley, February 9, 1934, NAA Files.

4. Osborn and Riggs (eds.), *Mr. Mac,* 157, 179, 181; *Black Hearings,* 2112–19.

5. *Black Hearings,* 2193–220, 2222–45; Osborn and Riggs (eds.), *Mr. Mac,* 159–63. McCarran quotation from *Black Hearings,* 2198.

6. *Cong. Rec.*, 73d Cong., 2d sess., 1902–14.

7. *Ibid.*, 2304–308; Osborn and Riggs (eds.), *Mr. Mac*, 170–71.

8. Virginia Van Der Veer Hamilton, "Barnstorming the U.S. Mail," *American Heritage*, August 1974, 36; Osborn and Riggs (eds.), *Mr. Mac*, 165, 184; *Cong. Rec.*, 73d Cong., 2d sess., 2249.

9. Osborn and Riggs (eds.), *Mr. Mac*, 166–67, 184–85; *Cong. Rec.*, 73d Cong., 2d sess., 2494–98.

10. *Black Hearings*, 2611–12; *New York Sun*, April 25, 1934; Arthur M. Schlesinger, Jr., *The Coming of the New Deal* (Boston, 1958), 451; *Complete Presidential Press Conferences of Franklin D. Roosevelt* (25 vols.; New York, 1972), III, 112. See also *Fortune*, May 1934, 85.

11. *New York Sun*, April 25, 1934.

12. *Ibid.*; James A. Farley, *Jim Farley's Story* (New York, 1948), 46; U.S. Congress, House, *Air Mail, Hearings* before Committee on the Post Office and Post Roads, 73d Cong., 2d sess., 1934, 91; Hamilton, "Barnstorming," 36.

13. Benjamin D. Foulois with C. V. Glines, *From the Wright Brothers to the Astronauts: The Memoirs of Major General Benjamin D. Foulois* (New York, 1968), 236–38.

14. *Ibid.* 238–39.

15. Howard J. Hamstra, "Two Decades--Federal Aero-Regulation in Perspective," *Journal of Air Law and Commerce*, April 1941, 105–107. See also James A. Farley to Hugo L. Black, February 14, 1934, in *Cong. Rec.*, 73d Cong., 2d sess., 2471–72.

16. *U.S. Air Services*, December 1934, 7; *New York American*, February 14, 1934; *New York Times*, February 13, 1934; *Newsweek*, February 17, 1934, 7–8; *Cong. Rec.*, 73d Cong., 2d sess., 3010–11.

17. *Kansas City Star*, February 12, 1934; *Los Angeles Times*, February 20, 1934; *New York Sun*, February 12, 1934; address, Warren R. Austin, before the Union League Club of New York City, June 14, 1934, NAA Files; *Newark Sunday Ledger*, February 11, 1934.

18. [Washington] *Evening Star*, February 12, 1934; Schlesinger, *New Deal*, 452–53; *Newsweek*, February 17, 1934, 8; *Cong. Rec.*, 73d Cong., 2d sess., 2722–23; *New York Herald Tribune*, March 28, 1934.

19. *Cong. Rec.*, 73d Cong., 2d sess., February 24, 1934, 3141.

20. *Ibid.*, 7293–94.

21. Black's radio address reprinted in *ibid.*, 2716–17.

22. *Ibid.*, 7293; *House Air Mail Hearings*, 382, 384; *New Republic*, March 7, 1934, 85; *Nation*, February 28, 1934, 235; *New York Evening Post* poll results in *Newsweek*, March 24, 1934, 10.

23. Beirne Lay, Jr., *I Wanted Wings* (School edition; New York, 1937), 206; Hamilton, "Barnstorming," 87; Foulois, *Memoirs*, 240.

24. *House Air Mail Hearings*, 98; Lay, *I Wanted Wings*, 207; H. H. Arnold, *Global Mission* (New York, 1951), 142–44; Foulois, *Memoirs*, 242–43.

25. Hamilton, "Barnstorming," 36, 86; Foulois, *Memoirs*, 244–45.

26. *New York Evening Journal*, February 26, 1934; *Pittsburgh Post-Gazette*, February 24, 1934; *Literary Digest*, March 10, 1934, 7; *New York Times*, February 25, 1934. See also *Newsweek*, March 3, 1934, 9–10.

27. *New York Times*, February 25, 1934; Foulois, *Memoirs*, 253; *New York Sun*, March 10, 1934; *New York Herald Tribune*, February 27, 1934; *Aviation*, April 1934, 113; *Cong. Rec.*, 73d Cong., 2d sess., 4139; [Washington] *Evening Star*, March 10, 1934.

28. Elsbeth E. Freudenthal, *The Aviation Business* (New York, 1940), 196–97; Foulois, *Memoirs*, 253–55; *Aviation*, April 1934, 117; *Cong. Rec.*, 73d Cong., 2d sess., 4170.

29. Samuel I. Rosenman (ed.), *The Public Papers and Addresses of Franklin D. Roosevelt* (5 vols.; New York, 1938), III, 138–40; *Cong. Rec.*, 73d Cong., 2d sess., 4041; U.S. Congress, Senate, *Revision of Air-Mail Laws, Hearings* before the Committee on Post Offices and Post Roads, 73d Cong., 2d sess., 1934, 70.

30. Henry Ladd Smith, *Airways: The History of Commercial Aviation in the United States* (New York, 1942), 280; *Washington Daily News*, March 31, 1934.

31. *Newsweek*, April 7, 1934, 26; *House Air Mail Hearings*, 374; *Air-Mail Law Hearings*, 73; *New York Sun*, March 26, 1934; *FDR Press Conferences*, III, 292.

32. *New York Times*, March 14, 1934; *Philadelphia Inquirer*, March 16, 1934; Foulois, *Memoirs*, 257–58; Schlesinger, *New Deal*, 453–54.

33. Foulois, *Memoirs*, 257.

34. *Aviation*, April 1934, 118; Hamstra, "Two Decades," 126–29; *Washington Daily News*, May 3, 1934.

35. Foulois, *Memoirs*, 258–59.

36. *Aircraft Year Book* (1935), opposite 128; [Washington] *Evening Star*, April
     20, 1934; *San Francisco Chronicle*, April 24, 1934; *Philadelphia Inquirer*,
     April 22, 1934; *Aviation*, June 1934, 187; Gilbert Goodman, *Government
     Policy Toward Commercial Aviation* (New York, 1944), 45–46, 48–49;
     Hamstra, "Two Decades," 125; Smith, *Airways*, 280–81; *New York Herald
     Tribune*, February 23 & May 14, 1934.

37. *Statutes at Large*, Vol. 48, 933; *Aviation*, July 1934, 205; *New York Times*,
     July 1, 1934.

38. *FDR Press Conferences*, III, 116; *Aviation*, April 1934, 116; *Cong. Rec.*,
     73d Cong., 2d sess., 5384; Rosenman (ed.), *FDR Public Papers*, III, 183.

39. Hamstra, "Two Decades," 130–31; *Cong. Rec.*, 73d Cong., 2d sess., 7521,
     7615–28; *Aviation*, May 1934, 155; *Washington Herald*, April 26, 1934;
     Black Hearings, 3064–65, 3068; *House Air Mail Hearings*, 353.

40. Herbert Hoover, *The Memoirs of Herbert Hoover: The Cabinet and the
     Presidency, 1920–1933* (New York, 1952), 245n.

41. *Chicago Tribune*, May 29, 1934; *Indianapolis Star*, February 22, 1934.

42. Austin's argument is cited in Goodman, *Government Policy*, 39. Goodman
     gives Brown the benefit of any doubt. Compare: Smith, *Airways*, 241;
     Hamstra, "Two Decades," 107; Charles J. Kelly, Jr., *The Sky's the Limit:
     The History of the Airlines* (New York, 1963), 187ff.

43. U.S. Congress, Senate, *Regulation of Transportation of Passengers and
     Property by Aircraft, Hearings* before a subcommittee of the Committee on
     Interstate Commerce, 75th Cong., 1st sess., 1937, 202–204; Paul M.
     Godehn and Frank E. Quindry, "Air Mail Contract Cancellations of 1934
     and Resulting Litigation," *Journal of Air Law and Commerce*, Summer
     1954, 256–57, 259, 272.

44. *New York Herald Tribune*, March 20, 1934.

45. *Ibid.*

46. *Cong. Rec.*, 73d Cong., 2d sess., 8537; *Aircraft Year Book* (1935), 467;
     Hamilton, "Barnstorming," 87.

47. Arnold, *Global Mission*, 144; Schlesinger, *New Deal*, 455; Foulois, *Memoirs*, 274.

48. *New York Times*, March 12, 1934; *Aviation*, November 1934, 25; *Aero
     Digest*, November 1935, 13.

49. Smith, *Airways*, 282; Goodman, *Government Policy*, 41; Hamstra, "Two
     Decades," 125; *Aviation*, January 1935, 1–2.

Chapter 11

1. Memo, Malcolm Kerlin to Mr. Trimble, March 27, 1934, E. L. Vidal to the Secretary of Commerce, April 14, 1934, Daniel C. Roper to Senator William H. King, June 11, 1934, RG 40, FN 83272; *U.S. Statutes at Large*, Vol. 48, 1113.

2. *New York Times*, May 7, 1935; Ray Tucker and Frederick R. Barkley, *Sons of the Wild Jackass* (Boston, 1932), 196; *Time*, May 13, 1935, 55; Raymond Moley, *After Seven Years* (New York, 1939), 125-26, 191-193; Arthur M. Schlesinger, Jr., *The Politics of Upheaval* (Boston, 1960), 140; Harold L. Ickes, *The Secret Diary of Harold L. Ickes*, Vol. I: *The First Thousand Days* (New York, 1953), 359.

3. *New Republic*. December 31, 1934; Schlesinger, *Politics of Upheaval*, 140; Ernest K. Lindley, *Half Way with Roosevelt* (New York, 1937), 82; Ickes, *First Thousand Days*, 359; *Time*, May 13, 1935, 49; Oswald Garrison Villard, "Issues and Men: Senator Cutting," *Nation*, May 22, 1935, 591; Richard L. Neuberger and Stephen B. Kann, *Integrity: The Life of George W. Norris* (New York, 1937), 308; *Congressional Record*, 74th Cong., 1st sess., 8420, 8485, 8823-24; *New York Times*, June 18, 1935; Ewing Y. Mitchell, *Kicked In and Kicked Out of the President's Little Cabinet* (Washington, 1936), 342.

4. James T. Patterson, *Congressional Conservatives and the New Deal* (Lexington, Ky., 1967), 349; *Dictionary of American Biography*, XI, 120-23.

5. For a fuller discussion of the accident see Nick A. Komons, *The Cutting Air Crash: A Case Study in Early Federal Aviation Policy* (Washington, 1973), 13-16, 20-25.

6. "Statement of Probable Cause Concerning an Aircraft Accident which Occured to Plane of Transcontinental and Western Air, Inc., on May 6, 1935, near Atlanta, Macon County, Mo.," *Air Commerce Bulletin*, July 15, 1935, 16-18.

7. Memo, Eugene L. Vidal to Secretary of Commerce Roper, June 12, 1935, in *Air Commerce Bulletin*, July 15, 1935, 15-16; Daniel C. Roper to the Attorney General of the United States, October 28, 1935, RG 237.

8. *Washington Herald*, June 14, 1935, cited in U.S. Congress, Senate, *Safety in Air, Hearings* before a subcommittee of the Committee on Commerce, pursuant to S. Res. 146, 74th Cong., 2d sess., & 75th Cong., 1st sess., 1936-37, 1565-66, hereinafter cited as *Copeland Hearings*.

9. Eugene L. Vidal, transcript of personal interview with Charles E. Planck, 1962, FAA History Files.

10. Komons, *Cutting Crash*, 35-41.

11. *Ibid.*, 43-48; *Copeland Hearings*, 378-79; 473-79.

12. *Copeland Hearings*, 272-76.

13. *Ibid.*, 257-65, 267-68.

14. *Ibid.*, 735ff; Frank A. Tichenor, "Five Billion Dollars for Relief! How Much for Accident Reports?" *Aero Digest*, July 1935, 19.

15. *Copeland Hearings*, 81-83, 654, 826-27; Fred D. Fagg, transcript of personal interview with Charles E. Planck, 1962, FAA History Files.

16. *Copeland Hearings*, 155-58, 684-85, 707, 827; "Report of Proceedings of Airline Safety Conference," Washington, D.C., February 4, 1937, 213, FAA Library.

17. *U.S. Air Services*, October 1935, 8.

18. U.S. Congress, Senate, *Civil Aviation and Air Transport, Hearings* before a subcommittee of the Committee on Interstate Commerce, 75th Cong., 3d sess., 1938, 25; Komons, *Cutting Crash*, 70-71.

19. *Copeland Hearings*, 828-29.

20. *Ibid.*, 91, 154, 189, 602, 1212, 1216, 1228; *U.S. Air Services*, April 1936, 9.

21. Tichenor, "How Much for Accident Reports?" 19; Cy Caldwell to Harold Hartney, February 17, 1936, in *Copeland Hearings*, 601. See also *Business Week*, April 18, 1936, 9-10.

22. *U.S. Air Services*, November 1936, 8; Charles F. Horner to J. Monroe Johnson, July 31, 1936, Johnson to Clark Howell, September 25, 1936, RG 40, FN 83272.

23. Ray Brown to Clarence M. Young, August 10, 1931, RG 237, FN 846; "Regulations Governing Scheduled Operation of Interstate Passenger Air Transport Services," *Air Commerce Bulletin*, September 15, 1931, 131-35.

24. *Copeland Hearings*, 676-77; David L. Behncke to All Air Line Inspectors, July 29, 1933, Jack Oates to R. W. Schroeder, June 7, 1934, Behncke to Eugene L. Vidal, June 20, 1934, Behncke to Vidal, June 23, 1934, J. H. Burns to Vidal, September 19, 1934, Behncke to Schroeder, July 26, 1934, RG 237, FN 846.

25. *U.S. Statutes at Large*, Vol. 48, 933; *Copeland Hearings*, 677; "Air Commerce Regulations Governing Scheduled Operation of Interstate Air-Line Services," *Air Commerce Bulletin*, December 15, 1934, 133-44.

26. David L. Behncke to R. W. Schroeder, August 17, 1934, Joe B. Glass to Eugene L. Vidal, September 5, 1934, Tom Hardin to Vidal, September 17,

1934, J. G. Ingram to Vidal, September 6, 1934; Vidal to William Green, October 5, 1934, RG 237, FN 611.41; *Copeland Hearings,* 681; Behncke to J. Carroll Cone, October 1, 1934, RG 237.

27. *Air Commerce Bulletin,* July 15, 1935, 14 & January 15, 1936, 167; *Copeland Hearings,* 701-702.

28. Arnold E. Briddon, Ellmore A. Champie, and Peter A. Marraine, *FAA Historical Fact Book: A Chronology, 1926-1971* (Washington, 1974), 278; *CAA Statistical Handbook of Civil Aviation* (1954), 33, 60; Charles I. Stanton, "Federal Airways Modernization Program," *Air Commerce Bulletin,* September 15, 1937, 45-56; *Copeland Hearings,* 731; U.S. Congress, House, *Department of Commerce Appropriation Bill for 1936, Hearings* before a subcommittee of the Committee on Appropriations, 74th Cong., 1st sess., 1935, 8, 29; U.S. Congress, House, *Department of Commerce Appropriation Bill for 1937, Hearings* before a subcommittee of the Committee on Appropriations, 74th Cong., 2d sess., 1936, 217; *Fortune,* April 1937, 168.

29. Fred L. Smith, "Cooperation Between the Federal Bureau of Air Commerce and State Aviation Officials," *Journal of Air Law,* October 1936, 504; *Copeland Hearings,* 21, 138, 243; U.S. Congress, Senate, *Departments of State, Justice, Commerce, and Labor Appropriation Bill for 1937, Hearings* before a subcommittee of the Committee on Appropriations, 74th Cong., 2d sess., 1936, 83; night ltr., J. M. Johnson to S. Gordon Taylor, April 9, 1936, RG 237, Box 327.

30. U.S. Congress, Senate, *Departments of State, Justice, Commerce, and Labor Appropriation Bill for 1938, Hearings* before a subcommittee of the Committee on Appropriations, 75th Cong., 1st sess., 1937, 169; *Copeland Hearings,* 818-19, 836.

31. *Copeland Hearings,* 947-48; U.S. House of Representatives, *Fiscal 1937 DOC Appropriation Hearings,* 153, 158-59.

32. *New York Times,* May 17, 1936; doc., Eugene L. Vidal, "Statement as to Why No Reserve Has Been Provided in Appropriations for Bureau of Air Commerce," ca. July 1936, RG 237, Box 69; *Copeland Hearings,* 812-13; Edgar S. Gorrell to Franklin D. Roosevelt, September 23, 1936, J. M. Johnson to M. H. McIntyre, October 15, 1936, RG 40, Box 573.

33. *Copeland Hearings,* 526, 732, 1163; U.S. House of Representatives, *Fiscal 1937 DOC Appropriation Hearings,* 222-34, 225; Briddon *et al., FAA Fact Book,* 278.

34. *CAA Statistical Handbook of Civil Aviation* (1944), 49; *Copeland Hearings,* 682, 730; Caldwell to Hartney, February 17, 1936, in *Copeland Hearings,* 600.

35. U.S. Congress, Senate, *Safety in the Air,* S. Rpt. 2455 pursuant to S. Res. 146, 74th Cong., 2d sess., 1936.

36. John H. Wigmore to J. M. Johnson, June 23, 1936, RG 237.

37. S. Rpt. 2455. See also Komons, *Cutting Crash*, 77-79.

Chapter 12

1. *Business Week*, July 11, 1936, 26.

2. Speech, Harry H. Blee, "Air Transportation," May 1932, FAA Historical Files.

3. Chester A. Church, Lecture No. 2, Course TA-311, "Air Traffic Control," 6, FAA Historical Files; David S. Little, "Airport Traffic Control," *Aero Digest*, October 1935, 42-44; *Aviation*, February 1932, 99; Theodore Maher, "ATC--And How It Used to Be," *FAA World*, March 1973, 3.

4. Little, "Airport Traffic Control," 42-44; *Aviation*, January 1932, 40; Church, "ATC Lecture," 6.

5. U.S. Congress, House, *Department of Commerce Appropriation Bill for 1937, Supplemental Hearings* before a subcommittee of the Committee on Appropriations, 74th Cong., 2d sess., 1936, 5; Jerome Lederer, "'Go Ahead, Newark,'" *Aviation*, July 1936, 23-24; Jerome Lederer, *Safety in the Operation of Air Transportation* (A James Jackson Cabot Professorship Lecture; Northfield, Vt., 1939), 62; *Aviation*, August 1935, 25-26.

6. U.S. Congress, Senate, *Safety in Air, Hearings* before a subcommittee of the Committee on Commerce, pursuant to S. Res. 146, 74th Cong., 1st sess., 1936-37, 32 (hereinafter cited as *Copeland Hearings*); *Journal of Air Law*, October 1936, 517; Church, "ATC Lecture," 2; *Congressional Record*, 74th Cong., 2d sess., April 1, 1936, 4932-33; Fowler W. Barker, Secretary, Air Line Operations Committee, Aero Chamber, to Air Line Operations Committee, October 23, 1935, RG 237, FN 846. See also R. S. Roose, "Airway Traffic Control," *Journal of Air Law*, April 1938, 271.

7. *Journal of Air Law*, October 1936, 517; *Congressional Record*, 74th Cong., 2d sess., April 1, 1936, 4933; Paul E. Richter to Harold E. Hartney, October 30, 1935, in *Copeland Hearings*, 25-32.

8. *Air Commerce Bulletin*, December 15, 1935, 128; Eugene L. Vidal to Admiral E. J. King, April 15, 1935, Admiral King to Vidal, April 20, 1935, Fowler W. Barker to Members of Air Line Operations Committee, ACC, RG 237, FN 611.01 & 846.

9. Memo, R. W. Schroeder to Colonel Cone, August 21, 1935, RG 237, FN 611.01; *Air Commerce Bulletin*, December 15, 1935, 128; *New York Times*, November 8, November 24, & December 1, 1935; *Copeland Hear-

ings, 1237; U.S. Congress, House, *Air Safety, Hearings* before the Committee on the Post Office and Post Roads, 74th Cong., 2d sess., 1936, 96; J. Carroll Cone, "Federal Control of Air Traffic," *Journal of Air Law*, October 1936, 519.

10. *Air Commerce Bulletin*, December 15, 1935, 135; U.S. House of Representatives, *Supplemental Appropriation Hearings for 1937*, 514.

11. Memo, Earl F. Ward to Chief, Air Line Inspection Service, March 14, 1936, RG 237, FN 611.3.

12. *Ibid.*; DOC News Release, November 22, 1935, RG 237, FN 611.3; *Air Commerce Bulletin*, December 15, 1935, 129; doc., "Newark Airway Traffic Control," April 17, 1936, FAA Historical Files.

13. Edgar S. Gorrell to J. M. Johnson, March 11, 1936, in U.S. House of Representatives, *Supplemental Appropriation Hearings for 1937*, 7-9; Ward to Chief, Air Line Inspection, March 14, 1936.

14. Gorrell to Johnson, March 11, 1936; U.S. House of Representatives, *Supplemental Appropriation Hearings for 1937*, 6; Church, "ATC Lecture," 3.

15. Ward to Chief, Air Line Inspection, March 14, 1936.

16. *New York Times*, March 7, 1936; U.S. House of Representatives, *Supplemental Appropriation Hearings for 1937*, 6-7.

17. James J. O'Hara to Director of Air Commerce, December 6, 1935, Denis Mulligan to Director of Air Commerce, March 16, 1936, J. Carroll Cone to Mr. Vidal, March 24, 1936, J. Monroe Johnson to DOC Solicitor, March 23, 1936, RG 237, FN 611.3; J. Monroe Johnson to Edgar S. Gorrell, March 28, 1936, RG 40, FN 83272.

18. U.S. House of Representatives, *Supplemental Appropriation Hearings for 1937*, 2, 5-13.

19. J. Carroll Cone to R. W. Schroeder, August 2, 1936, James J. O'Hara to Colonel Johnson, July 3, 1936, RG 237, FN 611.3; DOC News Release, July 1, 1936; *New York Times*, July 2, 1936; *Air Commerce Bulletin*, August 15, 1936, 42-45.

20. Church, "ATC Lecture," 3; E. R. Mehrling, telephone conversation with N. A. Komons, June 26, 1975; Robert Baker, "History of Air Traffic Control," unpublished manuscript, July 1971, FAA Historical Files; Clifford P. Burton to Frederick H. Ottersberg, January 22, 1972, FAA Historical Files.

21. DOC News Release, July 1, 1936; Earl F. Ward, "Airway Traffic Control," *Air Commerce Bulletin*, October 15, 1937, 74.

22. Roose, "Air Traffic Control," 271.

23. Memo, Earl F. Ward to Airways Traffic Control Personnel, ca. June 1936, RG 237, FN 611.3.

24. Roose, "Air Traffic Control," 272.

25. Earl F. Ward to Hugh L. Smith, July 1, 1937, Earl F. Ward to Colonel Cone, June 29, 1936, RG 237, FN 611.3.

26. Doc., Eugene L. Vidal, "General [ATC] Instructions," August 15, 1936, RG 237, FN 611.3; DOC News Release, July 16, 1936; War Department Circular 60-28, November 9, 1936, FAA Historical Files.

27. Roose, "Air Traffic Control," 273; *Air Commerce Bulletin*, August 15, 1936, 36.

28. U.S. Department of Commerce, "Aeronautic Radio," Aeronautics Bulletin No. 27, July 1, 1937, 31-32; Roose, "Air Traffic Control," 271-72.

29. *Air Commerce Bulletin*, August 15, 1936, 33; Ward, "Air Traffic Control," 74-75; Roose, "Air Traffic Control," 271.

30. *Air Commerce Bulletin*, August 15, 1936, 33-38; Lederer, "'Go Ahead,'" 23; Roose, "Air Traffic Control," 273-74; Earl F. Ward, "The Federal Government in Private Flying," *Air Commerce Bulletin*, February 15, 1938, 181-83.

31. Doc., Earl F. Ward, "Air Traffic Control Now and in the Future," June 11, 1937, Earl F. Ward to United Airports Company of California, August 12, 1936, RG 237, FN 611.3.

32. J. Carroll Cone to R. W. Schroeder, August 21, 1936, Cone to J. Monroe Johnson, November 10, 1936, Cone to Edgar Gorrell, August 24, 1936, Cone to Fowler W. Barker, November 23, 1936, RG 237, FN 611.3.

33. Cone to Johnson, November 10, 1936, Eugene L. Vidal to Assistant Director, Air Navigation, August 11, 1936, RG 237, FN 611.3.

34. U.S. Congress, House, *Department of Commerce Appropriation Bill for 1938, Hearings* before a subcommittee of the Committee on Appropriations, 75th Cong., 1st sess., 1937, 220; Cone to James B. Watson, January 29, 1937, FAA Historical Files; United States Civil Service Examination No. 102, October 3, 1938, FAA Historical Files; Cone to Schroeder, August 21, 1936, Earl F. Ward to Chief, Air Line Inspection Service, July 25, 1936, Ward to Chief, Air Line Inspection, June 1, 1936, RG 237, FN 611.3; enclosure to ltr., Lee E. Warren to Nick A. Komons, April 2, 1977, FAA Historical Files.

35. *New York Times*, June 5, 1936; [Pittsburgh] *Daily News*, August 17, 1937; *Baltimore Sun*, August 30, 1936; *Washington Herald*, October 22, 1936; [McKeesport, Pa.] *Daily News*, November 14, 1936; [Washington] *Evening Star*, February 15, 1937; *Washington Daily News*, May 25, 1937; *Cleveland Plain Dealer*, August 8, 1937; H. W. Magee, "Traffic Officers of

the Skyways," *Popular Mechanics*, October 1936, 514; NBC Radio Script, "Airway and Airport Traffic Control," August 2, 1936, FAA Historical Files; J. Carroll Cone to J. Monroe Johnson, July 25, 1936, Cone to John H. Hartley, August 4, 1936, telegram, C. E. Harmon to Cone, September 3, 1936, Earl F. Ward to Director, Bureau of Federal Airways, April 4, 1939, RG 237, FN 611.3.

36. Lee E. Warren to Base Operations Officer, March Field, February 10, 1937, R. E. Sturtevant to Earl F. Ward, December 6, 1937, RG 237, FN 611.3; Briddon *et al.*, *FAA Fact Book*, 275.

37. Cone to Hartley, August 4, 1936; Eugene L. Vidal to Rex Martin, August 11, 1936, RG 237, FN 611.3; Cone, "Federal Control," 514; Church, "ATC Lecture," 4; enclosure to ltr., Lee E. Warren to Nick A. Komons, April 2, 1977, FAA Historical Files; L. G. Fritiz, Superintendent, Eastern Region, TWA, to Station Managers & Radio Men, July 18, 1936, Earl F. Ward to Fowler Barkner, May 26, 1938, H. F. Cole to Ward, November 3, 1936, RG 237, FN 611.3.

38. Cone, "Federal Control," 514.

39. U.S. House of Representatives, *Appropriation Hearings for 1938*, 221; Cone, "Federal Control," 518, 520; William Barclay Harding to Fred D. Fagg, June 22, 1937, B. D. DeWeese to Fagg, June 10, 1937, Robert L. Montgomery to Fagg, June 28, 1937, W. S. Weiant to Fagg, June 23, 1937, RG 237, FN 611.01.

40. L. Ponton de Arce to Glen A. Gilbert, December 21, 1937, Earl F. Ward to Manager, Airway Traffic Control, Oakland, December 28, 1937, RG 237, FN 611.3; [Pittsburgh] *Daily News*, August 17, 1937.

41. U.S. House of Representatives, *Appropriation Hearings for 1938*, 231-32, 234; Civil Air Reg No. 27, "Airline Dispatcher Rating," November 1, 1937 & as amended May 31, 1938.

42. J. Carroll Cone to Rex Martin, January 26, 1937, Lee E. Warren to Glen A. Gilbert, April 11, 1938, Ward to Chief, Administrative Division, March 30, 1938, Warren to BOAC Section 52, August 1, 1938, RG 237, FN 611.3.

43. Memo, A. C. Mills to Mr. Kerlin, April 9, 1937, RG 40, FN 83272; R. E. Sturtevant to Glen Gilbert, April 5, 1938, Harry D. Copland to Chief, Airway Traffic Control Section, July 25, 1938, RG 237, FN 611.3; Warren to Komons, April 2, 1977, enclosure to ltr., Chester A. Church to N. A. Komons, April 4, 1977, FAA Historical Files.

44. C. W. Schott to Manager, Detroit Airway Traffic Control Station, February 10, 1938, RG 237, FN 611.3.

45. Ward, "Air Traffic Control," 74; H. D. Copland to E. F. Ward, March 17, 1937; D. S. Brachman to P. E. Whitehead, October 24, 1936, E. Sibley to

K. R. Ferguson, September 29, 1937, R. W. Schroeder to Assistant Director, Air Regulation, August 27, 1936, John Berry to Earl F. Ward, November 4, 1936, RG 237, FN 611.3; J. M. Johnson to Maurice J. Tobin, March 28, 1938, RG 40, FN 83272; Civil Air Reg No. 60, "Air Traffic Rules," May 31, 1938, 37; Civil Air Reg No. 26, "Airport Control Tower Operator Rating," November 1, 1937, & as amended May 31, 1938; Fred L. Smith to Mr. Mehrling, June 10, 1939, David L. Behncke to Donald H. Connolly, November 7, 1940, Earl F. Ward to CAA Administrator, May 29, 1940, RG 237, FN 611.3. U.S. Congress, Senate, *Safety in the Air*, S. Rept. 185, 75th Cong., 1st sess., 1937, 15.

46. *Washington Herald*, October 22, 1936.

Chapter 13

1. J. M. Johnson to T. E. Braniff, December 29, 1936, RG 40, FN 83272; L. E. Hanchett to Daniel C. Roper, January 8, 1937, C. Wm. Wittman, Jr., to J. Monroe Johnson, January 6, 1937, RG 237, FN 845; E. V. Rickenbacker to J. M. Johnson, December 28, 1936, RG 237, FN 671.6; *Aviation*, February 1937, 52–53.

2. *Time*, March 28, 1937, 13–14; *Business Week*, March 6, 1937, 16; *Aviation*, April 1937, 92; *U.S. Air Services*, April 1937, 8; *New York Times*, March 1, 1937.

3. *New York Times*, March 2, 1937; *Time*, March 28, 1937, 14; *Aviation*, September 1937, 65, 72.

4. Arthur M. Schlesinger, Jr., *The Coming of the New Deal* (Boston, 1958), 16–17.

5. For Fagg biographical details see Fred D. Fagg, transcript of personal interview with Charles E. Planck, 1962, FAA History Files. See also Howard C. Westwood and Alexander E. Bennett, "A Footnote to the Legislative History of the Civil Aeronautics Act of 1938 and Afterword," *Notre Dame Lawyer*, February 1967, 326.

6. J. M. Johnson to John H. Wigmore, May 26, 1936, RG 40, FN 83272.

7. Nick A. Komons, *The Cutting Air Crash: A Case Study in Early Federal Aviation Policy* (Washington, 1973), 51–52.

8. John H. Wigmore, "Form and Scope of the Civil Air Regulations," *Journal of Air Law and Commerce*, January 1939, 1–3.

9. Hessel E. Yntema, "The Civil Air Regulations and the Code of Federal Regulations," *Journal of Air Law and Commerce*, January 1939, 42; Louis

L. Jaffe, *Judicial Control of Administrative Action* (Boston, 1965), 61; *Congressional Record*, 74th Cong., 1st sess., 4788–89.

10. Jaffe, *Judicial Control*, 62; *Panama Refining Co.*, v. *Ryan*, in Felix Frankfurter and J. Forrester Davison, *Cases and Materials on Administrative Law* (Chicago, 1935), 131–36.

11. Denis Mulligan to Aeronautics Information Division, March 4, 1935, RG 237, FN 611.01; Komons, *Cutting Crash*, 52.

12. *Congressional Record*, 74th Cong., 1st sess., 4788–89; *U.S. Statutes at Large*, Vol. 49, 500–503.

13. Wigmore, "Form and Scope," 1, 4–5; *U.S. Statutes at Large*, Vol. 50, 304–305.

14. Fagg, personal interview with Planck, 1962; Wigmore, "Form and Scope," 2; *Aviation*, November 1937, 51; Fred D. Fagg, Jr., to the Secretary of Commerce, September 20, 1937, John H. Geisse to the Assistant Secretary of Commerce, November 22, 1937, Geisse to H. C. Knotts, January 7, 1938, RG 237, FN 611.00; *New York Times*, October 31, 1937.

15. Fagg, personal interview with Planck, 1962; *Newsweek*, March 13, 1937, 43.

16. *New York Times*, April 30, 1937; *Aviation*, June 1937, 48; *Business Week*, May 8, 1937, 46; *Air Commerce Bulletin*, May 15, 1937, 242; U.S. Congress, House, *Department of Commerce Appropriation Bill for 1939*, *Hearings* before a subcommittee of the Committee on Appropriations, 75th Cong., 3d sess., 1938, 45; Richard C. Gazley, "Development of a Safety and Planning Program," Civil Aeronautics Authority Technical Development Report No. 7, April 1938, 1; Gazley, "Planning for Safety," *Journal of Air Law*, April 1938, 254, 257–58.

17. Arnold E. Briddon, "Washington-Field Relationships in FAA's Predecessor Agencies," unpublished manuscript, June 1966, FAA Historical Files.

18. Fagg, Personal interview with Planck, 1962.

19. U.S. Congress, Senate, *Departments of State, Justice, Commerce, and Labor Appropriation Bill for 1938, Hearings* before a subcommittee of the Committee on Appropriations, 75th Cong., 1st sess., 1937, 362; *Aviation*, December 1937, 23–24; *Time*, October 18, 1937, 45.

20. *Air Commerce Bulletin*, March 15, 1937, 202–203; *Aviation*, March 1937, 46; *New York Times*, March 21, 1937; U.S. Congress, Senate, *Safety in the Air*, S. Rept. 185, 75th Cong., 1st sess., 1937, 19–23, 47.

21. U.S. Congress, Senate, *Departments of State, Justice, Commerce, and Labor Appropriation Bill for 1937, Hearings* before a subcommittee of the Committee on Appropriations, 74th Cong., 2d sess., 1936, 78; Fagg, personal interview with Planck, 1962; U.S. Congress, Senate, *Departments*

of *State, Justice, Commerce, and Labor Appropriation Bill for 1938, Hearings* before a subcommittee of the Committee on Appropriations, 75th Cong., 1st sess., 1937, 197, 363; U.S. Congress, House, *Aviation, Hearings* before the Committee on Interstate and Foreign Commerce, 75th Cong., 1st sess., 1937, 289; U.S. Congress Senate, *Regulation of Transportation of Passengers and Property by Aircraft, Hearings* before a subcommittee of the Committee on Interstate Commerce, 75th Cong., 1st sess., 1937, 451, 452, 453.

22. *Dictionary of American Biography*, XI, 120–23; U.S. Senate, *Appropriation Hearings for 1938, 196, 277.*

23. Arnold E. Briddon, Ellmore A. Champie, and Peter A. Marraine, *FAA Historical Fact Book: A Chronology, 1926–1971* (Washington, 1974), 31–32; Henry W. Roberts, "Radio Developments of the Bureau of Air Commerce," *Aero Digest*, December 1937, 34; Fagg, personal interview with Planck, 1962; Department of Commerce News Release, July 20, 1937.

24. P. V. H. Weems and Charles A. Zweng, *Instrument Flying* (Annapolis, Md., 1940), 66; Karl S. Day, *Instrument and Radio Flying* (Garden City, N. Y., 1938), 67; U.S. Department of Commerce, "Aeronautic Radio," Aeronautics Bulletin No. 27, July 1, 1937, 24; W. E. Jackson and H. I. Metz, "The Development, Adjustment, and Application of the Z-Marker," Civil Aeronautics Authority Technical Development Rept. No. 14, July 1938, 1–2.

25. Rex Martin to W. S. Rosenberger, December 11, 1935, Harlan Hull, *et. al.,* to P. E. Richter, April 28, 1936, RG 237, Box 265, 267; *Aero Digest*, April 1937, 62; U.S. Congress, House, *Department of Commerce Appropriation Bill for 1938, Hearings* before a subcommittee of the Committee on Appropriations, 75th Cong., 1st sess., 1937, 202; Jackson and Metz, "Z-Marker," 3, 9.

26. Henry I. Metz, "The Development of Fan-Type Ultra-High-Frequency Radio Markers as a Traffic Control and Let-Down Aid," Civil Aeronautics Authority Technical Development Rept. No. 5, January 1938, 1–2.

27. Doc., R. G. Nichols, Report of Radio Conditions to the Assistant Director (Air Regulations), September 1, 1936, 14, FAA Historical Files; Metz, "Fan-Type Marker," 2; W. E. Jackson, P. D. McKeel, and H. I. Metz, "Tests of the First Manufactured Fan Marker," Civil Aeronautics Authority Technical Development Rept. No. 15, July 1938, 1, 16.

28. *Air Commerce Bulletin*, October 15, 1938, 116.

29. See a series of articles by Henry W. Roberts in *Aero Digest*: "Practical Aspects of Radio Navigation of Aircraft," February 1937, 56; "Flying the Radio Ranges," July 1937, 56; "Ultra-Short Waves for Air Navigation," November 1937, 66.

30. Radio Technical Commission for Aeronautics, *The Air Traffic Story* (Washington, 1952), 26; Roberts, "Ultra-Short Waves," 66, 71; J. C.

Hromada, "Preliminary Report on a Four Course Ultra-High-Frequency Radio Range," Civil Aeronautics Authority Technical Development Rept. No. 3, January 1938, 1; Roberts, "Radio Developments," 37.

31. W. S. Rosenberger to R. W. Schroeder, December 2, 1935, RG 237, Box 265; D. M. Stuart, "Cone of Silence Tests at Knoxville, Tennessee," Civil Aeronautics Authority Technical Rept. No. 8, April 1938, 3; Roberts, "Flying the Radio Ranges," 55.

32. Roberts, "Flying the Radio Ranges," 55; Day, *Instrument Flying*, 64–65; Hull to Richter, April 28, 1936; U.S. House of Representatives, *Appropriation Hearings for 1937*, 156–57; U.S. Department of Commerce, "Report of Proceedings of Airline Safety Conference," February 4, 1937, FAA Library; U.S. Congress, House, *Department of Commerce Appropriation Bill 1933, Hearings* before a subcommittee of the Committee on Appropriations, 72d Cong., 1st sess., 1932, 226–27.

33. Roberts, "Ultra-Short Waves," 66; Day, *Instrument Flying*, 66–67.

34. *Air Commerce Bulletin*, July 15, 1932, 33, December 15, 1932, 293, & August 15, 1933, 34; *Aero Digest*, January 1933, 32; D. M. Stuart, "Circuit Design for Low-Frequency Radio Ranges," Civil Aeronautics Authority Technical Development Rept. No. 23, November 1939, 2; Briddon *et. al.*, *FAA Fact Book*, 21; doc., Nichols, Report of Radio Conditions, 13; U.S. House of Representatives, *Appropriation Hearings for 1938*, 197.

35. DOC, "Aeronautic Radio," 16–17.

36. *Ibid.*; Day, *Instrument Flying*, 61–63; Jerome Lederer, *Safety in the Operation of Air Transportation* (A James Jackson Cabot Professorship Lecture; Northfield, Vt., 1939), 18; U.S. Congress, Senate, *Safety in Air, Hearings* before a subcommittee of the Committee on Commerce, pursuant to S. Res. 146, 74th Cong., 2d sess. & 75th Cong., 1st sess., 1936–37, 645; *Air Commerce Bulletin*, April 15, 1935, 225; Paul H. Brattain to Rex Martin, January 1936, Martin to Brattain, February 3, 1936, RG 237, Box 263.

37. *Air Commerce Bulletin*, July 15, 1933, 16, & July 15, 1935, 1–5; Rex Martin, "Improvements on the Federal Airways," *Aero Digest*, August 1934, 17; Day, *Instrument Flying*, 62–63.

38. Department of Commerce News Release, June 29, 1934; *Air Commerce Bulletin*, October 15, 1936, 83–84, April 15, 1938, 260, & June 15, 1938, 308; Stuart, "Radio Ranges," 1; DOC, "Airline Safety Conference," 71.

Chapter 14

1. William Orr to James A. Farley, October 6, 1936, RG 40, Box 573; U.S. Congress, Senate, *Safety in Air, Hearings* before a subcommittee of the

Committee on Commerce, 74th Cong., 2d sess., & 75th Cong., 1st sess., 1936-37, 136-37 (hereinafter cited as *Copeland Hearings*); *Literary Digest*, January 25, 1936, 33-34; Howard C. Westwood and Alexander E. Bennett, "A Footnote to the Legislative History of the Civil Aeronautics Act of 1938 and Afterword," *Notre Dame Lawyer*, February 1967, 320.

2. U.S. Congress, Senate, *Report of the Federal Aviation Commission*, S. Doc. 15, 74th Cong., 1st sess., 1935, 1, 49, 52-53, 54-55, 63, 243-45, hereinafter cited as *FAC Report.*

3. Fred L. Smith, address delivered before the National Association of State Aviation Officials, Detroit, September 27, 1935, in *Copeland Hearings*, 202; *Aviation*, November 1934; 367; *U.S. Air Services*, February 1935, 7; *Business Week*, February 2, 1935, 12.

4. Arnold E. Briddon, Ellmore A. Champie, and Peter A. Marraine, *FAA Historical Fact Book: A Chronology, 1926-1971* (Washington, 1974), 29; Westwood and Bennett, "Civil Aeronautics Act," 325; *FAC Report*, ii-iv.

5. Charles S. Rhyne, *The Civil Aeronautics Act Annotated* (Washington, 1939), 195-99; *Congressional Record*, 74th Cong., 1st sess., 8925; U.S. Congress, Senate, *Civil Aviation and Air Transport, Hearings* before a subcommittee of the Committee on Interstate Commerce, 75th Cong., 3d sess., 1938, 7-8, hereinafter cited as *Truman Hearings, 1938.*

6. U.S. Congress, Senate, *Regulation of Transportation of Passengers and Property by Aircraft, Hearings* before a subcommittee of the Committee on Interstate Commerce, 74th Cong., 1st sess., 1935, 27, 31, 47, 57, 61, 89-90, 108-13, 114-22, hereinafter cited as *Donahey Hearings.*

7. Gilbert Goodman, *Government Policy Toward Commercial Aviation* (New York, 1944), 19; U.S. Congress, Senate, *Air Transport Act, 1935*, S. Rept. 1329, 74th Cong., 1st sess., 1935, 2-3.

8. *Donahey Hearings*, 47, 114-15; U.S. Congress, Senate, *To Amend the Air Mail Act of 1934, Hearings* before a subcommittee of the Committee on Post Roads, 74th Cong., 1st sess., 1935, 7-8; *U.S. Statutes at Large*, Vol. 49, 614.

9. U.S. Congress, Senate, *Regulation of Transportation of Passengers and Property by Aircraft, Hearings* before a subcommittee of the Committee on Interstate Commerce, 75th Cong., 1st sess., 1937, 259, 278, 279, 291, 299, hereinafter cited as *Truman Hearings, 1937.*

10. *U.S. Air Services*, March 1937, 8-9; *Truman Hearings, 1937*, 116-17.

11. U.S. Congress, House, *Civil Aeronautics Bill*, H. Rept. 2254, 75th Cong., 3d sess., 1938, 2; *U.S. Air Services*, August 1937, 7; John H. Frederick, *Commercial Air Transportation* (5th edition; Homewood, Ill., 1961), 75.

12. H. Rept. 2254, 2; *Truman Hearings, 1937*, 173-74, 252; U.S. Congress, House, *Air Safety, Hearings* before the Committee on the Post Office and

Post Roads, 74th Cong., 2d sess., 1936, 84; Elsbeth E. Freudenthal, *The Aviation Business* (New York, 1940), 218-20; Goodman, *Government Policy*, 19; *Time*, June 14, 1937, 61-62; Rhyne, *Civil Aeronautics Act*, 35.

13. Edward P. Warner, *Technical Development and Its Effect On Air Transportation* (A James Jackson Cabot Professorship Lecture; Northfield, Vt., 1938), 40; Peter W. Brooks, *The Modern Airliner: Its Origins and Development* (London, 1961), 84-86, 88; Frederick W. Gill and Gilbert L. Bates, *Airline Competition* (Boston, 1949), 3, 60, 65; Lloyd Morris and Kendall Smith, *Ceiling Unlimited* (New York, 1953), 301, 319.

14. *U.S. Air Services*, July 1937, 8; *Truman Hearings, 1937*, 376, 377; U.S. Congress, House, *Aviation, Hearings* before the Committee on Interstate and Foreign Commerce, 75th Cong., 1st sess., 1937, 81 (hereinafter cited as *Lea Hearings, 1937*); *Truman Hearings, 1938*, 31-32.

15. *Aviation*, August 1937, 61; *Truman Hearings, 1937*, 226, 288, 335-39, 344, 447-50; *Lea Hearings, 1937*, 52.

16. *Truman Hearings, 1937*, 118; *Lea Hearings, 1937*, 147, 240, 241; Clarence F. Lea to Franklin D. Roosevelt, July 23, 1937, FDR Papers.

17. *Truman Hearings, 1937*, 221-27, 277-78, 313, 345; Westwood and Bennett, "Civil Aeronautics Act," 324; *U.S. Air Services*, September 1937, 9.

18. Westwood and Bennett, "Civil Aeronautics Act," 324; Lea to Roosevelt, July 30, 1937, Lea to Roosevelt, July 23, 1937, Roosevelt to Lea, August 5, 1937, FDR Papers.

19. *Copeland Hearings*, 602, 684-85; U.S. Department of Commerce, "Report of Proceedings of Airline Safety Conference," Washington, D.C., February 4, 1937, FAA Library.

20. Rhyne, *Civil Aeronautics Act*, 200, 208, 213; S. Rept. 687, June 7, 1937, 3; *Truman Hearings, 1937*, 390-93; Malcolm B. Ronald, "Dividends and Death," *Forum*, February 1937, 77.

21. *Truman Hearings, 1937*, 400-401.

22. *Ibid.*, 337, 450; S. Rept. 687, June 7, 1937, 3.

23. *Lea Hearings, 1937*, 253.

24. *Ibid.*, 243.

25. Richard Polenberg, *Reorganizing Roosevelt's Government* (Cambridge, Mass., 1966), 15, 28; U.S. Congress, Senate, *Reorganization of the Executive Departments*, S. Doc. 8, 75th Cong., 1st sess., 1937, 67-68, 69-70.

26. Franklin D. Roosevelt to Harllee Branch, July 31, 1937, FDR Papers.

27. Westwood and Bennett, "Civil Aeronautics Act," 327; Fred D. Fagg, Jr., to Nick A. Komons, May 6, 1977, FAA Historical Files; U.S. Congress, House, *To Create A Civil Aeronautics Authority, Hearings,* before the Committee on Interstate and Foreign Commerce, 75th Cong., 3d sess., 1938, 64 (hereinafter cited as *Lea Hearings, 1938; Complete Presidential Press Conferences of Franklin D. Roosevelt* (25 vols; New York, 1972), XI, 59-60.

28. Telegram, Edgar S. Gorrell to Danial C. Roper, September 21, 1937, RG 40, FN 83272; Westwood and Bennett, "Civil Aeronautics Act," 327; *Lea Hearings, 1938,* 48; Rhyne, *Civil Aeronautics Act,* 78-79.

29. *Aviation,* November 1937, 55; Westwood and Bennett, "Civil Aeronautics Act," 332.

30. Polenberg, *Roosevelt's Government,* 165-66.

31. The Interdepartmental Committee bill is printed in full as an appendix to Westwood and Bennett, "Civil Aeronautics Act," 363-81.

32. *Truman Hearings, 1938,* 14; Westwood and Bennett, "Civil Aeronautics Act," 329-30, 340; Rhyne, *Civil Aeronautics Act,* 206; *FDR Press Conferences,* XI, 217; *Aviation,* February 1938, 67.

33. *New York Times,* November 29, 1937; *Truman Hearings, 1938,* 6-7; Westwood and Bennett, "Civil Aeronautics Act," 346.

34. *Truman Hearings, 1938,* 1-2; Westwood and Bennett, "Civil Aeronautics Act," 332-33.

35. Denis Mulligan, transcript of personal interview with Charles A. Planck, April 23, 1962, FAA Historical Files.

36. Text of unamended Lea bill printed in full in *Lea Hearings, 1938,* 1-35.

37. *Lea Hearings, 1938,* 63-78, 84, 177, 151.

38. *Ibid.,* 38, 52-54.

39. Westwood and Bennett, "Civil Aeronautics Act," 344-46; U.S. Congress, House, *Civil Aeronautics Bill,* H. Rept. 2254, pt. 2, 75th Cong., 3d sess., 1938, 1.

40. Fred D. Fagg, Jr., memo for the record, April 5, 1938, RG 237, FN 846.

41. *Ibid.;* Ellmore A. Champie, *The Federal Turnaround on Air to Airports, 1926-38* (Washington, 1937), 14-17.

42. *Lea Hearings, 1938,* 101, 105, 121, 335, 336, 355; Champie, *Turnaround,* 4-6.

43. *Lea Hearings, 1938,* 120. A brilliant presentation of the forces undermining the dock concept of airports can be found in Champie, *Turnaround.*

44. *Lea Hearings, 1938,* 424.

45. U.S. Congress, House, *Civil Aeronautics Bill,* H. Rept. 2254, pt. 1, 75th Cong., 3d sess., 1938, 3, 6; U.S. Congress, House, *Creation of Civil Aeronautics Authority,* H. Rept. 2635, 75th Cong., 3d sess., 1938, 66.

46. Westwood and Bennett, "Civil Aeronautics Act," 346-48; Rhyne, *Civil Aeronautics Act,* 216; *Truman Hearings, 1938,* 2.

47. *Truman Hearings, 1938,* 13, 15, 26; Westwood and Bennett, "Civil Aeronautics Act," 348-49.

48. *Congressional Record,* 75th Cong., 3d sess., 6856, 6868, 6879; *Aviation,* June 1938, 52.

49. *Congressional Record,* 75th Cong., 3d sess., 7104.

50. H. Rept. 2635, 65, 75-76; *Congressional Record,* 75th Cong., 3d sess., 7222-24.

51. *Congressional Record,* 75th Cong., 3d sess., 7457-58.

52. *Ibid.,* 7459; Harry S. Truman, *Memoirs,* Vol. I: *Year of Decisions* (New York, 1955), 156.

53. H. Rept. 2635, 65, 75-76; Briddon *et al., FAA Fact Book,* 34-35, 36.

54. *CAA Statistical Handbook of Civil Aviation* (1945), 32-33, 36; *New York Times,* August 22, 1938; Rhyne, *Civil Aeronautics Act,* 1.

Index

Accident investigation, 286, 336
  and public reporting, 178-83
  function misplaced, 277-78, 285-86
Advertising, and aviation, 13
Aero Club of America, 26
  supports Federal safety regulation, 36, 45-46, 47
  demise of, 54
Aero Limited, 16
Aeromarine Airways, 16-17, 29
Aero Medical Association, 290, 292
Aeronautical Chamber of Commerce, 53, 60, 96, 119, 302
Aeronautics Branch, 135, 165, 172, 176-77, 181-85, 189
  organized, 92-93
  budget of, 100, 101, 102, 158-59
  regulatory activities of, 100-20
  and airport development, 123-24, 173

relationship with industry, 167, 170
  and New Deal austerity, 236-39
  reorganized, 239-41
  See also airway development & Bureau of Air Commerce
Agriculture, U.S. Department of, 14
Ahlers, John, 59, 63
Air carriers, 379
  independents, 195-96, 215
  mail operators, 191, 201-203
  and economic regulation, 347, 351, 378
  operations under Kelly Act, 192-94, 199
  operations under Watres Act, 210-11, 223
  reorganized, 264-65
  and 1934 airmail bids, 265-66
  safety record in 1930's, 277, 295-96

441

operations under Black-McKellar Act, 352-55
See also aviation, civil
Air Commerce Act, 88, 91-92, 101, 132, 137, 165, 173-74, 178, 181, 212, 252, 307, 359, 378
enacted, 86
amended, 278
See also Bingham bill
Air Commerce Regulations, 285, 290-92, 303, 324-25
promulgated, 93-96
detailed, 97-99
amended, 114-20
codified, 330-33
Aircraft-engine noise, 166-67
Aircraft Production Board, 37-39
Air Law Institute, 329
Airline dispatchers, 321
Air Line Pilots Association, 213, 290-92, 359-60, 370
Air Mail Act of 1925, 66-67, 132, 191, 192-94, 200
Air Mail Act of 1930, 105, 150, 201-203, 210-11, 214-15, 250, 255, 271
Air Mail Act of 1934, 266-68, 291, 352
Air Mail Act of 1935, 353, 355, 356, 378-79
Air Mail Service, U.S., 25, 135-36, 148, 153-54
origins, 17-21
reliance on ground transportation, 126-32
Airport development, 241-42
encouragement of, 172-73
and Air Commerce Act, 173

dock theory of, 85
Federal aid to, 174-75
and Civil Aeronautics Act, 372-75

Air navigation aids, 125, 127, 129
light beacons, 130-31, 134-37, 144-45, 238
intermediate landing fields, 137-38, 238
two-way radio communication, 148-50
four-course radio range, 153-57, 159, 294
"M" marker, 157-58, 159
maintenance of, 160-63
Z-marker, 294, 338, 339
fan marker, 294, 338, 340
See also airway development

Air safety, 21, 23, 24, 124, 277, 294, 327-28

Air safety regulation, 91, 295
before 1926, 7
movement for, 8, 21-25, 78-79
in foreign countries, 25-26
in individual 48 States, 27-28, 120-22
by Federal Government, 26, 93-96, 100-20
See also Air Commerce Regulations

Air traffic control (airway):
conference on, 303-305
established by airlines, 305
assumed by Bureau of Air Commerce, 308
procedures, 309-16
and pilot resistance to, 318-19

Transcontinental & Western Air (TWA), 207-208, 209-10, 214, 265, 266, 271-72, 293-94, 352
and Cutting crash, 278, 281-85
Trenchard, Hugh, 39, 40
Truman, Harry S., 288, 353, 358, 369
and Civil Aeronautics Act, 375-78

Underwood & Underwood, 13
United Aircraft & Transport, Inc. 192, 196, 263
United Air Lines, 68, 185, 202, 206, 209, 210, 213-14, 216, 249, 263, 265, 266, 269, 271-72, 352
United Avigation Company, 206-208, 209
United States Airways, 206-208

Vidal, Eugene L., 215, 234, 235, 238, 242, 249, 255-56, 260, 293, 294, 295, 306, 307-308, 316, 317, 320, 336, 361
relationship with Cone and Martin, 230, 232-33, 289-90
characterized, 231-32
and $700 airplane, 244-48
on accident investigations, 278, 286-87
Copeland report on, 297-98
calls ATC conference, 303-305
resigns, 327-28
Vincent, Jesse G., 38
Vinson, Carl, 75
Vorys, John M., 175
Vought, Chance M., 17-18, 31

Wadsworth, Earl B., 207

Wadsworth, James W., 37, 46, 47, 57, 58, 371, 374
Wadsworth bill, 46-47, 58, 81, 82, 83
Walcott, Charles D., 21, 32, 44, 46, 84-85, 86
Walsh, Thomas T., 229
Ward, Earl F., 306, 309, 311-12, 317, 319, 321, 323, 325
Warner, Edward P., 61, 79, 86, 113, 144-45, 193, 225, 233, 268, 287, 348
Warren, Lee E., 309n, 322
Watres, Laurence Hawley, 201
Watres Act. See Air Mail Act of 1930.
Weather Bureau, U.S., 151-52
Wedell-Williams Air Service, 208, 251, 266
Weeks, John W., 70, 71-72, 73
Western Air Express, 205-207, 210, 271-72, 327
Westlake, E.A., 309n
Westwood, Howard C., 369
Wheeler, Burton K., 351
White, Wallace H., Jr., 250, 252, 279-80
White, William Allen, 221
Wigmore, John H., 297, 330, 331, 332-33, 365
Wilson, Gill Robb, 302, 374
Wilson, Woodrow, 26, 35, 36, 37, 39, 40, 126
Winslow, Samuel E., 52, 55, 56, 57, 62-63, 64
Winslow bill, 55-58, 61, 62-64, 81, 82, 83
Wolverton, Charles A., 370-71